Lecture Notes in Computer Scien

Commenced Publication in 1973
Founding and Former Series Editors:
Gerhard Goos, Juris Hartmanis, and Jan van Leeuwen

Per Stenström   Michael O'Boyle   François Bodin
Marcelo Cintra   Sally A. McKee (Eds.)

Transactions on High-Performance Embedded Architectures and Compilers I

 Springer

Editor-in-Chief

Per Stenström
Chalmers University of Technology
Department of Computer Science and Engineering
412 96 Gothenburg, Sweden
E-mail: pers@ce.chalmers.se

Volume Editors

Michael O'Boyle
Marcelo Cintra
Institute for Computing Systems Architecture, School of Informatics
King's Buildings, Mayfield Road, Edinburgh EH9 3JZ, UK
E-mail: {mob,mc}@inf.ed.ac.uk

François Bodin
IRISA, Campus de Beaulieu
35042 Rennes Cedex, France
E-mail: bodin@irisa.fr

Sally A. McKee
Cornell University, School of Electrical and Computer Engineering
324 Rhodes Hall, Ithaca, NY 14853, USA
E-mail: sam@csl.cornell.edu

Library of Congress Control Number: 2007923068

CR Subject Classification (1998): B.2, C.1, D.3.4, B.5, C.2, D.4

LNCS Sublibrary: SL 1 – Theoretical Computer Science and General Issues

ISSN	0302-9743 (Lecture Notes in Computer Science)
ISSN	1864-306X (Transactions on HiPEAC)
ISBN-10	3-540-71527-4 Springer Berlin Heidelberg New York
ISBN-13	978-3-540-71527-6 Springer Berlin Heidelberg New York

Springer is a part of Springer Science+Business Media

springer.com

© Springer-Verlag Berlin Heidelberg 2007
Printed in Germany

Typesetting: Camera-ready by author, data conversion by Scientific Publishing Services, Chennai, India
Printed on acid-free paper   SPIN: 12039449   06/3180   5 4 3 2 1 0

Editor-in-Chief's Message

It is my pleasure to introduce the first volume of *Transactions on High-Performance Embedded Architectures and Compilers*, or *Transactions on HiPEAC* for short. *Transactions on HiPEAC* is a new journal which aims at timely dissemination of research contributions in computer architecture and/or compilation methods for high-performance embedded computer systems. Recognizing the convergence of embedded and general-purpose computer systems, this journal intends to publish original research and surveys on systems targeted at specific computing tasks as well as systems with broader application bases. The scope of the journal, therefore, covers all aspects of computer architecture as well as code generation and compiler optimization methods of interest to researchers and practitioners designing future embedded systems. Examples of topics of interest include:

- Processor architecture, e.g., network and security architectures, application-specific processors and accelerators, and reconfigurable architectures
- Memory system design
- Power, temperature, performance, and reliability constrained designs
- Evaluation methodologies, program characterization, and analysis techniques
- Compiler techniques for embedded systems, e.g, feedback-directed optimization, dynamic compilation, adaptive execution, continuous profiling/optimization, back-end code generation, and binary translation/optimization
- Code size/memory footprint optimizations

Journal publications are usually associated with a significant delay between submission and final publication. *Transactions on HiPEAC* will rectify this by seriously cutting down on manuscript handling time. The time to the first response will not exceed ten weeks. If minor revisions only are requested, the goal is to publish such papers within six months. Articles that are requested to undergo a major revision will be requested to be resubmitted within three months. Articles that are accepted will immediately be available electronically. By the end of each year, a printed volume will be published by Springer.

In This Volume

First, I am very delighted that Sir Maurice Wilkes accepted to write the leading article of the first volume of the journal. Having contributed to our field ever since the beginning of the electronic computer era, he has an unprecedented broad perspective of the exciting evolution of computers to the point that we know them today. In his leading article, which is partly based on the keynote address he contributed to the first HiPEAC summer school (ACACES 2005), Prof. Wilkes shares with us his reflections on the evolution in computer architecture over the last few decades. He also provides his outlook on the forces that will be important over the next decade. His article appears as the first regular paper in this volume.

An important deliverable for the HiPEAC Network of Excellence is a roadmap of the challenges facing high-performance embedded architectures and compilers. The HiPEAC community has put together a roadmap along ten themes that highlights the research challenges we are faced with in the next decade. I am pleased that the roadmap appears in this volume. It is the second regular paper.

Apart from publishing regular papers, *Transactions on HiPEAC* will sometimes publish papers on special topics or highlights from conferences. This volume contains three such specialized themes organized into three parts: Part 1, Part 2, and Part 3. Part 1 is devoted to the best papers of the 2005 International Conference on High-Performance Embedded Architectures and Compilers (HiPEAC 2005). Part 2 is devoted to the topic of optimizing compilers and is edited by Mike O'Boyle, University of Edinburgh, François Bodin, IRISA, and Marcelo Cintra, University of Edinburgh. Finally, Part 3 is devoted to the best papers on embedded architectures and compilers from the 2006 ACM International Conference on Computing Frontiers and is edited by Sally A. McKee, Cornell University. Organizing specific themes in this journal will be a recurring activity in the future and I encourage prospective guest editors to propose themes for future volumes.

Finally, I have been fortunate to engage a set of distinguished members of our community to form the first editorial board. It is my pleasure to introduce this set of fine people.

Per Stenström
Chalmers University of Technology
Editor-in-chief
Transactions on HiPEAC

Editorial Board

Per Stenström is a professor of computer engineering of Chalmers University of Technology and a deputy dean of the IT University of Göteborg. His research interests are devoted to design principles for high-performance computer systems. He is an author of two textbooks and 100 research publications. He is regularly serving program committees of major conferences in the computer architecture field as well as actively contributing to editorial boards: He has been an editor of *IEEE Transactions on Computers* and is an editor of the *Journal of Parallel and Distributed Computing* and the *IEEE Computer Architecture Letters*. Further, he served as the General as well as the Program Chair of the ACM/IEEE Int. Symposium on Computer Architecture. He is a member of the ACM and the SIGARCH, a Fellow of the IEEE, and a founding member of the Network of Excellence in High-Performance Embedded Architectures and Compilation Methods funded by the European Commission.

Koen De Bosschere obtained his PhD from Ghent University in 1992. Currently, he is research professor at the engineering school of the same university where he teaches courses on computer architecture and operating systems. He is the head of a research group of 20 researchers and has co-authored 150 contributions in the domain of optimization, performance modeling, microarchitecture, and debugging. He is the coordinator of the Flemish research network on Architectures and Compilers for Embedded Systems (ACES), and he is the Belgian representative of the HiPEAC network of Excellence. Contact him at Koen.DeBosschere@elis.UGent.be.

Jose Duato is Professor in the Department of Computer Engineering (DISCA) at UPV, Spain. His research interests include interconnection networks and multiprocessor architectures. He has published over 340 papers. His research results have been used in the design of the Alpha 21364 microprocessor, and the Cray T3E, IBM BlueGene/L, and Cray Black Widow supercomputers. Dr. Duato is the first author of the book "Interconnection Networks: An Engineering Approach". He served as associate editor of IEEE TPDS and IEEE TC. He was General Co-chair of ICPP 2001, Program Chair of HPCA-10, and Program Co-chair of ICPP 2005. Also, he served as Co-chair, Steering Committee member, Vice-Chair, and Program Committee member in more than 55 conferences, including HPCA, ISCA, IPPS/SPDP, IPDPS, ICPP, ICDCS, Europar, and HiPC.

Manolis Katevenis received his PhD degree from U.C. Berkeley in 1983 and the ACM Doctoral Dissertation Award in 1984 for his thesis on "Reduced Instruction Set Computer Architectures for VLSI". After a brief term on the faculty of Computer Science at Stanford University, he is now based in Greece, with the University of Crete and with FORTH since 1986. After RISC, his research has been on interconnection networks and interprocessor communication. In packet switch architectures, his contributions since 1987 have been mostly in per-flow queueing, credit-based flow control, congestion management, weighted round-robin scheduling, buffered crossbars, and non-blocking switching fabrics. In multiprocessing and clustering, his contributions since 1993 have been on remote-write-based, protected, user-level communication.

His home URL is http://archvlsi.ics.forth.gr/~kateveni

Michael O'Boyle is a Reader in the School of Informatics at the University of Edinburgh and an EPSRC Advanced Research Fellow. He received his PhD in Computer Science from the University of Manchester in 1992. He was formerly a SERC Postdoctoral Research Fellow, a Visiting Research Scientist at IRISA/INRIA Rennes, a Visiting Research Fellow at the University of Vienna and a Visiting Scholar at Stanford University. More recently he was a Visiting Professor at UPC, Barcelona. Dr.O'Boyle's main research interests are in adaptive compilation, formal program transformation representations, the compiler impact on embedded systems, compiler-directed low-power optimization and automatic compilation for parallel single-address space architectures. He has published over 50 papers in international journals and conferences in this area and manages the Compiler and Architecture Design group consisting of 18 members.

Cosimo Antonio Prete is Full Professor of Computer Systems at the University of Pisa, Italy, and a faculty member of the PhD School in Computer Science and Engineering (IMT), Italy. He is Coordinator of the Graduate Degree Program in Computer Engineering and Rector's Adviser for Innovative Training Technologies at the University of Pisa. His research interests are focused on multiprocessor architectures, cache memory, performance evaluation, and embedded systems. He is an author of more than 100 papers published in international journals and conference proceedings. He has been project manager for several research projects, including: the SPP project, OMI, Esprit IV; the CCO project, supported by VLSI Technology, Sophia Antipolis; the ChArm project, supported by VLSI Technology, San Jose, and the Esprit III Tracs project.

André Seznec is "Directeur de Recherches" at IRISA/INRIA. Since 1994, he has been the head of the CAPS (Compiler Architecture for Superscalar and Special-purpose Processors) research team. He has been conducting research on computer architecture for more than 20 years. His research topics have included memory hierarchy, pipeline organization, simultaneous multithreading and branch prediction. In 1999-2000, he spent a sabbatical with the Alpha Group at Compaq.

Olivier Temam obtained a PhD in computer science from University of Rennes in 1993. He was Assistant Professor at the University of Versailles from 1994 to 1999, and then Professor at the University of Paris Sud until 2004. Since then, he has been a senior researcher at INRIA Futurs in Paris, where he heads the Alchemy group. His research interests include program optimization, processor architecture, and emerging technologies, with a general emphasis on long-term research.

Theo Ungerer is Chair of Systems and Networking at the University of Augsburg, Germany, and Scientific Director of the Computing Center of the University of Augsburg. He received a Diploma in Mathematics at the Technical University of Berlin in 1981, a Doctoral Degree at the University of Augsburg in 1986, and a second Doctoral Degree (Habilitation) at the University of Augsburg in 1992. Before his current position, he was scientific assistant at the University of Augsburg (1982-89 and 1990-92), visiting assistant professor at the University of California, Irvine (1989-90), professor of computer architecture at the University of Jena (1992-1993) and the Technical University of Karlsruhe (1993-2001). He is a Steering Committee member of HiPEAC and of the German Science Foundation's priority programme on "Organic Computing". His current research interests are in the areas of embedded processor architectures, embedded real-time systems, organic, bionic and ubiquitous systems.

Mateo Valero obtained his PhD at UPC in 1980. He is a professor in the Computer Architecture Department at UPC. His research interests focus on high-performance architectures. He has published approximately 400 papers on these topics. He is the director of the Barcelona Supercomputing Center, the National Center of Supercomputing in Spain. Dr. Valero has been honored with several awards, including the King Jaime I by the Generalitat Valenciana, and the Spanish national award "Julio Rey Pastor" for his research on IT technologies. In 2001, he was appointed Fellow of the IEEE, in 2002 Intel Distinguished Research Fellow and since 2003 he is a Fellow of the ACM. Since 1994, he has been a foundational member of the Royal Spanish Academy of Engineering. In 2005 he was elected Correspondant Academic of the Spanish Royal Academy of Sciences, and his home town of Alfamén named their public college after him.

Stamatis Vassiliadis is currently the chairperson of computer engineering and a T.U. Delft chair professor in the Faculty of Electrical Engineering, Mathematics and Computer Science. He has also served in the ECE faculties of Cornell University, Ithaca, NY and State University of New York (S.U.N.Y.), Binghamton, NY. He worked for a decade with IBM in the Advanced Workstations and Systems laboratory in Austin TX, the Mid-Hudson Valley laboratory in Poughkeepsie NY and the Glendale laboratory in Endicott NY. In IBM he was involved in a number of projects regarding computer design, organizations, and architectures and the leadership to advanced research projects. He has been involved in the design and implementation of several computers. For his work he received numerous awards including 24 publication awards, 15 invention achievement awards and an Outstanding Innovation Award for Engineering/Scientific Hardware Design in 1989. Six of his patents have been rated with the highest patent ranking in IBM and in 1990 he was awarded the highest number of patents in IBM. While at IBM, he was awarded 73 USA patents ranking him as the top all-time IBM inventor. Dr. Vassiliadis received best paper awards at the PDCS (2002), the IEEE CAS(1998, 2001),the IEEE ICCD (2001) and honorable mention best paper award at the IEEE/ACM MICRO 25(1992). He is an IEEE and ACM fellow.

Table of Contents

Part 3: ACM International Conference on Computing Frontiers 2006. Best Papers

High Performance Processor Chips

Maurice V. Wilkes

Computer Laboratory
University of Cambridge
U.K.

The development during the last 15 years in single-chip computers has been striking. It is a development that I have followed in detail, and some of you may have heard me talk about it before. It started in 1989 when a desktop computer first outperformed the most powerful minicomputer on the market, namely the VAX 8600. The desktop computer in question was a workstation based on a processor chip developed and marketed by the MIPS Computer Company, of which Professor John Hennessy of Stanford University was a leading light. Subsequent developments were very rapid and led to the demise of the minicomputer as we used to know it and to love it.

As time went on, desktop computers became more powerful. This enabled designers of operating systems to embody various speed enhancing techniques that were already in widespread use in large minicomputers. One of these techniques was branch prediction,that is the prediction ahead of time of the way a branch in the program would go. It surprised me how accurate branch prediction soon became. It made possible speculative execution. On arriving at a branch, the processor would go ahead along the predicted route, and only rarely was that found wrong. If it did happen to be wrong, then the instructions taken speculatively were cancelled and the correct branch was taken instead. This happened so rarely that the amount of time that was lost did not matter.

The same principle, namely speculation, was soon applied to situations other than branch prediction. Some of the techniques used came from minicomputers, but others had never reached minicomputers and came directly from the largest mainframes in existence. Among them were techniques that had been first used in the IBM model 92, which was the largest of the IBM 360 range.

The dramatic progress that I have just described has now been going on for 15 years, with no slackening of pace. It has of course been mainly the result of shrinkage. As it has become possible to make transistors smaller, the laws of physics have resulted in their becoming faster. The surprising thing is that it has been possible to carry out the shrinkage in such a way that the cost per transistor has actually gone down. In consequence, we have not had to make the choice between slow and cheap transistors on the one hand and fast and more expensive transistors on the other. We could have the best of both worlds. By some miracle, the fastest transistors available were also the cheapest. There were parallel developments in DRAM chips. As a result, it became possible to have large main memories, also at decreasing cost measured in cost per bit. The latest high-performance processor chips have thus always been more cost effective than older lower-performance chips. As you will appreciate, this fact has been of profound importance for the economics of the semiconductor industry.

P. Stenström (Ed.): Transactions on HiPEAC I, LNCS 4050, pp. 1–4, 2007.

In 1987 the semiconductor industry in the United States was going through a difficult period and it was no longer in a leading position worldwide. This naturally caused concern both within the US industry itself and also in US government circles. It was clear that improved cooperation and a common vision were required. Otherwise, there was a significant danger that the US industry would not be able to continue to uphold Moore's law as it always had done. Widespread consultation took place in the United States; best advice was sought, not only on the technical situation, but also on the best way to secure cooperation.

The proposal that emerged was that the US semiconducter companies should operate in two phases. The first would be a pre-competitive phase in which the basic research and development would be done using the pooled resources of the industry. The plan for this phase, the pre-competitive phase, was known as the semiconductor roadmap. In a second phase, the same companies would build plants, or foundries as they are often called, to manufacture chips which they would then market in a normal competitive manner. These chips specifically included processor chips and DRAM chips. The proposal was adopted, and it was very successful. It was so successful that it was agreed that a new roadmap should be produced at regular intervals. Each would give rise to a new generation of chips.

Originally, the roadmaps were an initiative of the US industry. They were started with the support of the United States government. By 1998 the government was felt to have played its part and, by agreement with the industry, it withdrew. This laid the way open to the US industry to issue an invitation to other areas of the world to participate. The areas were Europe, Japan, Korea, and Taiwan. The invitation was issued in April 1998. Any company in those areas able and willing to contribute might apply to do so. As a result, what had been the National Technology Roadmaps for Semiconductors became the International Technology Roadmaps for Semiconductors. This began with the issue published for 1999. Since then, a new edition of the roadmap has appeared every two years, with an update in between. The roadmaps and their updates have always been available for purchase by the public. They are now freely available on the Web and may be downloaded.

At this point I should stress that the roadmaps are not only research plans; they are also business plans. The principal business requirement that is built into the roadmaps is that the cost per transistor, or cost per bit of memory, should fall with each generation of chips. It is important to note that this is far from being an automatic consequence of shrinkage. If it had not been built into the roadmap as a business requirement, it might very well not have happened.

The principal step taken to meet the cost target was to move to larger wafers. This took place at an early point in the history of the roadmap. Specifically, it was a move from wafers of 200 mm in diameter to wafers of 300 mm in diameter. The larger wafer yielded nearly two and a half times as many chips as the smaller one. This increase in productivity has been a major factor in meeting the cost target.

What I have described is an ongoing activity. As time goes on, new editions of the roadmap come out and lead to the building of new foundries, or the upgrading of existing ones. In this way, the industry continually re-equips itself for the manufacture of chips of steadily increasing performance and also of falling cost, measured in terms of the work done.

It has always been realised that shrinkage cannot go on forever. There was a time when some people thought that, if we got down to using a few hundred electrons only to represent a one as distinct from a zero, then statistical effects would lead to unreliability and make it impracticable to go down any further. However, it was soon realised that this was not the way the end was likely to come. Later, it was a widely held view that difficulties with lithography would bring progress to an end. Lithography is, of course, the photographic process by which chips are made. As transistors get smaller and smaller, it is necessary to use light of shorter and shorter wavelength. The problem is that, eventually, all known transparent materials that could be used for lenses become opaque. We are very near that point, We are well into the ultraviolet, but, somehow, to everyone's great surprise, optical lithography still works. It only just works, but work it does. This is fortunate, because although the use of x-rays for lithography is not impossible and we may one day need it, it presents many technical difficulties.

More recently, we have met a different and very fundamental problem, one that is likely to be fatal. It is that the insulating layers in the transistors have become so thin that they are becoming porous. The layers are in fact only about eight atoms thick, and the porosity is to be explained in terms of quantum physics. We have now reached the point at which, because of porosity, traditional shrinkage can hardly go much further.

A search is going on for less porous insulating materials; this may take us a little further but not much. And so, are we finished? Well, the answer is: not quite. In fact, if you believe the roadmap, we still have a good way to go. It is true that conventional CMOS, as we know it, will not scale any further. But we should be able to get one step further, perhaps a bit more, by using non-conventional forms of CMOS. In addition, there are various other once-only expedients, known as technological boosters, by which further speeding up may be obtained. One of these, namely, the use of copper instead of aluminum for interconnect, has already found its way into production. Another, known as stretched silicon, is coming in. The active silicon is deposited on top of another crystalline material which has a slightly larger lattice than silicon. The silicon manages to conform by stretching its own lattice slightly. This stretching has the effect of increasing electron mobility, and it results in an increase in switching speed of about 10 to 15 percent. The second material is silicon carbide.

One can sum up by saying that we are now going to enter a period in which Moore's law is maintained, not by shrinkage, but by a series of once-only technological advances. I had always realised that we would enter such a period, but I felt that it would not be of long duration. However, the roadmap shows that there is a much wider range of technological boosters than I had expected, and their combined effort may be substantial. On this basis, the roadmap is very optimistic about maintaining Moore's law for the next five years.

Whether things will actually go this way or not will depend on whether the industry will be able to maintain the necessary investment in the changed circumstances that will exist after the end of routine shrinkage. I do not have a good enough knowledge of the economics of the semiconductor industry to enter into a discussion of this issue. Nor would I feel confident of being able to make a sufficiently accurate prediction of the future general economic climate, and this will obviously be a critical factor.

There is one incipient problem that I would like to mention. It is a problem that is beginning to concern designers and users of all high-performance computers. Its origins lie in an assumption which was built into the roadmaps from the beginning and which has been steadily ticking away like a timebomb ever since. I mean the assumption that DRAMs, while not as fast as SRAMs, are amply fast enough to be used for main memory. This statement was once true, but processors are now so fast that it is no longer true. We are beginning to experience a gap between the speed of the processor and the speed of its main memory. The gap is small at the moment, but it will become worse as long as processor speeds continue to increase.

There are, as you know, two parameters that characterize the performance of memory chips: latency and streaming bandwidth. Latency refers to the delay which occurs after a block of words has been requested from a memory chip before the first bits of the first word arrive. That is latency. Streaming bandwidth refers to the rate at which the bits of subsequent words follow on. I am sure that you all understand this distinction. I mention it because I find that there are people in the computer world who do not. It is, of course, latency that gives rise to the memory gap problem.

Small amounts of latency can be hidden by the overlapping of threads, for example by symmetric multithreading, or hyperthreading as Intel now call it, and this is actually being done. But ultimately, if Moore's law continues to hold long enough, a direct attack on latency itself will be needed. It would not be right to rule out a breakthrough in memory technology. Otherwise, I would expect there to be a movement in high-performance computers away from the use of DRAM for main memory to some form of SRAM.

High-Performance Embedded Architecture and Compilation Roadmap

Koen De Bosschere[1,2], Wayne Luk[1,3], Xavier Martorell[1,4], Nacho Navarro[1,4],
Mike O'Boyle[1,5], Dionisios Pnevmatikatos[1,6], Alex Ramirez[1,4],
Pascal Sainrat[1,7], André Seznec[1,8], Per Stenström[1,9], and Olivier Temam[1,10]

[1] HiPEAC Network of Excellence
http://www.HiPEAC.net
[2] Ghent University, Belgium
[3] Imperial College, UK
[4] UPC, Spain
[5] University of Edinburgh, UK
[6] ICS FORTH, Greece
[7] CNRS, France
[8] IRISA, France
[9] Chalmers, Sweden
[10] INRIA Futurs, France

Abstract. One of the key deliverables of the EU HiPEAC FP6 Network of Excellence is a roadmap on high-performance embedded architecture and compilation – the HiPEAC Roadmap for short. This paper is the result of the roadmapping process that took place within the HiPEAC community and beyond. It concisely describes the key research challenges ahead of us and it will be used to steer the HiPEAC research efforts.

The roadmap details several of the key challenges that need to be tackled in the coming decade, in order to achieve scalable performance in multi-core systems, and in order to make them a practical mainstream technology for high-performance embedded systems.

The HiPEAC roadmap is organized around 10 central themes: (i) single core architecture, (ii) multi-core architecture, (iii) interconnection networks, (iv) programming models and tools, (v) compilation, (vi) run-time systems, (vii) benchmarking, (viii) simulation and system modeling, (ix) reconfigurable computing, and (x) real-time systems. Per theme, a list of challenges is identified. In total 55 key challenges are listed in this roadmap. The list of challenges can serve as a valuable source of reference for researchers active in the field, it can help companies building their own R&D roadmap, and – although not intended as a tutorial document – it can even serve as an introduction to scientists and professionals interested in learning about high-performance embedded architecture and compilation.

Key words: HiPEAC, roadmap, single core architecture, multi-core architecture, interconnection networks, programming models and tools, compilation, run-time systems, benchmarking, simulation and system modelling, reconfigurable computing, real-time systems

P. Stenström (Ed.): Transactions on HiPEAC I, LNCS 4050, pp. 5–29, 2007.

Introduction

Modern embedded systems have computing resources that by far surpass the computing power of the mainframes of the sixties. This has been made possible thanks to technology scaling, architectural innovations, and advances in compilation. The driving force was the ability to speed-up existing binaries without much help of the compiler. However, since 2000 and despite new progress in integration technology, the efforts to design very aggressive and very complex wide issue superscalar processors have essentially come to a stop. The exponentially increasing number of transistors has since then been invested in ever larger on-chip caches, but even there we have reached the point of diminishing return.

Therefore, for the last five years, it has become more and more obvious that the quest for the ultimate performance on a single chip uniprocessor is becoming a dead-end. Although there are still significant amounts of unexploited instruction-level parallelism left, the complexities involved to extract it and the increased impact of wire-delay on the communication have left us with few ideas on how to further exploit it. Alternatively, further increasing the clock frequency is also getting more and more difficult because (i) of heat problems and (ii) of too high energy consumption. The latter is not only a technical problem for both server farms and mobile systems, but in the future, it is also going to become a marketing weapon targeted at the growing number of environmentally-aware consumers and companies in search of a greener computer.

For these and other reasons, there is currently a massive paradigm shift towards multi-core architectures. Instead of scaling performance by improving single core performance, performance is now scaled by putting multiple cores on a single chip, effectively integrating a complete multiprocessor on one chip. Since the total performance of a multi-core is improved without increasing the clock frequency, multi-cores offer a better performance/Watt ratio than a single core solution with similar performance. The interesting new opportunity is now that Moore's Law (which is still going to bring higher transistor density in the coming years) will make it possible to double the number of cores every 18 months. Hence, with 4 cores of the complexity of high-performance general-purpose processors already on a chip today, we can expect to fit as many as 256 such cores on a chip in ten years from now. The future scaling in the number of cores is called the multi-core roadmap hereafter.

This paradigm shift has a profound impact on all aspects of the design of future high-performance systems. In the multi-core roadmap, the processor becomes the functional unit, and just like floating-point units were added to single-core processors to accelerate scientific computations, special-purpose computing nodes will be added to accelerate particular application types (media processing, cryptographic algorithms, digital signal processing, . . .) leading to heterogeneous multi-cores. Heterogeneous multi-cores add a new design complexity issue, because special-purpose computing nodes can have a significant impact on the memory hierarchy of the system. This will require specially designed communication paths for which bus-based interconnects are no longer suited.

On the multi-core roadmap, cheaper and more reliable high-performance switched serial interconnects will be used. This trend is evident in all recent high-performance interconnects such as PCI Express, ASI, FSB, HyperTransport.

Programming these (heterogeneous) multi-core systems requires an advanced parallel programming environment enabling the user to manually express concurrency as well as to automatically discover thread-level parallelism (in contrast to instruction-level parallelism) in sequential code. Automatically extracting thread-level parallelism or auto-parallelization has been extensively studied for scientific programs since the 1970s. Despite impressive gains for certain applications it is highly sensitive to the programming idiom. Common programming languages featuring arbitrary pointer manipulations (like C or C++) make this auto-parallelization extremely difficult. Due to this difficulty in exploiting parallelism and the easier option of waiting for the next technology generation to provide greater performance, parallel computing has failed to deliver in the past. However, now it seems that thread-level parallelism is the only route to performance scalability together with customization. If we cannot extract sufficient thread-level parallelism from the user's code, it does not matter how many cores are available – there will be no performance gain. This situation has implications far beyond architecture and compilation as it will affect all consumers used to the steady improvement of application performance across computer generations. Such improvements will no longer occur unless the application is parallelized.

The increased computing power for a given power budget will pave the way for new high-performance embedded applications: more demanding multimedia applications, advanced online biomedical signal processing, software-defined radio, biometric data processing like voice processing and image recognition. Many of these applications have hard or soft real-time requirements. This is challenging in a multi-core system because all cores share common resources like the lower level caches and the off-chip communication bandwidth – making it more difficult to compute the worst case execution time. Due to the better performance/Watt metric for multi-cores, they will also be used as elementary computing nodes in supercomputers where they will be used to run traditional scientific workloads. Hence, multi-cores will span the complete computational spectrum.

It is clear that this paradigm shift is so profound that it is affecting almost all aspects of system design (from the components of a single core up to the complete system), and that a lot of research and tool development will be needed before it will be possible to bring many-core processors to the masses.

The remainder of this paper details several of the key challenges that need to be tackled in the coming decade, in order to achieve scalable performance in multi-core systems, and in order to make them a practical mainstream technology for embedded systems. It is in the first place a roadmap for research and is not meant to be a roadmap on industrial R&D. Furthermore it is a roadmap on high-performance embedded architecture and compilation, hence it is about future embedded hardware and tools to exploit that hardware in the broad sense. It is neither a technology roadmap, nor an embedded application roadmap as these aspects are already covered by other documents like the ITRS roadmap and the ISTAG documents.

The roadmap is structured around 10 themes: (i) single core architecture, (ii) multi-core architecture, (iii) interconnection networks, (iv) programming models and tools, (v) compilation, (vi) run-time systems, (vii) benchmarking, (viii) simulation and system modeling, (ix) reconfigurable computing, and (x) real-time systems. Per theme, a list of challenges is identified. More important challenges are put higher in the list.

The fact that we distinguish 10 themes does not mean that these themes are independent; it is just a way to structure this document. In fact, some of the challenges have moved from one theme to another several times during the roadmapping process. Other issues like power are popping up as a challenge in different themes.

The description of the individual challenges is kept concise, and we have tried to describe just the challenge, not the solutions as we did not want to impose our vision on the possible solutions. For the same reason, we decided not to include references per challenge.

1   Single Core Architecture

Many of the classical uniprocessor trade-offs of the last 20 years will have to be reconsidered when uniprocessors are used as building blocks in a multi-core system. Devoting precious silicon area to aggressive out-of-order execution hardware might no longer lead to an optimal solution, and using the area to implement two simpler cores can result in a better performance and/or lower power consumption (in a sense we might be witnessing the CISC-RISC transition again – this time at the core level). However, since many existing workloads are inherently sequential, and since even a parallelized application will contain significant amounts of sequential code, giving up on single core performance might cause serious problems for this class of applications. The research on processor micro-architecture must therefore continue to focus on the trade-off between performance and complexity of the micro-architecture. The following challenges are identified for future single core architectures.

Challenge 1.1:   Complexity Reduction

The aggressive out-of-order execution mechanism is very complex, its verification is very time-consuming, its implementation is using up a lot of silicon area, and its operation is consuming a lot of power. In order to make it a suitable candidate as a basic building block in a multi-core system, its complexity has to be reduced, without compromising the single-core performance too much.

Challenge 1.2:   Power Management

Besides the creation of specialized hardware modules, Dynamic-Voltage-Frequency-Scaling (DVFS) has been a prevailing power managing technique so far. It not only helps in reducing the dynamic power consumption, but it also helps fighting static (leakage) power consumption. Unfortunately, scaling down the voltage leads to an increase in the number of soft errors which creates a reliability problem in future systems. As a result, while DVFS has been an important technique so far, it will be less attractive as we move along. Hence, novel techniques will be needed to manage both dynamic and static power consumption in single cores. If not, it is expected that future architectural designs will be more and more constrained by leakage power consumption.

Challenge 1.3:   Thermal Management

With the increasing integration density, power consumption is not the only concern. Power density has also risen to very high levels in several parts of the processor. Temperature hotspots are therefore becoming a major concern on processors, since they can result in transient or permanent failure. The temperature hotspots have also a major impact of the aging of the components. While systems are now designed with a predetermined power budget, they will also have to be designed with a fixed thermal envelope. In order to fix this issue, architects first have to build reliable models able to represent both dynamic power consumption and temperature behavior of modern cores. Then they have to propose hardware/software solutions to optimize performance while respecting the thermal envelope. Such proposals might include more uniform power density distribution through the chip, but also thermally-guided dynamic activity migration.

Challenge 1.4:   Design Automation for Special-Purpose Cores

Future embedded systems will take advantage of special-purpose hardware accelerators to speed up execution, and to dramatically reduce power consumption. Such accelerators can be made available as independent IP blocks or can be custom designed. A major challenge in the custom design of special-purpose cores is the fully automatic generation of the hardware and the software tools from a single architecture description or an application.

Challenge 1.5:   Transparent Micro-architecture

Modern execution environments such as just-in-time compilers, code morphers, and virtualization systems rely on run-time information about the code being executed. Most processors already provide a set of performance counters that are used to steer the optimization or translation process. Given the raising popularity of this type of applications, and in order to enable more advanced optimizations, there will be a growing demand to provide more information about the dynamic processor operation. An important issue is to come up with a standardized set of performance counters in order to make the optimizations that use them more portable.

Challenge 1.6:   Software-Controlled Reconfiguration

Cores should provide a number of controls to the compiler to allow the latter to better control the detailed operation of the processor (e.g. the ability to power down particular components of the processor). The compiler has often a better view on the behavior of a program than the core executing it (e.g. it has information about the type of algorithm, the memory usage, the amount of thread-level parallelism). By allowing the compiler to adapt or reconfigure the core to the needs of the application, a better performance/Watt ratio can be obtained.

Challenge 1.7:   Reliability and Fault Tolerance

Electronic circuit reliability is decreasing as CMOS technology scales to smaller feature sizes. Single event upsets will soon become a common phenomenon instead of being extremely rare. Furthermore, permanent faults can occur due to device fatigue and other reasons. Functionality must be added to the cores that allow them to operate in the presence of transient and permanent faults perhaps with degraded performance.

Challenge 1.8:   Security

By putting multiple cores on one chip, security is getting increasingly important for single cores. Hardware protection mechanisms are needed to help the software staying secure and to prevent against on-chip attacks like denial-of-service attacks against cores, the exploitation of hidden channels leaking information between cores, etc.

Challenge 1.9:   Virtualization

Virtualization is a technology that will gain importance. Hardware support is needed to keep the virtualization layer slim, fast and secure. For some types of applications, strong performance isolation guarantees will be required between multiple containers.

2   Multi-core Architecture

A multi-core architecture is a MIMD (multiple-instruction multiple-data) multiprocessor using the terminology that has been prevailing for many decades. In the last decade, chip multiprocessing (mostly heterogeneous, up to 6-8 cores) has been commonly used in embedded SOCs, thus anticipating some of the trends that have since then been adopted also by mainstream general-purpose processors. However, the ad-hoc programmability of such embedded system has been far from satisfactory, and we now have enough transistors to integrate even more complex cores on a single chip. Envisioning a multi-core microprocessor with 256 cores by 2015, several opportunities and system challenges arise at the architecture level. Multi-core challenges are identified at the hardware and the software level. Hardware challenges are discussed in this section, the software challenges in the sections on programming models and compilation.

Challenge 2.1:   Hardware Support for Parallel Programming

When moving on the multi-core roadmap, at some point traditional software-based synchronization methods will no longer be feasible and new (hardware-based) methods will have to be introduced. Transactional memory is one candidate, but it is probably just the initial approach. In fact, the hardware/software interface, i.e., the instruction-set architecture has more or less stayed unaltered for several decades. An important challenge is to understand which hardware/software abstraction can enhance the productivity of parallel software development and then find suitable implementation approaches to realize it. In fact, the abundance of transistors available in the next decade can find good use in realizing enhanced abstractions for programmers.

Challenge 2.2:   On-Chip Interconnects and Memory Subsystem

The critical infrastructure to host a large core count (say 100-1000 cores in ten years from now) consists of the on-chip memory subsystem and network-on-chip (NoC) technologies. Scaling these subsystems in a resource-efficient manner to accommodate the foreseen core count is a major challenge. According to ITRS, the off-chip bandwidth is expected to increase linearly rather than exponentially. As a result, a high on-chip cache performance is crucial to cut down on bandwidth. However, we have seen a diminishing return of investments in the real-estate devoted to caches, so clearly cache hierarchies are in need of innovation to make better use of the resources.

Challenge 2.3:   Cache Coherence Schemes

At the scale of cores that is foreseeable within the next decade, it seems reasonable to support a shared memory model. On the other hand, a shared memory model requires efficient support for cache coherence. A great deal of attention was devoted to scalable cache coherence protocols in the late 80s and the beginning of the 90s and enabled industrial offerings of shared memory multiprocessors with a processor count of several hundred, e.g., SGI Origin 2000. More recently, the latency/bandwidth trade-off between broadcast-based (snooping) and point-to-point based (directory) cache coherency protocols has been studied in detail. However, now that we can soon host a system with hundreds of cores on a chip, technological parameters and constraints will be quite different. For example, cache-to-cache miss latencies are relatively shorter and the bandwidth on-chip is much larger than for the "off-chip" systems of the 90s. On the other hand, design decisions are severely constrained by power consumption. All these differences make it important to revisit the design of scalable cache coherence protocols for the multi-cores in this new context.

Challenge 2.4:   Hardware Support for Heterogeneity

Multiple heterogeneous cores have their own design complexity issues, as special-purpose cores have significant impact on the memory hierarchy of the system, and require specially designed communication protocols for fast data exchange among them. A major challenge is the design of a suitable high-performance and flexible communication interface between less traditional computing cores (e.g. FPGAs) and the rest of the multi-core system.

Challenge 2.5:   Hardware Support for Debugging

Debugging a multi-core multi-ISA application is a complex task. The debugger needs to be both powerful and must cause very low overhead to avoid timing violations and so-called Heisenbugs. This is currently a big problem for existing debuggers, since providing a global view of a multi-core machine is virtually impossible without specialized hardware support. Much more so than a classic single-core device, multi-core chips have to be designed to support debugging tools. The proper hardware support is needed to non-intrusively observe an execution, to produce synchronized traces of execution from multiple cores, to get debug data into and out of the chip.

3   Interconnection Networks

Bus-based interconnects, like PCI or AMBA have been the dominant method for interconnecting components. They feature low cost (simple wires), convenience in adding nodes, and some reliability advantages (no active elements other than end-nodes). However, they do not scale to high performance or to high number of nodes as they are limited by higher parasitic capacitance (multiple devices attached to the wires), arbitration delay (who will transmit next), turn-around overhead (idle time when the transmitting node changes, due to the bidirectionality of the medium), and lack of parallelism (only one transmission at a time).

Point-to-point links do not suffer from arbitration delays or turn-around overheads. For external connections, high-speed serial link technology has advanced and offers single link performance at the level of 6.25 GBaud in the immediate future, making it the preferred solution to support high throughput applications. Similarly, on-chip networks can use transmission lines and compensation or re-timing techniques to minimize timing skew between long parallel wires, enabling the use of wide paths. To further increase aggregate system throughput, multiple links interconnected via switches offer parallelism, and hence even higher performance. The switch is becoming the basic building block for wired interconnections, much like the microprocessor is for processing and the RAM is for memory. Finally, embedded system components are slowly turning to packet-based transfers, aiding in this way the convergence to switched-based interconnects. Lately memory chips such as FBDIMM have appeared and directly support packet-style transfers.

Future on-chip interconnects will connect hundreds of nodes (processors, memories, etc) reaching the realm of today's off-chip networks. To build these networks we can use today's ideas and techniques, adapting them to the requirements and technologies of future embedded systems. The new applications, requirements, level of integration and implementation technologies will also open new possibilities for innovation and fresh ideas. In this context, the challenges for the near future are the following:

Challenge 3.1:   Interconnect Performance and Interfaces

Increasing levels of functionality and integration are pushing the size and the performance requirements of future embedded systems to unprecedented levels. Networks-on-chips will need to provide the necessary throughput at the lowest possible latency. Besides implementation technology innovations, important research areas include the long-standing, deep and difficult problems of interconnection network architecture: lossless flow control and congestion management. Recent research results in these areas have shown good progress: regional explicit congestion notification (RECN), and hierarchical request-grant-credit flow control. New research directions are opening to fully exploit the implementation technologies, for example techniques to exploit the different characteristics of multiple metal layers to provide links with shorter latencies.

Network interface design and its related buffering issues are also important for the system-level performance and cost. The simple bus interfaces of the past are rapidly evolving to full-fledged, tightly coupled network interfaces. To improve end-to-end application throughput, we need both a new breed of simplified protocol stacks, and analogously architected network interfaces. The solutions may include key research findings from the parallel computing community: user-level protected communication protocols, network interface virtualization, and communication primitives for remote DMA and remote queues.

Challenge 3.2:   Interconnect Power Consumption and Management

Meeting the required interconnect performance at the lowest power consumption is becoming increasingly important as the technology moves into the nanometer scale. Power consumption is affected by many interconnect design parameters such as implementation technology, link driver design, network topology, congestion and buffer management. For example, power consumption for off-chip networks is dominated by chip crossings, suggesting higher-radix switches for lower power consumption. In addition, power management functionality will extend from the processing nodes to the system level, creating a need for NoC power-management features and protocols. These features will enable performance for power dissipation trade-offs according to system-level processing requirements. Such features can also be used for thermal management that is also becoming important in sub-micron technologies.

Challenge 3.3:   Quality of Service

Embedded systems are often real-time systems, and in these cases, the interconnection network has to provide guarantees in communication parameters such as bandwidth and latency. Predicable interconnect behaviour is cornerstone to providing these guarantees, and Quality of Service (QoS) differentiation can be the vehicle towards this goal. The requirements can vary greatly from best effort, soft- and hard-real time applications, and the entire range should be supported in the most uniform and transparent way to aid component reuse. Effectiveness in providing these guarantees (for example the size of buffers that hold low priority traffic) is also an important issue as it directly influences the interconnect cost. A similar need for QoS is created by resource virtualization, where a single system (even a single processor) is viewed as a set of virtual entities that operate independently and must have a fair access to the network resources. This can be achieved either through a physical partitioning of the network, or by virtualizing the network itself using the traditional QoS mechanisms.

Challenge 3.4:   Reliability and Fault Tolerance

Single event upsets will introduce uncertainties even in fully controlled environments such as on-chip networks. While traditional networking solutions exist for dealing with transmission errors, they often come at a significant implementation cost. Efficient protocols that expose part of the necessary buffering to the application and possibly to the compiler in order to jointly manage the required space can offer an efficient solution to this problem. To deal with permanent faults techniques such as automatic path migration and network reconfiguration can be used. However, errors can affect not only the data links and switches, but also the network interface logic which needs to be designed to tolerate this type of upsets.

Challenge 3.5:   Interconnect Design Space Exploration

To explore the large interconnect design space, and to create efficient interconnect topologies, while at the same time providing support and guarantees for Quality-of-Service requirements is a complex, time-consuming and error-prone process. Many individual aspects of this process can however be automated and provide feedback to the designer. However, there is a lack of integrated toolchains that will operate from the requirement level allowing early design-space exploration, all the way to the implementation dealing with all the intermediate parameters. Such tool-chains will improve productivity and allow for faster and smaller designs and faster system verification.

Challenge 3.6:   Protection and Security

Embedded systems traditionally have been "flat" systems with direct control of all resources aminimal – if any – protection domains. The increase in the number of nodes, the need for programmability and extensibility, and the ever-increasing complexity are creating the need for support of protected operation. This functionality can be implemented in the network interfaces but is an integral part of and has to be designed in coordination with the overall system-level protection architecture. The system also needs modularity to support virtualization features. At the next level is the interconnection of systems and devices, where there is a need for secure communications.

4   Programming Models and Tools

Exploiting the parallelism offered by a multi-core architecture requires powerful new programming models. The programming model has to allow the programmer to express parallelism, data access, and synchronization. Parallelism can be expressed as parallel constructs and/or tasks that should be executed on each of the processing elements. The data access and the synchronization models can be distributed – through message passing – or can be shared – using global memory.

As a result, the programming model has to deal with all those different features, allowing the programmer to use such a wide range of multiprocessors, and their functionality. At the same time, the programming model has to be simple for the programmers, because a large majority of them will now be confronted with parallel programming. Therefore, to a certain extent, the simplicity of parallel programming approaches is becoming as important as the performance they yield. For the programming of reconfigurable hardware, a combination of procedural (time) and structural (space) programming views should be considered. Debuggers, instrumentation, and performance analysis tools have to be updated accordingly to support the new features supported by the programming model. This is important to reduce the time to market of both run-time systems, and applications developed on multi-core processors.

Challenge 4.1:   Passing More Semantics

A first challenge is how to get the correct combination of programming constructs for expressing parallelism. Most probably, they will be taken from different programming paradigms. OpenMP 3.0 will incorporate the task concept, and with it, it will be easy to program in a pthreads-like way without the burden of having to manually outline the code executed in parallel with other tasks. Incremental parallelization will be also possible, as OpenMP already allows it. Along with this, new approaches at the higher level will include techniques from the productivity programming models area: The definition of "places" (X10), "regions" (Fortress), "locales" (Chapel) or addressable domains from the language perspective, allowing to distribute the computation across a set of machines in clustered environments; Futures (X10, Cilk), allowing the execution of function calls in parallel with the code calling the function.

Challenge 4.2:   Transparent Data Access

A second challenge is to build a programming model that allows the programmer to transparently work with shared and distributed memory at the same time. Current attempts, like Co-Array Fortran, UPC, X10, Fortress, Chapel..., still reflect in the language the fact that there are such different and separate addressable domains. This interferes with data access and synchronization, because depending on where the computation is performed, different ways to access data and synchronization must be used. As hardware accelerators can also be seen as different execution domains with local memory, it is interesting to note that solving this challenge will also provide transparent support to run on accelerators (see also Challenge 5.4).

Challenge 4.3:   Adaptive Data Structures

An observation is that at the low level all code is structured as procedures: (i) programmers break the different functionality they put in the application as subroutines or functions; (ii) parallelizing compilers outline as a subroutine the code to be executed in parallel; (iii) even accelerators can be used through a well-defined procedure interface, hiding the details of data transfer and synchronization; and (iv) most hardware vendors already provide libraries with optimized primitives in the form of procedures. But there is no such mechanism for data structures. A mechanism is needed to allow the compiler and the run-time system to tune – optimize – data structures, adapting them to the execution conditions. In such a way that a data structure can be automatically distributed in a cluster or accessed by a set of accelerators, while all data transfer involved is managed by the run-time system. Knowing the restrictions on the arguments of the procedures (atomicity, asynchrony ...) will also be needed to ensure correct data transfers and manipulation.

Challenge 4.4:   Advanced Development Environments

An easy to program multi-core system requires sophisticated support for threading management, synchronization, memory allocation and access. When different threads run different ISA's, a single debugging session must show all types of machine instructions, and the information related to variables and functions, and must be able to automatically detect non-local bugs like race conditions, dangling pointers, memory leaks, etc. Debugging a multi-core system running hundreds of threads is a major unsolved challenge, which will require hardware support in order to be effectively solved.

Challenge 4.5:   Instrumentation and Performance Analysis

Tools obtaining run-time information from the execution are essential for performance debugging, and to steer dynamic code translation (Just-in-Time compilation, code morphing,...). Hardware designs must take observability into consideration. The amount of information that can possibly be generated by a multi-core system is however overwhelming. The challenge is to find techniques to efficiently analyze the data (e.g. searching for periods or phases), to significantly reduce the amount of data, and to find effective ways to conveniently represent the data generated by hundreds of threads.

5   Compilation

Modern hardware needs a sophisticated compiler to generate highly optimized code. This increasing rate of architectural change has placed enormous stress on compiler technology such that current compiler technology can no longer keep up with architectural change. The key point is that traditional approaches to compiler optimizations are based on hardwired static analysis and transformation which can no longer be used in a computing environment that is continually changing. What is required is an approach which evolves and adapts to applications and architectural change along the multi-core roadmap and takes into account the various program specifications: from MATLAB programs to old already parallelized code. For future multi-core based high-performance embedded systems, the following challenges are identified.

Challenge 5.1:   Automatic Parallelization

Automatic parallelization has been quite successful in the past for scientific programs, array-based programming languages (FORTRAN), and for homogeneous shared memory architectures. This work has to be extended to a much wider set of application types, to pointer-based programming languages, and to a wide variety of potentially heterogeneous multi-core processors with different memory models. This requires the development of new static analysis techniques to analyze pointer-based programs (maybe already parallelized) and manage the mapping of memory accesses to systems without explicit hardware-based shared memory. By providing hints or assertions, the programmer might be able to considerably improve the parallelization process.

It will incorporate speculative parallelization to extract greater levels of parallelism. Furthermore by adding certain architectural features, the compiler could communicate its assumptions at run-time and enable the violations to be detected by the hardware, causing more optimal overall program execution. Examples of these techniques include speculative load instructions, and speculative multithreading. These ideas enable the compiler to make better optimization choices without over-burdening the hardware with complexity. Finally, speculative parallelization can be combined with dynamic optimization such that as the program evolves in time, the (just-in-time) compiler can learn about the relative success of speculation and dynamically recompile the code accordingly.

Challenge 5.2:   Automatic Compiler Adaptation

Tuning the optimization heuristics for new processor architectures is a time-consuming process, which can be automated by machine learning. The machine learning based optimizer will try many different transformations and optimizations on a set of benchmarks recording their performance and behavior. From this data set it will build an optimizing model based on the real processor performance.

This approach can also be used for long running iterative optimization where we want to tune important libraries and embedded applications for a particular configuration. Alternatively, it can be used by dynamic just-in-time compilers to modify their compilation policy based on feedback information. In addition, if we wish to optimize for space, power and size simultaneously we just alter the objective function of the model to be learned and this happens automatically.

Challenge 5.3:   Architecture/Compilation Cooperation

The role compilation will have in optimization will be defined by the architectural parameters available to it. Longer term work will require strong compiler/architecture co-design opening up the architecture infrastructure to compiler manipulation or conversely passing run-time information to the architecture to allow it to best use resources.

This is part of a larger trend where the distinction between decisions currently made separately in the compiler and in the hardware is blurred. If the compiler has exact knowledge of behavior within an up-coming phase of a program (a so-called scenario), then the hardware should be appropriately directed. If, however, analysis fails, then the hardware should employ an appropriate general mechanism possibly aided by hardware-based prediction. In between these two extremes, the compiler can provide hints to the hardware and can modify its behavior based on run-time analysis.

Challenge 5.4:   Mapping Computations on Accelerators

Some approaches already offer access to accelerators through well defined interfaces, thus summarizing computation, data access and synchronization on a single procedure call. This challenge seeks to enable the compiler to automatically detect and map parts of the application code to such "accelerated" routines. This may be easy for well-known procedures from the HPC environment, like FFT or DGEMM, but there is no general solution yet for general application code. The problem is especially challenging for less conventional computing nodes such as FPGAs.

Challenge 5.5:   Power-Aware Compilation

As the demand for power efficient devices grows, compilers will have to consider energy consumption in the same way space and time are considered now. The key challenge is to exploit compile-time knowledge about the program to use only those resources necessary for the program to execute efficiently. The compiler is then responsible for generating code where special instructions direct the architecture to work in the desired way. The primary area of interest of such compiler analysis is in gating off unused parts or in dynamically resizing expensive resources with the help of the run-time system. Another compiler technique for reducing power is the generation of compressed or compacted binaries which will stay important in the embedded domain.

Challenge 5.6:   Just-in-Time Compilation

Given the popularity of programming languages that use just-in-time compilation (Java and C# being very popular programming languages of the moment), more research is needed in Just-in-Time compilation for heterogeneous multi-core platforms. Since the compilation time is part of the execution time, the optimization algorithms have to be both accurate and efficient. The challenge in Just-in-Time compilation for heterogeneous multi-cores is not only to predict (i) when to optimize, (ii) what to optimize and (iii) how to optimize, but also (i) when to parallelize, (ii) what to parallelize, and (iii) how to parallelize. Appropriate hardware performance counters or possibly additional run-time information can help making these decisions.

Challenge 5.7:   Full System Optimization

Given the component-based nature of modern software, the massive use of libraries, and the widespread use of separate compilation, run-time optimization, and on-line profiling, no single tool has an overview of the complete application, and many optimization opportunities are left unexploited (addresses, function parameters, final layout,...). One of the challenges in full system optimization is to bring the information provided at all these levels together in one tool, and then to use this information to optimize the application. This will enable cross-boundary optimization: between ISAs in a heterogeneous multi-core, between a processor and reconfigurable hardware, between the application and the kernel. An underlying technical challenge is often the design of scalable algorithms to analyze and optimize a full system.

6   Run-Time Systems

The run-time system aims at controlling the environment of the embedded system during system operation. It is concerned mainly with issues related to dynamic behavior that cannot be determined through static analysis (by the compiler). The run-time system consists of a collection of facilities, such as dynamic memory allocation, thread management and synchronization, middleware, virtual machines, garbage collection, dynamic optimization, just-in-time compilation and execution resources management.

The current trend in embedded systems is to customize automatically or by hand the operating systems developed for general-purpose platforms. There is a large opportunity for improving operating system and run-time performance via hardware support for certain features and functions (e.g., fault management and resource monitoring). Operating system and runtime research should be more closely coupled to hardware research in the future in order to integrate multicore heterogeneous systems (medium term challenges) and to seamlessly support dynamic reconfiguration and interoperability (long term challenges).

Challenge 6.1:   Execution Environments for Heterogeneous Systems

Runtimes and operating systems have to be aware that the architecture is a heterogeneous multi-core. Currently, most specific accelerators are considered as devices or slave coprocessors. They need to be treated as first class objects at all levels of management and scheduling. The scheduler will map fine grain tasks to the appropriate computing element, being processors with different ISA or even specific logic engines. Memory will be distributed across the chip, so the runtime needs to graciously handle new local storages and sparse physical address spaces. Support for code morphing should be integrated. Hardware and software will be co-designed, and compilers should generate multiple binary versions for the software to run on and control the multiple cores.

Challenge 6.2:   Power Aware Run-Time Systems

Allocation of resources should take energy efficiency into account, for example the fair allocation of battery resources rather than just CPU time. Operating system functionalities and policies should consider: disk scheduling (spin down policies), security (adaptive cryptographic policy), CPU scheduling (voltage scaling, idle power modes, moving less critical tasks to less power-hungry cores), application/OS interaction for power management, memory allocation (placement, switch energy modes), resource protection/allocation (fair distribution, critical resources) and communication (adaptive network polling, routing, and servers).

Challenge 6.3:   Adaptable Run-Time Systems

The run-time systems should (semi-)automatically adapt to different heterogeneous multi-cores based on the requirements of the applications, available resources, and scheduling management policies. However, static application-specific tailoring of operating systems is not sufficient. An adaptable operating system is still tailored down for specific requirements, but can be reconfigured dynamically if the set of required features changes. We will need new run-time systems that leverage the OS modularity and configurability to improve efficiency and scalability, and provide support to new programming models or compilers that exploit phase and versioning systems. Reliability, availability and serviceability (RAS) management systems have to work cooperatively with the OS/Runtime to identify and resolve these issues. Advanced monitoring and adaptation can improve application performance and predictability.

Challenge 6.4:   Run-Time Support for Reconfiguration

Run-time support for reconfigurable (RC) applications is hampered by the fact that the execution model of dynamically reconfigurable devices is a paradigm currently not supported by existing run-time systems. Research challenges include reconfigurable resource management that deals with problems such as reconfiguration time scheduling, reconfigurable area management and so on. The need for real-time, light-weight operating systems support on RC platforms is also emerging. The problem of multi-tasking in dynamically reconfigurable RC context is largely unsolved. Transparent hardware/software boundaries are envisioned: a task can be dynamically scheduled in hardware or in software by the run-time system, while the rest of the system does not need to be aware of such activities. This challenge is about target-architecture and technology dependent automated run-time system customization needed to allow fine-tuning of RC-aware run-time systems.

Challenge 6.5:   Fault Tolerance

Providing new levels of fault tolerance and security in an increasingly networked embedded world by taking advantage of large degrees of replication and by designing fence mechanisms in the system itself (as opposed at the application level). Moreover, besides providing novel techniques that will increase system reliability and security, research should consider methods for allowing users/programmers to specify their intentions in this domain. Self-diagnosis mechanisms should detect and repair defective components while maintaining the system operation.

Challenge 6.6:   Seamless Interoperability

Due to the very nature of embedded applications (communication with the environment is a key part in embedded computation) many existent embedded devices are somehow (wired or wireless) connected. Mobility suggests support for wireless connectivity, and in the future the majority of the embedded systems platform will have a connection either with other similar devices through small area networks or with bigger infrastructures via the Internet or other private networks. Future embedded systems devices will gain enhanced new capabilities using the networks: they will be able to upgrade themselves (automatically or semi-automatically), maintain consistency with other devices (PCs, laptops), and perform backups and other useful administrative tasks. At least a dozen wireless networks along with their protocols and interfaces are available and cover the wide range from personal- and small-area to medium and long distance networks, offering different trade-offs in features, throughput, latency and power consumption. The challenge towards this goal is the seamless functional integration of vastly different communication media and methods, and the automatic adaptation to network performance both at the level of interconnect management as well as the application behaviour.

7 Benchmarking

The design of high-performance processor architecture is a matter of trade-offs, where a sea of design options is available, all of them having some performance/power/area impact. In order to reliably compare two design points, we must use realistic applications. Such is the role of a benchmark suite, which is a set of representative applications.

First of all, it is getting increasingly difficult to find useful benchmarks: realistic applications are generally carefully protected by companies. Even inside companies, strict Intellectual Property (IP) barriers isolate the application development groups from the hardware development groups, who only get a vague description of the real application needs. And then again, another set of IP barriers isolate the hardware development groups from the research groups, who only get access to distorted versions of the applications, or synthetic kernels. In the absence of real applications, academia generally relies on micro-benchmarks (kernels), synthetic applications or the widely spread SPEC benchmark suite. However, they only model particular aspects of an application.

Secondly, different application domains have different computing requirements, and hence need their own benchmarks. There are already a number of benchmark suites representing different application domains: SPEC for CPU performance, Mediabench for multimedia, TPC-H, TPC-C for databases, etc. The EEMBC embedded benchmark is already composed of different suites. As new application domains emerge, new benchmarks will have to be added. Besides the application domain, the software implementation technology is also changing rapidly. Virtualization is gaining popularity, and an increasing number of applications are being deployed for managed execution environments like the Java virtual machine or .NET. Currently, there are very few good benchmarks in this area.

Finally, the hardware is also evolving. Old benchmarks are not suited anymore to evaluate hardware extensions like MMX, SSE, Altivec, or 3DNow and hardware accelerators in general (including FPGAs). Since these hardware accelerators are getting increasingly common in heterogeneous multi-cores, there is a huge need for realistic benchmarks that can exploit these (parallel) hardware resources.

In the benchmarking domain, there are three major challenges:

Challenge 7.1: Multi-core Benchmarks

Multi-cores (and especially heterogeneous multi-cores) are less standardized than general-purpose processors. They can contain several special-purpose hardware accelerators, and even reconfigurable components. Benchmarking such architectures against one another is very difficult because there are almost no benchmarks available that fully exploit the resources of such a platform (computing cores, but also the interconnections and memory hierarchy). This challenge aims at creating a set of representative benchmark applications for this type of processing architectures.

Challenge 7.2: Synthetic Benchmarks

Creating a good benchmark is a tough job. First one has to get full access to a realistic, IP-free, relevant and representative application, and then this application has to be adapted in order to make it platform independent. This challenge aims at transforming an existing application into an IP-free and platform independent synthetic benchmark with a given execution time. Such a methodology would significantly facilitate the exchange of code between (departments of) companies, or between companies and academia. The fact that the execution time of the synthetic benchmark can be chosen, will have a dramatic effect on simulation time. One particularly challenging task is to come up with a synthetic benchmark that models the behavior of an application that runs in a virtual machine.

Challenge 7.3: Benchmark Characterization

Traditionally, benchmarks are divided in application domains: floating-point (scientific) applications, CPU-intensive applications, media processing, digital signal processing kernels. Recently, some application domains have been added: bio-informatics, gaming, software-defined radio,... There is no solid methodology to characterize all these different types of benchmarks in such a way that the characterization could be used to steer the selection of benchmarks or eventually prune the system design space. More research is needed to come up with (mathematical) models describing benchmark behavior – including benchmarks that run in a virtual machine.

8 Simulation and System Modelling

Simulation technology and methodology is at the crux of computer architecture research and development. Given the steadily increasing complexity of modern computer systems, simulation has become the de facto standard for making accurate design trade-offs efficiently.

Simulation technology and methodology need to meet high standards. Computer architects want simulation software to be fast, accurate, modular, extensible, etc. We expect these requirements to simulation software to expand drastically in the multi-core era. We observe at least five major challenges for the near future.

Challenge 8.1: Simulator Building

Being able to quickly build simulators by reusing previously built modules is a first key challenge for future simulation technology. Too often until now, computer architects have been building monolithic simulators which are hard to reuse across projects. Modular simulators on the other hand, which provide an intuitive mapping of hardware blocks to software modules, enable the easy exchange of architecture components.

Challenge 8.2:   Simulation Modeling Capabilities

A related issue is that simulation software should be extensible in the sense that novel capabilities of interest that crosscut the entire simulator should be easy to add in a plug-and-play fashion. Example capabilities are architectural power/energy modeling, temperature modeling, reliability modeling, etc. In addition, the modeling itself needs further research.

Challenge 8.3:   Simulation Speed

Simulation speed is a critical concern to simulation technology. Simulating one second of real hardware execution takes around one day of simulation time, even on today's fastest simulators and machines. And this is to simulate a single core. With the advent of multi-core systems, the simulation time is expected to increase more than proportional with the number of cores in a multi-core system. Exploring large design spaces with slow simulation technology obviously is infeasible. As such, we need to develop simulation technology that is capable of coping with the increased complexity of future computer systems.

There are a number of potential avenues that could be walked for improving simulation speed. One avenue is to consider modeling techniques, such as analytical modeling and transaction-level modeling, which operate at a higher level of abstraction than the cycle-by-cycle models in use today. A second avenue is to study techniques that strive at shortening the number of instructions that need to be simulated. Example techniques are sampled simulation and statistical simulation; these techniques are well understood in the uniprocessor domain but need non-trivial extensions to be useful in the multiprocessor domain. A third avenue is to parallelize the simulation engine. This could be achieved by parallelizing the simulation software to run on parallel (multi-core) hardware, or by embracing hardware acceleration approaches using for example FPGAs for offloading (parts of) the simulation. A fourth avenue consists in building slightly less accurate but very fast architecture models using machine-learning techniques such as neural networks.

Challenge 8.4:   Design Space Exploration

The previous challenge concerned the simulation speed in a single design point. However, computer architects, both researchers and developers, need to cull large design spaces in order to identify a region of interesting design points. This requires running multiple simulations. Although this process is embarrassingly parallel, the multi-billion design points in any realistic design space obviously make exhaustive searching infeasible. As such, efficient design space exploration techniques are required. The expertise from other domains such as operational research, data mining and machine learning could be promising avenues in the search for efficient but accurate design space exploration.

Challenge 8.5:   Simulator Validation

As alluded to before, designing a computer system involves modeling the system-under-design at different modeling abstractions. The idea is to make high-level design decisions using high-level abstraction models that are subsequently refined using low-level abstraction models. The key point however is to validate the various abstraction models throughout the design cycle to make sure high-level design decisions are valid decisions as more details become available throughout the design process. Since this already is an issue for a uniprocessor design flow, it is likely to increase for multi-core designs where high-level abstraction models will be used to cope with the simulation speed problem.

9   Reconfigurable Computing

Reconfigurable computing (RC) is becoming an exciting approach for embedded systems in general, and for application-specific designs in particular. The main advantage of such systems is that they can adapt to static and dynamic application requirements better than those with fixed hardware. Furthermore, the power/performance ratio for reconfigurable hardware is at least an order of magnitude better than that of general-purpose processors. However, for RC technology to be deployed on a large scale, a number of (but not limited to) important gaps in theory and in practice have to be bridged.

Challenge 9.1:   Application Domain Extension

Currently, RC technology has much success for selected applications in networking, communications, and in defense where cost is not a limiting factor. One future challenge here is to combine high-performance with high reliability, durability and robustness, by exploiting the properties inherent to RC devices. Future research on RC is expected to enable new application domains: medical and automotive (reliability and safety), office applications (scientific, engineering and media processing), and high-end consumer electronics (trade-offs in speed/size/power/cost/development time). A set of relevant (realistic) benchmarks is needed for analysis and comparison investigations.

Challenge 9.2:   Improved Run-Time Reconfiguration

Techniques for supporting fast and reliable reconfiguration, including those for dynamic and partial run-time reconfiguration are rapidly gaining importance. Novel configuration memories that overcome soft errors are desirable; they can be used to support technologies for rapid reconfiguration, such as multi-context organization. These would be useful for designs that make use of reconfiguration to adapt to environmental changes, and for evolutionary computing applications.

Challenge 9.3:   Interfacing

Techniques to enable components on an RC device to be efficiently interfaced to each other and to external devices are required. Within the RC device, improved communication bandwidth between processors, memories and peripherals will tend to reduce power and energy consumption. Dynamically adaptable network-on-chip technologies and main memory interfaces, such as packet-based routing, flux networks and memory controllers on demand will become relevant.

Challenge 9.4:   Granularity

Efficient support for special-purpose units is important. Commercial FPGAs are becoming more heterogeneous, since common functional blocks such as arithmetic units or a complete DSP are hardwired to reduce area, speed and power consumption overheads associated with reconfigurability; it is useful to develop theory and practice to enable optimal inclusion of such special-purpose hardwired units in a reconfigurable fabric for given applications, to get the best trade-offs in adaptability and performance.

Understanding the pros and cons of the granularity of the reconfigurable fabric is also of particular interest. Fine-grained architectures are more flexible, but less efficient than coarse-grained architectures which have fewer reconfigurable interconnects. The challenge is to determine, for a given application, the optimal RC fabric granularity or the optimal combination of RC fabrics with different granularities. This is related to RC technologies for special-purpose units described earlier, since an array of special-purpose units with limited programmability can be seen as a coarse-grained RC array.

Challenge 9.5:   Efficient Softcores

Support for efficient hardwired and softcore instruction processors, and determining, for a given application, the optimal number for each type and how they can be combined optimally will become important. One direction is to investigate facilities for instruction extension, exploiting customizability of RC technology to produce Application Specific Instruction Processors (ASIP). Multiple instructions in an inner loop can, for instance, be replaced by fewer custom instructions to reduce overhead in fetching and decoding. Another direction is to explore how processor architectures can be customized at design time and at run time, so that unused resources can be reconfigured, for instance, to speed up given tasks. Relevant topics include caching of multiple configurations, dedicated configuration memory controllers, and dedicated memory organizations.

Challenge 9.6:   RC Design Methods and Tools

RC design methods and tools, including run-time support, are key to improving designer productivity and design quality; they are responsible for mapping applications, usually captured in high-level descriptions, into efficient implementations involving RC technology and architectures.

Design methods and tools can be classified as either synthesis or analysis tools. The synthesis tools are required to map high-level descriptions into implementations with the best trade-offs in speed, size, power consumption, programmability, upgradeability, reliability, cost, and development time. Their satisfactory operation relies on extending current synthesis algorithms to take, for instance, dynamic reconfigurability into account. They need to integrate with analysis tools, which characterize a design at multiple levels of abstraction, and to support verification of functionality and other properties such as timing and testability.

Even for a given application targeting specific RC systems, there is currently no coherent tool- chain that covers all the main synthesis and analysis steps, including domain-specific design capture, performance profiling, design space exploration, multi-chip partitioning, hardware/software partitioning, multi-level algorithmic, architectural and data representation optimization, static and dynamic reconfiguration mapping, optimal instruction set generation, technology mapping, floor planning, placement and routing, functional simulation, timing and power consumption analysis, and hardware prototyping.

10   Real-Time Systems

The computing requirements of real-time systems are increasing rapidly: video-coding and decoding in tv-sets, set-top boxes, DVD recorders, compute-intensive energy saving and safety algorithms in automotive, railway, and avionic applications. Processors in most current real-time systems are characterized by a simple architecture, encompassing short pipelines and in-order execution. These types of pipelines ease the computation of the worst-case execution time (WCET). Due to the use of hard-to-predict components (caches, branch predictors,...) or due to resource sharing in multi-core processors, the worst-case execution time is either (i) hard to compute, or (ii) if computed, it is way beyond the real execution time (RET). Hence, on the one hand, multi-core processors will be needed to meet the computing demand of future real-time systems, but on the other hand they also pose serious challenges for real-time applications.

Challenge 10.1:   Timing-Analyzable High-Performance Hardware and Software

In soft real-time systems, the time constraints of applications are relaxed. Instead of ensuring that every instance of a task meets its deadline, a guaranteed mean performance is required. This allows more freedom in the processor design. A matter of great concern is however the parallel execution of the tasks on general-purpose hardware while ensuring the access to shared resources. Often, it is realized by specific hardware but, more and more, we would like to rely on "general-purpose" hardware to reduce costs. Thus, the aim of the research is to define how, on a multithreaded processor, the hardware can observe the behavior of the tasks in order to dynamically decide which resources (or which percentage of resources) should be devoted to each task.

On the one hand, a high resource sharing (SMT) implies that chips are smaller and that the performance per resource is higher. But also, a high resource sharing causes a high interference between threads, which causes more variable execution times. On the other hand, a reduced resource sharing (like CMPs) causes much smaller execution time variability, but implies that many hardware resources are duplicated, increasing area and cost of the chip. Hence there is a large space of architectural solutions to explore like creating private processors for time-critical processing, or providing hardware components that warn when deadlines are not met or are getting too close.

Challenge 10.2:   WCET Computation for Shared Resources

Research on hard real-time architectures is also needed because some applications (mainly in automotive, aeronautics and space) render current embedded hardware solutions obsolete. Indeed, these applications will require much more performance than today while preserving the need for a static WCET analysis to determine and guarantee the maximum execution time of a task. Furthermore, this maximum execution time should not be (too much) overestimated to be useful. Thus, in addition to enhancing static analysis, there is a need for new architectural features, some of them being managed by software, which increase performance while favoring static analysis.

Challenge 10.3:   Alternative Real-Time Modeling Methodologies

In absence of analyzable hardware, more sophisticated (probabilistic) models need to be developed that can model the probability of not meeting the deadline. This relaxed real-time demand only guarantees that no more than x% of all real execution times will exceed a boundary called LET (longest execution time). The LET (which can be determined through extensive simulation) should be much closer to the RET than the WCET.

Conclusion

The paradigm shift to multi-core architectures is having a profound effect on research challenges for the next decade. The exponential improvement of application performance across computer generations will come to an end if we do not succeed in adapting our applications to the parallel resources of the future computer systems. This requires a massive effort to improve all aspects of computing, as detailed in the 55 challenges in this HiPEAC Roadmap.

Acknowledgements. This work was funded by the 6th European Framework Programme (FP6), under contract no. IST-004408 High-Performance Embedded Architecture and Compilation (HiPEAC) Network of Excellence.

Compiling a roadmap and making it into a coherent document is not an easy task and builds on the expertise of many. Therefore, the authors of this research roadmap would like to thank the following people for their contributions to the roadmap effort: (in alphabetical order) Angelos Bilas (FORTH, Greece), Doug Burger (University of Texas at Austin, USA), Francisco Cazorla (UPC, Spain), Albert Cohen (INRIA, France), Sorin Cotofana (TU Delft, The Netherlands), Bruno De Bus (Ghent University, Belgium), José Duato (University of Valencia, Spain), Lieven Eeckhout (Ghent University, Belgium), Jakob Engblom (Virtutech), Paolo Faraboschi (HP), Piero Foglia (University of Pisa, Italy), Georgi Gaydadjiev (Tu Delft, The Netherlands), Marisa Gil (UPC, Spain), Christoforos Kachris (TU Delft, The Netherlands), Manolis Katevenis (FORTH, Greece), Stefanos Kaxiras (University of Patras, Greece), Kathryn McKinley (University of Texas at Austin, USA), Osman Unsal (BSC, Spain), Barbara Ryder (Rutgers University, USA), Guri Sohi (University of Wisconsin-Madison, USA), Theo Ungerer (University of Augsburg, Germany), Mateo Valero (UPC, Spain), Hans Vandierendonck (Ghent University, Belgium), David Whalley (Florida State University, USA), Sami Yehia (ARM), Ayal Zaks (IBM).

Part 1

First International Conference on High-Performance Embedded Architectures and Compilers, HiPEAC 2005
Best Papers

Introduction to Part 1

In November 2005, the first in the series of International Conferences on High-Performance Embedded Architectures and Compilers (HiPEAC 2005) was held in Barcelona. We were fortunate to attract close to 100 submissions of which only 18 were selected for presentation. Among these, we asked the authors of the five most highly rated contributions to make extended versions of them. They all accepted to do that and their articles appear in this section of the volume.

The first article by Fursin et al. reports on an interesting approach to evaluate a large number of program optimizations. The aim is to self-tune a program against a specific architecture so as to achieve a shorter running time. In the second article by Geiger et al., the topic is energy-efficient cache design – also an important topic for embedded systems. They report on a multi-lateral cache design that is better tailored to the access characteristics of applications. In the third article by Buytaert et al., the topic is garbage collection – a performance-costly operation for object-oriented software systems. They propose a methodology by which garbage collection points, called hints, can be identified that reduces the cost of garbage collection. The fourth article, by Shi et al., addresses system designs that protect software confidentiality and integrity. To this end, they describe a new security model – MESA – that takes a memory-centric approach towards enhancing security in architectures. In the last article by Ning and Kaeli, the topic is energy-efficient bus design. They particularly address the power-inefficiency of bus arbitration algorithms and propose and evaluate novel algorithms that are shown to improve power-efficiency as well as performance.

Per Stenström
Chalmers University of Technology
Editor-in-chief
Transactions on HiPEAC

P. Stenström (Ed.): Transactions on HiPEAC I, LNCS 4050, p. 33, 2007.

Quick and Practical Run-Time Evaluation of Multiple Program Optimizations

Grigori Fursin[1,2], Albert Cohen[1], Michael O'Boyle[2], and Olivier Temam[1]

[1] Members of HiPEAC, ALCHEMY Group, INRIA Futurs and LRI, Paris-Sud University,
France
{grigori.fursin,albert.cohen,olivier.temam}@inria.fr
[2] Member of HiPEAC, Institute for Computing Systems Architecture, University of Edinburgh,
UK
mob@inf.ed.ac.uk

Abstract. This article aims at making iterative optimization practical and usable by speeding up the evaluation of a large range of optimizations. Instead of using a full run to evaluate a single program optimization, we take advantage of periods of stable performance, called phases. For that purpose, we propose a low-overhead phase detection scheme geared toward fast optimization space pruning, using code instrumentation and versioning implemented in a production compiler.

Our approach is driven by simplicity and practicality. We show that a simple phase detection scheme can be sufficient for optimization space pruning. We also show it is possible to search for complex optimizations at run-time without resorting to sophisticated dynamic compilation frameworks. Beyond iterative optimization, our approach also enables one to quickly design self-tuned applications.

Considering 5 representative SpecFP2000 benchmarks, our approach speeds up iterative search for the best program optimizations by a factor of 32 to 962. Phase prediction is 99.4% accurate on average, with an overhead of only 2.6%. The resulting self-tuned implementations bring an average speed-up of 1.4.

1   Introduction

Recently, iterative optimization has become an increasingly popular approach for tackling the growing complexity of processor architectures. Bodin et al. [7] and Kisuki et al. [25] have initially demonstrated that exhaustively searching an optimization parameter space can bring performance improvements higher than the best existing static models, Cooper et al. [17] have provided additional evidence for finding best sequences of various compiler transformations. Since then, recent studies [42,21,3] demonstrate the potential of iterative optimization for a large range of optimization techniques.

Some studies show how iterative optimization can be used *in practice*, for instance, for tuning optimization parameters in libraries [46,6] or for building static models for compiler optimization parameters. Such models derive from the automatic discovery of the mapping function between key program characteristics and compiler optimization parameters; e.g., Stephenson et al. [39] successfully applied this approach to unrolling.

However, most other articles on iterative optimization take the same approach: several benchmarks are repeatedly executed with the same data set, a new optimization

P. Stenström (Ed.): Transactions on HiPEAC I, LNCS 4050, pp. 34–53, 2007.

parameter (e.g., tile size, unrolling factor, inlining decision,...) being tested at each execution. So, while these studies demonstrate the *potential* for iterative optimization, few provide a *practical* approach for effectively applying iterative optimization. The issue at stake is: what do we need to do to make iterative optimization a reality? There are three main caveats to iterative optimization: quickly scanning a large search space, optimizing based on and across multiple data sets, and extending iterative optimization to complex composed optimizations beyond simple optimization parameter tuning.

In this article, we aim at the general goal of making iterative optimization a usable technique and especially focus on the first issue, i.e., how to speed up the scanning of a large optimization space. As iterative optimization moves beyond simple parameter tuning to composition of multiple transformations [21,31,27,13] (the third issue mentioned above), this search space can become potentially huge, calling for faster evaluation techniques. There are two possible ways to speeding up the search space scanning: search more smartly by exploring points with the highest potential using genetic algorithms and machine learning techniques [16,17,43,40,1,29,22,39], or scan more points within the same amount of time. Up to now, speeding up the search has mostly focused on the former approach, while this article is focused on the latter one.

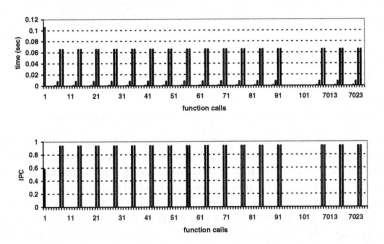

Fig. 1. Execution time and IPC for subroutine `resid` of benchmark `mgrid` across calls

The principle of our approach is to improve the efficiency of iterative optimization by taking advantage of program *performance stability* at run-time. There is ample evidence that many programs exhibit phases [37,26], i.e., program trace intervals of several millions instructions where performance is similar. What is the point of waiting for the end of the execution in order to evaluate an optimization decision (e.g., evaluating a tiling or unrolling factor, or a given composition of transformations) if the program performance is stable within phases or the whole execution? One could take advantage of phase intervals with the same performance to evaluate a different optimization option at each interval. As in standard iterative optimization, many options are evaluated, except that multiple options are evaluated within the same run.

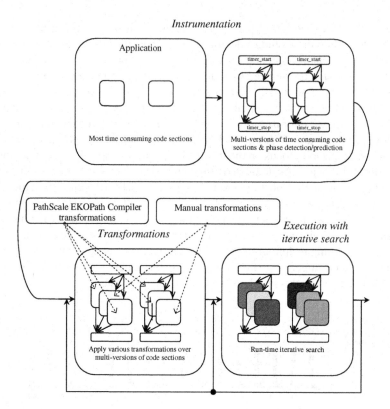

Fig. 2. Application instrumentation and multi-versioning for run-time iterative optimization

The main assets of our approach over previous techniques are simplicity and practicality. We show that a low-overhead performance stability/phase detection scheme is sufficient for optimization space pruning for loop-based floating point benchmarks. We also show that it is possible to search (even complex) optimizations at run-time without resorting to sophisticated dynamic optimization/recompilation frameworks. Beyond iterative optimization, our approach also enables one to quickly design self-tuned applications, significantly easier than manually tuned libraries.

Phase detection and optimization evaluation are respectively implemented using code instrumentation and versioning within the EKOPath compiler. Considering 5 self-tuned SpecFP2000 benchmarks, our space pruning approach speeds up iterative search by a factor of 32 to 962, with a 99.4% accurate phase prediction and a 2.6% performance overhead on average; we achieve speedups ranging from 1.10 to 1.72.

The paper is structured as follows. Section 2 provides the motivation, showing how our technique can speedup iterative optimization, and including a brief description of how it may be applied in different contexts. Section 3 describes our novel approach to runtime program stability detection. This is followed in Section 4 by a description of our dynamic transformation evaluation technique. Section 5 describes the results of applying these techniques to well known benchmarks and is followed in Section 6 by a brief survey of related work. Section 7 concludes the paper.

2 Motivation

This section provide a motivating example for our technique and outlines the ways in which it can be used in program optimization.

2.1 Example

Let us consider the `mgrid` SpecFP2000 benchmark. For the sake of simplicity, we have tested only 16 random combinations of traditional transformations, known to be efficient, on the two most time consuming subroutines `resid` and `psinv`. These transformations include loop fusion/fission, loop interchange, loop and register tiling, loop unrolling, prefetching. Since the original execution time of `mgrid` is 290 seconds (for the reference data set), a typical iterative approach for selecting the best optimization option would take approximately $290 \times 32 = 9280$ seconds (more than 2 hours). Moreover, all these tests are conducted with the same data set, which does not make much sense from a practical point of view.

However, considering the execution time of every call to the original subroutine `resid` in Figure 1, one notices fairly stable performance across pairs of consecutive calls with period 7.[1] Therefore, we propose to conduct most of these iterations at run-time, evaluating multiple versions during a single or a few runs of the application. The overall iterative program optimization scheme is depicted in Figure 2.

Practically, we insert all 16 different optimized versions of `resid` and `psinv` into the original code. As shown in the second box of Figure 2, each version is enclosed by calls to monitoring functions before and after the instrumented section. These timer functions monitor the execution time and performance of any active subroutine version using the high-precision PAPI hardware counters library [8], allowing to switch at run-time among the different versions of this subroutine. This low-overhead instrumentation barely skews the program execution time (less than 1%) as shown in Figure 3.

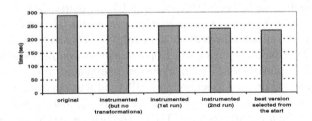

Fig. 3. Execution times for different versions of benchmark `mgrid`

If one run is not enough to optimize the application, it is possible to iterate on the multi-version program, the fourth box in Figure 2. Eventually, if new program transformations need to be evaluated, or when releasing an optimized application restricted

---

[1] Calls that take less than 0.01s are ignored to avoid startup or instrumentation overhead, therefore their IPC bars are not shown in this figure.

```
                Original code
SUBROUTINE RESID(U,V,R,N,A)
REAL*8 U(N,N,N),V(N,N,N),R(N,N,N),A(0:3)
INTEGER N, I3, I2, I1
   BODY OF THE SUBROUTINE
RETURN
END

              Instrumented code
SUBROUTINE RESID(U,V,R,N,A)
REAL*8 U(N,N,N),V(N,N,N),R(N,N,N),A(0:3)
INTEGER N, I3, I2, I1
INTEGER FSELECT

CALL TIMER_START(00001, FSELECT)
GOTO (1100, 1101, 1102, 1103, 1104, 1105,
   (...)
+1115, 1116), FSELECT+1
   (...)
1100 CONTINUE
CALL RESID_00(U,V,R,N,A)
GOTO 1199
```

```
1101 CONTINUE
     CALL RESID_01(U,V,R,N,A)
     GOTO 1199
        (...)
1199 CONTINUE
     CALL TIMER_STOP(00001)
     RETURN
     END

     SUBROUTINE RESID_00(U,V,R,N,A)
     REAL*8 U(N,N,N),V(N,N,N),R(N,N,N),A(0:3)
     INTEGER N, I3, I2, I1
        BODY OF THE SUBROUTINE
     RETURN
     END

     SUBROUTINE RESID_01(U,V,R,N,A)
     REAL*8 U(N,N,N),V(N,N,N),R(N,N,N),A(0:3)
     INTEGER N, I3, I2, I1
        BODY OF THE SUBROUTINE
     RETURN
     END
```

Fig. 4. Instrumentation example for subroutine `resid` of benchmark `mgrid`

to the most effective optimizations, one may also iterate back to apply a new set of transformations, the third box in Figure 2.

Figure 4 details the instrumentation and versioning scheme. Besides starting and stopping performance monitoring, `timer_start` and `timer_stop` have two more functions: `timer_stop` detects performance stability for consecutive or periodic executions of the selected section, using execution time and IPC; then `timer_start` predicts that performance will remain stable, in order to evaluate and compare new options. After stability is detected, `timer_start` redirects execution sequentially to the optimized versions of the original subroutine. When the currently evaluated version has exhibited stable performance for a few executions (2 in our case), we can measure its impact on performance *if* the phase did not change in the meantime. To validate this, the original code is executed again a few times (2 in our case to avoid transitional effects). In the same way all 16 versions are evaluated during program execution and the best one is selected at the end, as shown in Figure 5a.

Overall, evaluating all 16 optimization options for subroutine `resid` requires only 17 seconds instead of 9280 thus speeding up iterative search 546 times. Furthermore, since the best optimization has been found after only 6% of the code has been executed, the remainder of the execution uses the best optimization option and the overall `mgrid` execution time is improved by 13.7% all in one run (one data set) as shown in Figure 5b. The results containing original execution time, IPC and the corresponding best option which included loop blocking, unrolling and prefetching in our example, is saved in the database after the program execution. Therefore, during a second run with the same dataset (assuming standard across-runs iterative optimization), the best optimization option is selected immediately after the period is detected and the overall execution time is improved by 16.1% as shown in Figure 5c. If a different dataset is used and the behavior of the program changed, the new best option will be found for this context and saved into the database. Finally, the execution time of the non-instrumented code with the best version implemented from the start (no run-time convergence) brings almost the same performance of 17.2% as shown in Figure 5d and 3. The spikes on the graphs in Figure 5b,c are due to the periodic change in calling context of subroutine `resid`. At

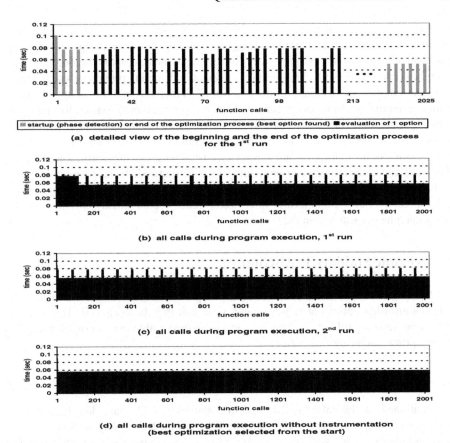

Fig. 5. Execution times for subroutine `resid` of benchmark `mgrid` during run-time optimization

such change points, the phase detection mechanism produces a miss and starts executing *the original non-transformed version* of the subroutine, to quickly detect the continuation of this phase or the beginning of another one (new or with a known behavior).

2.2 Application Scenarios

The previous example illustrates the two main applications of our approach. The first one is iterative optimization, and the second is dynamic self-tuning code.

In the first case, each run — and each phase within this run — exercises multiple optimization options, including complex sequences of compiler or manual transformations. The phase analysis and optimization decisions are dumped into a database. This facility can be used for across-runs iterative optimization. There are two cases where this approach is practical. First, some applications may exhibit similar performance across multiple data sets, providing key parameters do not change (e.g., matrix dimensions do not change, but matrix values do); second, even when the performance of a code section varies with the data set, it is likely that a few optimizations will be able to achieve good results for a large range of data sets. In both cases, run-time iterative optimization can speed up optimization space search: a selection of optimizations is evaluated during each run, progressively converging to the best optimization.

In the second case, our technique allows to create self-tuning programs which adjust to the current data set, within a production run. This method smoothly adapts the program to maximize performance, unlike static cloning techniques that specialize function to input parameters using decision trees and often fail to correctly associate performance anomalies with the right version. Assuming the optimized versions known to perform best (in general, for multiple benchmarks) have been progressively learned across previous runs and data sets, one can implement a self-tuning code by selecting only a few of those versions. Even if some of the selected versions perform poorly, they do not really affect overall execution time since convergence occurs quickly and most of the execution time is spent within the best ones.

3   Dynamic Stability Prediction

The two key difficulties with dynamic iterative optimization are how to evaluate multiple optimization options at run-time and when can they be evaluated. This section tackles the second problem by detecting and predicting stable regions of the program where optimizations may be evaluated.

3.1   Performance Stability and Phases

As mentioned in the introduction, multiple studies [37,33] have highlighted that programs exhibit *phases*, i.e., performance can remain stable for many millions instructions and performance patterns can recur within the program execution. Phase analysis is now extensively used for selecting sampling intervals in processor architecture simulation, such as in SimPoint [33]. More recently, phase-based analysis has been used to tune program power optimizations by dynamically adapting sizes of L1 and L2 caches [23].

For iterative optimization, phases mean that the performance of a given code section will remain stable for multiple consecutive or periodic executions of that code section. One can take advantage of this stability to compare the effect of multiple different optimization options. For instance, assuming one knows that two consecutive executions $E1$ and $E2$ of a code section will exhibit the same performance P, one can collect P in $E1$, apply a program transformation to the code section, and collect its performance P' in $E2$; by comparing P and P', one can decide if the program transformation is useful. Obviously, this comparison makes sense only if $E1$ and $E2$ exhibit the same baseline performance P, i.e., if $E1$ and $E2$ belong to the same phase. So, the key is to detect when phases occur, i.e., where are the regions with identical baseline performance. Also, IPC may not always be a sufficient performance metric, because some program transformations may increase or reduce the number of instructions, such as unrolling or scalar promotion. Therefore, we monitor not only performance stability but also execution time stability across calls, depending on the program transformations.

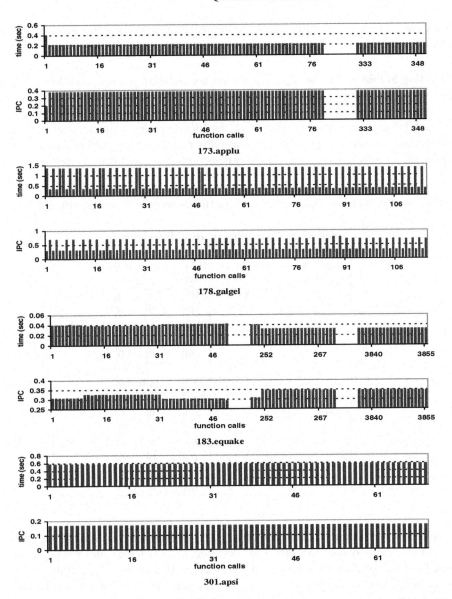

Fig. 6. Execution time and IPC for one representative subroutine per benchmark (across calls)

Figures 6 and 1 illustrate IPC and execution time stability of one representative subroutine for 5 SpecFP2000 benchmarks by showing variations across calls to the same subroutine. These benchmarks are selected to demonstrate various representative behavior for floating point programs. For instance, the applu subroutine has a stable performance across all calls except for the first one; the galgel subroutine has periodic performance changes with 5 shifts during overall execution; the equake most time-consuming section exhibits unstable performance for 250 calls and then becomes stable; the `apsi` subroutine has a stable performance across all calls; finally, the `mgrid` subroutine exhibits periodic stable performance.

Detecting Stability. For the moment, we do not consider program transformations, and two instances are compared solely using IPC. We then simply define stability by 3 consecutive or periodic code section execution instances with the same IPC. Naturally, this stability characterization is speculative, the 4th instance performance may vary, but in practice as graphs in Figure 6 suggest, stability regions are long and regular enough so that the probability of incorrect stability detections (miss rate) is fairly low.

Table 1. Number of phases, phase prediction hits and misses per code section for each application

Application	Code sections	Phases	Hits	Misses	Miss rate
mgrid	a	1	1924	27	0.014
	b	1	998	1	0.001
applu	a	1	348	0	0
	b	2	349	0	0
	c	2	349	0	0
	d	1	350	0	0
	e	1	350	0	0
galgel	a	2	86	12	0.140
	b	2	83	14	0.169
equake	a	2	3853	1	0.000
apsi	a	1	69	0	0
	b	1	69	0	0
	c	1	69	0	0
	d	1	69	0	0
	e	1	70	0	0
	f	1	69	0	0

Note however, that the occurrence of a phase (an execution instance with a given performance) is only detected *after* it has occurred, i.e., when the counter value is collected and the code section instance already executed. If changes in the calling context occur faster than the evaluation of a new optimization option, there may not be long enough consecutive executions with stable performance to measure the impact of the optimization. Therefore, it is not sufficient to *react* to phase changes: within a phase, it is necessary to detect the *length of consecutive regions* of stable performance and to *predict* their occurrence. Fortunately, Figure 6 shows that phases tend to recur regularly, especially in scientific applications which usually have simple control flow behavior, which is further confirmed by other broader experiments [38].

To predict the occurrence of regular phases, for each instrumented code section, we store the performance measurement along with the number of calls exhibiting the same performance (phase length) in a Phase Detection and Prediction Table (PDPT) as shown in Figure 7. If a performance variation occured, we check the table to see if a phase with such behavior already occurred, and if so, we also record the distance (in number of calls) since it occurred. At the third occurrence of the same performance behavior, we conclude the phase becomes stable and recurs regularly, i.e., with a fixed period, and we can predict its next occurrence. Then, program transformations are applied to the code section, and the performance effects are only compared within the same phase, i.e., for the same baseline performance, avoiding to reset the search each time the phase changes. The length parameter indicates when the phase will change. Thus, the transformation space is searched independently for all phases of a code section. This property has the added benefit of allowing per-phase optimization, i.e., converging towards different optimizations for different phases of the same code section.

Table 1 shows how the phase prediction scheme performs. Due to the high regularity of scientific applications, our simple phase prediction scheme has a miss rate lower than 1.4% in most of the cases, except for `galgel` which exhibits miss rates of 14% and 17% for two time-consuming subroutines. Also, note that we assumed two performance measurements were identical provided they differ by less than a threshold determined by observed measurement error, of the order of 2% with our experimental environment.

3.2 Compiler Instrumentation

Since, program transformations target specific code sections, phase detection should target code sections rather than the whole program. In order to monitor code sections performance, we instrument a code section, e.g., a loop nest or a function, with performance counter calls from the hardware counters PAPI library. Figure 4 shows an example instrumentation at the subroutine/function level for `mgrid` (Fortran 77) and its `resid` subroutine. Figure 7 shows the details of our instrumentation.

Each instrumented code section gets a unique identifier, and before and after each section, monitoring routines `timer_start` and `timer_stop` are called. These routines record the number of cycles and number of instructions to compute the IPC (the first argument is the unique identifier of the section). At the same time, `timer_stop` detects phases and stability, and `timer_start` decides which optimization option should be evaluated next and returns variable `FSELECT` to branch to the appropriate optimization option (versioning), see the `GOTO` statement.

Instrumentation is currently applied before and after the call functions and the outer loops of all loop nests with depth 2 or more (though the approach is naturally useful for the most time-consuming loop nests and functions only). Note that instrumented loop nests can themselves contain subroutine calls to evaluate inlining; however we forbid nested instrumentations, so we systematically remove outer instrumentations if nested calls correspond to loop nests.

4   Evaluating Optimizations

Once a stable period has been detected we need a mechanism to evaluate program transformations and evaluate their worth.

4.1   Comparing Optimization Options

As soon as performance stability is observed, the evaluation of optimization options starts. A new optimization option is said to be evaluated only after 2 consecutive executions with the same performance. The main issue is to combine the detection of phases with the evaluation of optimizations, because, if the phase detection scheme does not predict that a new phase starts, baseline performance will change, and we would not know whether performance variations are due to the optimization option being evaluated or to a new phase.

In order to verify the prediction, the instrumentation routine periodically checks whether baseline performance has changed (and in the process, it monitors the occurrence of new phases). After any optimization option evaluation, i.e., after 2 consecutive executions of the optimized version with the same performance, the code switches back to the original code section for two additional iterations. The first iteration is ignored to avoid transition effects because it can be argued that the previous optimized version of the code section can have performance side-effects that would skew the performance evaluation of the next iteration (the original code section). However, we did not find empirical evidence of such side-effects; most likely because code sections have to be long enough that instrumentation and start-up induces only a negligible overhead. If the performance of the second iteration is similar to the initial baseline performance, the effect of the current option is validated and further optimization options evaluation resumes. Therefore, evaluating an optimization option requires at least 4 executions of a given code section (2 for detecting optimization performance stability and 2 for checking baseline performance). For example, see the groups of black bars in Figure 5a of the motivation section (on benchmark mgrid). If the baseline performance is later found to differ, the optimization search for this other phase is restarted (or started if it is the first occurrence of that phase).[2]

Practically, the Phase Detection and Prediction Table (PDPT) shown in Figure 7 holds information about phases and their current state (detection and prediction), new option evaluation or option validation (stability check). It also records the best option found for every phase.

4.2   Multiple Evaluations at Run-Time

Many optimizations are parameterized, e.g., tile size or unroll factor. However, in the context of run-time iterative optimization, whether changing a parameter just means changing a program variable (e.g., a parametric tile size), or changing the code structure (e.g., unroll factor) matters. The former type of optimization can be easily verified by updating the parameter variable. In order to accommodate the latter type of complex optimizations, we use versioning: we generate and optimize differently multiple versions of the same code section (usually a subroutine or a loop nest), plus the additional control/switching code driven by the monitoring routine as shown in Figures 7 and 4, using the EKOPath compiler.

The main drawback of versioning is obviously increased code size. While this issue matters for embedded applications, it should not be a serious inconvenience for desktop

---

[2] Note that it is *restarted* not *reset*.

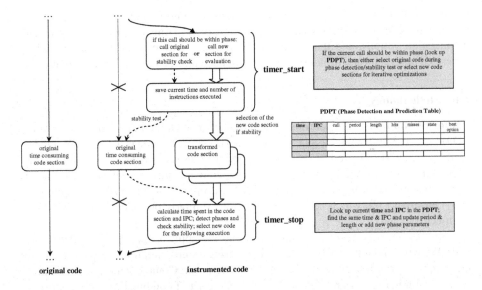

Fig. 7. Code instrumentation for run-time adaptive iterative optimizations

applications, provided the number of optimization options is not excessive. Considering only one subroutine or loop nest version will be active at any time, even the impact of versioning on instruction cache misses is limited. However, depending on what run-time adaptation is used for, the number of versions can vary greatly. If it is used for evaluating a large number of program transformations, including across runs, the greater the number of versions the better, and the only limitation is the code size increase. If it is used for creating self-adjusting codes that find the best option for the current run, it is best to limit the number of options, because if many options perform worse than the original version, the overall performance may either degrade or marginally improve. In our experiments, we limited the number of versions to 16.

This versioning scheme is simple but has practical benefits. Alongside the optimized versions generated by the compiler, the user can add subroutines or loop nests modified by hand, and either test them as is or combine them with compiler optimizations. User-suggested program transformations can often serve as starting points of the optimization search, and recent studies [15,42] highlight the key role played by well selected starting points, adding to the benefit of combined optimizations. Moreover, another study [13] suggests that iterative optimization should not be restricted to program transformation parameter tuning, but should expand to selecting program transformations themselves, beyond the strict composition order imposed by the compiler. Versioning is a simple approach for testing a variety of program transformations compositions.

5   Experiments

The goal of this article is to speedup the evaluation of optimization options, rather than to speedup programs themselves. Still, we later report program speedups to highlight that the run-time overhead has no significant impact on program performance, that the run-time performance analysis strategy is capable of selecting appropriate and efficient optimization options, and that it can easily accommodate both traditional compiler-generated program transformations and user-defined ad-hoc program transformations.

5.1 Methodology

Platforms and tools. All experiments are conducted on an Intel Pentium 4 Northwood (ID9) Core at 2.4GHz (bus frequency of 533MHz), the L1 cache is 4-way 8KB, the L2 cache is 8-way 512KB, and 512MB of memory; the O/S is Linux SUSE 9.1. We use the latest PAPI hardware counter library [30] for program instrumentation and performance measurements. All programs are compiled with the open-source EKOPath 2.0 compiler and -Ofast flag [32], which, in average, performs similarly or better than the Intel 8.1 compiler for Linux.

Compiler-generated program transformations are applied using the EKOPath compiler. We have created an EKOPath API that triggers program transformations, using the compiler's optimization strategy as a starting point. Complementing the compiler strategy with iterative search enables to test a large set of combinations of transformations such as inlining, local padding, loop fusion/fission, loop interchange, loop/register tiling, loop unrolling and prefetching.

Target benchmarks. We considered five representative SpecFP2000 benchmarks with different behavior, as shown in Figure 6 (mgrid, applu, galgel, equake, apsi), using the ref data sets. We apply optimization only on the most-time consuming sections of these benchmarks. We handpicked these codes based on the study by Parello et al. [31] which suggests which SpecFP2000 benchmarks have the best potential for improvement (on an Alpha 21264 platform, though). Since the role of seed points in iterative search has been previously highlighted [1,42], we also used the latter study as an indication for seed points, i.e., initial points for a space search.

5.2 Results

This section shows that the full power of iterative optimization can be achieved at the cost of profile-directed optimization: one or two runs of each benchmark are sufficient to discover the best optimization options for every phase.

Boosting Search Rate. For each benchmark, Table 2 shows the actual number of evaluated options, which is the number of versions multiplied by the number of instrumented code sections and by the number of phases with significant execution time.

However, the maximum number of potential optimization options (program transformations or compositions of program transformations) that can be evaluated during one execution of a benchmark can be much higher depending on the application behavior. Thanks to run-time adaptation it is now possible to evaluate 32 to 962 more optimization options than through traditional across-runs iterative optimization. The discrepancy among maximum number of evaluations is explained by the differences in phase behavior of programs and in the instrumentation placement. If the instrumentation is located

Table 2. Maximum number of potential evaluations or iterative search speedup vs. the real number of options evaluated during single execution and the associated overhead

Application	Max. number of potential evaluations	Number of options evaluated	Code size increase (times)	Instrumentation overhead
mgrid	699	32	4.3	0%
applu	430	80	5.5	0.01%
galgel	32	32	2.6	0.01%
equake	962	16	2.5	13.17%
apsi	96	96	5.3	0%

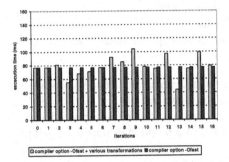

Fig. 8. Execution time variations of the resid subroutine of the mgrid benchmark over iterations (subroutine calls)

Fig. 9. Speedups of instrumented program over original program after first run, second run or if the best option is selected from the start

at a lower loop nest level, it enables a greater number of evaluations but it can also induce excessive overhead and may limit applicable transformations. On the other hand, instrumentation at a higher level enables all spectrum of complex sequences of transformations but can limit the number of potential evaluations during one execution. For example, the number of potential optimization evaluations is small for galgel due to chaotic behavior and frequent performance mispredictions, and is high for equake due to relatively low level instrumentation.

To quantify the instrumentation overhead, the last column in Table 2 shows the ratio of the execution time of the instrumented program over the original program, assuming all optimization options are replaced with exact copies of the original code section. As a result, this ratio only measures the slowdown due to instrumentation. The overhead is negligible for 4 out of 5 benchmarks, and reaches 13% for equake. Note however that equake still achieves one of the best speedups at 1.7, as shown in Figure 9.

Finally, Table 2 shows the code size increase after the program instrumentation. In all cases it is modest, and the expansion factor is considerably smaller than the number of optimization versions we evaluate at run-time. This is easily explained by observing that time-consuming sections are generally small in scientific codes. Furthermore, for self-tuning applications which will retain only a few versions with the best optimizations, their code size increase should not be significant.

Self-Tuned Speedup. For each selected benchmark we have created a self-tuning program with 16 versions of each most time consuming sections of these benchmarks. For each of these versions we applied either combinations of compiler-generated program transformations or manual program transformations suggested by Parello et al. [31] for the Alpha platform, or combinations of both:

- Compiler-generated transformations were obtained through our EKOPath compiler API, using randomly selected parameters (this API wraps internal compiler phases to allow external control on transformations such as loop fusion/fission, loop interchange, loop and register tiling, loop unrolling and prefetching on any part of the code).
- We manually optimized the code wherever the EKOPath compiler failed to apply a transformation as directed through the API (due to internal limitations or to consavative static analysis information), or whenever unsupported transformations were required.

The overall number of evaluations per each benchmark varied from 16 to 96 depending on the number of most-time consuming sections, as shown in table 2.

Figure 8 shows an example of execution time variations for the triple-nested loop in the `resid` subroutine of the `mgrid` benchmark for each option evaluation all within one execution of this program. The baseline performance is shown in a straight gray line and the best version is found at iteration 13. The final best sequence of transformations for the loop in the subroutine `resid` is loop tiling with tile size 60, loop unrolling with factor 16 and prefetching switched off. The best parameters found for subroutine `psinv` of the same benchmark are 9 for loop tiling and 14 for loop unrolling. Note also that the static algorithm of the EKOPath compiler suggested unrolling factors of 2 for loops of both subroutines. This factor is a kind of tradeoff value across all possible data sets, while the self-tuning code converged toward a different value dynamically. It is important to note that this adjustment occurred at run-time, during a single run, and that the optimization was selected soon enough to improve the remainder of the run.

Figure 9 shows the speedups obtained for all benchmarks after two executions as well as the speedups assuming there is no instrumentation overhead and the best optimization option is used from the start; speedups vary from 1.10 to 1.72. The difference in the speedups between successive runs of the application depends mainly on the percentage of overall execution time spent evaluating different options. Naturally, the higher the ratio of the maximum number of potential evaluations to the number of real evaluations, the faster the convergence to the maximal performance level. The difference in the speedups achived using our new technique and when selecting the best option from the start depends on the quality of our phase detection and prediction scheme. This difference is quite high for `galgel` due to frequent performance mispredictions and for `equake` due to relatively low level instrumentation. This suggests further improvements are needed for our performance stability detection scheme. It is also interesting to note that, though the manual transformations were designed for a different architecture (Alpha 21264), for 4 out of 5 benchmarks, they were eventually adjusted through transformation parameter tuning to our target architecture, and still perform well. In other terms, beyond performance improvement on a single platform, self-adjusting codes also provide a form of cross-platform portability by selecting the optimization option best suited for the new platform.

6 Related Work

Some of the first techniques to select differently optimized versions of code sections are cloning and multi-versioning [9,14,18]. They use simple version selection mechanisms according to the input run-time function or loop parameters. Such techniques are used to some extent in current compilers but lack flexibility and prediction and cannot cope with various cases where input parameters are too complex or differ while the behavior of the code section remains the same and vice versa.

To improve cloning effectiveness, many studies defer code versioning to the run-time execution. Program hot spots and input/context parameters are detected at run-time, to drive dynamic recompilation. For example, the Dynamo system [4] can optimize streams of native instructions at run-time using hot traces and can be easily implemented inside JIT compilers. Insertion of prefetching instructions or changing prefetching distance dynamically depending on hardware counter metrics is presented in [35].

Dynamic optimization on object code is limited by the lack of abstract semantical information (types, control structures, abstract variable names). Many run-time techniques thus resort to dynamic code generation and compilation. Multi-stage programming is one general computing paradigm that fits well with the dynamic optimization context [10,41]: it denotes the syntactic and semantic support allowing a program to generate another program and execute it, having multiple program levels cooperate and share data. Multi-stage programming has been applied to adaptive optimization of high-performance applications [12,5]. Yet these source-level approaches will only see a limited applicability to continuous optimization due to run-time compilation overhead. Alternatively, languages like 'C [34] (spelled Tick-C, a multi-stage extension of C) emphasize code generation speed: 'C is based on VCODE, a very fast framework to produce native code at run-time [20]. To reduce run-time code generation overhead, [2] presents a technique which produces pre-optimized machine-code templates and later dynamically patch those templates with run-time constants. ADAPT [45,44] applies high-level optimizations to program hot spots using dynamic recompilation in a separate process or on a separate workstation and describes a language to write self-tuned applications. ADORE [11,28] uses a sampling-based phase analysis to detect performance bottlenecks and apply simple transformations such as prefetching dynamically. Finally, dynamic code regions (DCR) improve on sampling-based analysis, focusing the monitoring on procedure and loops [24] only.

Recently, software-only solutions have been proposed to effectively detect, classify and predict phase transitions, with very low run-time overhead [4,19]. In particular, [19] decouples this detection from the dynamic code generation or translation process, relying on a separate process sampling hardware performance counters at a fixed interval. Selection of a good sampling interval is critical, to avoid missing fine-grain phase changes while minimizing overhead [33,36].

In contrast with the above-mentioned projects, our approach is a novel combination of versioning, code instrumentation and software-only phase detection to enable practical iterative evaluation of complex transformations at run-time. We choose static versioning rather than dynamic code generation, allowing low-overhead adaptability to program phases and input contexts. Associating static instrumentation and dynamic detection avoids most pitfalls of either isolated instrumentation-based or sampling-based phase analyses, including sensitivity to calling contexts [24] and sampling interval selection [26]. Finally, we rely on predictive rather than reactive phase detection, although it is not for the reasons advocated in [19]: we do not have to amortize the overhead of run-time code generation, but we need to predict phase changes to improve the evaluation rate for new optimization options.

7   Conclusions and Perspectives

Several practical issues still prevent iterative optimization from being widely used, the time required to search the huge program transformations space being one of the main issues. In this article, we present a method for speeding up search space pruning by a factor of 32 to 962 over a set of benchmarks, by taking advantage of the phase behavior (performance stability) of applications. The method, implemented in the EKOPath compiler, can be readily applied to a large range of applications. The method has other benefits: such self-tuned programs facilitate portability across different architectures and software environments, they can self-adjust at the level of phases and to particular data sets (as opposed to the trade-off proposed by current iterative techniques), they can build a catalog of per-phase appropriate program transformations (code section/performance pairs) across runs, and they can easily combine user-suggested and compiler-suggested transformations thanks to their versioning approach.

Future work will include fast analysis of large complex transformation spaces, improving our phase detection and prediction scheme to capture more complex performance behaviors for integer and DSP-type benchmarks, and improving the instrumentation placement, especially using self-placement of instrumentation at the most proper loop nest levels, by instrumenting all loop nests levels, then dynamically switching off instrumentation at all levels but one, either using predication or versioning again. We are currently extending our work to create self-tuning applications on embedded systems where the size of the application is critical and on multi-core architectures.

Acknowledgments. Grigori Fursin has been supported by a grant from European Network of Excellence on High-Performance Embedded Architecture and Compilation (HiPEAC). We would also like to thank all our colleagues and reviewers for their comments.

References

1. L. Almagor, K. D. Cooper, A. Grosul, T. Harvey, S. Reeves, D. Subramanian, L. Torczon, and T. Waterman. Finding effective compilation sequences. In *Proc. Languages, Compilers, and Tools for Embedded Systems (LCTES)*, pages 231–239, 2004.
2. J. Auslander, M. Philipose, C. Chambers, S. J. Eggers, and B. N. Bershad. Fast, effective dynamic compilation. In *Conference on Programming Language Design and Implementation (PLDI)*, pages 149–159, 1996.

3. J. T. B. Franke, M. O'Boyle and G. Fursin. Probabilistic source-level optimisation of embedded systems software. In *ACM SIGPLAN/SIGBED Conference on Languages, Compilers, and Tools for Embedded Systems (LCTES'05)*, 2005.

4. V. Bala, E. Duesterwald, and S. Banerjia. Dynamo: A transparent dynamic optimization system. In *ACM SIGPLAN Notices*, 2000.

5. O. Beckmann, A. Houghton, P. H. J. Kelly, and M. Mellor. Run-time code generation in c++ as a foundation for domain-specific optimisation. In *Proceedings of the 2003 Dagstuhl Workshop on Domain-Specific Program Generation*, 2003.

6. J. Bilmes, K. Asanović, C. Chin, and J. Demmel. Optimizing matrix multiply using PHiPAC: A portable, high-performance, ANSI C coding methodology. In *Proc. ICS*, pages 340–347, 1997.

7. F. Bodin, T. Kisuki, P. Knijnenburg, M. O'Boyle, and E. Rohou. Iterative compilation in a non-linear optimisation space. In *Proc. ACM Workshop on Profile and Feedback Directed Compilation*, 1998. Organized in conjunction with PACT98.

8. S. Browne, J. Dongarra, N. Garner, G. Ho, and P. Mucci. A portable programming interface for performance evaluation on modern processors. *The International Journal of High Performance Computing Applications*, 14(3):189–204, 2000.

9. M. Byler, M. Wolfe, J. R. B. Davies, C. Huson, and B. Leasure. Multiple version loops. In *ICPP 1987*, pages 312–318, 2005.

10. C. Calcagno, W. Taha, L. Huang, and X. Leroy. Implementing multi-stage languages using ASTs, Gensym, and reflection. In *ACM SIGPLAN/SIGSOFT Intl. Conf. Generative Programming and Component Engineering (GPCE'03)*, pages 57–76, 2003.

11. H. Chen, J. Lu, W.-C. Hsu, and P.-C. Yew. Continuous adaptive object-code re-optimization framework. In *Ninth Asia-Pacific Computer Systems Architecture Conference (ACSAC 2004)*, pages 241–255, 2004.

12. A. Cohen, S. Donadio, M.-J. Garzaran, C. Herrmann, and D. Padua. In search of a program generator to implement generic transformations for high-performance computing. *Science of Computer Programming*, 2006. To appear.

13. A. Cohen, S. Girbal, D. Parello, M. Sigler, O. Temam, and N. Vasilache. Facilitating the search for compositions of program transformations. *ACM Int. Conf on Supercomputing (ICS'05)*, June 2005.

14. K. D. Cooper, M. W. Hall, and K. Kennedy. Procedure cloning. In *Proceedings of the 1992 IEEE International Conference on Computer Language*, pages 96–105, 1992.

15. K. D. Cooper, K. Kennedy, and L. Torczon. The impact of interprocedural analysis and optimization in the R^n programming environment. *ACM Transactions on Programming Languages and Systems*, 8:491–523, 1986.

16. K. D. Cooper, P. Schielke, and D. Subramanian. Optimizing for reduced code space using genetic algorithms. In *Proc. Languages, Compilers, and Tools for Embedded Systems (LCTES)*, pages 1–9, 1999.

17. K. D. Cooper, D. Subramanian, and L. Torczon. Adaptive optimizing compilers for the 21st century. *J. of Supercomputing*, 23(1), 2002.

18. P. Diniz and M. Rinard. Dynamic feedback: An effective technique for adaptive computing. In *Proc. PLDI*, pages 71–84, 1997.

19. E. Duesterwald, C. Cascaval, and S. Dwarkadas. Characterizing and predicting program behavior and its variability. In *IEEE PACT 2003*, pages 220–231, 2003.

20. D. Engler. Vcode: a portable, very fast dynamic code generation system. In *Proceedings of PLDI*, 1996.

21. G. Fursin, M. O'Boyle, and P. Knijnenburg. Evaluating iterative compilation. In *Proc. Languages and Compilers for Parallel Computers (LCPC)*, pages 305–315, 2002.

22. K. Heydeman, F. Bodin, P. Knijnenburg, and L. Morin. UFC: a global trade-off strategy for loop unrolling for VLIW architectures. In *Proc. Compilers for Parallel Computers (CPC)*, pages 59–70, 2003.

23. S. Hu, M. Valluri, and L. K. John. Effective adaptive computing environment management via dynamic optimization. In *IEEE / ACM International Symposium on Code Generation and Optimization (CGO 2005)*, 2005.

24. J. Kim, S. V. Kodakara, W.-C. Hsu, D. J. Lilja, and P.-C. Yew. Dynamic code region (DCR)-based program phase tracking and prediction for dynamic optimizations. In *Intl. Conf. on High Performance Embedded Architectures & Compilers (HiPEAC'05)*, number 3793 in LNCS, Barcelona, Spain, Sept. 2005. Springer Verlag.

25. T. Kisuki, P. Knijnenburg, M. O'Boyle, and H. Wijshoff. Iterative compilation in program optimization. In *Proc. Compilers for Parallel Computers (CPC2000)*, pages 35–44, 2000.

26. J. Lau, S. Schoenmackers, and B. Calder. Transition phase classification and prediction. In *International Symposium on High Performance Computer Architecture*, 2005.

27. S. Long and G. Fursin. A heuristic search algorithm based on unified transformation framework. In *7th International Workshop on High Performance Scientific and Engineering Computing (HPSEC-05)*, 2005.

28. J. Lu, H. Chen, P.-C. Yew, and W.-C. Hsu. Design and implementation of a lightweight dynamic optimization system. In *The Journal of Instruction-Level Parallelism*, volume 6, 2004.

29. A. Monsifrot, F. Bodin, and R. Quiniou. A machine learning approach to automatic production of compiler heuristics. In *Proc. AIMSA*, LNCS 2443, pages 41–50, 2002.

30. PAPI: A   Portable   Interface   to   Hardware   Performance   Counters. http://icl.cs.utk.edu/papi, 2005.

31. D. Parello, O. Temam, A. Cohen, and J.-M. Verdun. Toward a systematic, pragmatic and architecture-aware program optimization process for complex processors. In *Proc. Int. Conference on Supercomputing*, 2004.

32. PathScale EKOPath Compilers. http://www.pathscale.com, 2005.

33. E. Perelman, G. Hamerly, M. V. Biesbrouck, T. Sherwood, and B. Calder. Using simpoint for accurate and efficient simulation. In *ACM SIGMETRICS the International Conference on Measurement and Modeling of Computer Systems*, 2003.

34. M. Poletto, W. C. Hsieh, D. R. Engler, and M. F. Kaashoek. 'C and tcc: A language and compiler for dynamic code generation. *ACM Trans. Prog. Lang. Syst.*, 21(2):324–369, Mar. 1999.

35. R. H. Saavedra and D. Park. Improving the effectiveness of software prefetching with adaptive execution. In *Conference on Parallel Architectures and Compilation Techniques (PACT'96)*, 1996.

36. X. Shen, Y. Zhong, and C. Ding. Locality phase prediction. In *ACM SIGARCH Computer Architecture News*, pages 165–176, 2004.

37. T. Sherwood, E. Perelman, G. Hamerly, and B. Calder. Automatically characterizing large scale program behavior. In *10th International Conference on Architectural Support for Programming Languages and Operating Systems*, 2002.

38. T. Sherwood, E. Perelman, G. Hamerly, and B. Calder. Automatically characterizing large scale program behavior. In *Proceedings of ASPLOS-X*, 2002.

39. M. Stephenson and S. Amarasinghe. Predicting unroll factors using supervised classification. In *IEEE / ACM International Symposium on Code Generation and Optimization (CGO 2005)*. IEEE Computer Society, 2005.

40. M. Stephenson, M. Martin, and U. O'Reilly. Meta optimization: Improving compiler heuristics with machine learning. In *Proc. PLDI*, pages 77–90, 2003.

41. W. Taha. *Multi-Stage Programming: Its Theory and Applications*. PhD thesis, Oregon Graduate Institute of Science and Technology, Nov. 1999.

42. S. Triantafyllis, M. Vachharajani, and D. I. August. Compiler optimization-space exploration. In *Journal of Instruction-level Parallelism*, 2005.
43. X. Vera, J. Abella, A. González, and J. Llosa. Optimizing program locality through CMEs and GAs. In *Proc. PACT*, pages 68–78, 2003.
44. M. Voss and R. Eigemann. High-level adaptive program optimization with adapt. In *Proceedings of the Symposium on Principles and practices of parallel programming*, 2001.
45. M. Voss and R. Eigenmann. Adapt: Automated de-coupled adaptive program transformation. In *Proc. ICPP*, 2000.
46. R. C. Whaley and J. J. Dongarra. Automatically tuned linear algebra software. In *Proc. Alliance*, 1998.

Specializing Cache Structures for High Performance and Energy Conservation in Embedded Systems

Michael J. Geiger[1], Sally A. McKee[2], and Gary S. Tyson[3]

[1] ECE and CIS Departments, University of Massachusetts Dartmouth
North Dartmouth, MA 02747-2300
mgeiger@umassd.edu
[2] Computer Systems Lab, Cornell University
Ithaca, NY 14853-3801
sam@csl.cornell.edu
[3] Department of Computer Science, Florida State University
Tallahassee, FL 32306-4530
tyson@cs.fsu.edu

Abstract. Increasingly tight energy design goals require processor architects to rethink the organizational structure of microarchitectural resources. We examine a new multilateral cache organization, replacing a conventional data cache with a set of smaller region caches that significantly reduces energy consumption with little performance impact. This is achieved by tailoring the cache resources to the specific reference characteristics of each application. In applications with small heap footprints, we save about 85% of the total cache energy. In the remaining applications, we employ a small cache for frequently accessed heap data and a larger cache for low locality data, achieving an energy savings of 80%.

1 Introduction

Energy conservation continues to grow in importance for everything from high performance supercomputers down to embedded systems. Many of the latter must simultaneously deliver both high performance and low energy consumption. In light of these constraints, architects must rethink system design with respect to general versus specific structures. Consider memory hierarchies: the current norm is to use very general cache structures, splitting memory references only according to instructions versus data. Nonetheless, different kinds of data are used in different ways (i.e., they exhibit different locality characteristics), and even a given set of data may exhibit different usage characteristics during different program phases. On-chip caches can consume over 40% of total chip power [1]: as an alternative to general caching designs, specializing memory structures to better match data usage characteristics can improve performance and significantly reduce total energy expended.

One form of such heterogeneous memory structures, *region-based caching* [2][3][4], replaces a single unified data cache with multiple caches optimized for global, stack, and heap references. This approach works well precisely because these types of references exhibit different locality characteristics. Furthermore, many

P. Stenström (Ed.): Transactions on HiPEAC I, LNCS 4050, pp. 54–73, 2007.

applications are dominated by data from a particular region, and thus greater speciali-zation of region structures should allow both quantitative (in terms of performance and energy) and qualitative (in terms of security and robustness) improvements in system operation. This approach slightly increases required chip area, but using mul-tiple, smaller, specialized caches that together constitute a given "level" of a tradi-tional cache hierarchy and only routing data to a cache that matches those data's usage characteristics provides many potential benefits: faster access times, lower en-ergy consumption per access, and the ability to turn off structures that are not required for (parts of) a given application.

Given the promise of this general approach, in this paper we first look at the heap cache, the region-based memory structure that most data populate for most applica-tions (in fact, the majority of a unified L1 cache is generally populated by heap data). Furthermore, the heap represents the most difficult region of memory to manage well in a cache structure. We propose a simple modification to demonstrate the benefits of increased specialization: large and small heap caches. If the application exhibits a small heap footprint, we save energy by using the smaller structure and turning off the larger. For applications with larger footprints, we use both caches, but save energy by keeping highly used "hot" data in the smaller, faster, lower-energy cache. The com-piler determines (through profiled feedback or heuristics) which data belong where, and it conveys this information to the architecture via two different malloc() func-tions that allocate data structures in two disparate regions of memory. This allows the microarchitecture to determine what data to cache where without requiring additional bits in memory reference instructions or complex coherence mechanisms.

This architectural approach addresses dynamic or switching energy consumption via smaller caches that reduce the cost of each data access. The second kind of energy consumption that power-efficient caching structures must address is static or leakage energy; for this, we add *drowsy caching* [5][6][7], an architectural technique exploit-ing dynamic voltage scaling. Reducing supply voltage to inactive lines lowers their static power dissipation. When a drowsy line is accessed, the supply voltage must be returned to its original value before the data are available. Drowsy caches save less power than many other leakage reduction techniques, but do not suffer the dramatic latency increases of other methods.

Using the MiBench suite [8], we study application data usage properties and the design space for split heap caches. The contributions of this paper are:

- We perform a detailed analysis of heap data characteristics to determine the best heap caching strategy and necessary cache size for each application.
- We show that a significant number of embedded applications do not require a large heap cache and demonstrate significant energy savings with minimal performance loss for these by using a smaller cache. We show energy savings of about 85% for both normal and drowsy reduced heap caches.
- For applications with large heap footprints that require a bigger cache, we demon-strate that we can still achieve significant energy savings by identifying a subset of data responsible for the majority of accesses to the heap region and splitting the heap cache into two structures. Using a small cache for hot data and a large cache for the remaining data, we show energy savings of up to 79% using non-drowsy split-heap caches and up to 80% using drowsy split heap caches.

2   Related Work

Since dissipated power per access is proportional to cache size, partitioning techniques reduce power by accessing smaller structures. Cache partitioning schemes may be vertical or horizontal. Vertical partitioning adds a level between the L1 and the processor; examples include line buffers [9][10] and filter caches [11]. These structures provide low-power accesses for data with temporal locality, but typically incur many misses, increasing average observed L1 latency. Horizontal partitioning divides entities at a given level in the memory hierarchy to create multiple entities at that level. For instance, cache sub-banking [9][10] divides cache lines into smaller segments. Memory references are routed to the proper segment, reducing dynamic power per data access.

Fig. 1 illustrates a simple example of region-based caching [3][4], a horizontal partitioning scheme that replaces a unified data cache with heterogeneous caches optimized for global, stack, and heap references. Any non-global, non-stack reference is directed to a normal L1 cache, but since most non-global, non-stack references are to heap data, (with a small number of accesses to text and read-only regions), this L1 is referred to as the *heap cache*. On a memory reference, only the appropriate region cache is activated and draws power. Relatively small working sets for stack and global regions allow those caches to be small, dissipating even less power on hits. Splitting references among caches eliminates inter-region conflicts, thus each cache may implement lower associativity, reducing complexity and access time. The region-based paradigm can be extended to other areas of the memory system; for example, Lee and Ballapuram [12] propose partitioning the data TLB by semantic region.

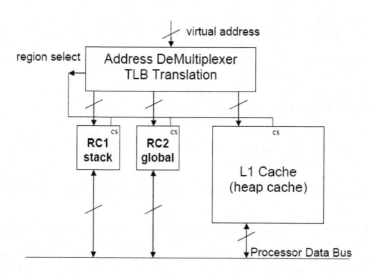

Fig. 1. Memory design for region-based caching

Other approaches to partitioning data by region aim to improve cache performance, not energy consumption. Several efforts focus on stack data, the most localized and frequently referenced data in most applications. Early machines like the HP3000 Series II [13] and the CRISP processor [14][15] contain caches specifically for stack references; in both cases, the stack cache is the only data cache in the processor. Cho et al. [16] decouple stack accesses from the rest of the data reference stream and route each stream to its own cache. The stack value file [17] and specialized stack cache [18] are two examples of cache-like structures customized to exploit characteristics of stack references. Techniques specifically addressing non-stack data are less common. In their analysis of the CRISP stack cache [14], Ditzel and McLellan note that global variables are also well suited to caching. The pointer cache [19] stores mappings between heap pointers and targets, but the structure a prefetching aid, not a data cache.

The downside to region-based caching is that increasing total cache capacity leads to higher static energy dissipation. Drowsy region-based caching [2] attacks this problem by implementing a leakage energy reduction technique [5][6][7] within the region-based caches. In a drowsy cache, inactive lines use a reduced supply voltage; an access to a drowsy line must wait for the supply voltage to return to its full value. Drowsy caches usually update cache line states after a given interval: lines may switch state from active to drowsy. Depending on the policy, lines accessed within an interval may remain active, and non-accessed lines become or continue to be drowsy. Geiger et al. [2] show that combining drowsy and region-based caching yields more benefits than either alone because each technique improves the performance of the other. Drowsy caching effectively eliminates static power increases due to additional region caches, while the partitioning strategy used in region-based caching permits more aggressive drowsy policies. The drowsy interval of each region cache can be tuned according to reference characteristics of that region, allowing highly active regions to be less drowsy than inactive regions.

The primary advantage of drowsy caching over other leakage reduction techniques is that drowsy cache lines preserve their state in low-leakage mode. Techniques that turn off unused cache lines by gating supply voltage [10][20][21] provide larger reductions in leakage energy. In these schemes, however, inactive lines must reload their state from L2 cache when accessed, and resulting performance penalties often outweigh power savings. Parikh et al. [22] dispute the notion that state-preserving techniques are superior, noting that the cost of drowsy caching depends on the latency of the transition between leakage modes.

Geiger et al. [2] introduce split heap caches. They find that for their application suite the ideal drowsy interval for the heap cache is the same as for the stack cache, a result that implies at least some heap data have locality similar to stack data. The authors observe that moving high-locality data to a separate structure allows a more aggressive drowsy caching policy for low-locality data, further reducing static energy consumption of region-based caches. Using a 4KB cache for hot heap data and maintaining a 32KB cache for low-locality heap data, they show an average energy reduction of 71.7% over a unified drowsy L1 data cache.

3   Characteristics of Heap Data

In this section, we analyze characteristics of heap cache accesses in applications from the MiBench [8] benchmark suite to determine best heap caching strategies for each program. We begin by assessing the significance of the heap region within each target application, looking at overall size and number of accesses relative to the other semantic regions. Table 1 provides this information. The second and third columns of the table show number of unique block addresses accessed in the heap cache and number of accesses to those addresses, respectively. Since our simulations assume 32B cache blocks, 1KB of data contains 32 unique block addresses. The fourth and fifth columns show this same data as a percentage of the corresponding values for all regions (i.e., the fourth column shows the ratio of unique data addresses in the heap region to all unique data addresses in the application). Several cases bear out our assertions about heap data: they have a large footprint and low locality. In these applications, the heap cache accesses occupy a much larger percentage of the overall footprint than of the total accesses. The most extreme cases are applications such as

Table 1. Characteristics of heap cache accesses in MiBench applications, including total footprint size, total number of accesses, and relative contribution of heap data to overall data footprint and reference count

Benchmark	# unique addresses	Accesses to heap cache	% total unique addresses	% total accesses
adpcm.encode	69	39971743	27.6%	39.9%
adpcm.decode	68	39971781	27.0%	39.9%
basicmath	252	49181748	61.2%	4.5%
blowfish.decode	213	39190633	39.0%	10.2%
blowfish.encode	212	39190621	38.9%	10.2%
bitcount	112	12377683	42.7%	6.7%
jpeg.encode	26012	10214537	99.2%	29.3%
CRC32	90	159955061	41.1%	16.7%
dijkstra	347	44917851	19.7%	38.3%
jpeg.decode	1510	7036942	90.2%	62.9%
FFT	16629	15262360	99.2%	8.6%
FFT.inverse	16630	14013100	99.2%	6.3%
ghostscript	59594	56805375	98.0%	15.3%
ispell	13286	28000346	96.5%	6.4%
mad	2123	40545761	82.3%	36.4%
patricia	110010	16900929	99.9%	6.6%
pgp.encode	298	252620	7.4%	1.9%
pgp.decode	738	425414	44.9%	1.5%
quicksort	62770	152206224	66.7%	12.9%
rijndael.decode	229	37374614	31.0%	21.7%
rijndael.encode	236	35791440	40.0%	19.6%
rsynth	143825	104084186	99.2%	21.4%
stringsearch	203	90920	18.2%	6.2%
sha	90	263617	20.9%	0.7%
susan.corners	18479	9614163	97.1%	63.6%
susan.edges	21028	22090676	99.1%	62.3%
susan.smoothing	7507	179696772	97.0%	41.7%
tiff2bw	2259	57427236	92.1%	98.5%
tiffdither	1602	162086279	83.1%	62.8%
tiffmedian	4867	165489090	53.0%	79.8%
tiff2rgba	1191987	81257094	100.0%	98.5%
gsm.encode	302	157036702	68.0%	11.7%
typeset	168075	153470300	98.0%	49.0%
gsm.decode	285	78866326	55.6%	21.5%
AVERAGE			65.7%	29.8%

FFT.inverse and *patricia* in which heap accesses account for over 99% of unique addresses accessed throughout the programs but comprise less than 7% of total data accesses. This relationship holds in most applications; heap accesses cover an average of 65.67% of unique block addresses and account for 29.81% of total data accesses. In some cases, we see a correlation between footprint size and number of accesses—applications that have few heap lines and few accesses, like *pgp.encode*, and applications that have large percentages of both cache lines and accesses, like *tiff2rgba*. A few outliers like *dijkstra* buck the trend entirely, containing frequently accessed heap data with small footprints.

We see that about half the applications have a small number of lines in the heap, with 16 of the 34 applications containing fewer than 1000 unique addresses. The *adpcm* application has the smallest footprint, using 69 and 68 unique addresses in the encode and decode phases, respectively. The typical 32KB L1 heap cache is likely far larger than these applications need; if we use a smaller heap cache, we dissipate less dynamic power per access with minimal effects on performance. Since heap cache accesses still comprise a significant percentage of total data accesses, this change should have a noticeable effect on dynamic energy consumption of these benchmarks. Shrinking the heap cache will also reduce static energy consumption. Previous resizable caches disable unused ways [23][24] or sets [24][25] in set-associative caches; we can use similar logic to simply disable the entire large heap cache and route all accesses to the small cache when appropriate. In Section 4, we show effects of this optimization on energy and performance.

Shrinking the heap cache may reduce the energy consumption for benchmarks with large heap footprints, but resulting performance losses may be intolerable for those applications. However, we can still benefit by identifying a small subset of addresses with good locality, and routing their accesses to a smaller structure. Because we want the majority of references to dissipate less power, we strive to choose the most frequently accessed lines. The access count gives a sense of the degree of temporal locality for a given address.

Usually, a small number of blocks are responsible for the majority of the heap accesses, as shown in Table 2. The table gives the number of lines needed to cover different percentages—50%, 75%, 90%, 95%, and 99%—of the total accesses to the heap cache. We can see that, on average, just 2.1% of the cache lines cover 50% of the accesses. Although the rate of coverage decreases somewhat as you add more blocks—in other words, the first N blocks account for more accesses than the next N blocks—we still only need 5.8% to cover 75% of the accesses, 13.2% to cover 90% of the accesses, 24.5% to cover 95% of the accesses, and 45.5% to cover 99% of the accesses. The percentages do not tell the whole story, as the footprint sizes are wildly disparate for these applications. However, the table also shows that in applications with large footprints (defined as footprints of 1000 unique addresses or more), the percentage of addresses is lower for the first two coverage points (50% and 75%). This statistic implies that we can identify a relatively small subset of frequently accessed lines for all applications, regardless of overall footprint size.

Table 2. Number of unique addresses required to cover different fractions of accesses to the heap cache in MiBench applications. The data show that a small number of lines account for the majority of heap cache accesses, indicating that some of these lines possess better locality than previously believed. This trend is more apparent in applications with large heap cache footprints.

Benchmark	# unique addresses	% unique addresses needed to cover given percentage of heap cache accesses				
		50%	75%	90%	95%	99%
adpcm.encode	69	1.4%	2.9%	2.9%	2.9%	2.9%
adpcm.decode	68	1.5%	1.5%	1.5%	1.5%	1.5%
basicmath	252	4.0%	25.4%	48.0%	55.6%	61.9%
blowfish.decode	213	0.9%	1.4%	2.3%	26.8%	55.9%
blowfish.encode	212	0.9%	1.4%	2.4%	26.9%	56.1%
bitcount	112	0.9%	1.8%	2.7%	3.6%	3.6%
jpeg.encode	26012	0.1%	0.6%	2.9%	38.2%	87.3%
CRC32	90	2.2%	3.3%	4.4%	4.4%	4.4%
dijkstra	347	0.3%	18.2%	39.2%	49.6%	63.1%
jpeg.decode	1510	4.8%	12.3%	31.9%	44.1%	59.5%
FFT	16629	0.0%	0.1%	4.8%	40.7%	85.3%
FFT.inverse	16630	0.0%	0.1%	13.0%	44.0%	86.5%
ghostscript	59594	0.0%	0.0%	0.6%	6.6%	57.5%
ispell	13286	0.1%	0.2%	0.5%	0.7%	1.3%
mad	2123	1.3%	2.6%	9.7%	14.9%	24.5%
patricia	110010	0.0%	0.1%	0.3%	36.6%	86.0%
pgp.encode	298	0.7%	1.0%	3.7%	6.7%	26.8%
pgp.decode	738	0.3%	0.4%	1.1%	2.3%	29.7%
quicksort	62770	0.0%	0.0%	0.2%	22.1%	49.1%
rijndael.decode	229	1.3%	2.2%	6.6%	31.4%	57.2%
rijndael.encode	236	1.3%	3.0%	7.6%	32.6%	56.8%
rsynth	143825	0.0%	0.0%	0.0%	1.3%	77.3%
stringsearch	203	17.2%	42.9%	59.6%	65.5%	72.9%
sha	90	1.1%	2.2%	3.3%	3.3%	8.9%
susan.corners	18479	0.0%	3.0%	11.0%	14.9%	32.7%
susan.edges	21028	0.0%	4.9%	15.1%	20.2%	30.4%
susan.smoothing	7507	0.0%	0.1%	13.7%	30.3%	44.1%
tiff2bw	2259	10.3%	15.4%	24.3%	29.4%	37.1%
tiffdither	1602	9.4%	19.6%	25.7%	29.6%	40.8%
tiffmedian	4867	4.0%	10.9%	16.7%	20.8%	47.8%
tiff2rgba	1191987	0.0%	0.1%	57.4%	78.7%	95.7%
gsm.encode	302	2.3%	4.0%	6.0%	7.6%	10.6%
typeset	168075	5.5%	15.4%	25.5%	33.0%	60.1%
gsm.decode	285	0.7%	1.4%	4.2%	6.0%	30.5%
AVERAGE (all apps)		2.1%	5.8%	13.2%	24.5%	45.5%
AVERAGE (>1k unique addrs)		2.0%	4.8%	14.1%	28.1%	55.7%

Since a small number of addresses account for a significant portion of the heap cache accesses, we can route these frequently accessed data to a smaller structure to reduce the energy consumption of the L1 data cache. Our goal is to maximize the low-power accesses without a large performance penalty, so we need to judiciously choose which data to place in the hot heap cache. To estimate performance impact, we use the Cheetah cache simulator [26] to find a lower bound on the miss rate for a given number of input data lines. We simulate fully-associative 2 KB, 4 KB, and 8 KB caches with optimal replacement [27] and route the N most frequently accessed lines to the cache, varying N by powers of 2. We use optimal replacement to minimize conflict misses and give a sense of when the cache is filled to capacity; the actual miss rate for our direct-mapped hot heap cache will be higher.

Tables 3, 4, and 5 show the results of these simulations for 2 KB, 4 KB, and 8 KB caches, respectively. We present only a subset of the applications, omitting programs with small heap footprints and a worst-case miss rate less than 1% because they will perform well at any cache size. As these tables show, the miss rate rises precipitously for small values of N, but levels off around $N = 512$ or 1024 in most cases. This result reflects the fact that the majority of accesses are concentrated at a small number of addresses. Note, however, that the miss rates remain tolerable for all applications for N values up to 256, regardless of cache size. The miss rate alone does not establish the suitability of a given caching scheme for heap data. Applications in which these accesses comprise a significant percentage of the total data references are less likely to be able to tolerate a higher miss rate. In order to gain the maximum benefit from split heap caching, we would like to route as many accesses as possible to a small cache. These simulations indicate that varying the cache size will not have a dramatic effect on performance, so we choose the smallest cache size studied—2 KB—and route the 256 most accessed lines to that cache when splitting the heap. This approach should give us a significant energy reduction without compromising performance.

This approach for determining what data is routed to the small cache does require some refinement. In practice, the compiler would use a profiling run of the application to determine the appropriate caching strategy, applying a well-defined heuristic to the profiling data. We use a simple heuristic in this work to show the potential effectiveness of our caching strategies; a more refined method that effectively incorporates miss rate estimates as well as footprint size and access percentages would likely yield better results.

Table 3. Miss rates for a fully-associative 2 KB cache using optimal replacement for different numbers of input addresses, N. These results establish a lower bound for the miss rate when caching these data. Applications shown either have a large heap footprint, which we define as a footprint of at least 1000 unique addresses, or a worst-case miss rate above 1%.

Benchmark	Miss rate for given N value						
	128	256	512	1024	2048	4096	8192
jpeg.encode	0.2%	0.8%	1.8%	2.5%	2.5%	2.5%	2.5%
dijkstra	4.2%	8.0%	8.0%	8.0%	8.0%	8.0%	8.0%
jpeg.decode	0.4%	0.9%	1.7%	2.8%	2.8%	2.8%	2.8%
FFT	0.1%	0.1%	0.2%	0.3%	0.4%	0.8%	1.4%
FFT.inverse	0.1%	0.1%	0.2%	0.3%	0.5%	0.8%	1.5%
ghostscript	0.0%	0.2%	0.3%	0.5%	0.6%	0.6%	0.8%
ispell	0.2%	0.4%	0.4%	0.4%	0.4%	0.4%	0.4%
mad	0.7%	1.6%	2.4%	2.4%	2.4%	2.4%	2.4%
patricia	0.7%	1.3%	1.8%	1.9%	2.0%	2.0%	2.1%
quicksort	0.0%	0.0%	0.1%	0.1%	0.1%	0.2%	0.2%
rsynth	0.0%	0.0%	0.0%	0.0%	0.1%	0.1%	0.1%
stringsearch	1.8%	2.0%	2.0%	2.0%	2.0%	2.0%	2.0%
susan.corners	0.0%	0.0%	0.0%	0.0%	0.1%	0.1%	0.2%
susan.edges	0.0%	0.0%	0.0%	0.0%	0.1%	0.1%	0.2%
susan.smoothing	0.0%	0.0%	0.0%	0.0%	0.0%	0.0%	0.0%
tiff2bw	2.5%	3.8%	4.7%	5.7%	5.7%	5.7%	5.7%
tiffdither	0.4%	0.8%	1.3%	1.6%	1.6%	1.6%	1.6%
tiffmedian	0.5%	1.2%	2.0%	3.4%	3.5%	3.4%	3.4%
tiff2rgba	2.5%	3.8%	4.6%	6.1%	7.1%	7.1%	7.1%
typeset	1.4%	2.6%	2.7%	3.0%	3.4%	4.0%	5.0%

Table 4. Miss rates for a fully-associative 4 KB cache using optimal replacement for different numbers of input addresses. Applications are the same set shown in Table 3

Benchmark	Miss rate for given N value						
	128	256	512	1024	2048	4096	8192
jpeg.encode	0.0%	0.3%	0.9%	1.4%	1.5%	1.5%	1.5%
dijkstra	0.0%	2.7%	2.7%	2.7%	2.7%	2.7%	2.7%
jpeg.decode	0.0%	0.3%	0.7%	1.4%	1.5%	1.5%	1.5%
FFT	0.0%	0.0%	0.1%	0.1%	0.3%	0.6%	1.3%
FFT.inverse	0.0%	0.0%	0.1%	0.2%	0.4%	0.7%	1.4%
ghostscript	0.0%	0.0%	0.0%	0.1%	0.2%	0.3%	0.4%
ispell	0.0%	0.1%	0.1%	0.1%	0.1%	0.1%	0.1%
mad	0.0%	0.8%	1.6%	1.6%	1.6%	1.6%	1.6%
patricia	0.0%	0.3%	0.5%	0.6%	0.6%	0.6%	0.7%
quicksort	0.0%	0.0%	0.0%	0.1%	0.1%	0.1%	0.2%
rsynth	0.0%	0.0%	0.0%	0.0%	0.0%	0.1%	0.1%
stringsearch	0.2%	0.5%	0.5%	0.5%	0.5%	0.5%	0.5%
susan.corners	0.0%	0.0%	0.0%	0.0%	0.0%	0.1%	0.1%
susan.edges	0.0%	0.0%	0.0%	0.0%	0.0%	0.1%	0.1%
susan.smoothing	0.0%	0.0%	0.0%	0.0%	0.0%	0.0%	0.0%
tiff2bw	0.0%	2.5%	3.9%	5.0%	5.0%	5.0%	5.0%
tiffdither	0.0%	0.5%	1.1%	1.3%	1.3%	1.3%	1.3%
tiffmedian	0.0%	0.8%	1.3%	2.9%	3.0%	3.0%	3.0%
tiff2rgba	0.0%	2.5%	3.1%	4.6%	5.8%	5.8%	5.8%
typeset	0.0%	0.1%	0.2%	0.5%	0.9%	1.4%	2.3%

Table 5. Miss rates for a fully-associative 8 KB cache using optimal replacement for different numbers of input addresses. Applications shown are the same set shown in Table 3

Benchmark	Miss rate for given N value						
	128	256	512	1024	2048	4096	8192
jpeg.encode	0.0%	0.0%	0.2%	0.6%	0.6%	0.7%	0.7%
dijkstra	0.0%	0.0%	0.0%	0.0%	0.0%	0.0%	0.0%
jpeg.decode	0.0%	0.0%	0.2%	0.7%	0.7%	0.7%	0.7%
FFT	0.0%	0.0%	0.0%	0.1%	0.3%	0.6%	1.2%
FFT.inverse	0.0%	0.0%	0.0%	0.1%	0.3%	0.7%	1.4%
ghostscript	0.0%	0.0%	0.0%	0.0%	0.1%	0.1%	0.2%
ispell	0.0%	0.0%	0.0%	0.0%	0.0%	0.0%	0.0%
mad	0.0%	0.0%	0.8%	0.9%	0.9%	0.9%	0.9%
patricia	0.0%	0.0%	0.1%	0.2%	0.3%	0.3%	0.3%
quicksort	0.0%	0.0%	0.0%	0.0%	0.1%	0.1%	0.1%
rsynth	0.0%	0.0%	0.0%	0.0%	0.0%	0.1%	0.1%
stringsearch	0.2%	0.2%	0.2%	0.2%	0.2%	0.2%	0.2%
susan.corners	0.0%	0.0%	0.0%	0.0%	0.0%	0.1%	0.1%
susan.edges	0.0%	0.0%	0.0%	0.0%	0.0%	0.1%	0.1%
susan.smoothing	0.0%	0.0%	0.0%	0.0%	0.0%	0.0%	0.0%
tiff2bw	0.0%	0.0%	2.4%	3.6%	3.7%	3.7%	3.7%
tiffdither	0.0%	0.0%	0.6%	0.8%	0.8%	0.8%	0.8%
tiffmedian	0.0%	0.0%	0.2%	1.9%	2.0%	2.0%	2.0%
tiff2rgba	0.0%	0.0%	0.5%	1.7%	3.2%	3.3%	3.3%
typeset	0.0%	0.0%	0.0%	0.0%	0.2%	0.6%	1.3%

4   Experiments

The previous section motivates the need for two separate heap caches, one large and one small, to accommodate the needs of all applications. As shown in Table 1, many applications have small heap footprints and therefore do not require a large heap cache; in these cases, we can disable the large cache and place all heap data in the smaller structure. This approach will reduce dynamic energy by routing accesses to a smaller structure and reduce static energy by decreasing the active cache area. Applications with large heap footprints are more likely to require both caches to maintain performance. We showed in Table 2 that most heap references access a small subset of the data; by keeping hot data in the smaller structure, we save dynamic energy. In all cases, we further lower static energy consumption by making the caches drowsy.

Our simulations use a modified version of the SimpleScalar ARM target [28]. We use Wattch [29] for dynamic power modeling and Zhang et al.'s HotLeakage [30] for static power modeling. HotLeakage contains a detailed drowsy cache model, which was used by Parikh et al. [22] to compare state-preserving and non-state-preserving techniques for leakage control. HotLeakage tracks the number of lines in both active and drowsy modes and calculates leakage power appropriately. It also models the power of the additional hardware required to support drowsy caching. All simulations use an in-order processor model similar to the Intel StrongARM SA-110 [1]; the configuration details are shown in Table 6. We assume 130 nm technology with a 1.7 GHz clock frequency.

Table 6. Processor model parameters for heap caching simulations. All simulations use an in-order model based on the Intel StrongARM SA-110 [1].

Memory system	
Line size (all caches)	32 bytes
L1 stack/global cache configuration	4 KB, direct-mapped, single-ported, 1 cycle hit latency
L1 heap cache configuration	32KB, direct-mapped, single-ported, 2 cycle hit latency
L1 instruction cache configuration	16 KB, 32-way set associative, 1 cycle hit latency
L2 cache configuration	512 KB, 4-way set-associative, unified data/inst., 12 cycle hit latency
Main memory latency	88 cycles (first chunk) 3 cycles (inter chunk)

Execution engine	
Fetch/decode/ issue/commit width	1/1/1/1
IFQ size	8
Branch predictor	not taken
Integer ALU/multiplier	1 each
FP ALU/multiplier	1 each
Memory port(s) to CPU	1

Figures 2 and 3 show simulation results for region-based caches using three different heap cache configurations: a large (32KB) unified heap cache, a small (2KB) unified heap cache, and a split heap cache using both the large and small caches. We present normalized energy and performance numbers, using a single 32KB direct-mapped L1 data cache as the baseline. Because all region-based caches are

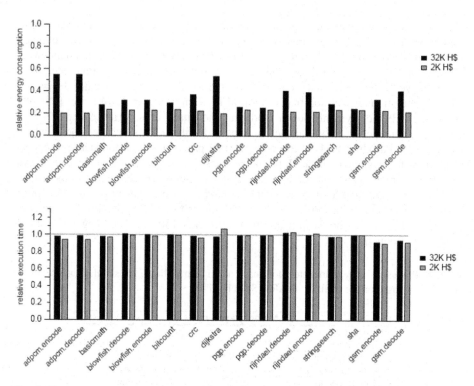

Fig. 2. Energy (top graph) and performance (bottom graph) results for MiBench applications with small heap footprints (less than 1000 unique addresses) using region-based caches with large and small unified heap caches. The baseline is a 32KB direct-mapped unified L1 data cache. Speedups for the large heap cache are due to reduced conflicts between regions.

direct-mapped to minimize energy consumption, we use a direct-mapped baseline to ensure a fair comparison. We consider the most effective configuration to be the cache organization with the lowest energy-delay product ratio [31].

For applications with a heap footprint under 1000 lines, the split cache is unnecessary. Fig. 2 shows the results from these applications. Fig. 3, which shows applications with large heap footprints, adds the energy and performance numbers for the split cache. As expected, using the small heap cache and disabling the large offers the best energy savings across the board. Most applications consume close to 80% less energy in this case; however, some applications suffer significant performance losses, most notably *susan.corners* and *susan.edges*. 18 of the 34 applications in the MiBench suite experience performance losses of less than 1%, including *ghostscript*, *mad*, *patricia*, *rsynth*, and *susan.smoothing*—all applications with large heap footprints. This result suggests that heap data in these applications have good locality characteristics and are frequently accessed while present in the cache. Another application, *quicksort*, suffers significant performance losses for all configurations due to an increased number of global misses, and therefore still benefits most from using the

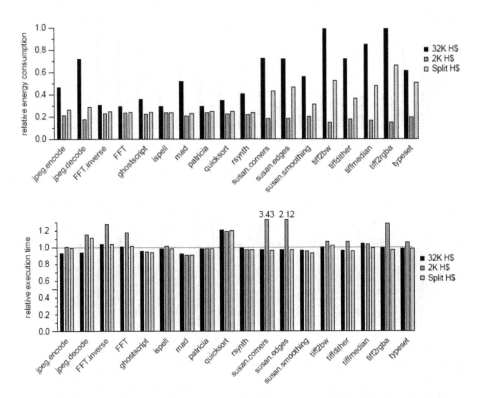

Fig. 3. Energy (top graph) and performance (bottom graph) results for MiBench applications with large heap footprints (greater than 1000 unique addresses) using three different heap cache configurations: a large unified heap cache, a small unified heap cache, and a split heap cache employing both large and small caches. The baseline is a 32KB direct-mapped unified L1 data cache. Speedups for the large heap cache are due to reduced conflicts between regions.

small heap cache. In all of these cases, we gain substantial energy savings with virtually no performance loss, reducing overall energy consumption by up to 86%. Several applications actually experience small speedups, a result of reduced conflict between regions and the lower hit latency for the smaller cache.

For those applications that suffer substantial performance losses with the small cache alone, the split heap cache offers a higher-performance alternative that still saves some energy. The most dramatic improvements can be seen in *susan.corners* and *susan.edges*. With the large heap cache disabled, these two applications see their runtime more than double; with a split heap cache, they experience small speedups. Other applications, such as *FFT* and *tiff2rgba*, run close to 30% slower with the small cache alone and appear to be candidates for a split heap cache. However, the energy required to keep the large cache active overwhelms the performance benefit of splitting the heap, leading to a higher energy-delay product.

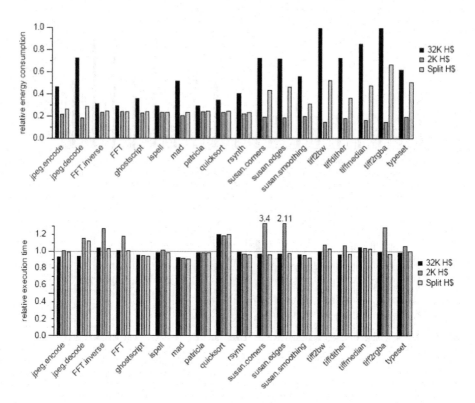

Fig. 4. Energy (top graph) and performance (bottom graph) results for MiBench applications with large heap footprints (greater than 1000 unique addresses) using three different heap cache configurations: a large unified heap cache, a small unified heap cache, and a split heap cache employing both large and small caches. The baseline is a 32KB direct-mapped unified L1 data cache with a 512-cycle drowsy interval.

Fig. 4 shows simulation results for drowsy heap caching configurations. In all cases, we use the ideal drowsy intervals derived in [2]—for the unified heap caches, 512 cycles; for the split heap cache, 512 cycles for the hot heap cache and 1 cycle for the cold heap cache. The stack and global caches use 512 and 256 cycle windows, respectively. We assume a 1 cycle latency for transitions to and from drowsy mode. Note that drowsy caching alone offers a 35% energy reduction over a non-drowsy unified cache for this set of benchmarks [2].

Although all caches benefit from the static energy reduction offered by drowsy caching, this technique has the most profound effect on the split heap caches. Since the applications with small heap footprints do not require a split cache, the figure only shows the larger benchmarks. Drowsy caching all but eliminates the leakage energy of the large heap cache, as it contains rarely accessed data with low locality and is therefore usually inactive. Since the small cache experiences fewer conflicts in the split heap scheme than by itself, its lines are also less active and therefore more conducive to drowsy caching. Both techniques are very effective at reducing the energy consumption of these benchmarks. Drowsy split heap caches save up to 80% of the

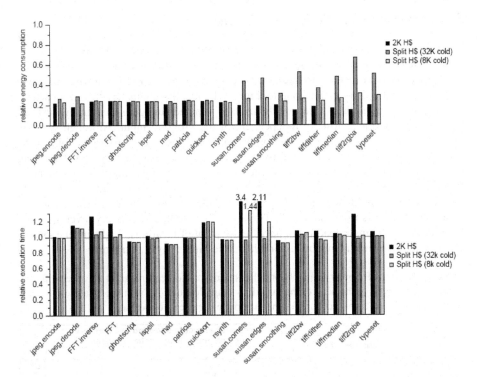

Fig. 5. Energy (top graph) and performance (bottom graph) results for MiBench applications with large heap footprints (greater than 1000 unique addresses) using three different heap cache configurations: a small unified heap cache, and split heap caches using either a 32KB cache or an 8KB cache for low-locality heap data. The baseline is a 32KB direct-mapped unified L1 data cache with a 512-cycle drowsy interval.

total energy, while the small caches alone save between 76% and 85%. Because drowsy caching has a minimal performance cost, the runtime numbers are similar to those shown in the previous figure. The small cache alone and the split heap cache produce comparable energy-delay values for several applications; *ispell* is one example. In these cases, performance-conscious users can employ a split heap cache, while users desiring lower energy consumption can choose the small unified heap cache.

Shrinking the large heap cache further alleviates its effect on energy consumption. The data remaining in that cache is infrequently accessed and can therefore tolerate an increased number of conflicts. Fig. 5 shows simulation results for two different split heap configurations—one using a 32KB cache for cold heap data, the other using an 8KB cache—as well as the 2KB unified heap cache. All caches are drowsy. The unified cache is still most efficient for the majority of applications, but shrinking the cold heap cache narrows the gap between unified and split heap configurations. Applications such as *susan.corners* and *tiff2rgba*, which contain a non-trivial number of accesses to the cold heap cache, see the greatest benefit from this modification, with *tiff2rgba* consuming 36% less energy with the smaller cold heap cache. Overall, these applications save between 69% and 79% of the total energy.

5 Instruction-Centric Heap Caching

To this point, we have focused on analyzing heap data to determine how best to cache them. When only a subset of the data displays good locality, we use access frequency to identify hot data to store in a smaller cache. We now approach the same problem from a different angle—rather than looking at the locality characteristics of a particular line, we examine the references themselves. One advantage is that an instruction-based profile is often virtually independent of the program input. Although the data may affect how often a particular instruction executes, most programs follow the same general execution and therefore display the same relative behavior. Choosing hot data through their referencing instructions exploits locality in a different manner. Regularly accessed cache lines have high temporal locality. We cannot necessarily say the same about the targets of frequently executed memory instructions, as each instruction can access many addresses. However, this method effectively leverages spatial locality, as a single load often accesses sequential locations. Tight inner loops of program kernels display this behavior when accessing arrays or streams.

Table 7. Number of memory instructions that reference the heap required to cover different fractions of accesses to the heap cache in MiBench applications. As with the data itself, a small number of loads and stores account for the majority of heap cache accesses.

Benchmark	# memory instructions	% memory instructions needed to cover given percentage of heap cache accesses				
		50%	75%	90%	95%	99%
adpcm.encode	171	1.2%	1.8%	1.8%	1.8%	1.8%
adpcm.decode	173	1.2%	1.7%	1.7%	1.7%	1.7%
basicmath	373	1.1%	4.8%	8.6%	10.5%	18.2%
blowfish.decode	325	1.2%	2.2%	2.5%	2.8%	2.8%
blowfish.encode	325	1.2%	2.2%	2.5%	2.8%	2.8%
bitcount	244	0.4%	0.8%	1.2%	1.6%	1.6%
jpeg.encode	1406	1.1%	3.0%	6.5%	8.9%	15.3%
CRC32	329	0.9%	1.2%	1.5%	1.5%	1.5%
dijkstra	383	0.8%	1.0%	1.3%	5.7%	14.4%
jpeg.decode	1192	1.2%	2.6%	4.9%	6.8%	11.8%
FFT	329	5.2%	11.2%	17.0%	20.4%	24.3%
FFT.inverse	327	4.9%	11.3%	17.7%	21.4%	25.1%
ghostscript	7501	0.2%	0.3%	1.5%	4.1%	13.5%
ispell	649	2.3%	4.2%	7.1%	10.8%	18.3%
mad	1043	2.9%	4.5%	7.2%	11.2%	15.0%
patricia	420	3.3%	10.7%	20.5%	23.8%	26.7%
pgp.encode	1119	0.4%	0.5%	2.1%	4.8%	22.5%
pgp.decode	1022	0.4%	0.6%	1.2%	2.7%	17.7%
quicksort	337	2.4%	5.9%	10.4%	12.5%	14.8%
rijndael.decode	540	13.7%	22.2%	27.4%	29.3%	31.1%
rijndael.encode	617	11.2%	18.3%	22.5%	24.1%	25.3%
rsynth	889	2.2%	4.2%	5.5%	7.6%	15.0%
stringsearch	210	1.9%	7.1%	11.9%	15.7%	21.9%
sha	276	1.1%	1.4%	1.8%	1.8%	8.0%
susan.corners	691	4.2%	8.0%	15.6%	18.5%	21.1%
susan.edges	878	6.8%	13.4%	21.5%	25.3%	28.6%
susan.smoothing	517	0.4%	0.6%	0.6%	0.6%	0.6%
tiff2bw	1036	0.4%	0.7%	1.1%	1.4%	1.8%
tiffdither	1314	0.6%	0.9%	2.8%	4.3%	6.8%
tiffmedian	1359	0.7%	1.0%	1.5%	1.8%	3.0%
tiff2rgba	1154	0.8%	1.6%	2.6%	2.9%	3.1%
gsm.encode	736	3.0%	5.3%	7.1%	8.2%	13.5%
typeset	17235	0.6%	1.9%	3.8%	6.7%	16.2%
gsm.decode	555	0.9%	1.4%	2.9%	3.4%	7.6%
AVERAGE		2.4%	4.7%	7.2%	9.0%	13.3%

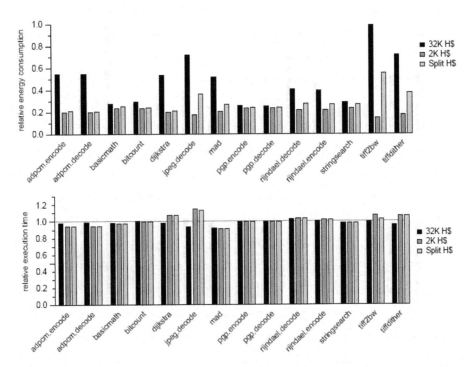

Fig. 6. Energy (top graph) and performance (bottom graph) for a subset of MiBench applications using different non-drowsy heap cache configurations. The baseline is a 32 KB direct-mapped unified L1 data cache. The hardware configurations are the same as in Figures 2 and 3, but in the split heap cache, data are routed to the hot heap cache based on the frequency of the accessing instructions, not references to specific blocks.

In Table 2, we showed that a small number of blocks are responsible for the majority of heap accesses. This trend is even more apparent for memory instructions, as shown in Table 7. Just 2.4% of the loads and stores to the heap cache cover 50% of the accesses—a similar figure to the 2.1% of heap addresses required to cover the same percentage of accesses. The numbers do not increase greatly as we look at different coverage points, with approximately 13% of the memory instructions accounting for 99% of the heap references. These results reflect the oft-quoted maxim that programs spend 90% of their time in 10% of the code. Note that the number of instructions accessing the heap cache remains fairly consistent across applications, unlike the size of the heap data footprint. Our studies show that a small percentage of loads and stores access multiple regions.

The data suggest that we can treat heap references in a similar manner to heap data when determining how to cache this region. Because a small number of instructions account for most accesses, we can move their targets to a smaller cache, maintaining a larger cache for the remaining references. Note that only identifying the most frequently executed memory instructions will not sufficiently capture the appropriate accesses. Other memory references that share the same targets must also access the hot heap cache. Choosing appropriate instructions involves an iterative routine that ceases when the set of target addresses overlaps with no remaining references.

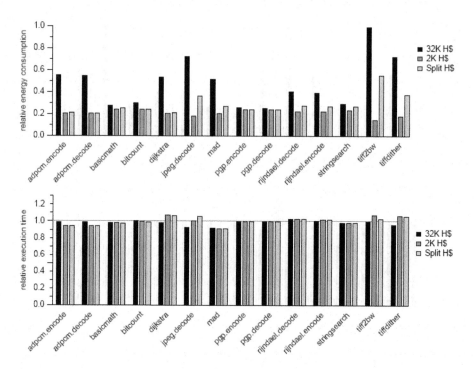

Fig. 7. Energy (top graph) and performance (bottom graph) results for a subset of MiBench applications using different drowsy heap cache configurations. The baseline is a 32 KB direct-mapped unified L1 data cache with a 512-cycle drowsy interval. The hardware configurations are the same as in Fig. 4, but in the split heap cache, data are routed to the hot heap cache based on the frequency of the accessing instructions, not references to specific blocks.

Fig. 6 shows some preliminary results from this approach. As in Figures 2 and 3, we compare three non-drowsy cache configurations: a large (32 KB) unified heap cache, a small (2 KB) unified heap cache, and a split cache employing both large and small caches. We use the 128 most executed load instructions as a starting point for routing data between the caches. The table shows a subset of the MiBench applications, as the space requirements for the memory instruction profiles currently prevents the execution of some of the larger applications. Therefore, the small unified heap cache unsurprisingly represents the ideal design point for the benchmarks shown. For the most part, the results for the split heap configuration are similar to those shown in Figures 2 and 3, with energy savings ranging between 45% and 79%.

In Fig. 7, we evaluate drowsy heap cache configurations using the same routing methodology. As with the data shown in Fig. 4, the addition of drowsy caching significantly improves the energy consumption of the split cache, leading to comparable results for the small cache and split cache in several cases. Energy savings range from 45% to 79% in the split heap caches for the applications shown. These reductions match the reductions shown in the non-drowsy case; however, recall that the drowsy baseline already provides a significant energy savings over the non-drowsy baseline.

6 Conclusions

In this paper, we have evaluated a new multilateral cache organization designed to tailor cache resources to the individual reference characteristics of an application. We examined the characteristics of heap data for a broad suite of embedded applications, showing that the heap data cache footprint varies widely. To ensure that all applications perform well, we maintain two heap caches: a small, low-energy cache for frequently accessed heap data, and a larger structure for low-locality data. In the majority of embedded applications we studied, the heap footprint is small and the data possesses good locality characteristics. We can save energy in these applications by disabling the larger cache and routing data to the smaller cache, thus reducing both dynamic energy per access and static energy. This modification incurs a minimal performance penalty while reducing energy consumption by up to 86%. Those applications that do have a large heap footprint can use both heap caches, routing a frequently-accessed subset of the data to the smaller structure. Because a small number of addresses account for the majority of heap accesses, we can still reduce energy with both heap caches active—using up to 79% less energy—while maintaining high performance across all applications. When we implement drowsy caching on top of our split heap caching scheme, we can achieve even greater savings. With drowsy heap caches, disabling the larger structure allows for energy reductions between 76% and 85%, while activating both heap caches at once allows us to save up to 80% of the total energy.

In the future, we plan to further explore a few different aspects of this problem. We believe that the instruction-based selection of hot heap data may ultimately hold more promise than the initial approach, and plan to explore this topic further through more detailed analysis of memory reference behavior. Also, the studies we ran using Cheetah suggest we can significantly lower the heap cache miss rate by reducing conflicts within it. We plan to investigate data placement methods as a means of ensuring fewer conflicts and better performance.

References

1. J. Montanaro, et al. A 160-MHz, 32-b, 0.5-W CMOS RISC Microprocessor. *Digital Technical Journal*, 9(1):49-62, January 1997.
2. M.J. Geiger, S.A. McKee, and G.S. Tyson. Drowsy Region-Based Caches: Minimizing Both Dynamic and Static Power Dissipation. *Proc. ACM International Conference on Computing Frontiers*, pp. 378-384, May 2005.
3. H.S. Lee and G.S. Tyson. Region-Based Caching: An Energy-Delay Efficient Memory Architecture for Embedded Processors. *Proc. International Conference on Compilers, Architecture, and Synthesis for Embedded Systems*, pp. 120-127, November 2000.
4. H-H.S. Lee. Improving Energy and Performance of Data Cache Architectures by Exploiting Memory Reference Characteristics. Doctoral thesis, The University of Michigan, 2001.
5. K. Flautner, N.S. Kim, S. Martin, D. Blaauw, and T. Mudge. Drowsy Caches: Simple Techniques for Reducing Leakage Power. *Proc. 29ᵗʰ International Symposium on Computer Architecture*, pp. 147-157, May 2002.

6. N.S. Kim, K. Flautner, D. Blaauw, and T. Mudge. Drowsy Instruction Caches: Leakage Power Reduction using Dynamic Voltage Scaling and Cache Sub-bank Prediction. *Proc. 35th International Symposium on Microarchitecure*, pp. 219-230, November 2002.
7. N.S. Kim, K. Flautner, D. Blaauw, and T. Mudge. Circuit and Microarchitectural Techniques for Reducing Cache Leakage Power. *IEEE Transactions on VLSI*, 12(2):167-184, February 2004.
8. M.R. Guthaus, J. Ringenberg, D. Ernst, T. Austin, T. Mudge, and R. Brown. MiBench: A Free, Commercially Representative Embedded Benchmark Suite. *Proc. 4th IEEE Workshop on Workload Characterization*, pp. 3-14, December 2001.
9. K. Ghose and M.B. Kamble. Reducing Power in Superscalar Processor Caches using Sub-banking, Multiple Line Buffers and Bit-Line Segmentation. *Proc. International Symposium on Low Power Electronics and Design*, pp. 70-75, August 1999.
10. C-L. Su and A.M. Despain. Cache Designs for Energy Efficiency. *Proc. 28th Hawaii International Conference on System Sciences*, pp. 306-315, January 1995.
11. J. Kin, M. Gupta, and W.H. Mangione-Smith. Filtering Memory References to Increase Energy Efficiency. *IEEE Transactions on Computers*, 49(1):1-15, January 2000.
12. H.S. Lee and C.S. Ballapuram. Energy Efficient D-TLB and Data Cache using Semantic-Aware Multilateral Partitioning. *Proc. International Symposium on Low Power Electronics and Design*, pp. 306-311, August 2003.
13. R.P. Blake. Exploring a stack architecture. *IEEE Computer*, 10 (5):30-39, May 1977.
14. D.R. Ditzel and H.R. McLellan. Register Allocation for Free: The C Machine Stack Cache. *Proc. 1st International Symposium on Architectural Support for Programming Languages and Operating Systems*, pp. 48-56, March 1982.
15. A.D. Berenbaum, B.W. Colbry, D.R. Ditzel, R.D. Freeman, H.R. McLellan, K.J. O'Connor, and M. Shoji. CRISP: A Pipelined 32-bit Microprocessor with 13-kbit of Cache Memory. *IEEE Journal of Solid-State Circuits*, SC-22(5):776-782, October 1987.
16. S. Cho, P-C. Yew, and G. Lee. Decoupling Local Variable Accesses in a Wide-Issue Superscalar Processor. In *Proc. 26th International Symposium on Computer Architecture*, pp. 100-110, May 1999.
17. H-H. S. Lee, M. Smelyanskiy, C.J. Newburn, and G.S. Tyson. Stack Value File: Custom Microarchitecture for the Stack. *Proc. 7th International Symposium on High Performance Computer Architecture*, pp. 5-14, January 2001.
18. M. Huang, J. Renau, S.-M. Yoo, and J. Torellas. L1 Data Cache Decomposition for Energy Efficiency. *Proc. International Symposium on Low Power Electronics and Design*, pp. 10-15, August 2003.
19. J. Collins, S. Sair, B. Calder, and D.M. Tullsen. Pointer Cache Assisted Prefetching. *Proc.35th IEEE/ACM International Symposium on Microarchitecture*, pp. 62-73, November 2002.
20. S. Kaxiras, Z. Hu, and M. Martonosi. Cache decay: Exploiting Generational Behavior to Reduce Cache Leakage Power. *Proc. 28th International Symposium on Computer Architecture*, pp. 240-251, June 2001.
21. M. Powell, S-H. Yang, B. Falsafi, K. Roy, and T.N. Vijaykumar. Gated-Vdd: A Circuit Technique to Reduce Leakage in Deep-Submicron Cache Memories. *Proc. International Symposium on Low Power Electronics and Design*, pp. 90-95, July 2000.
22. D. Parikh, Y. Zhang, K. Sankaranarayanan, K. Skadron, and M. Stan. Comparison of State-Preserving vs. Non-State-Preserving Leakage Control in Caches. *Proc. 2nd Workshop on Duplicating, Deconstructing, and Debunking*, pp. 14-24, June 2003.
23. D.H. Albonesi. Selective Cache Ways: On-Demand Cache Resource Allocation. *Proc. 32nd International Symposium on Microarchitecture*, pp. 248–259, November 1999.

24. S.-H. Yang, M. Powell, B. Falsafi, and T.N. Vijaykumar. Exploiting Choice in Resizable Cache Design to Optimize Deep-Submicron Processor Energy-Delay. *Proc. 8th International Symposium on High-Performance Computer Architecture,* pp. 147-158, February 2002.

25. S.-H. Yang, M.D. Powell, B. Falsafi, K. Roy, and T.N. Vijaykumar. An Integrated Circuit/Architecture Approach to Reducing Leakage in Deep-Submicron High-Performance I-Caches. *Proc. 7th International Symposium on High-Performance Computer Architecture,* pp. 147-158, Jan. 2001.

26. R.A. Sugumar and S.G. Abraham. Efficient Simulation of Multiple Cache Configurations using Binomial Trees. Technical Report CSE-TR-111-91, CSE Division, University of Michigan, 1991.

27. L.A. Belady. A Study of Replacement Algorithms for a Virtual-Storage Computer. *IBM Systems Journal,* 5(2):78-101, 1966.

28. T. Austin. SimpleScalar 4.0 Release Note. http://www.simplescalar.com/.

29. D. Brooks, V. Tiwari, and M. Martonosi. Wattch: A Framework for Architectural-Level Power Analysis and Optimizations. *Proc. 27th International Symposium on Computer Architecture,* pp. 83-94, June 2000.

30. Y. Zhang, D. Parikh, K. Sankaranarayanan, K. Skadron, and M. Stan. HotLeakage: A Temperature-Aware Model of Subthreshold and Gate Leakage for Architects. Technical Report CS-2003-05, University of Virginia Department of Computer Science, March 2003.

31. R. Gonzales and M. Horowitz. Energy Dissipation In General Purpose Microprocessors. *IEEE Journal of Solid State Circuits,* 31(9):1277-1284, September 1996.

GCH: Hints for Triggering Garbage Collections*

Dries Buytaert, Kris Venstermans, Lieven Eeckhout, and Koen De Bosschere

ELIS Department, Ghent University – HiPEAC member
St.-Pietersnieuwstraat 41, B-9000 Gent, Belgium
{dbuytaer,kvenster,leeckhou,kdb}@elis.UGent.be

Abstract. This paper shows that Appel-style garbage collectors often make suboptimal decisions both in terms of *when* and *how* to collect. We argue that garbage collection should be done when the amount of live bytes is low (in order to minimize the collection cost) and when the amount of dead objects is high (in order to maximize the available heap size after collection). In addition, we observe that Appel-style collectors sometimes trigger a nursery collection in cases where a full-heap collection would have been better.

Based on these observations, we propose *garbage collection hints (GCH)* which is a profile-directed method for guiding garbage collection. Off-line profiling is used to identify favorable collection points in the program code. In those favorable collection points, the garbage collector dynamically chooses between nursery and full-heap collections based on an analytical garbage collector cost-benefit model. By doing so, GCH guides the collector in terms of *when* and *how* to collect. Experimental results using the SPECjvm98 benchmarks and two generational garbage collectors show that substantial reductions can be obtained in garbage collection time (up to 29X) and that the overall execution time can be reduced by more than 10%. In addition, we also show that GCH reduces the maximum pause times and outperforms user-inserted forced garbage collections.

1 Introduction

Garbage collection (GC) is an important subject of research as many of today's programming language systems employ automated memory management. Popular examples are Java and C#. Before discussing the contributions of this paper, we revisit some garbage collection background and terminology.

1.1 Garbage Collection

An Appel-style generational copying collector divides the heap into two generations [2], a variable-size *nursery* and a *mature generation*. Objects are allocated from the nursery. When the nursery fills up, a *nursery collection* is triggered

---

* The first two authors contributed equally to this paper.

P. Stenström (Ed.): Transactions on HiPEAC I, LNCS 4050, pp. 74–94, 2007.

and the surviving objects are copied into the mature generation. When the objects are copied, the size of the mature generation is grown and the size of the nursery is reduced accordingly. Because the nursery size decreases, the time between consecutive collections also decreases and objects have less time to die. When the nursery size drops below a given threshold, a *full-heap collection* is triggered. After a full-heap collection all free space is returned to the nursery.

In this paper we consider two flavors of generational copying collectors, namely *GenMS* and *GenCopy* from JMTk [3]. GenMS collects the mature generation using the mark-sweep garbage collection strategy. The GenCopy collector on the other hand, employs a semi-space strategy to manage its mature generation. The semi-space collector copies scanned objects, whereas the mark-sweep collector does not. These Appel-style garbage collectors are widely used. To partition the heap into generations, the collector has to keep track of references between different generations. Whenever an object in the nursery is assigned to an object in the mature generation—*i.e.*, there is a reference from an object in the mature space to an object in the nursery space—this information is tracked by using a so-called *remembered set*. When a nursery collection is triggered the remembered set must be processed to avoid erroneously collecting nursery objects that are referenced only from the mature generation.

1.2 Paper Contributions

While implicit garbage collection offers many benefits, for some applications the time spent reclaiming memory can account for a significant portion of the total execution time [1]. Although garbage collection research has been a hot research topic for many years, little research has been done to decide *when* and *how* garbage collectors should collect.

With Appel-style collectors, garbage is collected when either the heap or a generation is full. However, to reduce the time spent in GC, the heap is best collected when the live ratio is low: the fewer live objects, the fewer objects need to be scanned and/or copied, the more memory there is to be reclaimed, and the longer we can postpone the next garbage collection run. In this paper, we show that collecting at points where the live ratio is low, can yield reductions in GC time.

In addition, when using an Appel-style collector with two generations, a decision needs to be made whether to trigger a full-heap or nursery collection. We found that triggering nursery collections until the nursery size drops below a certain threshold is sometimes suboptimal. In this paper, we show how to trade off full-heap collections and nursery collections so that performance improves.

The approach presented in this paper to decide *when* and *how* to collect, is called *garbage collection hints (GCH)* and works as follows. GCH first determines

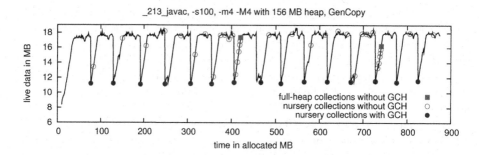

Fig. 1. Garbage collection points with and without GCH

favorable collection points (FCPs) for a given application through offline profiling. A favorable collection point is a location in the application code where the cost of a collection is relatively cheap. During program execution a cost function is then computed in each FCP to determine the best GC strategy: postpone GC, perform a nursery GC, or perform a full-heap GC. Our experimental results using the SPECjvm98 benchmarks and two generational collectors show that GCH can reduce the garbage collector time by up to 29X and can improve the overall execution time by more than 10%.

Figure 1 illustrates why GCH actually works for the _213_javac benchmark. This graph shows the number of live bytes as a function of the number of allocated bytes. The empty circles denote nursery collections and the squares denote full-heap collections when GCH is not enabled. Without GCH, GC is triggered at points where the number of live bytes is not necessarily low. In fact, the maximum GC time that we observed on our platform for these GC points is 225ms; and 12MB needs to be copied from the nursery to the mature generation. The GC time for a full-heap collection takes 330ms. When GCH is enabled (see the filled circles in Figure 1), garbage gets collected when the amount of live bytes reaches a minimum, *i.e.*, at an FCP. The GC time at an FCP takes at most 4.5ms since only 126KB needs to be copied. From this example, we observe two key features why GCH actually works: (i) GCH preferably collects when the amount of live data on the heap is low, and (ii) GCH eliminates full-heap collections by choosing to perform (cheaper) nursery collections at more valuable points in time.

The main contributions of this paper are as follows.

- We show that GC is usually not triggered when the amount of live data is low, *i.e.*, when the amount of garbage collection work is minimal.
- We show that the collector does not always make the best decision when choosing between a nursery and a full-heap collection.
- We propose GCH which is a feedback-directed technique based on profile information that provides hints to the collector about *when* and *how*

to collect. GCH tries to collect at FCPs when the amount of live data is minimal and dynamically chooses between nursery and full-heap collections. The end result is significant reductions in GC time and improved overall performance. GCH is especially beneficial for applications that exhibit a recurring phase behavior in the amount of live data allocated during program execution.

- We show that GCH reduces the pause time during garbage collection.
- And finally, we show that for our experimental setup, GCH improves overall performance compared to forced programmer-inserted GCs. The reason is that GCH takes into account the current live state of the heap whereas forced programmer-inserted GCs do not.

The remainder of this paper is organized as follows. Section 2 presents an overview of our experimental setup. In section 3, we describe the internals of GCH. The results are presented in section 4 after which we discuss related work in section 5. Finally, some conclusions are presented in section 6.

2   Experimental Setup

2.1   Java Virtual Machine

We use the Jikes Research Virtual Machine 2.3.2 (RVM) [4] on an AMD Athlon XP 1500+ at 1.3 GHz with a 256KB L2-cache, 1GB of physical memory, running Linux 2.6. Jikes RVM is a Java virtual machine (VM) written almost entirely in Java. Jikes RVM uses a compilation-only scheme for translating Java bytecodes to native machine instructions. For our experiments we use the *FastAdaptive* profile: all methods are initially compiled using a baseline compiler, and sampling is used to determine which methods to recompile using an optimizing compiler.

Because Jikes RVM is written almost entirely in Java, internal objects such as those created during class loading or those created by the runtime compilers are allocated from the Java heap. Thus, unlike with conventional Java virtual machines the heap contains both application data as well as VM data. We found that there is at least 8MB of VM data that is quasi-immortal. The presence of VM data has to be taken into account when interpreting the results presented in the remainder of this work.

Jikes RVM's memory management toolkit (JMTk) [3] offers several GC schemes. While the techniques presented in this paper are generally applicable to various garbage collectors, we focus on the *GenMS* and *GenCopy* collectors. Both are used in Jikes RVM's production builds that are optimized for performance.

To get around a bug in Jikes RVM 2.3.2 we increased the maximum size of the remembered set to 256MB. In order to be able to model the shrinking/growing behavior of the heap accurately, we made one modification to the original RVM. We placed the remembered set outside the heap.

Performance is measured using the Hardware Performance Monitor (HPM) subsystem of Jikes RVM. HPM uses (i) the `perfctr`[1] Linux kernel patch, which provides a kernel module to access the processor hardware, and (ii) PAPI [5], a library to capture the processor's performance counters. The hardware performance counters keep track of the number of retired instructions, elapsed clock cycles, etc.

2.2   Benchmarks

To evaluate our mechanism, we use the SPECjvm98[2] benchmark suite. The SPECjvm98 benchmark suite is a client-side Java benchmark suite consisting of seven benchmarks, each with three input sets: `-s1`, `-s10` and `-s100`. With the `-m` and `-M` parameters the benchmark can be configured to run multiple times without stopping the VM. Garbage collection hints work well for long running applications that show recurring phase behavior in the amount of live data. To mimic such workloads with SPECjvm98, we use the `-s100` input set in conjunction with running the benchmarks four times (`-m4 -M4`).

We used all SPECjvm98 benchmarks except one, namely _222_mpegaudio, because it merely allocates 15MB each run and triggers few GCs. The other benchmarks allocate a lot more memory.

All SPECjvm98 benchmarks are single-threaded except for _227_mtrt which is a multi-threaded raytracer. Note that because both Jikes RVM's sampling mechanism and the optimizing compiler run in separate threads all benchmarks are non-deterministic.

We ran all experiments with a range of different heap sizes. We vary the heap size between the minimum feasible heap size and the heap size at which our mechanism stops triggering GCs or shows constant behavior.

Some benchmarks, such as _213_javac, use *forced garbage collections* triggered through calls to `java.lang.System.gc()`. We disabled forced garbage collections unless stated otherwise.

3   Garbage Collection Hints

Our garbage collection hints approach consists of an offline and an online step, see Figure 2. The offline step breaks down into two parts: (i) offline profiling of the application and (ii) garbage collector analysis. The offline profiling computes the live/time function of the application, *i.e.*, the amount of live bytes as a function of the amount of bytes allocated. Based on this live/time function, favorable collection points (FCPs) can be determined. Determining the FCPs is a one-time cost per application. The garbage collector analysis characterizes the collection cost for a particular garbage collector and application, *i.e.*, the amount of time needed to process a given amount of live bytes. This is dependent on the collector and the platform on which the measurements are done. In the online

---

[1] http://user.it.uu.se/~mikpe/linux/perfctr/
[2] http://www.spec.org/jvm98/

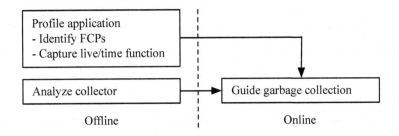

Fig. 2. An overview of the GCH methodology

part of GCH, the methods that have been identified as FCPs are instrumented to invoke a cost-benefit model that helps the garbage collector make decisions about *when* and *how* to collect. This decision making is based on the amount of heap space available, the live/time function of the application and the characteristics of the garbage collector. The following subsections discuss GCH in more detail.

3.1   Program Analysis

Live/Dead Ratio Behavior. The first step of the offline profiling is to collect the live/time function which quantifies the number of live bytes as a function of the bytes allocated so far. Moreover, we are interested in linking the live/time function to methods calls. We modified Jikes RVM to timestamp and report all method entries and exits. For each method invocation, we want to know how many objects/bytes died and how many objects are live. Therefore, a lifetime analysis is required at every point an object could have died. There are two reasons for an object to die: (i) an object's last reference is overwritten as a result of an assignment operation, or (ii) an object's last reference is on a stack frame and the stack frame gets popped because the frame's method returns or because an exception is thrown. To avoid having to do a lifetime analysis for every assignment operation, method return and exception, we used a modified version of the Merlin trace generator [6] that is part of Jikes RVM. Merlin is a tool that precisely computes every object's last reachable time. It has been modified to use our alternative timestamping method to correlate object death with method invocations.

Figure 3 shows the live/time function for the various benchmarks. As can be seen from these graphs, the live/time function shows recurring phase behavior. This recurring phase behavior will be exploited through GCH. Applications that do not exhibit a phased live/time function are not likely to benefit from GCH. Next, the live/time function is used to select FCPs and to compute the FCP live/time patterns.

Favorable Collection Points. For a method to represent a favorable collection point (FCP), it needs to satisfy three criteria:

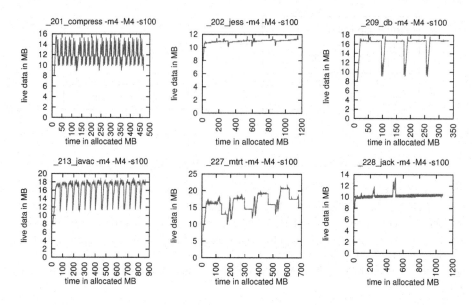

Fig. 3. The live/time function for the various benchmarks: number of live bytes as a function of the number of bytes allocated

1. An FCP's invocation should correspond to a local minimum in terms of the number of live bytes. In other words, we need to select methods that are executed in the minima of the live/time function. This will allow GCH to collect garbage with minimal effort.
2. An FCP should not be executed frequently. To minimize the overhead of the instrumentation code, FCPs that represent cold methods are preferred. A method that gets executed *only* in local minima is an ideal FCP.
3. The live/time pattern following the execution of the FCP should be fairly predictable, *i.e.*, each time the FCP gets executed, the live/time function should have a more or less similar shape after the FCP.

Given the live/time function, selecting FCPs is fairly straightforward. Table 1 shows the selected FCPs that we selected for the SPECjvm98 benchmarks. Some benchmarks have only one FCP (see for example Figure 1 for _213_javac); others such as _227_mtrt have three FCPs.

To illustrate the potential benefit of FCPs, Figure 4 plots the maximum time spent in GC when triggered at an FCP and when triggered otherwise. We make a distinction between full-heap and nursery collections, and plot data for a range of heap sizes. For most benchmarks we observe that the maximum GC time spent at an FCP is substantially lower than the GC time at other collection points. This reinforces our assumption that collecting at an FCP is cheaper than collecting elsewhere. However, there are two exceptions, _201_compress and _228_jack, for which GC time is insensitive to FCPs. For _201_compress, this is explained by the fact that the live/time function shown in Figure 3 is due to a few objects

Table 1. The selected FCPs for each of the benchmark applications. The method descriptors use the format specified in [7].

Benchmark	Favorable collection points
_201_compress	spec.io.FileInputStream.getContentLength()
_202_jess	spec.benchmarks._202_jess.jess._undefrule.<init>()V
	spec.harness.BenchmarkTime.toString()Ljava/lang/String;
_209_db	spec.harness.Context.setBenchmarkRelPath(Ljava/lang/String;)V
	spec.io.FileInputStream.getCachingtime()J
_213_javac	spec.benchmarks._213_javac.ClassPath.<init>(Ljava/lang/String;)V
_227_mtrt	spec.io.TableOfExistingFiles.<init>()V
	spec.harness.Context.clearIOtime()V
	spec.io.FileInputStream.getCachingtime()J
_228_jack	spec.benchmarks._228_jack.Jack_the_Parser_Generator_Internals.-
	compare(Ljava/lang/String;Ljava/lang/String;)V

that are allocated in the Large Object Space (LOS). Because objects in the LOS never get copied, GCH cannot reduce the copy cost. Furthermore, because there are only a few such objects it will not affect the scan cost either. For _228_jack, the height of the live/time function's peaks is very low, see Figure 3. Because _201_compress and _228_jack are insensitive to FCPs we exclude them from the other results that will be presented in this paper. (In fact, we applied GCH to these benchmarks and observed neutral impact on overall performance. Due to space constraints, we do not to include these benchmarks in the rest of this paper.)

It is also interesting to note that for _209_db, a nursery collection can be more costly than a full-heap collection. This is due to the fact that the remembered set needs to be scanned on a nursery collection. As such, for _209_db a full-heap collection can be more efficient than a nursery collection. This is exploited through GCH.

FCP's Live/Time Pattern. For each unique FCP we have to capture the *live/time pattern* following the FCP. This is a slice of the live/time function following the FCP that recurs throughout the complete program execution. We sample the FCP's live/time pattern at a frequency of one sample per 0.5MB of allocated memory and use it as input for the cost-benefit model. An FCP's live/time pattern is independent of the heap size (the same information is used for all heap sizes) and is independent of the collection scheme (the same information is used for both GenMS and GenCopy). And it only needs to be computed once for each benchmark.

3.2 Collector Analysis

So far, we discussed the offline application profiling that is required for GCH. We now discuss the characterization of the garbage collector. This characterization will be used in the cost model that will drive the decision making in GCH during program execution. The characterization of the garbage collector quantifies the cost of a collection. We identify three cost sources: the cost of a full-heap collection, the cost of a nursery collection and the cost of processing

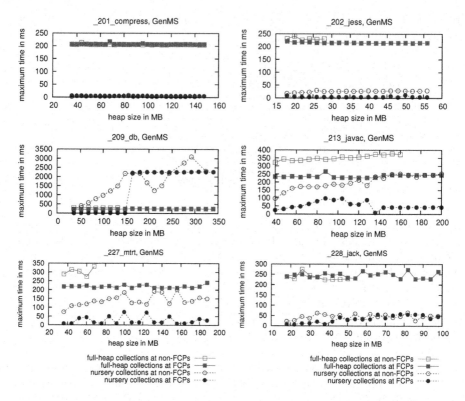

Fig. 4. The maximum times spent in garbage collection across different heap sizes for each of the different scenarios

the remembered set. The cost functions take as input the amount of live data and output the estimated collection time. These cost functions are dependent on the application, the collector and the given platform (VM, microprocessor, etc.).

Figure 5 shows how the cost functions are to be determined for the GenMS and GenCopy collectors. The graphs are obtained by running the benchmarks multiple times with different heap sizes using instrumented collectors. In these graphs we make a distinction between nursery collections, full-heap collections and processing of the remembered set. Hence, the processing times on the nursery collection graphs do not include the time required to process the remembered sets.

GC time can be modeled as a linear function of the amount of live data for both collectors. In other words, the scanning and copying cost is proportional to the amount of live bytes. Likewise, the processing cost of the remembered set can be modeled as a linear function of its size. In summary, we can compute linear functions that quantify the cost of a nursery collection, full-heap collection and processing of the remembered set.

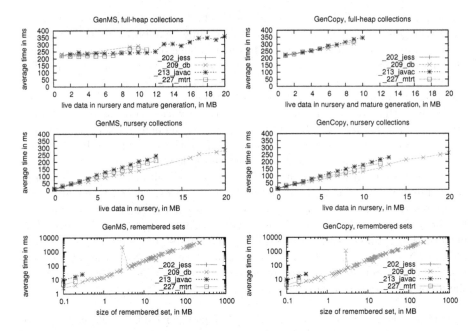

Fig. 5. The cost of a nursery and full-heap collection in terms of the amount of copied/live data

In this paper we employ both application-specific cost functions as well as cross-application cost functions. In fact, on a specialized system with dedicated long running applications, it is appropriate to consider a cost function that is specifically tuned for the given application. Nevertheless, given the fact that the cost functions appear to be fairly similar across the various applications, see Figure 5, choosing application-independent or cross-application cost functions could be a viable scenario for general-purpose environments. In this paper we evaluate both scenarios.

3.3   GCH at Work

The information that is collected through our offline analysis is now communicated to the VM to be used at runtime. Jikes RVM reads all profile information at startup. This contains (i) a list of methods that represent the FCPs, (ii) the live/time pattern per FCP, and (iii) the cost functions for the given garbage collector. Jikes RVM is also modified to dynamically instrument the FCPs. The instrumentation code added to the FCPs examines whether the current FCP should trigger a GC. The decision to collect or not is a difficult one as there exists a trade-off between reducing the amount of work per collection and having to collect more frequently. Clearly, triggering a collection will have an effect on subsequent collections. Because GC is invoked sooner due to GCH than without GCH, additional collections might get introduced. On the other hand, triggering a collection at an FCP can help reduce the GC overhead. A collection at an FCP will generally introduce modest pause times compared to collections at other points. Moreover, triggering a full-heap collection grows the nursery size and gives objects more time to die, while triggering a nursery collection when few objects are live will result in the mature generation filling up slower, reducing the need for more expensive full-heap collections.

To make this complex trade-off, the instrumentation code in the FCPs implements an *analytical cost-benefit model*. The cost-benefit model estimates the total GC time for getting from the current FCP to the end of its FCP's live/time pattern. The cost-benefit model considers the following three scenarios: (i) do not trigger a GC in the current FCP, (ii) trigger a full-heap GC, or (iii) trigger a nursery GC. For each of these three scenarios, the cost-benefit model computes the total GC time ($C_{total,i}$ with i one of the three scenarios above) by *analytically simulating* how the heap will evolve through the FCP's live/time pattern. The total GC time can be split up in a number of components: $C_{total,i} = C_{FCP,i} + \sum_{j=1}^{n} C_{profile,j} + C_{end}$. We now explain each component in more detail. First, the cost-benefit model computes the GC cost *in the current FCP* under the following three scenarios:

(i) The cost for not triggering a GC is obviously zero. The available heap size remains unchanged. So, $C_{FCP,notrigger} = 0$.

(ii) For computing the cost for triggering a full-heap collection in the current FCP, we first calculate the number of live bytes at the current FCP, $livebytes_{FCP}$. We get this information from the live/time pattern. We subsequently use the full-heap GC cost function to compute the GC time given the amount of live data in the current FCP. The available heap size after the current (hypothetical) full-heap collection then equals the maximum heap size minus the amount of live data in the current FCP. The cost of a full-heap collection at the current FCP, $C_{FCP,fullheap}$, can be computed using the linear function of the form $A \times x + B$ where are A and B are derived from Figure 5. So, $C_{FCP,fullheap} = A_{fullheap} \times livebytes_{FCP} + B_{fullheap}$.

(iii) To compute the cost for triggering a nursery GC in the current FCP, we assume that the amount of live bytes in the nursery at that FCP is close to zero. The GC cost is then computed based on the nursery GC cost function. This GC cost is incremented by an extra cost due to processing the remembered set. This extra cost is proportional to the size of the remembered set, which is known at runtime at an FCP. The heap size that was occupied by the nursery becomes available for allocation. The cost of a nursery collection at the current FCP, $C_{FCP,nursery}$, equals $(A_{nursery} \times livebytes_{FCP} + B_{nursery}) + (A_{remset} \times remsetsize_{FCP} + B_{remset})$ with the A and B coefficients extracted from Figure 5.

In the second step of the cost-benefit model we compute the cost of additional collections over the FCP's live/time pattern for each of the three scenarios. In fact, for each scenario, the cost-benefit model analytically simulates how the heap will evolve over time when going through an FCP's live/time pattern.

Therefore, we compute when the (nursery) heap will be full—when the application has allocated all memory available in the heap. In case the system would normally trigger a full collection (*i.e.*, when the nursery size drops below the given threshold), we need to compute the cost of a full-heap collection. This is done the same way as above, by getting the amount of live data from the FCP's live/time pattern—note that we linearly interpolate the live/time pattern—and use the full-heap GC cost function to compute its cost. In case the nursery size is above the given threshold, we need to compute the cost of a nursery collection. Computing the cost for a nursery collection is done by reading the number of live bytes from the FCP's live/time pattern and subtracting the number of live bytes in the previous GC point; this number gives us an estimate for the amount of live data in the nursery. This estimated amount of live nursery data is used through the nursery GC cost function to compute an estimated nursery GC cost. The number of terms n in $\sum_{j=1}^{n} C_{profile,j}$ equals the number of analytical simulations we perform going through the FCP's live/time pattern. If a sufficient amount of the heap is still free, or being freed by the simulated GC in the FCP, it is possible that $n = 0$.

When the end of the FCP's live/time pattern is reached within the model, an end cost C_{end} is added to the aggregated GC cost calculated so far. The purpose of the end cost is to take into account whether the next (expected) collection will be close by or far away. This end cost is proportional to the length of the FCP's live/time pattern after the last simulated GC divided by the fraction of calculated unused nursery space at that same last simulated GC point. The more data still needs to be allocated, the closer the next GC, the higher the end cost.

After computing all the costs for each of the three scenarios, the scenario that results in the minimal total cost is chosen. As such, it is decided whether a nursery, a full-heap or no collection needs to be triggered in the current FCP.

Note that the cost-benefit model presented above is specifically developed for GenMS and GenCopy, two Appel-style generational garbage collectors with a variable nursery size. However, a similar cost-benefit model could be constructed for other collectors.

3.4   GCH Across Inputs

GCH is a profile-driven garbage collection method which implies that the input used for the offline profiling run is typically different from the input used during online execution. Getting GCH to work across inputs needs a few enhancements since the size and the height of an FCP's live/time pattern varies across inputs; the general shape of the FCP's live/time pattern however is relatively insensitive to the given input. We define the height of an FCP's live/time pattern as the difference in live data at the top of an FCP's live/time pattern and at the FCP itself. For example, for _213_javac, see Figure 1, the height is approximately 6MB. The size of an FCP's live/time pattern is defined as the number of allocated bytes at an FCP's live/time pattern; this is approximately 60MB for _213_javac, see also Figure 1. To address this cross-input issue we just scale the size and the

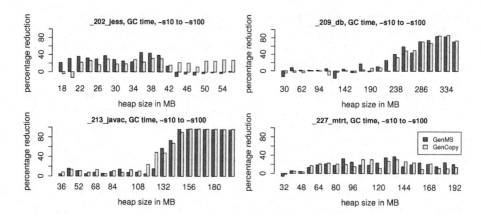

Fig. 6. Reduction in time spent in garbage collection through GCH across inputs. The profile input is -s10; the reported results are for -s100. Benchmark-specific GC cost functions are used.

height of the FCP live/time pattern. In practice, the amount of live data at the top of an FCP's live/time pattern can be computed at runtime when a GC is triggered at the top of an FCP's live/time pattern. The amount of allocated bytes over an FCP's live/time pattern can be computed at run-time as well. These scaling factors are then to be used to rescale the data in the FCP live/time pattern.

4   Evaluation

This section evaluates GCH through a number of measurements. First, we measure the GC time reduction. Second, we evaluate the impact on overall performance. Third, we quantify the impact on pause time. Fourth, we compare forced GC versus GCH. Finally, we quantify the runtime overhead due to GCH.

4.1   Garbage Collection Time

In order to evaluate the applicability of GCH, we have set up the following experiment. We used the profile information from the -s10 run to drive the execution of the -s100 run after cross-input rescaling as discussed in section 3.4.

Figure 6 shows the reduction through GCH in GC time over a range of heap sizes where reduction is defined as $100 \times (1 - \frac{time_{GCH}}{time_{old}})$. Each reduction number is an average number over three runs; numbers are shown for both GenMS and GenCopy. Figure 6 shows that GCH improves GC time for both collectors and for nearly all heap sizes. For both collectors, GCH achieves substantial speedups in terms of garbage collection time, up to 29X for _213_javac and 10X for _209_db.

Table 2. The average number of garbage collections across all heap sizes with and without GCH

	GenMS collector				GenCopy collector			
	Full-heap		Nursery		Full-heap		Nursery	
Benchmark	no GCH	GCH	no GCH	GCH	no GCH	GCH	no GCH	GCH
_202_jess	0	1	245	186	2	3	349	294
_209_db	1	3	16	14	2	4	25	25
_213_javac	2	2	80	62	6	5	93	61
_227_mtrt	0	1	45	36	2	2	81	67

The sources for these speedups are twofold. First, GCH generally results in fewer collections than without GCH, see Table 2 which shows the average number of GCs over all heap sizes; we observe fewer GCs with GCH for all benchmarks except one, namely _209_db for which the number of collections remains unchanged with and without GCH (we will discuss _209_db later on). For _213_javac we observe a 30% reduction in the number of collections. The second reason for these GC time speedups is the reduced work at each point of GC. This was already mentioned in Figure 4.

For _202_jess, GCH only occasionally triggers a collection for heap sizes larger than 44MB for GenMS. GCH then causes the same GC pattern as running without GCH, as the non-GCH directed pattern already is the optimal one.

Note that for _209_db, GCH is capable of substantially reducing the GC time for large heap sizes. The reason is not the reduced number of collections, but the intelligent selection of full-heap collections instead of nursery collections. The underlying reason is that _209_db suffers from a very large remembered set. GCH triggers more full-heap collections that do not suffer from having to process remembered sets, see Table 2. A full-heap collection typically only takes 250ms for this application whereas a nursery collection can take up to 2,000ms, see Figure 4. Note that the remembered set increases with larger heap sizes which explains the increased speedup for larger heap sizes. While the large remembered sets themselves are the consequence of the fact that JMTk uses sequential store buffers without a space cap, it shows that our analytical framework is robust in the face of extreme cases like this.

For _213_javac, GCH reduces the total number of collections. In addition, the cost of a nursery collection at an FCP is much cheaper than a nursery collection at another execution point because less data needs to be scanned and copied. As mentioned with our introductory example in Figure 1, at most 126KB needs to be copied at an FCP which takes about 4.5ms while up to 12MB needs to be copied otherwise, which takes about 225ms. From heap sizes of 132MB on, no other GCs are required than those triggered by GCH. As a direct result, the collector's performance improves by a factor 29.

Remind that because of the way Jikes RVM works, the heap contains both application data and VM data. We believe that our technique would be even more effective in a system where the collector does not have to trace VM data.

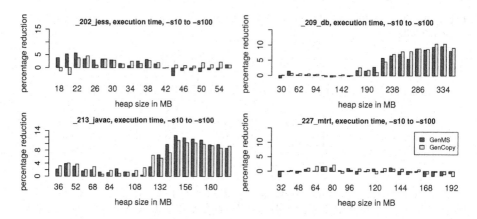

Fig. 7. Performance improvement in total execution time through GCH across inputs. The profile input is -s10; the reported results are for -s100. Benchmark-specific GC cost functions are used.

In such a system, full-heap collections would generally be cheaper opening up extra opportunities to replace nursery collections by full-heap collections.

4.2 Overall Execution Time

Figure 7 depicts the impact of GCH on the overall execution time. For _227_mtrt, the total execution time is more or less unaffected through GCH because the time spent collecting garbage is only a small fraction of the total execution time. The small slowdowns or speedups observed for _227_mtrt are probably due to changing data locality behavior because of the changed GCs. However, for _202_jess, _209_db and _213_javac, performance improves by up to 5.7%, 10.5% and 12.5%, respectively. For these benchmarks, the GC time speedups translate themselves in overall performance speedup.

4.3 Generic Cost Functions

So far we assumed application-specific GC cost functions, *i.e.*, the cost function for a nursery collection and a full-heap collection as well as the cost associated with scanning the remembered set was assumed to be application-specific. This is a viable assumption for application-specific designs. However, for application-domain specific (involving multiple applications) or general-purpose systems, this may no longer be feasible. Figures 8 and 9 evaluate the performance of GCH in case cross-application GC cost functions are employed instead of application-specific GC cost functions; this is done for the garbage collection time as well as for the overall execution time, respectively. Comparing these figures against Figures 6 and 7, we observe that there is no significant difference between the performance that is obtained from application-specific versus generic cost functions. As such, we conclude that GCH is robust to generic cost functions.

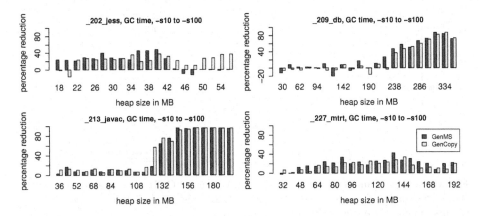

Fig. 8. Reduction in time spent in garbage collection through GCH across inputs using generic cost functions. The profile input is -s10; the reported results are for -s100.

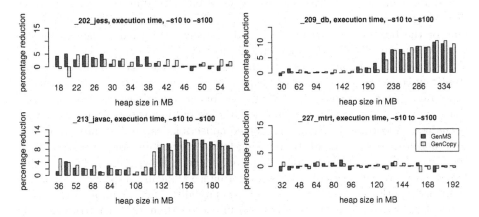

Fig. 9. Performance improvement in total execution time through GCH across inputs using generic cost functions. The profile input is -s10; the reported results are for -s100.

4.4 Pause Time

An important metric when evaluating garbage collection techniques is pause time. Pause time is especially important for interactive and (soft) real-time applications. Figure 10 presents the maximum pause times over all benchmark runs as a function of the heap size. We make a distinction between nursery and full-heap collections, and between with-GCH and without-GCH. The graphs show that the maximum pause time is reduced (or at least remains unchanged) through GCH. Note that the vertical axes are shown on a logarithmic scale. As such, we can conclude that GCH substantially reduces the maximum pause time that is observed during program execution.

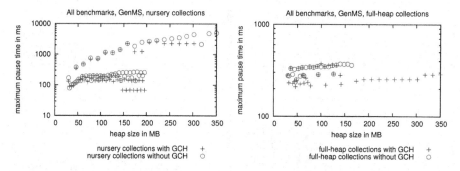

Fig. 10. The maximum pause time with and without GCH. The graph on the left shows the maximum pause time for nursery collections; the graph on the right shows the maximum pause time for full-heap collections.

4.5   Forced Versus Automatic Garbage Collection

A programmer can force the VM to trigger a GC by calling the java.lang.-System.gc() method. We refer to such collections as *forced garbage collections*. One of the benchmarks that we studied, namely _213_javac, triggers forced GCs. When run with -s100 -m4 -M4, 21 forced GCs are triggered. Figure 11 shows the GC times normalized to the fastest time for _213_javac using the GenCopy collector for a range of heap sizes. The graph depicts the collection times under four scenarios: the VM ignores forced collections, the forced collections are nursery collections, the forced GCs are full-heap collections, and GCH is enabled. According to Figure 11, forced collections can either improve or reduce performance compared to not using forced collections. More specifically, if the forced GCs are full-heap collections, performance is typically reduced; if the forced GCs are nursery collections, performance typically improves—for large heap sizes, performance even improves dramatically. Another important observation from Figure 11 is that GCH performs better than all other strategies for all heap sizes. This can be explained by the fact that while there are 21 forced collections, there are only 15 FCPs (see Figure 1). GCH correctly triggers no more than 15 times and takes the current state of the heap into account when making GC decisions. In summary, there are three reasons why GCH is preferable over forced collections. First, in large applications it can be difficult to identify favorable collection points without automated program analysis as presented in this paper. Second, forced GCs, in contrast to GCH, do not take into account the available heap size when deciding whether a GC should be triggered. Third, in our experimental setup, GCH is capable of deciding how garbage should be collected at runtime, *i.e.*, whether a nursery or full-heap collection should be triggered which is impossible through forced GCs.

4.6   Run-Time System Overhead

To explore the run-time overhead of our system, we compare the performance of a without-GCH Jikes RVM versus a with-GCH Jikes RVM. In the with-GCH

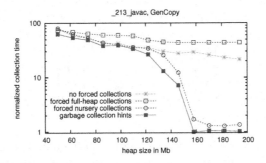

Fig. 11. Garbage collection time under forced garbage collection versus automatic garbage collection versus GCH

version, the profile information is read, the FCPs are instrumented and at each invocation of an FCP the cost-benefit model is computed, however, it will never trigger a collection. For computing the overhead per benchmark, each benchmark is run multiple times and the average overhead is computed over these runs. Table 3 shows the average overhead over all heap sizes with both collectors. The average overhead over all benchmarks is 0.3%; the maximum overhead is 1.3% for _227_mtrt. The negative overheads imply that the application ran faster with instrumentation that without instrumentation. We thus conclude that the overhead of GCH is negligible.

5   Related Work

We now discuss previously proposed GC strategies that are somehow related to GCH, *i.e.*, all these approaches implement a mechanism to decide when *or* how to collect. The work presented in this paper differs from previous work in that we combine the decision of both when *and* how to collect in a single framework.

The Boehm-Demers-Weiser (BDW) [8] garbage collector and memory allocator include a mechanism that determines whether to collect garbage or to grow the heap. The decision whether to collect or grow the heap is based on a static variable called the *free space divisor (FSD)*. If the amount of heap space allocated since the last garbage collection exceeds the heap size divided by FSD, garbage is collected. If not, the heap is grown. Brecht *et al.* [9] extended the BDW collector by taking into account the amount of physical memory available and by proposing dynamically varying thresholds for triggering collections and heap growths.

Wilson *et al.* [10] observe that (interactive) programs have phases of operation that are compute-bound. They suggest that tagging garbage collection onto the end of larger computational pauses, will not make those pauses significantly more disruptive. While the main goal of their work is to avoid or mitigate disruptive pauses, they reason that at these points, live data is likely to be relatively small

Table 3. The run-time overhead of GCH

Benchmark	GenMS	GenCopy
_202_jess	-0.1%	0.8%
_209_db	0.0%	-0.6%
_213_javac	0.2%	0.3%
_227_mtrt	1.3%	0.6%

since objects representing intermediate results of the previous computations have become garbage. They refer to this mechanism as *scavenge scheduling* but present no results.

More recently, Ding *et al.* [11] presented preliminary results of a garbage collection scheme called *preventive memory management* that also aims to exploit phase behavior. They unconditionally force a garbage collection at the beginning of certain execution phases. In addition, they avoid garbage collections in the middle of a phase by growing the heap size unless the heap size reaches the hard upper bound of the available memory. They evaluated their idea using a single Lisp program and measured performance improvements up to 44%.

Detlefs *et al.* [13] present the garbage-first garbage collectors which aims at satisfying soft real-time constraints. Their goal is to spend no more than x ms during garbage collection for each y ms interval. This is done by using a collector that uses many small spaces and a *concurrent marker* that keeps track of the amount of live data per space. The regions containing most garbage are then collected first. In addition, collection can be delayed in their system if they risk violating the real-time goal.

Velasco *et al.* [14] propose a mechanism that dynamically tunes the size of the copy reserve of an Appel collector [2]. Tuning the copy reserve's size is done based on the ratio of surviving objects after garbage collection. Their technique achieves performance improvements of up to 7%.

Stefanovic *et al.* [15] evaluate the older-first generational garbage collector which only copies the oldest objects in the nursery to the mature generation. The youngest objects are not copied yet; they are given enough time to die in the nursery. This could be viewed of as a way deciding when to collect.

Recent work [16,17,18] selects the most appropriate garbage collector during program execution out of a set of available garbage collectors. As such, the garbage collector is made adaptive to the program's dynamic execution behavior. The way GCH triggers nursery or full-heap collections could be viewed as a special form of what these papers proposed.

6   Summary and Future Work

This paper presented garbage collection hints which is a profile-directed approach to guide garbage collection. The goal of GCH is to guide in terms of *when* and *how* to collect. GCH uses offline profiling to identify favorable collection points in the program code where the amount of live data is relatively small (in order to reduce the amount of work per collection) and the amount of dead bytes is relatively large (in order to increase the amount of available heap after collection). Triggering collections in these FCPs can reduce the number of collections as well as the amount of work per collection. Next to guiding when to collect, GCH also uses an analytical cost-benefit model to decide how to collect, *i.e.*, whether to trigger a nursery or a full-heap collection. This decision is made based on the available heap size, and the cost for nursery and full-heap collections. Our experimental results using SPECjvm98 showed substantial reductions in GC time (up to 29X) and significant overall performance improvements (more than 10%); similar speedups are obtained for application-specific as well as cross-application, generic GC cost functions. In addition, we also showed that GCH dramatically reduces maximum pause times. And finally, we showed that, for a specific benchmark, GCH improves overall performance compared to forced programmer-inserted garbage collections.

In future work, we plan to extend and evaluate GCH for other collectors than the ones considered here. We also plan to study dynamically inserted garbage collection hints in which profiling is done online during program execution.

Acknowledgments

Dries Buytaert is supported by a grant from the Institute for the Promotion of Innovation by Science and Technology in Flanders (IWT). Kris Venstermans is supported by a BOF grant from Ghent University, Lieven Eeckhout is a Postdoctoral Fellow of the Fund for Scientific Research—Flanders (Belgium) (FWO—Vlaanderen). Ghent University is a member of the HiPEAC network. This work is an extended version of previous work [12]. We thank the reviewers for their insightful comments.

References

1. Blackburn, S.M., Cheng, P., McKinely, K.S.: Myths and realities: the performance impact of garbage collection. In: Proceedings of SIGMETRICS'04, ACM (2004)
2. Appel, A.W.: Simple generational garbage collection and fast allocation. Software practices and experience **19** (1989) 171–183
3. Blackburn, S.M., Cheng, P., McKinley., K.S.: Oil and water? High performance garbage collection in Java with JMTk. In: Proceedings of ICSE'04. (2004) 137–146
4. Alpern, B., Attanasio, C.R., Barton, J.J., Burke, M.G., Cheng, P., Choi, J.D., Cocchi, A., Fink, S.J., Grove, D., Hind, M., Hummel, S.F., Lieber, D., Litvinov, V., Mergen, M.F., Ngo, T., Russell, J.R., Sarkar, V., Serrano, M.J., Shepherd, J.C., Smith, S.E., Sreedhar, V.C., Srinivasan, H., Whaley, J.: The Jalapeño Virtual Machine. IBM Systems Journal **39** (2000) 211–238
5. Browne, S., Dongarra, J., Garner, N., Ho, G., Mucci, P.: A portable programming interface for performance evaluation on modern processors. The international journal of high performance computing applications **14** (2000) 189–204
6. Hertz, M., Blackburn, S.M., Moss, J.E.B., McKinley, K.S., Stefanovic, D.: Error free garbage collection traces: how to cheat and not get caught. In: Proceedings of SIGMETRICS'02, ACM (2002) 140–151

 7. Lindholm, T., Yellin, F.: The Java Virtual Machine Specification (second edition). Addison-Wesley (1999)
 8. Boehm, H., Weiser, M.: Garbage collection in an uncooperative environment. Software practices and experience **18** (1988) 807–820
 9. Brecht, T., Arjomandi, E., Li, C., Pham, H.: Controlling garbage collection and heap growth to reduce the execution time of Java applications. In: Proceedings of OOPSLA'01, ACM (2001) 353–366
10. Wilson, P.R., Moher, T.G.: Design of the opportunistic garbage collector. In: Proceedings of OOPSLA'89, ACM (1989) 23–35
11. Ding, C., Zhang, C., Shen, X., Ogihara, M.: Gated memory control for memory monitoring, leak detection and garbage collection. In: Proceedings of MSP'05, ACM (2005) 62–67
12. Buytaert, D., Venstermans, K., Eeckhout, L., De Bosschere, K.: Garbage collection hints. In: Proceedings of HiPEAC'05, LNCS 3793 (2005) 233–348
13. Detlefs, D., Flood, C., Heller, S., Printezis, T.: Garbage-first garbage collection. In: Proceedings of ISMM'04, ACM (2004) 37–48
14. J. M. Velasco, K. Olcoz, F.T.: Adaptive tuning of reserved space in an Appel collector. In: Proceedings of ECOOP'04, ACM (2004) 543–559
15. Stefanovic, D., Hertz, M., Blackburn, S.M., McKinley, K.S., Moss, J.E.B.: Older-first garbage collection in practice: evaluation in a Java virtual machine. In: Proceedings of MSP'02, ACM (2002) 25–36
16. Andreasson, E., Hoffmann, F., Lindholm, O.: Memory management through machine learning: to collect or not to collect? In: Proceedings of JVM'02, USENIX (2002)
17. Printezis, T.: Hot-swapping between a mark&sweep and a mark&compact garbage collector in a generational environment. In: Proceedings of JVM'01, USENIX (2001)
18. Soman, S., Krintz, C., Bacon, D.F.: Dynamic selection of application-specific garbage collectors. In: Proceedings of ISMM'04, ACM (2004) 49–60

Memory-Centric Security Architecture*

Weidong Shi, Chenghuai Lu, and Hsien-Hsin S. Lee

College of Computing
School of Electrical and Computer Engineering
Georgia Institute of Technology
Atlanta, GA 30332-0280
shiw@cc.gatech.edu, lulu@cc.gatech.edu, leehs@gatech.edu

Abstract. This article presents a new security model called MESA for protecting software confidentiality and integrity. Different from the previous process-centric systems designed for the same purpose, MESA ties cryptographic properties and security attributes to memory instead of each individual user process. The advantages of such a memory-centric design over the process-centric designs are many folds. First, it allows better access control on software privacy, which supports both selective and mixed tamper resistant protection on software components coming from heterogenous sources. Second, the new model supports and facilities tamper resistant secure information sharing in an open software system where both data and code components could be shared by different user processes. Third, the proposed security model and secure processor design allow software components protected with different security policies to inter-operate within the same memory space efficiently. The architectural support for MESA requires small silicon resources and its performance impact is minimal based on our experimental results using commercial MS Windows workloads and cycle based out-of-order processor simulator.

1 Introduction

Recently, there is a growing interest in creating tamper-resistant/copy protection systems that combine the strengths of security hardware and secure operating systems to fight against both software attacks and physical tampering of software [6,11,10,15,7,16]. Such systems aim at solving various problems in the security domain such as digital rights protection, virus/worm detection, system intrusion prevention, digital privacy, etc. For maximum protection, a tamper-resistant, copy protection system should provide protected software execution against both software and hardware based tampering including protections against duplication (copy protection), alteration (integrity and authentication), and reverse engineering (confidentiality).

Many secure processor based tamper resistant systems achieve protection by encrypting the instructions and data of a user process with a single master key.

---

* This research is supported by the National Science Foundation under award ITR/NGS-0325536 and a DOE Early CAREER PI Award.

P. Stenström (Ed.): Transactions on HiPEAC I, LNCS 4050, pp. 95–115, 2007.

Although such closed systems do provide security for software execution, they are less attractive for real world commercial implementation because of the gap between a closed tamper-resistant and real world software. Most of the real world applications are in fact multi-domained, in which a user process often comprises components from heterogeneous program sources with distinctive security requirements. For instance, almost all the commercial applications use statically linked libraries and/or dynamically linked libraries (DLL). It is quite natural that these library vendors would prefer a separate copy protection of their own intellectual properties decoupled from the user applications. Furthermore, it is also common for different autonomous software domains to share and exchange confidential information at both the inter- and intra- process levels. The nature of de-centralized development of software components by different vendors makes it difficult to enforce software and data confidentiality under a process-centric protection scheme.

Though it is plausible in theory to protect shared software modules by treating them as separately encrypted processes, such solution has many drawbacks. First, it destroys many advantages of DLL, which contribute to the popularity of DLL in certain OSs. For instance, DLL is faster with respect to separate process because DLL runs within the same process space of its client. DLL is also space efficient because it can be loaded or unloaded based on the need of software execution. Converting DLL into separate processes will be almost certain to introduce many space and processing overhead. Second, sometimes it is impracticable to convert DLL into process. One example is the DLL that resides in the kernel space. Many such DLLs are device drivers. What would a vendor of some device want to protect the architecture secret of its product from the others by releasing encrypted device drivers?

Traditional capability-based protection systems such as Hydra [4] and CAP [8] although provide access control on information, they were not designed for tamper resistance to prevent software duplication, alternation, and reverse engineering. Specifically, systems such as Hydra and CAP do not address how access control interacts with other tamper resistant protection mechanisms such as hardware-based memory encryption and integrity verification.

In this article, we present a framework called *MEmory-centric Security Architecture* or *MESA* to provide protection on software integrity and confidentiality using a new set of architectural and operating system features. It enables secure information sharing and exchange in a heterogeneous multi-domain software system. The major contributions of our work are the follows:

- Presented and evaluated a unique memory centric security model for tamper resistant secure software execution. It distinguishes from the existing systems by providing better support for inter-operation and information sharing between software components in an open heterogenous multi-domain software system.
- Introduced architecture innovations that allow efficient implementation of the proposed security model. The proposed secure processor design incorporates

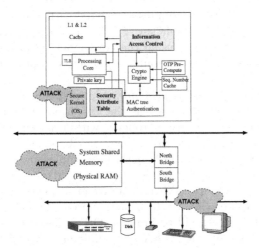

Fig. 1. Memory-Centric Security Architecture

and integrates fine-grained access control of software components, rigorous anti-reverse engineering and tamper resistant protection.

- Discussed novel system mechanisms to allow heterogenous program components to have their own tamper resistant protection requirements and still to be able to inter-operate and exchange information securely.

The rest of the article is organized as follows. Section 2 introduces MESA. Section 3 details each MESA component. Evaluation and results are in Section 4. Discussion of related work is presented in Section 5 and finally Section 6 concludes.

2   Memory-Centric Security Architecture

This section provides an overview of a security model, called *Memory-Centric Security Architecture* or MESA. Using novel architectural features, MESA enables high performance secure information sharing and exchange for multi-security domain software system. Figure 1 generalizes the security model and its operating environment.

Now we present MESA from the system's perspective. One critical concept of MESA is the *memory capsule*. A memory capsule is a virtual memory segment with a set of security attributes associated with it. It is an information container that may hold either data or code or both. It can be shared by multiple processes. For example, a DLL is simply a code memory capsule. A set of security attributes are defined for each memory capsule besides its location and size. These security attributes include security protection level, one or more symmetric memory encryption keys, memory authentication signature, accesses control information, etc. For each process, the secure OS kernel maintains a list of memory capsules and their attributes as process context. During software distribution, software vendors encrypt the security attributes associated with a memory capsule using the target secure processor's public key. The secure processor authenticates and extracts the security attributes using the corresponding private key. A secure processor never stores security attributes in the exposed physical RAM without encryption.

Another important concept is *principle*. A principle is an execution context smaller than a process. It is defined as the execution of secure code memory capsules having the same security property within a user process. Principles are associated with memory capsules. They can be considered as the owners of memory capsules. Based on the associated principles and security protection levels, access control of memory capsules can be carried out. An active principle is a currently executing principle. When an active principle accesses some memory capsule, the access will be checked. If the active principle is allowed to access the memory capsule, the access will be granted. Otherwise, a security exception of access violation will be thrown. MESA allows different crypto keys being used to protect separate memory capsules and enforces access control at runtime during program execution. Note that *principle* in MESA is not the same as the *principle* defined in capability systems [4,8].

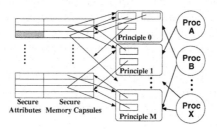

Fig. 2. Principles and the Secure Memory Capsules

Below we highlight certain assumptions of MESA:

- It is assumed that everything outside a secure processor is unprotected and subject to potential malicious tamper. The physical RAM can be read and overwritten directly by adversaries without CPU involvement. Furthermore, all the system/peripheral bus traffic are exposed and could be eavesdropped.
- MESA assumes hardware-based encryption/decryption and integrity protection using processor integrated crypto engine. Whenever an I- or D-cache line is brought into the processor, it is decrypted and its integrity is verified. Cache line is encrypted during eviction. The keys used for memory encryption/decryption and integrity verification are set by the software vendors. Software vendors distribute the memory encryption keys by encrypting them with the secure processor's public key;
- MESA assumes the existence of a secure BIOS stored in a securely sealed persistent storage device.

- Most of the OS codes are treated as regular program except a small set of core services, called *secure kernel*. The secure kernel is signed and authenticated by the secure BIOS during system boot [3].
- Security related process context information such as keys, integrity signatures, etc are managed by the secure kernel and securely preserved during process context switch.
- Secure processor can either run at debug mode or retail mode. Step execution or arbitrary break of protected software is only supported by the debug mode. While in the retail mode, processor exceptions and traps used for debugging are all disabled, thus preventing anyone from disclosing the software by running it in debug mode. A bit for setting the mode is defined as part of the signed binary image of an application.

2.1   Secure Capsule Management

Most functionality of the secure capsule management is achieved by the secure OS kernel. Some services provided by the secure kernel are, process and principle creation, principle authentication, principle access control.

First, during a process creation, the secure OS kernel will create a list of memory capsules associated with the process. The secure kernel creates application process from the binary images provided by a software vendor. Each binary image may comprise one or multiple protected code and data sections, each one with its own security attributes. Security attributes of binary images for the application itself, dependent middle-ware, and system shared code libraries are set independently by the corresponding vendors who developed them. The secure kernel creates a secure memory capsule context for each binary image based on it security attributes. Each memory capsule represents an instantiation of either a code module or data module and is uniquely identified with a randomly generated ID. For DLLs, a different capsule is created with a different ID when it is linked to a different process. However note that the code itself is not duplicated. It is simply mapped to the new process's memory space with a different capsule entry in the capsule context table.

Execution of a process can be represented as a sequence of executing principles. Heap and stack are two types of dynamic memory that a principle may access. Privacy of information stored in the heap and stack is optionally protected by allocating private heap or stack memory capsule to each principle. Another choice is to have one memory capsule to include both protected code image and memory space allocated as private heap and stack. When execution switches to a different principle, the processor stack register is re-loaded so that it will point to the next principle's private stack. Details of private stack are presented in the subsection of intra-process data sharing.

With the concept of private heap, there is the issue of memory management of private heaps associated with each principle. Does each principle require its own heap allocator? The answer is no. Heap management can be implemented in a protected shared system library. The key idea is that with hardware supported protection on memory integrity and confidentiality, the heap manager can manage usage of each principle's private heap but could not tamper its content.

To provide a secure sharing environment, support for authenticating principles is necessary. MESA supports three possible ways of principle authentication. The first approach is to authenticate a code memory capsule and its principle through a chain of certification. A code memory capsule could be signed and certificated by a trusted source. If the certification could be verified by the secure kernel, the created principle would become a trusted principle because it is certified by a trusted source. For example, application vendors can specify that the linked shared libraries must be certified by the system vendors such as Microsoft and the middle-ware image must be certified by the known middle-ware vendors. Failure of authenticating a code image will abort the corresponding process creation. Another approach is to authenticate a principle using a public key supplied by software vendors. This provides a way of private authentication. The third approach is to certify principle using secure processor's public key, in which security attributes are encrypted or signed by a secure processor's private key.

2.2   Intra Process Sharing

There are many scenarios that pointers need to be shared by multiple principles. One principle calls a routine of another principle and passes pointers to data of a confidential data memory capsule. In this scenario, information security will be violated if the callee's function attempts to exploit the caller's memory capsule more than what it is allowed. For instance, the caller may pass a memory pointer, *mp* and length *len*, to the callee and restricts the callee to access only the memory block *mp[0, len)*. However, the callee can spoil this privilege and try to access to

Intrinsic	Parameters	Explanation
sec_malloc(s,id)	s: *size*; id: *principle id*	Allocate memory from module's private heap
sec_free(p)	p: *memory pointer*	Free memory of private heap
sec_swap_stack (addr)	addr: *address*	Switch the active stack pointer to another capsule's private stack. Addr points to a location of the target principle. Save <active stack pointer, active principle id> to the stack context table
sec_get_id (name)	name: *capsule name*	Get id of a module (secure kernel service)
sec_push_stack_ptr()		Read the current executing principle's stack pointer from the stack context table and push it into its private stack
sec_return(addr)	addr: return addr	Assign addr to PC
sec_add_sharing_ptr (p, s, id, rw)	p: *pointer*; s: *size*; id: *principle id*; rw: *access right*	Allow target principle (id) to access memory region [p, p+s) with access right rw, return a security pointer that can be passed as function parameter (secure kernel service)
sec_remove_ptr (p)	p: *security pointer*	Remove access right granted to security pointer p
sec_save_security_ptr (reg, addr)	reg: *register holding security pointer*; addr: *address*	Save security pointer to memory
sec_load_security_ptr (reg, addr)	reg: *register holding security pointer*; addr: *address*	Load security pointer from memory

Fig. 3. MESA Security Intrinsics

the memory at *mp[-1]*. This must be prevented. Passing by value may solve the problem but it is less desired because of its cost on performance and compatibility problems. MESA facilitates information sharing using explicit declaration of shared subspace of memory capsules. The owner principle of a memory capsule is allowed to add additional principles to share data referenced by a pointer that points to data of its memory capsule. However, the modification is made on a single pointer basis. The principle can call *sec_add_sharing_ptr(addr, size, principle_p)* intrinsic to declare that *principle_p* is allowed to access the data in the range [addr, addr+size). The declaration is recorded in a pointer table. Dynamic access to the memory capsule is checked against both the memory capsule context and the pointer table. After the pointer is consumed, it is removed from the pointer table through another intrinsic *sec_remove_ptr(addr)*. This mechanism allows passing pointers of either private heap or private stack during a cross-principle call.

Aside from the above two intrinsics, MESA also proposes other necessary intrinsics for managing and sharing secure memory capsules as listed in Figure 3. Note that these security intrinsics are programming primitives not new instructions. Although a hardware implementation of MESA can implement many of them as CISCy instructions, yet it is not required.

```
// application called my_app
// middleware called my_middle, as dll
void* p;
unsigned int my_id, middle_id;
security void* sp;
int ret;



my_id = sec_get_id("my_app");
p = sec_malloc(0x20, my_id);
...
middle_id = sec_get_id("my_middle");
sp = sec_add_sharing_ptr(p, 0x20, middle_id, RD|WR);
ret = my_middle_foo(sp, 0x10);
sec_remove_ptr(sp);
...
sec_free(p);
```

```
// CALLER SIDE
push ebp //save stack frame pointer
sec_swap_stack addr_of_my_middle_foo
// stack pointer switched to the callee's stack
// caller's esp saved to the context table
push 0x10; // input parameter
call my_middle_goo
//push return PC to the callee's stack
pop ebp //get stack frame pointer back

// CALLEE SIDE
sec_push_stack_ptr
ebp = esp //ebp stack frame pointer
...
r1 = [ebp + 4] //return address
esp = [ebp]
sec_swap_stack r1
// restore stack pointer to the caller's stack
// callee's esp saved to the context table
sec_return r1//return to the caller
//return to the caller by loading return PC
```

Fig. 4. Pointer Sharing in Cross-Principle Function Call

Fig. 5. Securely Maintain Correct Stack Behavior in Cross-Principle Function Call

The code example in Figure 4 illustrates how to securely share data during a function call using MESA's security intrinsics. There are two principles. One is my_app and the other is a middle-ware library called my_middle. In the example, my_app allocates a 32-byte memory block from its own private heap by calling *sec_malloc(0x20, my_id)*. Then it declares a sharing pointer p using intrinsic *sec_add_sharing_ptr* that grants principle my_middle read/write access to the memory block pointed by p. The intrinsic call returns a security pointer, sp. After declaring the security pointer, principle my_app calls function

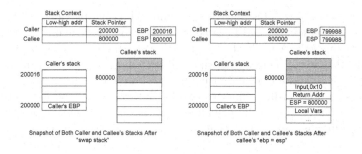

Fig. 6. Snapshot of Stacks Before and After Cross-Principle Call

my_middle_foo() of principle my_middle, passes the security pointer and another input argument. Inside my_middle_foo(), codes of principle my_middle can access the private memory block defined by the passed security pointer sp. After the function returns control back to principle my_app, my_app uses intrinsic *sec_remove_ptr* to remove the security pointer thus revoking my_middle's access to its private memory block. In addition to passing shared memory pointers, during cross-principle function call, program stack has to securely switch from the caller's private stack to the callee's private stack using some of the stack related security intrinsics.

To show how private stacks are protected during cross-principle function call, we show what happens at assembly code level when my_app calls my_middle_foo and the exit code of my_middle_foo in Figure 5. The assembly code uses x86 instruction set and MESA intrinsics. In the example, the caller switches stack pointer to the callee's private stack using *sec_swap_stack* intrinsic. Input addr is either a function entry address or return address if the intrinsic is used to switch stack pointer from the callee's private stack to the caller's stack. MESA maintains a table of stack pointer context for all the running principles. When *sec_swap_stack(addr)* is executed, it will save the current active stack pointer as a < principle, stack pointer > pair and set the active stack pointer to the target principle's. Then it pushes values to the callee's stack memory capsule. When the callee's stack capsule requires information to be encrypted, the pushed stack values will be encrypted with the callee's encryption key. Since the caller and the callee use different stacks, to maintain compatibility with the way how stack is used for local and input data, the callee uses *sec_push_stack_ptr* intrinsic at the function entry point to push its stack pointer value from the context table into its private stack. Figure 6 shows snapshot of both caller and callee's stacks before and after a principle crossing function call. When the execution switches back from my_middle to my_app, the callee copies the return value to the caller's stack capsule. Since the return PC address is saved in the callee's private stack (happens during execution of function call instruction after stack swap), the callee has to read the return address and put it into a temporary register using *sec_save_ret_addr*. Then the callee switches the stack pointer to the caller's.

Finally, the callee executes *sec_return* intrinsic that assigns the returned address stored in the temporary register to the current program counter. In the case where a large amount of data need to be returned, the caller could reserve the space for the returned value on its stack by declaring a security pointer pointing to its stack and passes it to the callee.

Note that MESA protects against tampering on the target principle's stack by only allowing one principle to push values to other principle's stack. A principle can not modify another principle's stack pointer context because only the owner principle can save the current active stack pointer as its stack pointer context according to the definition of *sec_swap_stack*. Explicitly assigning values to the active stack pointer owned by a different principle is prohibited.

2.3   Inter Process Sharing - Shared Memory

MESA supports tamper-resistant shared memory through access control. In MESA, each memory capsule can be owned by one or more principles as shown in Figure 2. Access rights (read/write) to a secure memory capsule could be granted to other principles. For secure sharing, the owner principle specifies the access right to be granted only to certain principles that are authenticated. Using this basic secure kernel service, secure inter-process communication such as secure shared memory and secure pipe can be implemented. For example, assume that P1 and P2 are two user principles belonging to different processes that want to share memory in a secure manner. Principle P1 can create a memory capsule and set a sharing criteria by providing a public authentication key. When principle P2 tries to share the memory created by P1, it will provide its credential, signed certificate by the corresponding private key to the secure kernel. The secure kernel then verifies that P2 can be trusted and maps the capsule to the memory space of P2's owning process.

3   Architectural Support for MESA

This section describes architectural support for MESA. Inside a typical secure processor, we assumed a few security features at the micro-architectural level that incorporate encryption schemes as well as integrity protection based on the prior art in [6,11,10]. In addition, we introduce new micro-architecture components for the MESA including a *Security Attribute Table (SAT)*, an *Access Control Mechanism (ACM)*, and a *Security Pointer Buffer (SPB)*. Other new system features are also proposed to cope with MESA in order to manage the security architecture asset.

3.1   Security Attribute Table

Secure memory capsule management is the heart of MESA. Most of the functionality for secure memory capsule management is implemented in the secure OS kernel that keeps track of a list of secure memory capsules used by a user

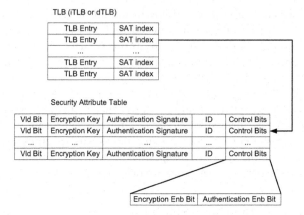

Fig. 7. Security Attribute Table (SAT) and TLB

process. Security attributes of frequently accessed secure memory capsules are cached on-chip in a structure called Security Attribute Table (SAT). Figure 7 shows the structure of a SAT attached to a TLB. Each entry caches a set of security attributes associated with a secure memory capsule. The crypto-key of each SAT entry is used to decrypt or encrypt information stored in the memory capsule. The secure kernel uses intrinsic *sec_SATld(addr)* to load security attributes from the memory capsule context stored in memory to SAT. The crypto-keys in the memory capsule context are encrypted using the secure processor's public key. The secure processor will decrypt the keys when they are loaded into the SAT.

A secure memory capsule could be bound to one or many virtual memory pages of a user process. When the entire user virtual memory space is bound to only one secure memory capsule, the model is equivalent to a process-centric security model. As Figure 7 shows, each TLB entry contains an index to SAT for retrieving the security attributes of the corresponding memory page. During context switches, the secure kernel authenticates the process's memory capsule context first, then loads security attributes into SAT. SAT is accessed for each external memory access. For a load operation, if it misses the cache, data in the external memory will be brought into the cache, decrypted using the encryption key in the SAT and its integrity verified against the root memory authentication signature, also stored in the SAT using hash tree algorithm [11]. On-chip caches maintain only plaintext data. SAT is also accessed when data is to be evicted from the on-chip caches. The evicted data will be encrypted using keys stored in the SAT and a new memory capsule root signature will be computed to replace the old root signature.

If the required security attributes could not be found in the SAT, a SAT miss fault is triggered and the secure kernel would take over. The secure kernel would load the required security attributes into the SAT. The SAT indexes stored in the TLB are also updated accordingly.

3.2   Access Control Mechanism

Efficient hardware-based access control plays a key role for protecting memory capsules from being accessed by un-trusted software components. It is important to point out that having software components or memory capsules encrypted does not imply that they can be trusted. A hacker can encrypt a malicious library and have the OS to load it into an application's virtual space. The encrypted malicious library despite encrypted can illegally access confidential data.

Access management is achieved by associating principles with memory capsules that they can access. The information is stored in a table. Based on the security requirements, the secure processor checks the table for every load/store memory operation and the operation is allowed to be completed only if it does not violate any access constraint. To speed up memory operations, frequently accessed entries of the rule table can be cached inside the processor by an *Access Lookup Cache*. Entries of ALC are matched based on the current executing principle's ID and the target memory capsule's ID. To avoid using a CAM for implementing ALC, executing principle's ID and the target memory capsule's ID can be XORed as the ALC index shown in Figure 8. This allows ALC to be implemented as a regular cache. For a memory operation and ID pair <running principle ID, memory capsule ID, rd, wr>, if a matching ALC entry can not be found, an ALC miss exception will be triggered and program execution will trap into the secure kernel. The secure kernel will check the complete access control table to see whether a matching entry can be found there. If an entry is found, it will be loaded into the ALC. Failure to find an entry in both the ALC and the complete access control table means detection of an illegal memory operation. Upon detection of such an operation, the secure kernel will switch to a special handling routine where proper action will be taken either terminating the process or nullifying the memory operation.

To minimize performance impact of ALC lookup on cache access, ALC checking can be conducted in parallel with storing information into the cache, thus incurs almost no performance loss since stores are typically not on the critical path. As shown in Figure 8, there is one pass bit in each cache line indicating whether the stored data yet passes access control security checking. When data is written to a cache line, the bit is clear. When ALC lookup returns a hit, the bit will be set. To guarantees that a secure memory capsule is not updated by instructions whose principles do not have write access right, cache lines with the checked bit clear are inhibited from being written back to the memory. Furthermore, read access to a cache line with the check bit set is stalled until the bit is set. The performance impact of the above mechanism on cache access is minimal because as our profiling study indicates the interval between access to the same dirty cache line is often long enough to cover the latency of ALC lookup.

For reading data from L1 cache, MESA also decouples access control verification with cache read. If access control takes more cycles then cache access, the processor pipeline is allowed to use the fetched data but it cannot commit the instruction until it receives the access control verification result. This would

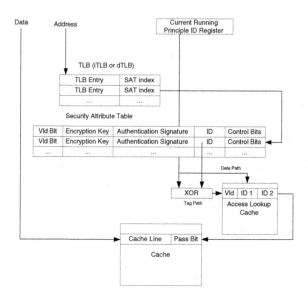

Fig. 8. Information Access Control Mechanism

not cause significant performance impact because the latency difference between cache access and access control verification is at most one or two cycles. Since ALC and TLB are often smaller, it is plausible to have both fetched data and access control verification result ready at the same time. But this is highly implementation dependent depending on the clock rate, size of L1 cache, size of ALC and TLB and the actual cache, TLB, ALC implementations.

3.3   Security Pointer Table and Security Pointer Buffer

MESA keeps track shared memory pointers in a security pointer table. To identify security pointer, MESA requires that an application explicitly declares temporarily shared memory regions. For each shared memory pointer, MESA assigns it a token. MESA allows pointer arithmetic where each computed address inherits the same pointer token. MESA adds a new programming data type, called security pointer to programming interface. The difference between a security pointer and a regular pointer is that aside from the address value, security pointer maintains additional information for identifying a pointer shared between principles such as the pointer's token value. For each security pointer value, a MESA friendly compiler will allocate enough memory space to hold both the address and the token value. For example, if the token is 16 bits long and memory address is 32 bits long. A security pointer type will be 48 bits. A strong typed langauge can guarantee that a security pointer only assigns its value to another security pointer. Each time, a security pointer is declared, MESA assigns a pointer token to it and inserts the address range (low, high address), access right, target principle, along with the token value into the security pointer table.

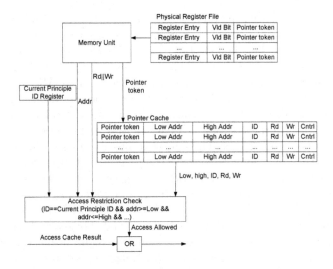

Fig. 9. Security Pointer Buffer

To speed up runtime access to the table, MESA can use a hardware facilitated hash function where hash key is calculated over pointer token value.

To support security pointer, MESA can choose one of the following designs. MESA can extend entries of register file with a pointer token field. If a register holds a security pointer, the corresponding register's pointer token will be set with the pointer's token value. When the register value is assigned to another register, the token value is also passed. When a null value is assigned to a register, its token value is cleared. When the address stored in a security pointer is used to access memory, the associated pointer token is used to retrieve the corresponding entry in the pointer table. The memory address is compared against the memory range stored in the security pointer table, and ID of the running principle is also compared with the ID stored in the corresponding pointer table entry. If the memory address is within the range, the principle's ID also matches, and the type of access (read/write) is compatible, the memory reference based on the security pointer is accepted. Otherwise, a security pointer exception will be raised. An alternative much less light-weighted solution is to simply add a new global security pointer token register. If an application intends to use a register value as security pointer, during pointer de-reference, the compiled application code has to explicitly set the token register with the security pointer's token value. For pointer assignment and pointer arithmetic, MESA friendly compiler will allocate two architecture registers for each security pointer, one for the address, the other for the pointer token. The compiler will insert additional instructions to maintain both registers properly during security pointer assignment and pointer arithmetic. Comparing with the first solution, this design is much simpler and requires only minor architecture changes, only one special register. But it may increases register allocation pressure.

Since for every security pointer based memory reference, MESA needs to consult the security pointer table, it is performance wise to cache entries of pointer table on chip. This is done by *Security Pointer Buffer (SPB)* as shown in Figure 9. For each memory access based on a security pointer, MESA searches the SPB using the pointer's token value. If there is a match, MESA will verify if it should allow the access according to the security pointer declaration. If there is no match in the SPB or the access address is outside the declared region or not permitted based on the access right, MESA will raise an exception. The exception is handled by the secure kernel. There are two possible reasons for a SPB access failure. First, the entry may be evicted from the SPB to the external security pointer table and replaced by some other security pointer declaration. In this case, a valid entry for that security pointer can be found in the security pointer table. If the entry is found and the access is consistent with the security pointer declaration, it should be allowed to continue as usual. The secure kernel may load the entry into the SPB as well in case it is needed again in future. Second, the security pointer declaration is revoked and no longer exists in both the SPB and the security pointer table. This represents an illegal memory reference. Execution will switch to a secure kernel handler on illegal memory reference and proper action will be taken.

If an implementation of MESA chooses the design of instrumenting register file with pointer token, two new instructions, sec_save_security_ptr and sec_load_security_ptr are used to support save/load security pointers in register file to/from the external memory. SPB and security pointer definition table are part of the protected process context. They are securely preserved during process context switch.

3.4   Integrity Protection Under MESA

The existing integrity protection schemes for security architectures are based on a m-ary hash/MAC tree [11]. Instead of using a m-ary hash tree [5], we designed a faster m-ary MAC (message authentication code) authentication tree. Under the memory-centric model in which information within a process space is usually encrypted by multiple encryption keys, the existing authentication methods cannot be directly applied. Toward this,

We protect individual memory capsules with their own MAC tree. For each memory capsule's MAC authentication tree, there is a root MAC. MESA uses this root MAC as the memory capsule's signature. To speed up integrity verification, frequently accessed nodes of the MAC tree nodes are cached on-chip. When a new cache line is fetched, the secure processor verifies its integrity by inserting it into the MAC tree. Starting from the bottom of the tree, recursively, a new MAC value based on the fetched value is computed and compared with the internal MAC tree node. The MAC tree is always updated whenever a dirty cache line is evicted from the secure processor. The secure processor can automatically determine the memory locations of MAC tree nodes and fetch them automatically during integrity check if they are needed. Root of the MAC tree is preserved securely when a process is swapped out of the processor pipeline.

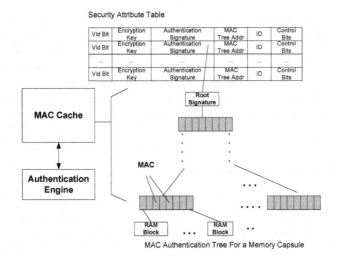

Security Attribute Table

Vld Bit	Encryption Key	Authentication Signature	MAC Tree Addr	ID	Control Bits
Vld Bit	Encryption Key	Authentication Signature	MAC Tree Addr	ID	Control Bits
...	...	...	...	...	...
Vld Bit	Encryption Key	Authentication Signature	MAC Tree Addr	ID	Control Bits

MAC Authentication Tree For a Memory Capsule

Fig. 10. Layered MAC Tree for Memory Integrity Verification

Details of the MAC tree operations are outside the range of this article. However, it is worth pointing out that our MAC tree implementation applies a number of optimizations to reduce the integrity verification latency overhead. For instance, MESA conducts parallel MAC verification for different MAC tree layers as much as possible. This is allowed because each internal MAC node of a layer is simply a MAC of a fixed number of MACs of the layer below (a block of MACs). Another optimization is that after an internal MAC node is verified against the root signature and cached inside the MAC cache, it does not need to be verified against the root signature again in future as along as the node is cached.

3.5   OS Implementation

The secure kernel is protected using its own key. The secure kernel maintains process and principle context using its protected memory capsule. Data exchanged between the secure processor and the secure kernel is protected as well.

Process Context Switch. When a process is swapped out of the secure processor, register context including the stack pointer is encrypted and preserved. Both the old SAT and ALC will be invalidated by the secure kernel. Security related context including the SPB must be preserved. The root signatures of memory capsules are also saved as part of a process context. Note the MESA authenticates every piece of information brought into the secure processor including the secure kernel. This means that portions of the memory authentication tree for the secure kernel code space have to be mapped to the application's memory authentication tree so that instructions of the secure kernel can be authenticated under application's MAC/hash tree after the secure kernel already switches address of authentication tree but yet switches execution control to the application.

Process Instantiation. To start execution of a process, the secure kernel has to set up SAT and ALC. Furthermore, it will load addresses of pointer lists for the removed and evicted security pointers and the associated security pointer buffer context. For a new process first time to be scheduled for execution, the SPB and security pointer table may be empty. Then, the secure kernel will load the base addresses of the authentication trees (MAC or hash tree) of memory capsules mapped to the application's memory space into the SAT.

4   Performance Evaluation

The purpose of performance evaluation is to show that MESA does not incur significant overall performance overhead. A cycle-based architecture model and simplified system software are implemented for detailed evaluation.

4.1   Simulation Framework

We used TAXI [13] as our simulation environment. TAXI includes two components, a functional open-source Pentium emulator called Bochs, and a cycle-based out-of-order x86 processor simulator. Bochs is an open source Pentium emulator capable of performing full system simulation. It models the entire platform including Ethernet device, VGA monitor, and sound card to support the execution of a complete operating system and its applications. We used out-of-the-box Windows NT (version 4.0, service pack 6) as our target. TAXI includes a SimpleScalar based x86 target. Both Bochs and the x86 SimpleScalar target are modified for performance evaluation for MESA. Proposed architecture components including SAT, ALC, and SPB are modelled. We measure the performance under two encryption schemes, XOM/Aegis like scheme and our counter mode based scheme, also called M-Tree(counter mode + MAC tree). The XOM/Aegis like scheme uses block cipher for software encryption/decryption where XOM uses triple-DES [2] and Aegis uses 128bit AES [1]. In our evaluation, we selected direct encryption mode such as ECB mode (electronic code block) similar to XOM as one of the encryption schemes. The other scheme is based on counter mode. It is known that counter mode is faster than many other standard encryption modes because in counter mode, the key stream used for encryption/decryption can be pre-computed or securely speculated [9].

Since we have no access to the windows OS source codes, simplification was taken to facilitate performance evaluation. Software handling of the MESA architecture is implemented as independent service routines triggered by the Bochs emulator. These routines maintains the SAT, ALC, and SPB using additional information on memory capsules provided by the application. Executing process is recognized by matching CR3 register (pointing to a unique physical address of process's page table) with process context.

To model the usage of MESA, we assumed that the application software and the system software are separately protected. The system software includes all the system dynamically linked libraries mapped to the application space, for instance including kernel32.dll, wsock32.dll, gdi32.dll, ddraw.dll, user32.dll, etc. If the application includes any middleware libraries. The middleware libraries are also separately protected. Note that all the system libraries mentioned above are linked to the user space by the windows OS and they are invoked through normal DLL function call. To track the data exchanged among the application, middleware DLLs, and system DLLs, dummy wrapper DLLs are implemented for the DLLs that interface with the application. These dummy DLLs are API hijackers. They can keep track of the pointers exchanged between an application and the system and update the security pointer table and the SPB accordingly. Usage of dynamic memory space such as heap and stack are traced and tagged. The assumption is that each protected code space uses its own separate encryption key to guarantee privacy of its stack and dynamically allocated memory space.

Table 1. Processor model parameters

Parameters	Values	Parameters	Values
Processor Frequency	1.0 GHz	Memory Frequency	200MHz
Fetch/Decode width	8	Issue/Commit width	8
L1 I-Cache	DM, 8KB, 32B line	L1 D-Cache	DM, 8KB, 32B line
L2 Cache	4way, Unified, 32B line, 512KB	L1/L2 Latency	1 cycle / 8 cycles
MAC cache size	32KB	AES latency	80ns
SHA256 latency	80ns	ALC latency	1 cycle
SPB size	64, random replacement	SPB latency	1 cycle

Table 1 lists the architectural parameters experimented. A default latency of 80ns for both SHA-256 and AES were used for the cryptographic engines in the simulation given that both units are assumed to be custom designed.

We chose seven windows NT applications as benchmarks, Microsoft Internet Explorer 6.0 (IE), Abobe Acrobat reader 5.0 (AcroReader), Windows Media Player 2 (MPlayer), Microsoft Visual Studio 6.0(VS), Winzip 8.0, Microsoft Word (Word), and Povray 3. The run of Explorer includes fetching web pages from yahoo.com using Bochs's simulated Ethernet driver. The run of Visual Studio includes compilation of Apache source code. Winzip run consists of decompressing package of Apache 2.0. Our run of Media Player includes play of a short AVI file of Olympics figure-skating. The input to Acrobat reader is Intel pdf document on IA64 system programming. The run includes search for all the appearance of word "virtual memory". The run of word consists of loading a word template for IEEE conference paper, type a short paragraph, cut/paste, and grammar checking. The run of Povray is the rendering of the default Povray image.

4.2 Performance Evaluation

We first evaluate the performance of access control, and security pointer table. We use a 32-entry SAT for storing keys and security attributes. This is large

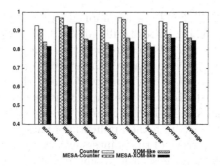

Fig. 11. Comparison of Normalized Performance Results for Counter Mode, Memory Centric Counter Mode, XOM/Aegis-like system(AES), and Memory Centric XOM/Aegis-like system

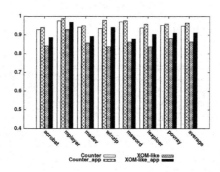

Fig. 12. Comparison of Normalized IPC Performance for Protecting of only User application vs. Protection of the Whole Process - both application and system libraries

enough to hold all the protected memory capsules in our study. The number of entries in the *security pointer buffer* is sixty-four which is large enough to handle most of the shared pointers. We evaluated three scenarios, baseline condition where security protection is turned off, *Counter mode* protection on the whole virtual space with one memory capsule, and protection using the proposed MESA. Baseline condition has the same setting as the security conditions for all the non-security related configurations.

Performance results for all the seven applications are reported in Figure 11. The figure shows relative results where IPC (instructions per cycle) is normalized to the performance of the baseline. According to the results, on average, *counter-mode* loses about 5% performance. When MESA is used, it further slows down by another 1%. Block cipher on average loses about 13% performance and introducing MESA will cause another 1.8% loss on performance. It is important to point out that when the whole user space is protected as one memory capsule (degenerated case), *security pointer buffer* and access control are no longer providing valuable services and could be turned off. There will be no further performance loss under this scenario.

One objective of MESA is to provide a secure environment so that software components co-existing in the same space could be selectively encrypted and protected. To evaluate the gain of selective protection, we selectively encrypt only application and its supporting DLLs, leave all the system libraries such as gdi32.dll, wsock32.dll, and etc un-encrypted. The performance results (IPC normalized to the baseline) are shown in Figure 12. For *counter-mode* architecture, the gain of performance is about 1.6% of total IPC comparing with encrypting everything in the memory space. This is substantial amount considering the slow down of *counter-mode* is only 5%. For the block ciphers, the gain is about 5.5%. This means that by ensuring a secure environment for information sharing, MESA could actually improve the overall system performance, especially for the block cipher based tamper resistant protection systems.

5   Related Work

Software protection and trusted computing are among the most important issues in the area of computer security. Traditionally, the protections on software are provided through a trusted OS. To improve the security model, some tamper resistant devices are embedded into a computer platform to ensure the loaded operating system is trusted. A typical example of such computer architecture is the trusted computing initiative (TCG) and the related OSs. TCG rely on a tamper-proof IC, called TPM (Trusted Platform Module), which is attached to the motherboard's south bridge as a peripheral device for security. Microsoft developed an operating system that can make use of TCG's TPM, called NGSCB (Next Generation Secure Computing Base) former known as Palladium. Intel has developed hardware for TCG based system, called LaGrande where TCG's TPM is also a part of the system. Certain security benefits offered by TCG are, secure boot, key management, attestation, protected storage, etc. Although TCG based systems improve trust computing on today's computing platform and prevent certain software attacks, they are not designed for protection of software confidentiality and privacy against physical tamper. They provide only weak protection on software and data confidentiality because the protection offered by the TPM as a south bridge peripheral device is very limited. For certain security applications that require strong anti-reverse engineering and anti-tampering features, a better solution is necessary. To address this issue, new secure processor architecture such as XOM and AEGIS emerged, which incorporates cryptographics units directly into the processor. However, as most closed system solutions, they too fail to address important issues such as inter-operation between heterogenous software components and information sharing.

MESA is different from the information flow based security model called RIFLE proposed in [12]. RIFLE tries to keep track of the flow of sensitive information dynamically at runtime by augmenting software's binary code. It prevents restricted information from flowing to a less secure or un-trusted channel. MESA is designed for a different purpose and usage model. The main purpose of MESA is to mitigate some of the drawbacks associated with the whole process based cryptographic protection of software instead of trying to solve the issue of secure information flow. MESA is also significantly different from the memory protection model called Mondrian [14]. Memory capsules in MESA are authenticated and encrypted memory spaces, concepts do not exist in Mondrian.

6   Conclusions

This article describes MESA, a high performance memory centric security system, that can protect software privacy and integrity against both software and physical tamper. Different from the previous process-based tamper-resistant systems designed for the same purpose, our new system allows different software components with different security policies to inter-operate in the same memory space. It allows software vendors to devise their own protection requirements on software components, therefore, it is more flexible and suitable for open software systems than the previous process-centric protection approaches.

References

1. Federal Information Processing Standard Draft, Advanced Encryption Standard (AES). National Institute of Standards and Technology, 2001.
2. National Institude of Standards and Technology, Recommendation for the Triple Data Encryption Algorithm (TDEA) Block Cipher. *SP-800-67*, 2004.
3. W. A. Arbaugh, D. J. Farber, and J. M. Smith. A Secure and Reliable Bootstrap Architecture. In *Proceedings of the Symposium on Security and Privacy*, 1997.
4. E. Cohen and D. Jefferson. Protection in the Hydra Operating System. In *Proceedings of the fifth ACM Symposium on Operating Systems Principles*, 1975.
5. B. Gassend, G. E. Suh, D. Clarke, M. van Dijk, and S. Devadas. Caches And Merkle Trees For Efficient Memory Integrity Verification. In *Proceedings of the 9th International Symposium on High Performance Computer Architecture*, 2003.
6. D. Lie, C. Thekkath, M. Mitchell, P.Lincoln, D. Boneh, J. Mitchell, and M. Horowitz. Architectual Support For Copy and Tamper Resistant Software. In *Proceedings of the 9th Symposium on Architectural Support for Programming Languages and Operating Systems*, 2000.
7. D. Lie, C. A. Thekkath, and M. Horowitz. Implementing an Untrusted Operating System on Trusted Hardware. In *Proceedings of the Symposium on Operating Systems Principles*, 2003.
8. R. M. Needham and R. D. Walker. The Cambridge CAP computer and its protection system. In *Proceedings of the Symposium on Operating Systems Principles*, 1977.
9. W. Shi, H.-H. S. Lee, M. Ghosh, C. Lu, and A. Boldyreva. High Efficiency Counter Mode Security Architecture via Prediction and Precomputation. In *Proceedings of the 32nd International Symposium on Computer Architecture*, 2005.
10. E. G. Suh, D. Clarke, B. Gassend, M. van Dijk, and S. Devadas. Efficient Memory Integrity Verification and Encryption for Secure Processors. In *Proceedings Of the 36th Annual International Symposium on Microarchitecture*, December, 2003.
11. E. G. Suh, D. Clarke, M. van Dijk, B. Gassend, and S.Devadas. AEGIS: Architecture for Tamper-Evident and Tamper-Resistant Processing . In *Proceedings of the International Conference on Supercomputing*, 2003.

12. N. Vachharajani, M. J. Bridges, J. Chang, R. Rangan, G. Ottoni, J. A. Blome, G. A. Reis, M. Vachharajani, and D. I. August. RIFLE: An Architectural Framework for User-Centric Information-Flow Security. In *Proceedings of the 37th annual International Symposium on Microarchitecture*, 2004.

13. S. Vlaovic and E. S. Davidson. TAXI: Trace Analysis for X86 Interpretation. In *Proceedings of the 2002 IEEE International Conference on Computer Design*, 2002.

14. E. J. Witchel. *Mondrian Memory Protection*. PhD thesis, Department of Electrical Engineering and Computer Science, Massachusetts Institute of Technology, 2004.

15. J. Yang, Y. Zhang, and L. Gao. Fast Secure Processor for Inhibiting Software Piracy and Tampering. In *Proceedings of the International Symposium on Microarchitecture*, 2003.

16. X. Zhuang, T. Zhang, S. Pande, and H.-H. S. Lee. HIDE: Hardware-support for Leakage-Immune Dynamic Execution. Report GIT-CERCS-03-21, Geogia Institute of Technology, Atlanta, GA, Nov. 2003.

Power Aware External Bus Arbitration for System-on-a-Chip Embedded Systems

Ke Ning[1,2] and David Kaeli[1]

[1] Northeastern University 360 Huntington Avenue, Boston MA 02115
[2] Analog Devices Inc. 3 Technology Way Norwood MA 02062

Abstract. Power efficiency has become a key design trade-off in embedded system designs. For system-on-a-chip embedded systems, an external bus interconnects embedded processor cores, I/O peripherals, a direct memory access (DMA) controller, and off-chip memory. External memory access activities are a major source of energy consumption in embedded systems, and especially in multimedia platforms. In this paper, we focus on the energy dissipated due to the address, data, and control activity on the external bus and supporting logic. We build our external bus power model on top of a cycle-accurate simulation framework that quantifies the bus power based on memory bus state transitions. We select the Analog Devices ADSP-BF533 Blackfin processor as our target architecture model. Using our power-aware external bus arbitration schemes, we can reduce overall external bus power by as much as 18% in video processing applications, and by 14% on average for the test suites studied. Besides reducing power consumption, we also obtained an average bus performance speedup of 21% when using our power-aware arbitration schemes.

Keywords: power-aware, external memory, bus arbitration, embedded systems, media processor.

1 Introduction

1.1 Background

Off-chip communication design plays a key role in today's system-on-a-chip (SoC) designs. While the performance of on-chip bus architectures can be improved, many industrial and academic efforts have been established to develop efficient system-level bus architectures. These architectures utilize a range of protocols including first-come-first-serve, fixed priority, time division multiplexing (TDMA) (on ARM's AMBA bus), token-ring mechanisms (on LotteryBus [1]), and network-on-chip architectures (on Arteris [2] and ST Microelectronics designs [3]). All of these efforts target reducing bus latency and access delay.

Modern embedded systems are becoming increasingly limited by memory performance and system power consumption. The portion of the total system power

P. Stenström (Ed.): Transactions on HiPEAC I, LNCS 4050, pp. 116–135, 2007.

attributable to off-chip accesses can dominate the overall power budget. Due to the intrinsic capacitance of the bus lines, a considerable amount of power is required at the I/O pins of a system-on-a-chip processor when data has to be transmitted through the external bus [4,5]. The capacitance associated with the external bus is much higher than the internal node capacitance inside a microprocessor. For example, a low-power embedded processor like an Analog Devices ADSP-BF533 Blackfin processor running at 500 MHz consumes about 374 mW on average during normal execution. Assuming a 3.65 V voltage supply, and a bus frequency of 133 MHz, the average external power consumed is around 170 mW, which accounts for approximately 30% of the overall system power dissipation [6].

The memory power performance problem is even more acute for embedded media processors that possess memory intensive access patterns and require streaming serial memory access that tends to exhibit low temporal locality (i.e., poor data cachablity). Without more effective bus communication strategies, media processors will continue to be limited by memory power and memory performance. One approach to addressing both power and performance issues is to consider how best to schedule off-chip accesses.

1.2   Power in External Bus

In modern CMOS circuit design, the power dissipation of the external bus is directly proportional to the capacitance of the bus and the number of transitions ($1 \rightarrow 0$ or $0 \rightarrow 1$) on bus lines [7,8]. Energy estimation has been studied for both software and hardware. Tiwari [9] investigate the instruction level power model for general purpose processors and Li [10] built a system frame work to conduct power analysis for embedded system. In general, the external bus power can be expressed as:

$$P_{bus} = C_{bus}V_{ext}^2 fk\mu + P_{leakage} \qquad (1)$$

In the above equation, C_{bus} denotes the capacitance of each line on the bus, V_{ext} is the bus supply voltage, f is the bus frequency, k is the number of bit toggles per transition on the full width of the bus, and μ is the bus utilization factor. This power equation is an activity-based model. It not only accounts for the dynamic power dissipated on the bus, but includes the pin power that drives the signal I/O's related to external bus communication. $P_{leakage}$ is the power dissipated on the bus due to leakage current.

Techniques to minimize the power dissipation in buses have been explored in previous research [4,11,12]. The main strategies have been to utilize improved bus encodings to minimize the bus activity. Various mixed-bus encoding techniques (e.g., Gray codes and redundant codes) were developed to save on bus power. Gray code addressing is based on the fact that bus values tend to change sequentially and they can be used to switch the least number of signals on the bus.

However, better power efficiency can be obtained by using redundant codes [4]. A number of redundant codes have been proposed that add signals on the bus lines in order to reduce the number of transitions. Bus-invert coding [12]is one class of the redundant codes. Bus-invert coding adds an INV signal on the bus to represent the polarity of the address on the bus. The INV signal value is chosen by considering how best to minimize the hamming distance between the last address on the bus and the current one. Some codes can be applied to both the data and address buses, though some are more appropriate for addresses.

In our previous work, we described a bus modeling system that can capture bus power in the same framework of a cycle-accurate simulator for an embedded media processor [13]. We discussed an initial design of a power-aware bus arbitration scheme. The main contributions of this paper are a completed design of our power-aware bus arbitration scheme that also considers using pipelined SDRAM, and we also consider a broader range of multimedia applications. This paper is organized as follows. In section 2 we describe the target architecture for our work, which contains a system-on-a-chip media processor, SDRAM memory, and an external bus interface unit. We also present our power modeling methodology. Section 3 describes a number of different bus arbitration algorithms that we consider for power and performance optimizations. Section 4 presents power/performance results of MPEG-2, JPEG, PGP and G721 benchmarks for traditional arbitration schemes and our power-aware schemes. Finally, Section 5 presents conclusions.

2   System-on-a-Chip Architectures

2.1   Interconnect Subsystem

Modern system-on-a-chip embedded media systems include many components: a high-speed processor core, hardware accelerators, a rich set of peripherals, direct memory access (DMA), on-chip cache and off-chip memory. The system architecture considered in our study includes a single core, several peripherals, and off-chip SDRAM memory, and is similar to many current embedded platforms.

For multimedia applications, throughput requirements are increasing faster and faster. Today, for a D1 (720x480) video codec (encoder/decoder) media node, we need to be able to process 10 million pixels per second. This workload requires a media processor for computation, devices to support high speed media streaming and data conversion via a parallel peripheral interface (PPI), and a synchronous serial port (SPORT) for interfacing to high speed telecom interfaces. The high data throughput requirements associated with this platform make it impossible to store all the data in an on-chip memory or cache. Therefore, a typical multimedia embedded system usually provides a high-speed system-on-a-chip microprocessor and a very large off-chip memory. The Analog Devices Blackfin processor family [14], the Texas Instrument OMAP [15], and the SigmaDesign EM8400 [16] series are all examples of low-power embedded media chipsets which share many similarities in system design and bus

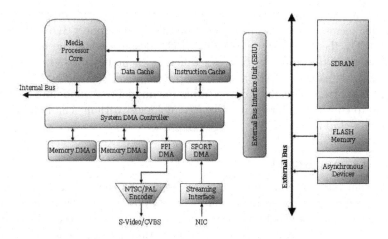

Fig. 1. Our target embedded media system architecture

structure. The system architecture assumed in this paper is based on these designs and is shown in Figure 1.

When trying to process streaming data in real-time, the greatest challenge is to provide enough memory bandwidth in order to sustain the necessary data rate. To insure sufficient bandwidth, hardware designers usually provide multiple buses in the system, each possessing different bus speeds and different protocols. An external bus is used to interface to the large off-chip memory system and other asynchronous memory-mapped devices. The external bus has a much longer physical length than other buses, and thus typically has higher bus capacitance and power dissipation. The goal of this work is to accurately model this power dissipation in a complete system power model so we can explore new power-efficient scheduling algorithms for the external memory bus.

2.2 External Bus Interface Unit

In the system design shown in Figure 1, there are two buses, one internal bus and one external bus, These two buses are bridged by an external bus interface unit (EBIU), which provides a glue-less interface to external devices (i.e., SDRAM memory, flash memory and asynchronous devices).

There are two sub-modules inside the EBIU, a bus arbitrator and a memory controller. When the units (processor or DMA's) in the system need to access external memory, they only need to issue a request to the EBIU buffer through the internal bus. The EBIU will read the request and handle the off-chip communication tasks through the external bus. Due to the potential contention between users on the bus, arbitration for the external bus interface is required. The bus arbitrator grants requests based on a pre-defined order. Only one access request can be granted at a time. When a request has been granted, the memory controller will communicate with the off-chip memory directly based on the specific memory type and protocol. The EBIU can support SDRAM, SRAM, ROM, FIFOs, flash memory and ASIC/FPGA designs, while the internal units do not need to discriminate between different memory types. In this paper, we use multi-banked SDRAM as an example memory technology and integrate SDRAM state transitions into our external bus model (our modeling framework allows us to consider different memory technologies, without changing the base system-on-a-chip model).

2.3 Bus Power Model

The external bus power includes dynamic power to charge and discharge the capacitance along the external bus, and the pin power to drive the bus current. The external bus power is highly dependent on the memory technology chosen. In past work on bus power modeling, little attention has been paid to the impact of the chosen memory technology. While we have assumed an SDRAM in our power model in this work, we can use the same approach with other types of memory modules. The external bus power associated with each transaction will be the total number of pins that toggle on the bus. We include in our model the power consumption due to the commands sent on the control bus, the row address and column address on the address bus, and the data on data bus. The corresponding leakage power is also considered in our model.

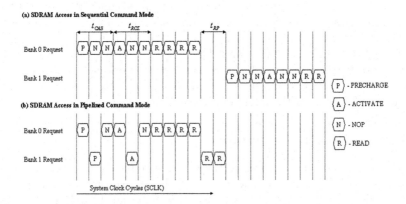

Fig. 2. Timing diagram showing two memory accesses for both sequential and pipelined command SDRAM

SDRAM is commonly used in cost-sensitive embedded applications that require large amounts of memory. SDRAM has a three-dimensional structure model. It is organized in multiple banks. Inside each bank, there are many pages, which are selected by row address. The memory access is on a command-by-command basis. An access involves processing a PRECHARGE and an

ACTIVATE command before a physical READ/WRITE command. At the same time of an ACTIVATE and READ/WRITE command, the corresponding row and column addresses are sent on the address bus.

To maximize memory bandwidth, modern SDRAM components allow for pipelining memory commands [17], which eliminates unnecessary stall cycles and NOP commands on the bus. While these features increase the memory bandwidth, they also reduce the bus command power. Consecutive accesses to different rows within one bank have high latency and cannot be pipelined, while consecutive accesses to different rows in different banks can be pipelined. Figure 2 is a timing diagram for processing two read operations in sequential access SDRAM and pipelined access SDRAM.

In our bus model, we assume that the power to drive the control bus and address bus are the similar. For each read/write request, we first determine the series of commands needed to complete that request. For each command, the bus state transitions, the number of pin toggles, and the bus utilization factor is recorded. Finally, the average bus power dissipated is calculated using Equation 1.

3 Bus Arbitration

The bandwidth and latency of external memory system are heavily dependent on the manner in which accesses interact with the three-dimensional SDRAM structure. The bus arbitration unit in the EBIU determines the sequencing of load/store requests to SDRAM, with the goals of reducing contention and maximizing bus performance. The requests from each unit will be queued in the EBIU's wait queue buffer. When a request is not immediately granted, the request enters stall mode. Each request can be represented as a tuple (t, s, b, l), where t is the arrival time, s identifies the request (load or store), b is the address of the block, and l is the extent of the block. The arbitration algorithm schedules requests sitting in the wait queue buffer with a particular performance goal in mind. The algorithm needs to guarantee that bus starvation will not occur.

3.1 Traditional Algorithms

A number of different arbitration algorithms have been used in microprocessor system bus designs. The simplest algorithm is *First Come First Serve* (FCFS). In this algorithm, requests are granted on the bus based on the order of arrival. This algorithm simply removes contention on the external bus without any optimization and pre-knowledge of the system configuration. Because FCFS schedules the bus naively, the system performs poorly due to instruction and data cache stalls. The priority of cache accesses and DMA access are equal (though cache accesses tend to be more performance critical than DMA accesses). An alternative is to have a *Fixed Priority* scheme where cache accesses are assigned higher priority than DMA accesses. For different DMA accesses, peripheral DMA accesses will have higher priority than memory DMA accesses. This differentiation is needed because if a peripheral device access is held off for a long period of time, it could cause the peripheral to lose data or time out. The Fixed Priority scheme selects the request with highest priority in the waiting queue instead of just selecting the oldest. Using Fixed Priority may provide similar external bus performance as the FCFS algorithm, but the overall system performance should be better if the application is dominated by cache accesses. For real-time embedded applications which are dominated by DMA accesses, cache accesses can be tuned such that cache misses are infrequent. Cache fetches can be controlled to occur only at non-critical times using cache prefetching and locking mechanisms. Therefore, for real-time embedded applications, the FCFS and Fixed Priority schemes produce very similar external bus behavior.

3.2   Power Aware Algorithms

To achieve efficient external bus performance, FCFS and Fixed Priority are not sufficient. Power and speed are two major factors of bus performance. In previous related work, dynamic external bus arbitration and scheduling decisions were primarily driven by bus performance and memory bandwidth [17,18]. If a power-efficient arbitration algorithm is aware of the power and cycle costs associated with each bus request in the queue, each request can be scheduled to achieve more balanced power/performance. The optimization target can be to minimize power P, minimize delay D, or more generally to minimize $P^n D^m$. Power P is measured as average power consumption for each external bus request, delay D is the average bus access request delay and $P^n D^m$ products of both measurements. This problem can be formulated as a shortest Hamiltonian path (SHP) on a properly defined graph. The Hamiltonian path is defined as the path in a directed graph that visits each vertex exactly once, without any cycles. The shortest Hamiltonian path is the Hamiltonian path that has the minimum weight. The problem is NP-complete, and in practice, heuristic methods are used to solve the problem [19].

Let R_0 denote the most recently serviced request on the external bus. R_1, R_2, ... R_L are the requests in the wait queue. Each request R_i consists of four elements (t_i, s_i, b_i, l_i), representing the arrival time, the access type (load/store), the starting address, and the access length. The bus power and delay are dependent on the current bus state and the following bus state for each request. The current bus state is the state of the bus after the previous bus access has completed. $P(i, j)$ represents the bus power dissipated for request R_j, given R_i was the immediate past request. $D(i, j)$ is the time between when request R_j is issued and when R_j is completed, where R_i was the immediate past request. The cost associated with scheduling request R_j after request R_i can be formulated as $P^n(i, j) D^m(i, j)$. We can define a directed graph $G = (V, E)$ whose vertices are the requests in the wait queue, with vertex 0 representing the last request completed. The edges of the graph include all pairs (i, j). Each edge is assigned

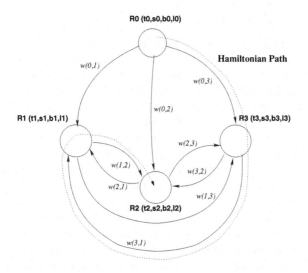

Fig. 3. Hamiltonian Path Graph

a weight $w(i, j)$, and is equal to the power delay product of processing request R_j after request R_i.

$$w(i, j) = P^n(i, j)D^m(i, j), n, m = 0, 1, ... \qquad (2)$$

The problem of optimal bus arbitration is equivalent to the problem of finding a Hamiltonian path starting from vertex 0 in graph G with a minimum path traversal weight. Figure 3 describes a case when there are 3 requests are in the wait queue. One of the Hamiltonian paths is illustrated with a dot line. The weight of this path is $w(0, 3) + w(3, 1) + w(1, 2)$. For each iteration, a shortest Hamiltonian path will be computed to produce the minimum weight path. The first request after request R_0 on that path will be the request selected in next bus cycle. After the next request is completed, a new graph will be constructed and a new minimum Hamiltonian path will be found.

Finding the shortest Hamiltonian path has been shown to be NP-complete. To produce a shortest path, we use heuristics. Whenever the path reaches vertex R_i, the next request R_k with minimum $w(i, k)$ will be chosen. This is a greedy algorithm, which selects the lowest weight for each step. The bus arbitration algorithm only selects the second vertex on that path. We avoid searching the full Hamiltonian path, and so the bus arbitration algorithm can simply select a request based on finding the minimum $w(0, k)$ from request R_0. The complexity of this heuristic is $O(L)$. When $w(i, j) = P(i, j)$, arbitration will try to minimize power. When $w(i, j) = D(i, j)$, then we can minimize delay. To consider the power efficiency, the power delay product can be used. Selecting different values for n and m change how we trade off power with delay using weights $w(i, j)$.

3.3   Target Architecture

In our experimental study, we used a power model of the Analog Devices Blackfin processor as our primary system model. We run code developed for ADSP-BF533 Blackfin EZ-Kit Lite board using the VisualDSP++ toolset. This board provides a 500 MHz ADSP-BF533 Blackfin processor, 16 MB of SDRAM, and a CCIR-656 video I/O interface. Inside the ADSP-BF533 Blackfin processor, there are both L1 instruction and data caches. The instruction cache is 16 KB 4-way set associative. The data cache is 16 KB 2-way set associative. Both caches use a 32 byte cache line size. The SDRAM module selected is the Micron MT48LC16M16A2 16 MB SDRAM. The SDRAM interface connects to 128 Mbit SDRAM devices to form one 16 MB of external memory. The SDRAM is organized in 4 banks, with a 1 KB page size. It also has following characteristics to match the on-chip SDRAM controller specification: 3.3V supply voltage, 133 MHz operating frequency, burst length of 1, column address strobe (CAS) latency t_{CAS} of 3 system clock cycles, t_{RP} and t_{RCD} equal to 2 system clock cycles, refresh rate programmed at 4095 system clock cycles. We used the Analog Devices Blackfin frio-eas-rev0.1.7 toolkit to integrate this model. The power model has been validated with physical measurements as described in [20]. To make sure the arbitration algorithm does not produce long-term starvation, a time-out mechanism was added for the requests. The timeout values for cache and memory DMA are 100 and 550 cycles, respectively.

Table 1. Benchmark descriptions and Cache Configuration

Name	Description	ICache Size	DCache Size
MPEG2-ENC	MPEG-2 Video encoder with 720x480 4:2:0 input frames.	16k	16k
MPEG2-DEC	MPEG-2 Video decoder of 720x480 sequence with 4:2:2 CCIR frame output.	16k	16k
JPEG-ENC	JPEG image encoder for 512x512 image.	8k	8k
JPEG-DEC	JPEG image decoder for 512x512 image.	8k	8k
PGP-ENC	Pretty Good Privacy encryption and digital signature of text message.	8k	4k
PGP-DEC	Pretty Good Privacy decryption of encrypted message.	8k	4k
G721-ENC	G.721 Voice Encoder of 16bit input audio samples.	4k	2k
G721-DEC	G.721 Voice Decoder of encoded bits.	4k	2k

4   Experimental Setup

4.1   Benchmarks

Experiments were run on a set of multimedia workloads. We chose MPEG-2 for video processing, JPEG for image compression, PGP for cryptography and

G721 for voice coding. All four benchmark suites are representative and commonly used applications for multimedia processing. For each benchmark, we used different cache configurations as shown in Table 1 in order to drive reasonable amount of external bus traffic.

MPEG-2 is the dominant standard for high-quality digital video transmission and DVD. We selected real-time MPEG-2 encoder and decoder source codes that include optimized Blackfin MPEG-2 libraries. The input datasets used are the *cheerleader* for encoding (the size is 720x480 and the format is interlaced video) and *tennis* for decoding (this image is encoded by the MPEG-2 reference encoder, the size is also 720x480, and the format is progressive video). Both inputs are commonly used by the commercial multimedia community.

JPEG is a standard lossy compression method for full color images. The JPEG encoder and decoder used also employ optimized Blackfin libraries. The input image is Lena (the size is 512x512 in a 4:2:2 color space).

PGP stands for *Pretty Good Privacy*, and provides for encryption and signing data. The signature we use is a 1024 bit cryptographically-strong one-way hash function of the message (MD5). To encrypt data, PGP uses a block-cipher IDEA and RSA for key management and digital signature.

G721 is specified in ITU recommendation G.721. G.721 is a 32kbps ADPCM (Adaptive Differential Pulse Code Modulation) voice compression algorithm. For G.721 encoder, we use 16bit audio input PCM samples called *clinton.pcm*, which is included in the MediaBench test suite. For G.721 decoder, the encoded file *clinton.g721* was fed into the decoder and output 16bits PCM samples.

In order to measure the external bus power and be able to assess the impact of our power-efficient bus arbitration algorithm, we developed the following simulation framework. First, we modified the Blackfin instruction-level simulator to include the system bus model and cache activity. From this model, we feed all accesses generated on the external bus to an EBIU model. The EBIU model faithfully simulates the external bus behavior, capturing detailed SDRAM state transitions and allows us to considered different bus arbitration schemes. The average bus power and performance are computed from the simulation results produced by our integrated simulator.

4.2   Results

There are eleven different bus arbitration schemes evaluated in our simulation environment. We considered two traditional schemes: (1) Fixed Priority (FP), (2) First Come First Serve (FCFS), and 9 different power-aware schemes. For Fixed Priority, we assign the following priority order (from highest to lowest): instruction cache, data cache, PPI DMA, SPORT DMA, memory DMA. In the power-aware schemes, each scheme is represented by the pair of power/delay coefficients (n, m) of the arbitration algorithm. n and m are the exponents shown in Equation 2. Different n and m values will favor either power or delay. $(1, 0)$ is the minimum power scheme, $(0, 1)$ is the minimum delay scheme, and $(1, 1), (1, 2), (2, 1), (1, 3), (2, 3), (3, 2), (3, 1)$ consider a balance between power and delay by using different optimization weights. We present experimental results for both power and delay. The MPEG-2 encoder and decoder simulation results are shown in Figure 4, JPEG encoder and decoder are shown in Figure 5, PGP encryptor and decryptor are shown in Figure 6 and G.721 voice encoder and decoder are shown in Figure 7. All the experiments consider both sequential command mode SDRAM and pipelined command mode SDRAM.

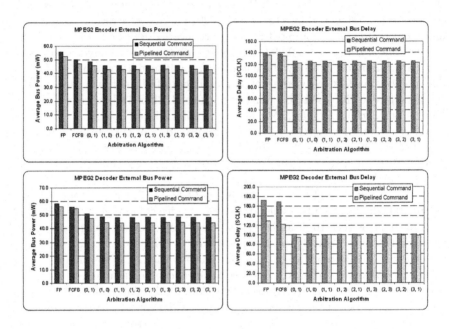

Fig. 4. External bus power/delay results for MPEG-2 video encoder and decoder

In all applications, the power dissipation for the power-aware arbitration schemes is much lower when compared to using Fixed Priority or FCFS. The power-aware schemes also benefit from fewer bus delays. These conclusions are consistent across all of the applications studied and are also consistent when using either sequential command SDRAM or pipelined command SDRAM. In the MPEG-2 case, the power-aware scheme (1, 0) enjoys an 18% power savings relative to a Fixed Priority scheme for encoder and 17% for decoder. The same power-aware scheme also achieved a 41% reduction in cycles when compared to the Fixed Priority scheme on MPEG-2 decoder, and a 10% reduction for MPEG-2 encoder.

To factor out the impact of sequential versus pipelined command mode from the power savings, we show in Table 2 the bus power savings. In Table 3 we show the cycle savings. Inspecting the two tables, we can see that the power-aware arbitration scheme achieves an average power savings of 14% and an average speedup of 21% over all eight applications. There exist some variations in the amount of power savings and speed up achieved. These variations are primarily

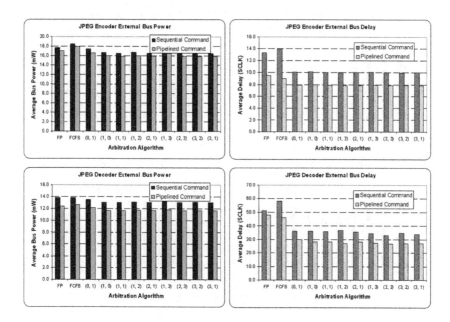

Fig. 5. External bus power/delay for JPEG image encoder and decoder

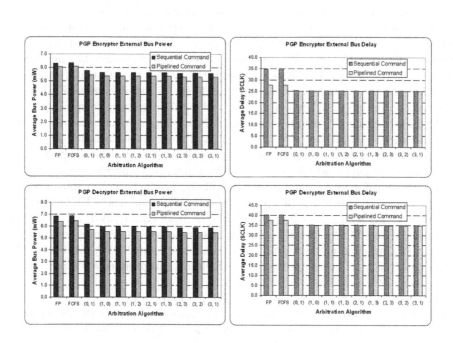

Fig. 6. External bus power/delay for PGP encryption and decryption

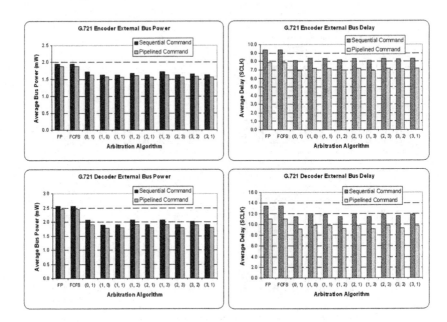

Fig. 7. External bus power/delay for G.721 Voice Encoder and Decoder

due to differences in bus utilization across the different applications. For high traffic applications, external memory access requests are more bursty, In those cases, our power-aware schemes provide a larger improvement than in low traffic applications, in which the requests are less bursty. The greater the number of requests in the queue, the greater the opportunity that the arbitrator can effect an improvement. Similarly, in Tables 4 and 5, the pipelined command SDRAM obtains on average a 15% power savings and a 16% performance speedup.

From inspecting the results shown in Tables 2-5, we can see that the choice of selecting sequential over pipelined command modes is not a factor when considering the performance impact of the bus arbitration algorithm. However, the pipelined command mode does decrease the request delay period by overlapping bus command stall cycles with other non-collision producing commands. Pipelining also helps to reduce the bus power by using one command's PRECHARGE or ACTIVATE stall cycles to prepare for the next READ/WRITE command (versus sending NOP commands). Table 6 summarizes the results between the sequential command mode and pipelined command mode SDRAMs. The results show that the pipelined command mode SDRAM can produce a 6% power savings and a 12% speedup.

Comparing the results across the different power-efficient schemes, we can see that the performance differences are insignificant. For all of the nine power-aware arbitration configurations modeled, there is no one scheme that clearly provides advantages over the rest. From our experimental results, we find that the

Table 2. External bus power savings of (1, 0) arbitration vs. fixed priority arbitration in sequential command SDRAM

	Fixed priority power (mW)	Arbitration (1, 0) Power (mW)	Power savings (%)
MPEG2-ENC	55.85	45.94	18%
MPEG2-DEC	58.47	48.62	17%
JPEG-ENC	17.64	16.57	6%
JPEG-DEC	13.77	12.99	6%
PGP-ENC	6.33	5.66	11%
PGP-DEC	6.81	5.94	13%
G721-ENC	1.95	1.63	16%
G721-DEC	2.56	1.90	26%
Average Savings			14%

Table 3. External bus speedup of (1, 0) arbitration vs. fixed priority in sequential command SDRAM

	Fixed priority delay (SCLK)	Arbitration (1, 0) Delay (SCLK)	Speedup (%)
MPEG2-ENC	140.36	126.10	10%
MPEG2-DEC	171.94	101.52	41%
JPEG-ENC	13.30	10.19	23%
JPEG-DEC	51.22	36.04	30%
PGP-ENC	34.87	25.21	28%
PGP-DEC	40.28	35.22	13%
G721-ENC	9.37	8.36	11%
G721-DEC	13.38	11.96	11%
Average Speedup			21%

minimun power approach and maximum speed approach have similar or equivalent effects when considering external memory bus optimizations. Even though an optimization approach is only focused on decreasing power consumption, the associated bus request access delay will decrease accordingly. Conversely, a speed optimization algorithm will increase the power performance as well. This fact will afford us the option to use power-oriented algorithms to optimize speed and power performance, which can lead to simpler and more efficient hardware implementations than those driven by speed alone.

5 Implementation Consideration

From our study of different hardware implementations for power-aware arbitration algorithms, we found that the (1, 0) scheme (i.e., the minimum power approach) was actually most favorable with regards to design implementation. The (1, 0) scheme involves several Hamming distance (XOR) computation units and integer adders to form a basic module for power estimation. The design also requires a power estimation unit (PEU) and multi-port integer comparator to select the minimum power request. Each power estimation unit (PEU) takes the current external memory state and address bus pin state as one input source.

Table 4. External bus power savings of (1, 0) arbitration vs. fixed priority arbitration in pipelined command SDRAM

	Fixed Priority Power (mW)	Arbitration (1, 0) Power (mW)	Power savings (%)
MPEG2-ENC	52.51	42.84	18%
MPEG2-DEC	56.29	44.58	21%
JPEG-ENC	16.97	15.93	6%
JPEG-DEC	12.41	11.68	6%
PGP-ENC	6.05	5.39	11%
PGP-DEC	6.40	5.54	13%
G721-ENC	1.89	1.57	17%
G721-DEC	2.44	1.78	27%
Average Savings			15%

Table 5. External bus speedup of (1, 0) arbitration vs. fixed priority in pipelined command SDRAM

	Fixed priority delay (SCLK)	Arbitration (1, 0) Delay (SCLK)	Speedup (%)
MPEG2-ENC	136.73	122.79	10%
MPEG2-DEC	128.82	97.57	24%
JPEG-ENC	9.50	7.93	16%
JPEG-DEC	48.02	28.20	41%
PGP-ENC	27.61	24.92	10%
PGP-DEC	37.34	34.78	7%
G721-ENC	7.88	7.17	9%
G721-DEC	10.98	9.88	10%
Average Speedup			16%

The other input is the request of interest that resides in the request queue. The memory/bus state includes the last bank address, the open row address (page address) for each bank and the last column address. Each of these states is updated after all memory access commands have been sent out to the external bus. In our case, we assume SDRAM is our memory technology, so the last bank address and row addresses are part of the state information for there SDRAM controller. Therefore, those fields can be shared between the power estimation unit and a SDRAM controller.

There are three steps to complete a power estimation. First, if the bank address is not equal to last bank address, a bank miss power number will be generated and sent to the accumulator. Second, we use the bank address as an index to inspect the open row address. If the row address is not the same as the next row address, a row miss (page miss) penalty power will be sent to the accumulator. The power penalty includes the SDRAM PRECHARGE command power and ACTIVATE command power. If a row address is sent to the bus, the

Table 6. Power and speed improvement comparison for pipelined vs. sequential command mode SDRAM over six benchmarks

	Avg. power in sequential mode (mW)	Avg. power in pipelined mode (mW)	Power saving of pipelined commands (%)	Avg. delay sequential mode (SCLK)	Avg. delay in pipelined mode (SCLK)	Speedup of in pipelined commands (%)
MPEG2-ENC	47.45	44.40	6%	128.31	124.99	3%
MPEG2-DEC	50.13	46.64	7%	113.38	103.38	9%
JPEG-ENC	16.86	16.26	4%	10.68	8.10	24%
JPEG-DEC	13.21	11.89	10%	38.74	31.28	19%
PGP-ENC	5.78	5.50	5%	26.95	25.40	6%
PGP-DEC	6.11	5.70	7%	36.09	35.25	2%
G721-ENC	1.71	1.64	4%	8.47	7.23	15%
G721-DEC	2.08	1.95	6%	11.99	9.80	18%
Avg. Gain			6%			12%

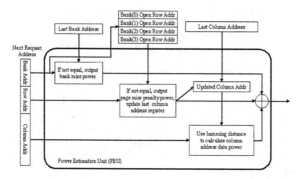

Fig. 8. Block Diagram of Power Estimation Unit(PEU)

address bus pin state will be changed. The last column address register needs to be updated, because the row address and the column address share the same bus pins. The third step involves comparing the last column address and the next column address to calculate the bus power due to switching in the column addresses. The major hardware component in this third step is the Hamming distance calculator. Finally, all the power is accumulated and output as an estimated power number. The data flow diagram for our power estimation unit (PEU) is shown in Figure 8.

Our power estimation unit(PEU) becomes a basic element for power-aware arbitrator. Figures 9 and 10 show two possible hardware designs of the (1, 0) power-aware arbitrator. They both contain three major components: 1) a request queue, 2) a minimum power comparator (which include one more more power estimation units), and 3) a memory access command generator (in our case, an SDRAM controller). As memory accesses arrive, they allocate storage space while waiting for service in the request queue. The power estimator computes a

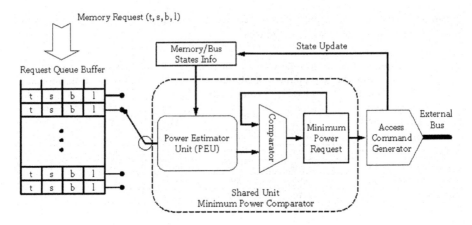

Fig. 9. Shared power estimator unit (1, 0) power-aware bus arbitrator architecture

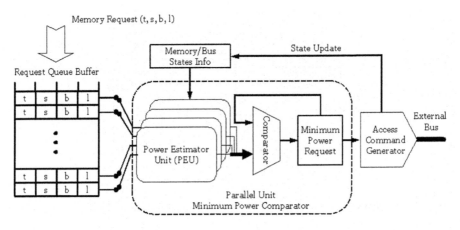

Fig. 10. Dedicated power estimator unit (1, 0) power-aware bus arbitrator architecture

latest request's power relative to the previous request. The comparator selects the minimum power request and stores it. When the currently active request finishes, the access with the lowest power requirements will be sent to the bus by the access command generator. The command generator also update the memory/bus state information register, which will be used to perform request selection in the next cycle.

The only difference between these two designs are the number of power estimation units (PEUs). Figure 9 has only one PEU. Power estimation is performed serially for each request in the queue. All requests will share the same power estimator logic. By sharing this structure, hardware complexity is reduced, but this can also introduce some extra delay due to limited computational resources. For instance, if the number of requests in the request queue is high, and the power estimation unit (PEU) cannot complete all estimations before the pre-

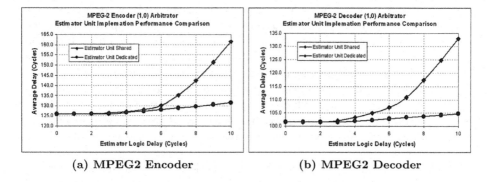

(a) MPEG2 Encoder   (b) MPEG2 Decoder

Fig. 11. MPEG2 benchmark shared/dedicated implementation performance

vious request finishes, the bus will insert idle commands until next request is ready. The bus idle cycle will increase the average request access delay. To minimize the probability of encountering idle bus cycles, multiple power estimation units can be used to performance the estimation job. In Figure 10, one power estimation unit(PEU) is dedicated to each slot in the request queue so that the power estimation task can be executed in parallel. The estimated power number for all requests in the queue will be ready at the same time. The hardware cost for providing such replication in the estimator design is much higher than the shared architecture, but the replication will result in better performance.

To investigate the performance differences between a shared and a dedicated PEU design, we implemented both designs and ran the MPEG-2 encoder and decoder benchmarks. Figures 11 shows the experimental results. As we can see, the average delay will increase for both shared and dedicated architectures when the logic delay for each power estimation unit (PEU) increases. However, when the PEU logic delay is 5 system clock cycles or higher, the performance degradation for the shared architecture become quite unacceptable. This is true in the results for both the MPEG-2 encoder and decoder. Therefore, if the latency of the PEU is less than 5 clock cycles, designers could consider sharing the PEU architecture. If the latency is higher, a dedicated architecture should be considered to avoid severe performance degradation.

6   Conclusions

Memory bandwidth has become a limiting factor in the design of high performance embedded computing. For future multimedia processing systems, bandwidth and power are both critical issues that need to be addressed. With memory speed and bus capacitance continually increasing, accesses on the external bus consume more and more of the total power budget on a system-on-a-chip embedded system.

In this paper, we proposed a set of new external bus arbitration schemes that balance bus power and delay. Our experiments are based on modeling a system-on-a-chip (SOC) embedded multimedia architecture while running six multimedia benchmarks. A simulation framework has been set up to estimate the power due to the switching activity of the processor-to-memory buses. Based on this environment, a set of simulation results has been derived to demonstrate how the external bus arbitration schemes can impact the overall system power budget. Our research is based on our power estimation model associated with the system-level address and data buses which expand our capability to evaluate the effects of bus arbitration schemes. The power model uses SDRAM as an implementation entity, however, the over implementation is to preserve the generality of the proposed approach.

Our results show that significant power reductions and performance gains can be achieved using power-aware bus arbitration schemes compared to traditional arbitration schemes. We also considered the impact of using both sequential and pipelined SDRAM models. Finally, two hardware implementations of (1, 0) power-aware arbitrator, shared PEU architecture and dedicated PEU architecture are described and the experimentals of those two designs are presented to illustrate the trade-off between design complexity and performance.

References

1. Lahiri, K., Raghunathan, A., Lakshminarayana, G.: LOTTERYBUS: A new high-performance communication architecture for system-on-chip designs. In: Design Automation Conference. (2001) 15–20
2. Arteris: Arteris Network on Chip technologies (2005) http://www.arteris.net/.
3. STMicroelectronics: STNoC (ST Network on Chip) technologies (2005) http://www.st.com/.
4. Benini, L., De Micheli, G., Macii, E., Sciuto, D., Silvano, C.: Address bus encoding techniques for system-level power optimization. In: Proceedings of the Conference on Design, Automation and Test in Europe, IEEE Computer Society (1998) 861–867
5. Panda, P.R., Dutt, N.D.: Reducing address bus transitions for low power memory mapping. In: Proceedings of the 1996 European Conference on Design and Test, IEEE Computer Society (1996) 63
6. Analog Devices Inc. Norwood, MA: Engineer-to-Engineer Note EE-229: Estimating Power for ADSP-BF533 Blackfin Processors (Rev 1.0). (2004)
7. Givargis, T.D., Vahid, F., Henkel, J.: Fast cache and bus power estimation for parameterized system-on-a-chip design. In: Proceedings of the Conference on Design, Automation and Test in Europe (DATE), ACM Press (2000) 333–339
8. Sotiriadis, P., Chandrakasan, A.: Low-power bus coding techniques considering inter-wire capacitances. In: Proceedings of IEEE Conference on Custom Integrated Circuits (CICC'00). (2000) 507–510
9. Tiwari, V., Malik, S., Wolfe, A.: Power analysis of embedded software: a first step towards software power minimization. IEEE Transactions on Very Large Scale Integration (VLSI) Systems **2** (1994) 437–445
10. Li, Y., Henkel, J.: A framework for estimating and minimizing energy dissipation of embedded hw/sw systems. (2002) 259–264
11. Lv, T., Henkel, J., Lekatsas, H., Wolf, W.: A dictionary-based en/decoding scheme for low-power data buses. IEEE Trans. Very Large Scale Integr. Syst. **11** (2003) 943–951

12. Stan, M., Burleson, W.: Bus-invert coding for low-power I/O. IEEE Transactions on Very Large Scale Integration (VLSI) Systems (1995) 49–58
13. Ning, K., Kaeli, D.: Bus power estimation and power-efficient bus arbitration for system-on-a-chip embedded systems. In: Workshop on Powre-Aware Computer Systems PACS'04, 37th Annual IEEE/ACM International Symposium on Microachitecture (2004)
14. Analog Devices Inc. Norwood, MA: ADSP-BF533 Blackfin Processor Hardware Reference (Rev 2.0). (2004)
15. Texas Instruments Inc. Dallas, Texas: OMAP5912 Multimedia Processor Device Overview and Architecture Reference Guide (Rev. A). (2004)
16. Sigma Designs, Inc. Milpitas, CA: EM8400: MPEG-2 Decoder for Set-top, DVD and Streaming Applications (Rev 01.09.03). (2003)
17. Rixner, S., Dally, W,J., Kapasi, U.J., Mattson, P., Owens, J.D.: Memory access scheduling. In: ISCA '00: Proceedings of the 27th Annual International Symposium on Computer Architecture, New York, NY, USA, ACM Press (2000) 128–138
18. Lyuh, C.G., Kim, T.: Memory access scheduling and binding considering energy minimization in multi-bank memory systems. In: DAC '04: Proceedings of the 41st Annual Conference on Design Automation, New York, NY, USA, ACM Press (2004) 81–86
19. Rubin, F.: A search procedure for hamilton paths and circuits. J. ACM **21** (1974) 576–580
20. VanderSanden, S., Gentile, R., Kaeli, D., Olivadoti, G.: Developing energy-aware strategies for the blackfin processor. In: Proceedings of Annual Workshop on High Performance Embedded Computing, MIT Lincoln Laboratory (2004)

Part 2

Optimizing Compilers

Introduction to Part 2

Current approaches to embedded compiler development are no longer sustainable. With each generation of embedded architecture, the development time increases and the performance improvement achieved decreases. As high-performance embedded systems move from application-specific integrated circuits to programmable multi-core parallel systems, this problem will become critical. This section of the volume investigates emerging alternative approaches to compiler construction exploring adaption, parallelization, speculation and automatic tuning.

The first paper by Nicholas Nethercote, Doug Burger and Kathryn S. McKinley investigates the idea of convergent compilation where optimization is refined on each specific compilation. This modification is based on a static evaluation of optimization effectiveness. When applied to loop unrolling on the TRIPS architecture, it automatically selects the best versions found by hand-tuning.

The second paper, by Harald Devos, Kristof Beyls, Mark Christiaens, Jan Van Campenhout, Erik H. D'Hollander, and Dirk Stroobandt, studies loop transformations, based on a polyhedral model, to better exploit FPGA. Important loops are detected in applications then refactored to finally issue VHDL code.

The third paper by Ghaffari Fakhreddine, Auguin Michel, Abid Mohammed, and Benjemaa Maher addresses the issue of partitioning code at run-time for soft real-time applications and an FPGA-based target. This method is particularly significant when the execution flow is dependent on the content of input data.

The fourth paper, by Shane Ryoo, Sain-Zee Ueng, Christopher I. Rodrigues, Robert E. Kidd, Matthew I. Frank, and Wen-mei W. Hwu, explores the impact that different static analysis techniques have, both in isolation and in conjunction, when used to automatically parallelize modern media applications. The paper then presents one case study using an MPEG-4 encoder.

Finally, the fifth paper, by Guilin Chen and Mahmut Kandemir, addresses the issue of minimizing the number of off-chip accesses in a chip-multiprocessor by ensuring that computations are organized such that adjacent cores that share data can share recently fetched values. The work is concerned with array transformations of stencil computations which are common in embedded applications.

Mike O'Boyle
University of Edinburgh

François Bodin
IRISA

Marcelo Cintra
University of Edinburgh

Guest editors
Transactions on HiPEAC

P. Stenström (Ed.): Transactions on HiPEAC I, LNCS 4050, p. 139, 2007.
© Springer-Verlag Berlin Heidelberg 2007

Convergent Compilation
Applied to Loop Unrolling*

Nicholas Nethercote, Doug Burger, and Kathryn S. McKinley

The University of Texas at Austin

Abstract. Well-engineered compilers use a carefully selected set of optimizations, heuristic optimization policies, and a phase ordering. Designing a single optimization heuristic that works well with other optimization phases is a challenging task. Although compiler designers evaluate heuristics and phase orderings before deployment, compilers typically do not statically evaluate nor refine the quality of their optimization decisions during a specific compilation.

This paper identifies a class of optimizations for which the compiler can statically evaluate the effectiveness of its heuristics and phase interactions. When necessary, it then modifies and reapplies its optimization policies. We call this approach *convergent compilation*, since it iterates to converge on high quality code. This model incurs additional compilation time to avoid some of the difficulties of predicting phase interactions and perfecting heuristics

This work was motivated by the TRIPS architecture which has resource constraints that have conflicting phase order requirements. For example, each atomic execution unit (a TRIPS block) has a maximum number of instructions (128) and a fixed minimum execution time cost. Loop unrolling and other optimizations thus seek to maximize the number of mostly full blocks. Because unrolling enables many downstream optimizations, it needs to occur well before code generation, but this position makes it impossible to accurately predict the final number of instructions. After the compiler generates code, it knows the exact instruction count and consequently if it unrolled too much or too little or just right. If necessary, convergent unrolling then goes back and adjusts the unroll amount accordingly and reapplies subsequent optimization phases. We implement convergent unrolling which automatically matches the best hand unrolled version for a set of microbenchmarks on the TRIPS architectural simulator.

Convergent compilation can help solve other phase ordering and heuristic tuning compilation challenges. It is particularly well suited for resource constraints that the compiler can statically evaluate such as register usage, instruction level parallelism, and code size. More importantly, these resource constraints are key performance indicators in embedded, VLIW, and partitioned hardware and indicate that convergent compilation should be broadly applicable.

* This work is supported by DARPA F33615-03-C-4106, DARPA NBCH30390004, NSF ITR CCR-0085792, NSF CCR-0311829, NSF EIA-0303609, and IBM. Any opinions, findings and conclusions are the authors' and do not necessarily reflect those of the sponsors.

P. Stenström (Ed.): Transactions on HiPEAC I, LNCS 4050, pp. 140–158, 2007.

1   Introduction

This paper introduces *convergent compilation* in which the compiler iteratively adjusts its optimization policies based on static self-evaluation.

1.1   Compiler Phase Ordering and Heuristic Design

Most compilers include numerous optimization phases. Because finding the optimal code transformation is often NP-complete, most optimizations use heuristic policies. Compiler writers typically tune individual heuristic policies experimentally, based on benchmark behaviors and optimization interactions with previous and subsequent phases. Since phases interact in complex ways, heuristics are not necessarily robust to changes made to another phase or due to phase reordering (e.g., when users specify optimization flags other than the default). To improve the design of individual heuristics, some researchers have turned to machine learning to tune transformation policies [1,2,3]. To solve the phase ordering problem, compilers have typically relied on a separation of concerns; they postpone handling resource constraints until the end of compilation. For instance, they assume infinite registers for most of compilation and perform register allocation near the end. Most compilers never evaluate during a specific compilation the quality of their upstream predictions. As more resources become constrained, this separation of concerns degrades the compiler's ability to produce high quality code due to the increasing difficulty of predicting how early decisions influence resource constraints.

Increasing hardware complexity is making this problem harder. For instance, shrinking technology increases clock-speed but exposes wire delays, causing less and less of the chip to be reachable in a single cycle [4]. To address this problem, architects are increasingly partitioning resources such as register banks, caches, ALUs (e.g., partitioned VLIW [5,6,7] and EDGE architectures [8,9]), and the entire chip (e.g., chip multiprocessors). Partitioning exposes on-chip latencies and resource constraints to the compiler and thus exacerbates the phase ordering problem and makes the separation of concerns solution with no subsequent static evaluation less appealing.

Convergent compilation was motivated by creating blocks full of useful instructions for the block atomic execution model in EDGE architectures. The TRIPS prototype EDGE architecture has a maximum block size of 128 instructions which the architecture maps at runtime on to a grid of 16 arithmetic units which each hold 8 instructions per block [8,9]. This array mapping has a fixed overhead. To amortize this overhead and maximize performance, the compiler tries to fill each block with useful instructions while minimizing the total number of blocks. For example, loop unrolling is one method the compiler uses to fill blocks. The compiler performs unrolling early to enable downstream optimizations such as redundant code elimination. However, if it unrolls too much, the resulting code has unnecessary blocks, and if it unrolls too little, each block is less efficient than it could be. Predicting the ideal unroll factor in a block early in the compilation cycle requires modeling down stream optimizations for each loop, and is thus virtually impossible.

A more conventional unrolling challenge tries to enables redundant code elimination and better scheduling while limiting instruction cache locality degredations and register spilling [10]. Spilling is almost always undesirable, since it increases (1) the number of instructions (loads and stores), (2) latency (two to three cycles in modern caches compared to single cycle register access), and (3) energy consumption due to the cache access. To gain the benefits of unrolling, compilers typically perform it well before register allocation and thus it is difficult for the unroller to predict how its decisions will affect register spilling.

1.2 Improving Optimization Quality

Previous solutions to solving the phase interaction problem include static evaluation of inlining's effect on other optimization phases [11] and iterated register allocation and instruction scheduling to resolve their tensions [12]. Both of these approaches require all participating phases to annotate and encode the results of their decisions. Thus, each phase must be appropriately engineered for all interacting optimizations, and must be cognizant of their phase ordering and influence on other optimization passes. Convergent compilation simplifies and generalizes over these approaches.

Instead of trying to model and perfect all the heuristics and phase interactions, convergent compilation improves one or more optimization heuristic by statically evaluating decisions after performing other interacting phases. If necessary, it then adjusts the heuristic for the particular code fragment and re-optimizes. More formally, given a sequence of ordered compilation phases $\{P_1, P_2, \ldots, P_n\}$, P_i records its optimization decisions. After some later phase P_k, $k > i$, a static evaluation phase P_{Eval_i} measures the effectiveness of P_i. If P_{Eval_i} decides P_i's decisions were poor, the compiler uses a checkpoint/rollback mechanism to reapply a modified P_i and subsequent phases by feeding back information from P_{Eval_i}'s static evaluation to help P_i adjust its heuristic and do a better job. To minimize the additional compile time, the compiler may choose a single optimization and iterate once, or to apply iteration only to key methods. To more thoroughly explore code quality sensitivities, the compiler may iterate on several key optimizations. Given repeated compilation of the same code, a repository could eliminate some of this overhead [13], or could enable the compiler to explore many phase interactions incrementally with modest per-compile overheads.

For example, in the TRIPS compiler we implement convergent unrolling (P_i) which checkpoints an intermediate representation, and records how many times it unrolls each loop. After other optimizations, the static evaluation phase (P_{Eval_i}) counts the instructions in a block. Assume the best unroll amount is n, if the compiler unrolls too little, P_{Eval_i} will go back and unroll more, if it unrolls too much, P_{Eval_i} will go back and unroll less. To roll back, the compiler discards the code fragments in question, reloads the checkpoint, improves the unroller's heuristic with the P_{Eval_i} feedback, invokes unrolling and subsequent phases.

Transformations that are suited to this approach must simply and statically record their decisions, and their corresponding evaluation function, P_{Eval_i}, must statically evaluate the resulting code quality. In unrolling, P_i records the number of iterations it unrolls, and the code generator (or a separate P_{Eval_i} phase) counts the instructions in a block. Suitable convergent optimizations include any that increase or change usage of limited resources (such as inlining, unrolling, register allocation, and scheduling), and have simple evaluation functions (such as instruction count, registers, loads/stores, or code size).

This paper makes the following contributions.

- Section 3 presents a convergent compilation model that simplifies and generalizes previous self-evaluating approaches. It mitigates the problem of selecting the perfect heuristic and phase ordering. It is suitable for both ahead-of-time and just-in-time compilation.
- Sections 4 and 5 shows convergent unrolling is effective for the TRIPS processor which is particularly sensitive to choosing the right unroll factor.
- Section 6 lists additional compiler transformations suited to this approach, and a useful variation called *convergent cloning*.

Although convergent compilation is motivated by our TRIPS compilation problems, it is applicable in many more settings. For instance, embedded programs have strict instruction space requirements and limited register files. Compilers for embedded processors could more easily assess the costs and benefits of code expanding (e.g., inlining, unrolling) and code size reduction (e.g., procedure abstraction, inlining) transformations with this approach.

2   Related Work

This section compares convergent compilation with related work on selecting good optimization heuristics, phase ordering, and other compiler feedback loops.

2.1   Designing Optimization Heuristics

The difficulty of designing good heuristics for individual optimizations is witnessed by a diversity of advanced approaches that to automate this process and search the optimization space [1,2,3,14,15]. For example, Cavazos and Moss use supervised learning to decide whether to schedule blocks in a Java JIT [3] and Cavazos et al. use code features to select between a linear scan or graph coloring register allocator [16]. Stephenson et al. use genetic algorithms to derive hyperblock formation, register allocation, and prefetching; and supervised learning for unrolling [1,2].

One difficulty for the learning algorithms is that they currently hold the rest of the compiler constant, thus learning one heuristic at a time. The convergent approach more naturally responds to changes in the other phases (which are numerous in our research compiler). This advantage may decrease in a production setting where phases change less frequently. Although we do not evaluate it, it may be possible to learn an unrolling heuristic that produces similar code quality to convergent unrolling. However, it is more likely that these approaches are complementary. Convergent compilation may produce better code starting with a "one-size-fits-all" learned heuristic and then further specializing for the specific program. Prior results that compare self and cross program learning [3,1,2] indicate that this specialization will improve performance.

2.2   Phase Interactions

The most closely related work performs static self-evaluation, but is not as general convergent compilation or requires more pervasive changes to the compiler [11,12]. Brasier et al. use a static feedback loop to reduce the antagonism between instruction scheduling and register allocation in a system called CRAIG [12]. It first performs instruction scheduling followed by register allocation; if it spills too much, it starts over and does register allocation before performing incremental instruction scheduling, moving towards late assignment. CRAIG thus reorders phases and refines its scheduling heuristic based on spill feedback. Convergent compilation generalizes beyond these two closely related phases by communicating more information across more phases.

Dean and Chambers use inlining trials to avoid designing a heuristic that models the exposed optimization opportunities for subsequent phases [11]. After inlining, each subsequent phase must carefully track how inlining influenced its decisions. If inlining does not enable optimizations that reduce the resulting code size (a static measure), the compiler reverses the inlining decision, recompiles the caller, and records the decision to prevent future inlining of this method and similar ones. This approach is limited because it requires changes to all subsequent phases for each optimization it wishes to evaluate. Section 6 describes how convergent inlining eliminates the need to change all intervening phases.

2.3   Iterative Compilation

Iterative compilation seeks to evaluate the extent of the phase ordering problem and to improve over default orderings. Iterative compilation reorders, repeats,and omits phases to empirically evaluate hundreds or thousands of compile-execute sequences to find the configuration that produces the fastest or smallest code for a particular program. Results show that default compiler phase orderings and settings are far from optimal [17,18,19,20,21,22]. Because the configuration space is huge, researchers use search techniques such as genetic algorithms and simulated annealing to reduce the number of compile-execute cycles and still attain benefits. For example, Lau et al. use performance measurement to select the best performing among a small set of pre-computed optimization strategies [23].

Convergent compilation is more robust to compiler changes (e.g., changing a policy or adding a heuristic), whereas iterative compilation must perform all the trials after any changes. However, convergent compilation could be a component of a system that attains benefits of phase selection and heuristic tuning at a reduced cost by using static objective functions. In fact, Triantafyllis et al. propose a compiler optimization-space exploration system that uses an iterative approach, but aggressively prunes the program to its most critical components based on dynamic behavior and then compares program versions using static performance estimation to reduce compile-time [22]. Performance estimation is a general approach. Convergent compilation instead couples optimization objective functions which are easy to measure with the final code quality on key resources such as register usage, instruction counts for blocks, and instruction level parallelism. Although we demonstrate only instruction counts for blocks with unrolling, many heuristic objective functions, such as adding spills to the register allocator is correlated with performance.

2.4   Feedback-Directed Optimization

Smith defines feedback-directed optimizations (FDO) [24,25,26,27,13] as a family of techniques that alter a program's execution based on tendencies observed in its present or past runs. FDO is orthogonal to convergent compilation since FDO typically uses dynamic edge, path, or method profiling to select which code to optimize, and to guide heuristics. Arnold et al. add a repository to combine online and offline (previously profiled) optimization plans that incorporate the costs and benefits of online optimization [13]. Convergent compilation instead feeds back static evaluations, e.g., code size or register usage, and then adjusts heuristics to avoid phase ordering problems, all without ever executing the program. Convergent compilation and FDO are thus complementary.

3   Convergent Compilation

This section describes convergent compilation in two parts. First, it explains its most general form for use in an ahead-of-time compiler. Second, it discusses three specific instances of the general approach, with different simplicity and compile-time trade-offs.

3.1   Convergent Compilation in the Abstract

Convergent compilation involves the following compiler phases.

P_{CP}:   Checkpoints code fragments (e.g. saves them to memory or file).

P_i: Transforms/optimizes the code using a heuristic.

P_{Eval_i}: Evaluates the effectiveness of the P_i transformation.

P_{LB}:   Determines if the current code fragment is acceptable or should be recompiled with a modified heuristic, based on the results of P_{Eval_i} and the number of times P_i has executed.

P_{RB}:   Rolls back to a checkpointed code fragment.

Figure 1 gives the pseudocode for the most general form of convergent compilation. Figure 2 shows its control flow and data flow in a diagram. The approach involves two main loops. The inner loop is the heart of convergent compilation. It processes one code fragment at a time, where a fragment could be a loop, a procedure, or a module. It performs the transformation phase P_i and subsequent phases, then runs P_{Eval_i} to evaluate P_i's decisions. It uses P_{RB} to roll back the

```
run pre(P_CP) on all fragments (e.g., loop, module, etc.)          1
for each fragment F                                                 2
    F_info := (empty);   N := 0                                     3
    run P_CP on F                                                   4
    while (true)                                                    5
        run between(P_CP, P_i) on F                                 6
        run P_i on F, using F_info if non-empty                     7
        run between(P_i, P_Eval_i) on F                             8
        if N < the loop limit                                       9
            run P_Eval_i on F, and record F_info                   10
        run between(P_Eval_i, P_LB) on F                           11
        run P_LB: if (N = loop limit or F evaluated ok)            12
            exit inner loop                                        13
        run P_RB on F                                              14
        N := N + 1                                                 15
    run post(P_LB) on all fragments                                16
```

Fig. 1. Convergent Compilation Pseudocode. $pre(P)$ gives the phases that precede P; $between(P, Q)$ gives the phases between P and Q; $post(Q)$ gives the phases that come after Q

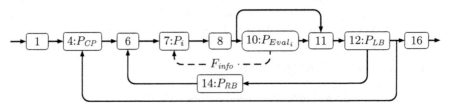

Fig. 2. Control flow of convergent compilation. Solid lines represent control flow, dashed lines represent data flow. The number labels correspond to pseudocode line numbers in Figure 1.

fragment to the version checkpointed by P_{CP} if necessary, and repeats until the fragment F is deemed "good enough," or it reaches a limit on its number of iterations (shown as the edge that skips P_{Eval_i}). The outer loop iterates through the code fragments one at a time.

P_i and P_{Eval_i} interact in three key ways. First, P_i must indicate to P_{Eval_i} what decisions it made. P_i annotates the code with this information. In our example, P_i identifies unrolled loops and their unroll factor. Second, P_{Eval_i} must be able to meaningfully evaluate P_i's decisions. P_{Eval_i} must include a static measurement that evaluates code quality. A simple example is "this unrolled loop has too many spills." Any performance improvements depend on the accuracy of P_{Eval_i}'s evaluations. Third, P_{Eval_i} should help P_i improve its decisions on any rejected fragment. In our example, P_{Eval_i} could indicate that the chosen unroll factor was too high (e.g., more blocks than necessary and an under-full block) or too low (e.g., one under-full with room for more unrolled iterations), or just right. If needed, the unrolling heuristic adjusts the unroll factor accordingly. Figure 2 depicts this information flow with a dashed line.

Thus far we have discussed using one P_i/P_{Eval_i} pair, but the compiler can use more. For example, one could employ a single large inner loop: perform all the P_i transformations on a fragment, then evaluate each P_{Eval_i}, and if any transformations were unsatisfactory, loop back and adjust them. This structure requires only checkpointing once, but performs all P_i phases even if only a single P_{Eval_i} evaluation failed. Alternatively, one could employ more checkpointing and have multiple inner loops, which might overlap or be entirely separate. The best configuration would depend on how the different P_i phases interact and the increase in compile time the system is willing to tolerate.

3.2   Instantiating Convergent Compilation

We can partially or fully instantiate this general convergent compilation framework by specifying some or all of its parameters: the size of each fragment F, the loop limit N, the workings of the phases P_i, P_{Eval_i}, P_{CP}, P_{RB}, P_{LB}, and the phases present in each of $pre(P_{CP})$, $between(P_{CP}, P_i)$, $between(P_i, P_{Eval_i})$, $between(P_{Eval_i}, P_{LB})$ and $post(P_{LB})$. The following paragraphs describe three such general instances of a single convergent optimization, and Section 4 presents convergent unrolling.

A complex but efficient instance of a convergent optimization. Code fragments are procedures, and the inner loop executes at most twice. P_{CP} and P_{RB} are simple: P_{CP} saves a copy of a procedure in memory, and P_{RB} discards the poorly optimized code and reverts to the saved code. The phase sequences $between(P_{CP}, P_i)$ and $between(P_{Eval_i}, P_{LB})$ are empty. We do not specify the other parameters—P_i, P_{Eval_i}, $pre(P_{CP})$, $between(P_i, P_{Eval_i})$ and $post(P_{LB})$—so this instance still has some generality.

This instance is efficient—it minimizes the number of phases that execute repeatedly, and the small fragment size reduces the cost of individual phase times and the size of the checkpoint. However, it requires some structural support in the compiler, e.g., the ability to run multiple phases in succession on a single procedure. Procedures are a good general choice for fragments as they are typically not too big, but are still stand-alone units. Smaller units are possible, but require more work to merge fragments. The efficiency of this instance depends on how often P_i makes bad decisions; if it makes no bad decisions, it will not iterate at all.

A simpler instance. A variant of the first instance involves changing the size of the code fragments to an entire module, which effectively removes the outer loop. This structure is less efficient—checkpointing and possibly repeating phases for the entire module—but simpler to implement. Note that although the fragment size is a whole module, the heuristics are adjusted at a finer level. For example, with loop unrolling P_{Eval_i} will include information about every unrolled loop in F_{info}. If any of the loops in the module are rejected by P_{LB} the whole module is recompiled. As a result, the fragment size does not affect accuracy, only the amount of checkpointing and number repeated phases.

An easy-to-implement instance. Figure 3 shows a simple way to implement this approach in which the compiler executes twice. In the first pass P_{Eval_i} writes F_{info} for the whole module to a file. In the second pass P_i reads F_{info} from

First pass   Second pass

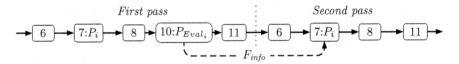

Fig. 3. Control flow of an easy-to-implement instance of convergent compilation. Solid lines represent control flow, dashed lines represent data flow. The number labels correspond to pseudocode line numbers in Figure 1.

this file and adjusts its decisions accordingly and P_{Eval_i} does not execute. Each code fragment is an entire module. P_{CP} and P_{RB} are no-ops; since the compiler runs twice, the original source code serves as the checkpoint. Both $pre(P_{CP})$ and $post(P_{LB})$ are empty.

This instance is an excellent way to trial convergent compilation in an existing compiler, since the only change needed is support for writing and reading the data file; a wrapper script can implement the inner loop. We implemented convergent unrolling exactly this way for our evaluation in Section 5. This structure sacrifices efficiency for simplicity by doubling compilation time.

4   Convergent Loop Unrolling for TRIPS

In this section, we review loop unrolling, describe the TRIPS architecture and the unique challenges it poses to the loop unroller, and explain how convergent unrolling helps to solve these problems.

4.1   Loop Unrolling

Loop unrolling is a common transformation which duplicates a loop's body one or more times. The *unroll factor* is the number of copies of the loop body in the final unrolled loop; an unroll factor of one means no unrolling. The simplest case is when the loop trip count is known statically and the unroll factor divides it evenly; the unrolled loop on the right has an unroll factor of three.

```
for (i = 0; i < 120; i++) {          for (i = 0; i < 118; i += 3) {
    b(i);                      =>         b(i);   b(i+1);   b(i+2);
}                                    }
```

We restrict this discussion to loops with sufficiently large trip counts, but the same framework flattens loops with small trip counts. If the loop trip count is known statically but the unroll factor does not divide it evenly, or the loop trip count is statically unknown but invariant, a "clean-up" loop performs the final few iterations. If the trip count is known statically, the clean-up loop can be flattened.

```
for (i = 0; i < n; i++) {            for (i = 0; i < n-2; i += 3) {
    b(i);                      =>         b(i);   b(i+1);   b(i+2);
}                                    }
                                     for ( ; i < n; i++) {
                                         b(i);
                                     }
```

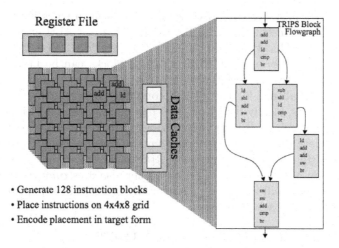

Fig. 4. The TRIPS prototype compilation target

Loop unrolling can improve program performance on traditional architectures in two ways. First, the unrolled loop requires fewer instructions, because there are fewer loop tests and backward branches, and in some forms, fewer updates of the index variable. On modern architectures, branch prediction and multiple issue mitigate these benefits, but the TRIPS block limit on instructions does benefit. Second and more importantly, unrolling enables other optimizations. For example, if the body loads or stores the same memory location on distinct adjacent iterations, scalar replacement can replace some memory accesses with register accesses. Loop unrolling also exposes instruction level parallelism (ILP) to static and dynamic instruction scheduling. The cost/benefit analysis for unrolling must also include the hard-to-model effect on code size which if increased too much degrades instruction cache performance, and increases in register pressure which cause spilling.

4.2   TRIPS

TRIPS is a prototype implementation of a new class of microprocessor architectures called EDGE (Explicit Data Graph Execution) designed to provide high performance and low power consumption in the face of technology trends such as increasing clock speed and increasing wire delays [8,9,28]. The prototype design is complete and working chips should be operational in 2006.

Unlike traditional architectures that operate at the granularity of a single instruction, EDGE architectures implement serial, block-atomic execution, mapping a block of instructions on to the ALU grid (as depicted in Figure 4), executing it atomically, committing it, and fetching the next block. Execution within blocks is dataflow; each instruction forwards its results directly to its consumers in that block without going through a shared register file (registers are only used for inter-block value passing). Each block orders its memory references to insure sequential consistency. Each block is a hyperblock—a single-entry, multiple-exit set of predicated basic blocks [29,30]—with some additional constraints [8].

In the TRIPS prototype, a key constraint is that each block is fixed-size and holds at most 128 instructions. Each ALU in the 4×4 ALU grid has up to 8 instructions in each block mapped onto it ($4 \times 4 \times 8 = 128$). Up to 16 instructions can execute per cycle, one per ALU. Up to 8 blocks can be in-flight at once (7 of them speculatively), resulting in a 1,024-wide instruction window.

The biggest challenge for the TRIPS compiler [9] is to create blocks full of useful instructions; ideally it will produce high quality blocks with close to 128 instructions, maximizing ILP and minimizing the fixed per-block execution overheads. To achieve this goal, the compiler's main tools are the use of predication to include multiple basic blocks in each TRIPS block (*hyperblock formation*), inlining, and loop unrolling. The TRIPS compiler also uses *convergent hyperblock formation* to create full blocks: it incrementally merges blocks, optimizes them, and if too full, rolls back [31].

4.3   Challenges for Loop Unrolling on TRIPS

To maximize TRIPS performance, the loop unroller would ideally produce loops containing exactly, or slightly fewer than, 128 instructions. Consider a loop with a known trip count of 120, in which each loop body has 31 instructions, and the loop test and exit are 4 instructions. If the unroll factor is 3, the block size is $31 \times 3 + 4 = 97$ instructions, and the loop will execute in 40 blocks. However, an unroll factor of 4 yields a block size of $31 \times 4 + 4 = 128$ instructions, and the loop will execute in only 30 blocks. If the size of the loop body is 32 instructions instead, an unroll factor of four produces a loop size of 132 instructions which requires two TRIPS blocks, and 60 block executions. An unroll factor of 2 produces this same result.

This example demonstrates that accurate instruction counts are vital for loop unrolling on TRIPS; in some cases, even underestimating the size of a loop body by one instruction can harm code quality. This example assumes that all duplicated loop bodies have the same size, but downstream optimizations like common subexpression elimination and test elision change the resulting code size further complicating the job of estimating the final number of instructions. The TRIPS compiler performs unrolling early in the optimization sequence because many optimizations, such as scalar replacement, further improve code quality after unrolling. Accurate instruction counts are not available to the unroller and become available only near the end of compilation.

4.4   Convergent Loop Unrolling

To solve this problem, we use a simple two-pass approach, as described in Section 3.2. In the first pass, the compiler performs the phases $pre(P_i)$ (represented by box 6 in Figure 3), which include parsing, inlining, and conversion to a static-single assignment, control-flow graph-based intermediate representation (IR). The loop unroller (P_i) then executes for the first time. For each candidate loop, it estimates the number of TRIPS instructions in the loop body (S_B), and the loop and exit tests (S_E) by examining each IR instruction in the loop. If $S_B + S_E > 128$, no unrolling takes place, otherwise it selects an unroll factor of

$U_1 = (128 - S_E)/S_B$. Loops that are larger than half a block are therefore never unrolled; we have experimented with trying to unroll to fit three loop bodies in two blocks, but with little success. One exception is that the unroller flattens loops with a known loop bound up to 512 instructions. Because flattened loops have no back edges, subsequent phases can easily merge them with surrounding blocks.

After unrolling, P_i marks the unrolled loops with the estimated sizes. The compiler then performs the phases in $between(P_i, P_{Eval_i})$ (box 8 in Figure 3), which in the TRIPS compiler include many optimizations (scalar replacement, constant propagation, global value numbering, etc.), code generation, and hyperblock formation. P_{Eval_i} then measures the actual sizes of the unrolled loops–accurate measurements are possible in this phase–and writes its measurements (F_{info}) to the data file. The final phases in $post(P_{Eval_i})$ then execute which include block splitting, register allocation, and instruction scheduling [9].

The second pass is like the first except P_i does not use IR-based loop size estimation. Instead, for each unrolled loop it reads from the data file (F_{info}) the measured size of the entire unrolled loop (S_L) and the loop test and exit (S_{E2}). It then estimates the size of each loop body as $S_{B2} = (S_L - S_{E2})/U_1$. This estimate is imperfect because all iterations in an unrolled loop are not always exactly the same size, but it improves over the IR-based estimate (Section 5.1 quantifies the difference). With this more accurate loop size estimate, it can now compute the new unroll factor, $U_2 = (128 - S_{E2})/S_{B2}$, and compilation continues to the end.

Convergent unrolling results in fuller TRIPS blocks, reducing the block execution count and speeding up programs, as the next section shows.

5   Evaluation

This section evaluates convergent unrolling's effectiveness in improving loop unrolling for TRIPS. Because TRIPS hardware is not yet available, we use a simulator for our experiments. It is cycle-accurate and slow, so we use only microbenchmarks for our evaluation. The suite consists of 14 microbenchmarks containing key inner loops extracted from SPEC2000, five kernels from an MIT Lincoln Laboratory radar benchmark (doppler_GMTI, fft2_GMTI, fft4_GMTI, transpose_GMTI, forward_GMTI), a vector add kernel (vadd), a ten-by-ten matrix multiply (matrix_1), and a discrete cosine transform (dct8x8). Because these benchmarks are all dominated by loops, the unrolling benefits should be large.

5.1   Goals

Convergent unrolling *statically* measures how full blocks are to *dynamically* reduce the number of blocks and thus execution time. Convergent unrolling therefore has three goals: 1) to improve the size estimates and thus produce fuller blocks; 2) to execute fewer blocks at runtime because each block is fuller; and thus 3) to speed up the program by a) exposing and exploiting more ILP

Table 1. Block and cycle results for unrolling. Column 1 gives the benchmark name. Column 2 (none) gives the number of blocks executed with no unrolling. Columns 3–5 give the percentage reduction in the number of blocks executed vs. no unrolling: column 3 (by 3) is default unrolling, column 4 (Est) is IR size estimation only, column 5 (CU) is convergent unrolling. Columns 6–9 give the corresponding cycle results.

		Unrolling Policies						
	Block Count Reduction				Cycle Count Reduction			
		%	%	%		%	%	%
	none	by 3	Est	CU	none	by 3	Est	CU
art_2	22061	66.3	66.3	84.9	504565	61.6	61.6	79.1
vadd	54334	84.0	84.1	84.1	439449	71.9	73.3	73.3
transpose_GMTI	78349	83.8	83.8	83.8	1027366	75.4	75.5	75.5
matrix_1	24665	81.5	81.5	81.5	383814	68.7	68.7	68.7
art_3	30051	49.9	76.8	80.9	443259	47.8	70.0	68.9
art_1	16651	64.3	66.2	78.9	233755	50.5	56.7	67.4
twolf_1	38631	53.7	65.3	76.6	689344	57.7	58.4	62.7
twolf_3	14051	49.8	49.7	66.3	673539	2.3	2.8	6.3
gzip_1	2395	32.9	54.7	57.3	24664	-10.1	-5.8	-2.3
bzip2_2	32911	44.7	51.7	52.5	426155	31.4	38.8	41.0
bzip2_1	15682	0.2	0.2	49.6	410409	30.9	31.2	39.5
doppler_GMTI	11190	43.8	12.5	37.5	396943	21.0	15.7	24.4
equake_1	16405	62.2	37.3	37.3	331378	55.1	43.9	43.9
gzip_2	8986	40.6	30.2	30.2	129110	48.5	31.7	31.7
forward_GMTI	11825	-5.1	13.5	13.5	392571	11.0	14.7	14.7
ammp_2	30951	5.5	16.5	11.0	910693	32.1	36.0	34.7
ammp_1	60751	0.0	8.9	8.9	1891762	0.0	-8.1	-8.1
dct8x8	3046	9.2	4.2	4.2	61756	11.8	41.2	41.2
parser_1	7051	-33.0	0.0	0.0	225255	11.6	6.1	0.0
bzip2_3	15531	0.0	-48.3	0.0	400906	14.0	-1.6	0.0
fft4_GMTI	9745	-9.2	-8.2	-8.2	142233	-8.8	-10.6	-10.6
fft2_GMTI	8378	-23.3	-9.5	-9.5	245022	-10.9	-2.7	-2.7
arith. mean		31.9	33.5	41.9		30.6	31.7	34.1

within a block and b) by fetching fewer blocks and thus reducing the time required to map blocks onto the ALU grid.

We measure static block size estimates, dynamic block executions, and execution times. We use as our straw-man unrolling by 3 which produces 4 loop bodies because we and others (e.g., gcc and the Alpha GEM compiler) have found it is a simple and reasonable heuristic for conventional architectures. We use the best intermediate representation (IR) estimator we were able to construct for our base TRIPS unroller, and then apply convergent unrolling to refine this estimator.

5.2   Results

Static Block Size Estimates. Convergent unrolling works well in improving the unroller's estimates of loop sizes, the first goal. The microbenchmark suite has 33 candidate loops. On the first pass, using the IR-based loop size estimator, the average relative error of this estimate was 61%. The errors include both under and overestimates. On the second pass, using the back end measurements of the resulting loop sizes, the average relative error was 6%. Most of the estimates by the second pass were within 1 or 2%; the worst result was a 24% underestimate. Poor final estimates correlated with the worst initial estimates, since the unroll factor chosen in the second pass was quite different from the first pass, and thus there was more room for error. Performing this cycle a third time attains small improvements, but is probably not worth the extra compilation time.

Dynamic Block and Cycle Results. Table 1 quantifies how well convergent unrolling achieves the second and third goals. We perform the following four experiments.

- No unrolling (none).
- Default unrolling (by 3): unroll by three for unknown loop bounds; for known bounds, flatten loops if the flattened size is fewer than 200 statements; otherwise choose an unroll factor based on an IR estimate.
- IR code estimation (Est): the compiler estimates the number of TRIPS instructions from the IR.
- Convergent unrolling corrected estimation (CU): uses the two-pass compiler structure and phases described above.

On average, convergent unrolling decreases the average number of blocks executed by 10% over the default unroller, and 8% over IR estimation (Est). It attains this result by substantial improvements over default unrolling on art_2, art_3, twolf_1, twolf_3, and bzip2_1, and avoiding the substantial degradations of IR estimation and default on parser_1, bzip2_3, and fft2_GMTI. For art_2 and art_3 the improvement is due to convergent unrolling using higher unroll factors (6 and 8 instead of 3) for loops with small bodies; for the others the improvement is caused by choosing lower unroll factors (e.g. 2 instead of 3, 3 instead of 6) for loops with larger bodies, so that the entire unrolled loop fits within one block. IR estimation is only marginally better than the default non-TRIPS-specific policy, which shows that the TRIPS-specific unrolling policy is of little use without convergent unrolling's accurate size estimates.

Although block counts are a good indicator of performance, they are not perfect (e.g., gzip_1 and ammp_1). The cycle count improvements with convergent unrolling are thus smaller than the block improvements. This result is due to architectural details that are beyond the scope of this paper. However, these results are more encouraging than they seem. Currently the TRIPS compiler does not perform instruction-level hyperblock optimizations, so the code it produces still has some "fat". Experiments with hand-coded microbenchmarks show that cycle count improvements due to loop unrolling increase as code quality goes up. For example, we have seen that better scalar replacement reduces twolf_3's run-time by around 20%.

Taken together, the dynamic block size and block execution results demonstrate that convergent unrolling can help bridge the phase ordering problem and provide improved heuristics for loop unrolling.

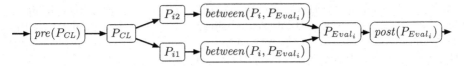

Fig. 5. Control flow of convergent cloning

6 Discussion

This section describes other potential convergent optimizations, mechanisms for mitigating increases in compilation time, and how to integrate convergent compilation into a JIT compiler.

6.1 Other Convergent Optimizations

This section describes other optimizations that interact with resource usage and are thus amenable to static evaluation.

- Loop unrolling can also increase register spilling. P_{Eval_i} could decide to reject any loop in which unrolling causes a register spill.
- We are also using this approach for convergent hyperblock formation in the TRIPS compiler [31]. When considering the inclusion of multiple basic blocks for a single TRIPS block, it is difficult to estimate the resulting block size beforehand because of subsequent optimizations (just like unrolling for block size). Instead, we optimistically and incrementally combine blocks, run the optimizations on the the resulting hyperblock, and roll back if it exceeds 128 instructions.

A variant we call *convergent cloning* removes the feedback loop but still uses static evaluation. Its control flow is shown in Figure 5. Instead of P_{CP} checkpointing the code, a cloning phase P_{CL} makes one or more temporary clones of a code fragment. P_i then operates in a different way on each clone. After the intervening phases operate on each clone, P_{Eval_i} then statically compares the clones and chooses the best one, discarding the others. This approach is most useful when P_i can choose between only a small number of possible transformations (e.g. whether to inline a particular procedure call or not). The following list gives some cases where this variation might be applicable.

- If P_i is an inliner, P_{Eval_i} could evaluate whether inlining increases register spills or bloats the code too much by comparing fragments in which calls were inlined and fragments in which they were not. This approach achieves a similar goal to inlining trials [11] but does not require the phases between P_i and P_{Eval_i} to track any additional information. This application is interesting for embedded platforms where code size is critical.
- Procedure abstraction—in which the compiler factors out matching code sequences into a procedure [32]—is sometimes used to reduce code size. However code size might increase if the register allocator must spill around the

call. Convergent cloning could choose the clone that did not have procedure abstraction applied if it ended up being smaller.

- The TRIPS compiler's back end estimates code size before splitting too-large blocks, as Section 4.3 described. Sometimes its estimates are inaccurate, partly because the compiler performs some optimizations (e.g. peephole optimizations) after block splitting, and partly because the estimation is conservative in various ways. Convergent cloning could select an unsplit block if it ends up fitting within 128 instructions.

- Vectorizing compilers targeting SIMD instruction sets will often unroll a loop by 2 or 4 with the goal of converting groups of scalar operations into single SIMD instructions. Scalar code in the loop body can prevent this transformation from working, in which case no unrolling is probably preferable, but it is difficult to predict at loop unrolling time. Convergent cloning could discard any unrolled loops that failed to be vectorized.

The common theme to these uses is that P_i transforms the code in a way that can result in better (faster and/or smaller) code, but puts stress on a limited machine resource such as registers or TRIPS block sizes. P_{Eval_i} then evaluates whether the increased resource stress is just right or too much or if more stress could be tolerated. However, the increases in compile time require judicious selection and application of convergent optimizations.

6.2 Just-In-Time and Interprocedural Compilation

Convergent compilation can be used as-is in a just-in-time (JIT) compiler. However, many JIT compilers use *staged dynamic optimization* on frequently executed code, also called *hotspot optimization*. This mechanism offers an opportunity to improve the efficiency of self-evaluation by eliminating the unnecessary recompilation. Instead, the JIT compiler can piggyback the inner loop phases P_{LB} and P_{RB} onto its existing recompilation loop. This formulation would also complement Arnold et al.'s repository for combining online and offline profiling in a JIT by providing more accurate benefit measurements [13].

Convergent optimizations would operate on the JIT's existing recompilation unit (e.g., methods) along with its existing P_{CP} and P_{RB} phases. When P_{Eval_i} evaluates P_i's decisions, rather than immediately rejecting substandard code, it records F_{info} (e.g., code size, register spills, etc.) and executes this initial version of the code. If a fragment is hot and worth recompiling, P_{RB} is invoked on it as usual, and P_i can use F_{info} to improve its heuristics during recompilation. This structure eliminates the additional compile-time cost that an ahead-of-time compiler must incur, requires no additional checkpointing cost (because it utilizes the JIT compiler's existing checkpointing mechanism), and still gains benefits for hot methods. The only addition required is the ability to record F_{info} (which is typically compact) for each code fragment.

Another important consideration for convergent compilation is interprocedural analysis. If the fragment size is less than a whole module, any interprocedural analysis must take place during $pre(P_{CP})$ or $post(P_{LB})$; any analysis between P_{CP} and P_{LB} might be invalidated by the per-fragment re-running of phases. This requirement is unlikely to cause problems in practice.

7   Conclusion

We presented a general model of convergent compilation, in which a compiler adjusts its heuristic policies based on static self-evaluation. Implementing convergent compilation efficiently in an ahead-of-time compiler requires significant effort, but one can easily test if it will be worthwhile with the simple two-pass instance from Section 3.2. JIT compilers with multiple levels of optimization can easily piggybacking this approach the additional evaluation and heuristic tuning on to their existing recompilation frameworks. These characteristics are desirable in a field that is full of clever but complex ideas that do not make it into production compilers—as Arch Robison noted [33]: "Compile-time program optimizations are similar to poetry: more are written than actually published in production compilers."

This paper also identified previous instances of the static self-evaluation in the literature, showed how convergent compilation generalizes them, and described a number of additional optimization heuristics and phase orderings which could benefit from this approach. It illustrated effective convergent unrolling on the TRIPS architecture in which the compiler corrected its unrolling heuristic to meet the TRIPS block size constraints using a simple two pass instance. Furthermore, simulation results demonstrated that convergent unrolling reduces the number of executed blocks and improves performance.

References

1. Stephenson, M., Amarasinghe, S., Martin, M.C., O'Reilly, U.M.: Meta optimization: Improving compiler heuristics with machine learning. In: Proceedings of PLDI 2003, San Diego, CA (2003) 77–90
2. Stephenson, M., Amarasinghe, S.: Predicting unroll factors using supervised classification. In: The International Conference on Code Generation and Optimization, San Jose, CA (2005) 123–134
3. Cavazos, J., Moss, J.E.B.: Inducing heuristics to decide whether to schedule. In: Proceedings of PLDI 2004, Washington, DC (2004) 183–194
4. Agarwal, V., Hrishikesh, M., Keckler, S.W., Burger, D.: Clock rate versus IPC: The end of the road for conventional microarchitectures. In: Proceedings of the 27th International Symposium on Computer Architecture. (2000) 248–259
5. Kailas, K., Ebcioglu, K., Agrawala, A.K.: CARS: A new code generation framework for clustered ILP processors. In: International Symposium on High-Performance Computer Architecture. (2001) 133–143
6. Kessler, C., Bednarski, A.: Optimal integrated code generation for clustered VLIW architectures. In: Joint Conference on Languages, Compilers and Tools for Embedded Systems. (2002) 102–111
7. Zhong, H., Fan, K., Mahlke, S., Schlansker, M.: A distributed control path architecture for vliw processors. In: International Conference on Parallel Architectures and Compilation Techniques, Washingotn, DC (2005) 197–206

8. Burger, D., Keckler, S.W., McKinley, K.S., et al.: Scaling to the end of silicon with EDGE architectures. IEEE Computer (2004) 44–55
9. Smith, A., Burrill, J., Gibson, J., Maher, B., Nethercote, N., Yoder, B., Buger, D., McKinley, K.S.: Compiling for edge architectures. In: The International Conference on Code Generation and Optimization. (2006) 185–195
10. Callahan, D., Carr, S., Kennedy, K.: Improving register allocation for subscripted variables. In: Proceedings of PLDI 1990, White Plains, NY (1990) 53–65
11. Dean, J., Chambers, C.: Towards better inlining decisions using inlining trials. In: Proceedings of LFP '94, Orlando, FL (1994) 273–282
12. Brasier, T.S., Sweany, P.H., Carr, S., Beaty, S.J.: CRAIG: A practical framework for combining instruction scheduling and register assignment. In: International Conference on Parallel Architecture and Compiler Techniques, Cyprus (1995)
13. Arnold, M.R., Welc, A., Rajan, V.T.: Improving virtual machine performance using a cross-run profile repository. In: ACM Conference Proceedings on Object–Oriented Programming Systems, Languages, and Applications. (2005) 297–311
14. Moss, J.E.B., Utgoff, P.E., Cavazos, J., Precup, D., Stefanovic, D., Brodley, C., Scheeff, D.: Learning to schedule straight-line code. In: Neural Information Processing Systems – Natural and Synthetic, Denver, CO (1997)
15. Yotov, K., Li, X., Ren, G., Cibulskis, M., DeJong, G., Garzaran, M.J., Padua, D., Pingali, K., Stodghill, P., Wu, P.: A comparison of empirical and model-driven optimization. In: Proceedings of PLDI 2003, San Diego, CA (2003) 63–76
16. Cavazos, J., Moss, J.E.B., O'Boyle, M.F.P.: Hybrid optimizations: Which optimization algorithm to use? In: International Conference on Compiler Construction, Vienna, Austria (2006)
17. Agakov, F., Bonilla, E., Cavazos, J., Franke, B., Fursin, G., O'Boyle, M.F.P., Thomson, J., Toussaint, M., Williams, C.K.I.: Using machine learning to focus iterative optimization. In: The International Conference on Code Generation and Optimization, New York, NY (2005) 295–305
18. Almagor, L., Cooper, K.D., Grosul, A., Harvey, T.J., Reeves, S.W., Subramanian, D., Torczon, L., Waterman, T.: Finding effective compilation sequences. In: Proceedings of LCTES 2004, Washington, DC (2004)
19. Cooper, K.D., Schielke, P.J., Subramanian, D.: Optimizing for reduced code space using genetic algorithms. In: Proceedings of LCTES '99, Atlanta (1999) 1–9
20. Haneda, M., Knijnenburg, P.M.W., Wijshoff, H.A.G.: Automatic selection of compiler options using non-parametric inferential statistics. In: International Conference on Parallel Architecture and Compiler Techniques, St. Louis, MO (2005) 123–132
21. Ladd, S.R.: Acovea: Using natural selection to investigate software complexities (2003) http://www.coyotegulch.com/products/acovea/.
22. Triantafyllis, S., Vachharajani, M., August, D.I.: Compiler optimization-space exploration. In: The Journal of Instruction-level Parallelism. (2005) 1–25
23. Lau, J., Arnold, M., Hind, M., Calder, B.: Online performance auditing: Using hot optimizations without getting burned. In: ACM Conference on Programming Language Design and Implementation. (2006) 239–251
24. Alpern, B., Attanasio, D., Barton, J.J., et al.: The Jalapeño virtual machine. IBM System Journal 39 (2000)
25. Arnold, M., Fink, S., Grove, D., Hind, M., Sweeney, P.: A survey of adaptive optimization in virtual machines. IEEE Computer 93 (2005)
26. Smith, M.D.: Overcoming the challenges to feedback-directed optimization. In: Proceedings of Dynamo '00, Boston, MA (2000) 1–11

27. Sun MicroSystems: The Sun HotSpot compiler (2005) http://java-sun.com.-products.hotspot.
28. Nagarajan, R., Sankaralingam, K., Burger, D., Keckler, S.W.: A design space evaluation of grid processor architectures. In: Proceedings of MICRO34, Austin, TX (2001) 40–53
29. Fisher, J.A.: Trace scheduling: A technique for global microcode compaction. IEEE Transactions on Computers **C-30** (1981) 478–490
30. Mahlke, S.A., Lin, D.C., Chen, W.Y., Hank, R.E., Bringmann, R.A.: Effective compiler support for predicated execution using the hyperblock. In: Proceedings of MICRO25, Portland, OR (1992) 45–54
31. Maher, B., Smith, A., Burger, D., McKinley, K.S.: Merging head and tail duplication for convergent hyperblock formation. Technical Report TR-06-36, University of Texas at Austin (2006)
32. Baker, B.S.: Parameterized pattern matching: Algorithms and applications. Journal of Computer and System Sciences **52** (1996) 28–42
33. Robison, A.D.: Impact of economics on compiler optimization. In: Proceedings of the ACM 2001 Java Grande Conference, Palo Alto, CA (2001) 1–10

Finding and Applying Loop Transformations for Generating Optimized FPGA Implementations

Harald Devos, Kristof Beyls, Mark Christiaens,
Jan Van Campenhout, Erik H. D'Hollander, and Dirk Stroobandt

Parallel Information Systems, ELIS-Dept., Faculty of Engineering,
Ghent University, Belgium
{harald.devos, kristof.beyls, mark.christiaens, jan.vancampenhout,
erik.dhollander, dirk.stroobandt}@elis.ugent.be
http://www.elis.ugent.be/paris

Abstract. When implementing multimedia applications, solutions in dedicated hardware are chosen only when the required performance or energy-efficiency cannot be met with a software solution. The performance of a hardware design critically depends upon having high levels of parallelism and data locality. Often a long sequence of high-level transformations is needed to sufficiently increase the locality and parallelism. The effect of the transformations is known only after translating the high-level code into a specific design at the circuit level. When the constraints are not met, hardware designers need to redo the high-level loop transformations, and repeat all subsequent translation steps, which leads to long design times.

We propose a method to reduce design time through the synergistic combination of techniques (a) to quickly pinpoint the loop transformations that increase locality; (b) to refactor loops in a polyhedral model and check whether a sequence of refactorings is legal; (c) to generate efficient structural VHDL from the optimized refactored algorithm.

The implementation of these techniques in a tool suite results in a far shorter design time of hours instead of days or weeks. A 2D-inverse discrete wavelet transform was taken as a case study. The results outperform those of a commercial C-to-VHDL compiler, and compare favorably with existing published approaches.

1   Introduction

Multimedia applications have made their way into all kinds of devices, from small mobile systems up to desktop computers, with varying ranges of computational power and requirements. They are part of a large class of signal processing applications that often need hardware acceleration. FPGAs (Field Programmable Gate Arrays) are a popular way to speed up designs [16]. They consist of a large array of elementary hardware blocks (LUTs, Memories, Multipliers, ...). The function of these blocks and the connections between them are programmed (configured) to implement a certain hardware design. All blocks can operate in

P. Stenström (Ed.): Transactions on HiPEAC I, LNCS 4050, pp. 159–178, 2007.

parallel, which offers a high computational power, provided that enough parallelism can be detected in the application.

Most multimedia applications require a significant amount of memory and have a streaming nature. The on-chip memory on FPGAs is often too small to contain all the data. Hence an external memory is added and buffer memories are used on-chip. This separation introduces the well-known memory bottleneck as the bandwidth to the external memory is limited. A FPGA is not useful if it wastes its time waiting for data. Hence optimizing the locality of the data accesses, e.g., by high-level loop transformations, is extremely important to reduce the bandwidth requirements.

Evaluating the impact of a high-level transformation is difficult and often requires further translation to low-level hardware structures. Despite the existence of behavioral compilers, in reality, the translation of algorithms described in a high-level language such as C or Matlab into a hardware description language such as VHDL or Verilog is often done manually, resulting in a long design time. An important reason is that these compilers perform insufficient high-level loop optimizations, even though these are usually needed to increase the amount of parallelism and locality. Currently several projects aim at hardware generation from high-level languages, e.g., Compaan/Laura [28], MMAlpha [20] and the PICO project [27]. Their main focus is on extracting parallelism.

In this paper we address the problem of locality optimization. Our approach is based on the concept of reuse distance [11]. The reuse distance is the amount of data accessed between two consecutive uses of the same data element. In this respect, it is a measure of temporal locality in an address stream. An analysis of the code executed between a data use and its consecutive reuse allows to pinpoint the required loop transformation to increase its temporal data locality and hence the usage of local memory resources.

Often, naively applying transformations, such as loop fusion, would violate data dependences. In order to make them valid, a sequence of enabling transformations is needed. Typically, the data locality has to be made worse first, in order to make subsequent optimizations possible. Because of this, optimizing compilers often fail to automatically find the best sequence of transformations [19]. Recently, iterative compilation has been proposed to automate the search for such sequences [18,23]. There, the strategy is to iteratively compile a program with different sequences of optimizations and to evaluate the result by profiling the resulting binary. Based on the results, new sequences of transformations are explored. Alternatively, Cohen et al. [15] propose to use a processor simulator to analyze the main performance bottlenecks in a manual iterative process.

In contrast, our analysis is based on tracing the data reuses and the code that is executed between them. For each reuse, the analysis unveils the key transformation needed to improve the temporal locality. By doing so, the set of critical transformations required to substantially improve the overall locality is discovered in a single profiling run. Consequently, the costly iterative cycle consisting of applying a transformation and subsequent profiling of the resulting binary to find a next profitable transformation is eliminated.

Next, a geometrical representation of the iteration space of a program, the polyhedral model [6], is used to facilitate combining loop transformations. Basically, programs are represented as a set of statements, where each statement is executed for a set of integer values of a number of iterator variables that are bounded by linear constraints. As such, the values of the iterators are described by a polytope, hence the name "polyhedral model". In the past decade, a number of effective methods have been developed to translate between an intermediate representation based on abstract syntax trees and the polyhedral model [5] and to represent traditional loop transformations [6]. Originally targeted at optimizing software, we use this method to optimize hardware. Therefore, we introduce a method to directly translate a polyhedral program representation into a VHDL description of interacting automata. The factorized architecture opens possibilities for scalability, i.e., quickly generating hardware designs with different trade-offs between speed, chip area and energy consumption.

The method outlined above has been partially automated and implemented in a tool suite. Our SLO tool [10,12] analyzes all data reuses in a program execution, and pinpoints the most promising loop transformations to increase data locality. Then, the URUK/WRaP-IT tool [6] is used to apply the loop transformations in the polyhedral model. Finally, our CLooGVHDL tool generates a factorized hardware controller block, described in synthesizable VHDL.

This paper is structured as follows. The analysis of data reuses with poor locality is introduced in Sect. 2. Sect. 3 briefly discusses the polyhedral model and how it supports combining sequences of transformations. In Sect. 4 the translation into a structural VHDL description is presented. The methods are applied to a 2D inverse discrete wavelet transform in Sect. 5. A comparison with related work is found in Sect. 6. Conclusions follow in Sect. 7.

2   Pinpointing the Most Effective Locality Transformations

During a program run, each data element is typically reused many times. When the reuses are close together, resulting in good temporal locality, it is feasible to retain the data in an on-chip buffer instead of repeatedly refetching it from the external memory. The goal of applying transformations to improve locality is to reduce the number of off-chip memory accesses. The difficulty in optimizing a program's locality lies in finding the appropriate sequence of transformations that, in the end, results in improved data locality. To support a designer in constructing an effective sequence of transformations, we introduce a program analysis that pinpoints the key transformation that is needed to improve locality for each individual data reuse. By focusing on the data reuses that generate poor locality, a small number of key transformations are identified.

2.1   Characterizing and Quantifying Locality by the Reuse Distance

We use the following terminology. A *memory reference* corresponds to a read or a write in the source code, while a particular execution of that read or write at

```
      for (i=0;i<=N;i++){              S1:  B[0]=B[0]*A[0][0];
          for (j=0;j<=N-i;j++)               for (i=1; i<=N; i++) {
S1:         B[i+j]=B[i+j]*A[i][j];              for (j=0; j<=i; j++)
      }                              S1:        B[i]=B[i]*A[j][i-j];
      for (k=0;k<=N-1;k++)           S2:        C[i-1]=B[i-1]+B[i];
S2:     C[k]=B[k]+B[k+1];                   }
```

(a) Original   (b) After locality optimizations

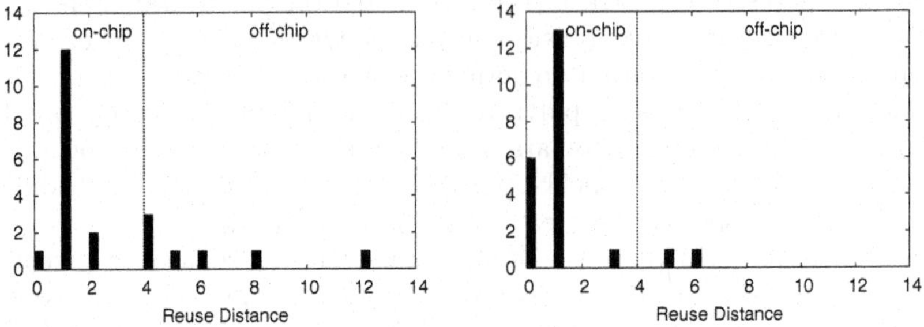

(c) Reuse distance histogram for code   (d) Reuse distance histogram for code
in (a)   in (b)

Fig. 1. Example code is shown in (a). After applying our methods, presented in Sections 2 and 3, its locality is optimized, resulting in the code shown in (b). The histograms (for N=3) in (c) and (d) show that the optimizations have reduced the distance of many reuses. The dotted line indicates the capacity of the local memory (=4). In this example, it is assumed that only the array references generate memory accesses. Therefore, the trace of accessed addresses starts with B[0], A[0][0], B[0], B[1], ...

runtime is called a *memory access*. A *reuse pair* is a pair of accesses to the same data element without intervening accesses to that data. The *use* of a reuse pair is the first access, the *reuse* is the second access. The *reuse distance* of a reuse pair is the number of unique data addresses accessed between use and reuse.

In a cache or local memory buffer with the Least Recently Used (LRU) replacement policy, data is retained between reuses if and only if the corresponding reuse distance is smaller than the cache or buffer size [11].

In Fig. 1, the histograms of reuse distances for two versions of the same algorithm are shown. In (a), the original program is shown, while an optimized version is shown in (b). A cache or buffer capacity of 4 elements is assumed. Consequently, the data will be retained in the buffer for the reuses with a distance smaller than 4, while for the other reuses the data needs to be refetched from external memory. In the original program (c), for 7 memory accesses, the data needs to be refetched. In the optimized program (d), only 2 refetches are needed.

2.2   Finding Locality-Improving Transformations

Poor temporal locality occurs when a large amount of other data is accessed between two consecutive uses of the same data. Improving the locality requires

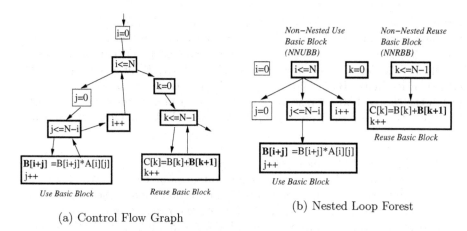

(a) Control Flow Graph

(b) Nested Loop Forest

Fig. 2. Flow graph and Nested Loop Forest for the code in Fig. 1(a). The basic blocks executed between the use of `B[3]` in statement S1 by reference `B[i+j]` in iteration $(i = 3, j = 0)$ and the reuse of the same element by reference `B[k+1]` in statement S2 at iteration $(k = 2)$ are indicated by bold boxes. N=3.

reducing the volume of data accessed between use and reuse. The source code executed between use and reuse is responsible for accessing the large data volume, leading to a long reuse distance. That source code is called the *Intermediately Executed Code (IEC)* of the corresponding reuse pair. Consequently, to improve the temporal locality, a refactoring of the IEC is needed. The analysis below examines the loop structure of the IEC and pinpoints the loop or pair of loops that need to be transformed to reduce the reuse distance for a specific reuse pair. Below we present the analysis for an intra-procedural context. Details of the extension to an inter-procedural context are presented in [10,12].

The analysis proceeds by determining a number of attributes for each reuse pair, as illustrated in Fig. 2 for the code of Fig. 1(a). In Fig. 2(a), the source codes corresponding to the basic blocks are shown in the control flow graph. The reuse pair under consideration consists of a pair of accesses to `B[3]`, where the use is generated by reference `B[i+j]` in iteration $(i = 3, j = 0)$ of statement S1 and the reuse is generated by `B[k+1]` in statement S2 at iteration $(k = 2)$. The basic blocks that are executed between use and reuse, assuming N=3, are highlighted by bold boxes. These basic blocks form the Intermediately Executed Code (IEC).

The basic block containing the use is called the *Use Basic Block (UBB)*, while the basic block containing the reuse is called the *Reuse Basic Block (RBB)*. The *Natural Loop Headers* are those basic blocks that control whether or not an iteration of a loop in the control flow graph gets executed [2]. The *Nested Loop Forest (NLF)* is a graph where each node represents a basic block, and there are edges to each basic block from the loop header of its closest surrounding natural loop. The NLF for the running example is shown in Fig. 2(b).

The *Outermost Executed Loop Header (OELH)* of a basic block BB with respect to a given reuse pair is the unique ancestor of BB in the nested loop forest that has been executed between the use and the reuse, but that does not have ancestors itself that are executed between use and reuse. The *Non-Nested Use Basic Block (NNUBB)* of a reuse pair is the OELH of its Use Basic Block. The *Non-Nested Reuse Basic Block (NNRBB)* of a reuse pair is the OELH of its Reuse Basic Block. The NNUBB and NNRBB are easily identified in the Nested Loop Forest, see Fig. 2(b). After determining the Non-Nested Use Basic Block and the Non-Nested Reuse Basic Block, the following cases may arise.

- *NNUBB = NNRBB and is a loop header.* In this case, the reuses occur across different iterations of a single (possibly outer) loop. This pattern arises when the loop traverses a "data structure"[1] in every iteration of the loop. The distance of reuses across iterations can be reduced by ensuring that only a small part of the data structure is traversed in any given iteration. As such, reuses of data elements between consecutive iterations are separated by only a small amount of data, instead of the complete data structure, and the data may remain in on-chip buffers between different loop iterations. A large number of transformations have been proposed that all aim at increasing temporal locality in this way, such as loop tiling [29], loop interchange [26] and loop chunking [7]. We call these transformations **tiling-like** optimizations.
- *NNUBB = NNRBB, but it is not a loop header.* The use and reuse occur at a close distance, inside the same basic block. If the reuse needs to be made shorter, some simple reordering of code in that basic block needs to be performed. This is a non loop-carried reuse.
- *NNUBB ≠ NNRBB.* When both NNUBB and NNRBB are different loop headers, reuses occur between different loops. A data structure is traversed by the NNUBB-loop, after which it is retraversed by the NNRBB-loop. The reuses can be brought closer together by only doing a single traversal, performing computations from both loops at the same time. This kind of optimization is known as loop fusion. We call the required transformation a **fusion-like** optimization. When one of NNUBB or NNRBB is not a loop header, similarly the NNUBB needs to be fused with the NNRBB.

For the reuse that is analyzed in Fig. 2, the NNUBB≠NNRBB. Therefore, to optimize the locality of that reuse, the i-loop needs to be fused with the k-loop.

We have implemented the required instrumentation and profiling to perform the above analysis in the GCC compiler. As an example, the result of profiling all reuses in the running example is shown in Fig. 3.

3   Polyhedral Program Model

Compilers and refactoring tools [30,31] that apply loop transformations need a way to represent loop nests and their corresponding boundaries. Usually, abstract

---

[1] The data structure could be as small as a single scalar variable or as large as all the data in the program.

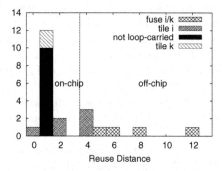

Fig. 3. Histogram of loop transformations needed versus the reuse distance at which reuses occur for the code in Fig. 1(a). It shows that fusing loop i with loop k is required to optimize the reuses with the longest distances. Next, a tiling-like transformation on loop i can reduce the distance of the other loop-carried reuses. N=3. The dotted line indicates the capacity of the local memory (=4).

```
Depth                          Ordering    Iteration   Scheduling
0    1    2                    vector      vector      vector
|    |    |
0: for i
     0: S1(i)                  (0,0)       (i)         (0,i,0)
     1: for j
          0: S2(i,j)           (0,1,0)     (i,j)       (0,i,1,j,0)
          1: S3(i,j)           (0,1,1)     (i,j)       (0,i,1,j,1)
1: for k
     0: S4(k)                  (1,0)       (k)         (1,k,0)
     1: S5(k)                  (1,1)       (k)         (1,k,1)
     2: S6(k)                  (1,2)       (k)         (1,k,2)
2: S7()                        (2)         ()          (2)
```

Fig. 4. Example illustrating the meaning of ordering, iteration and scheduling vector

syntax trees (AST) are used. In an AST, each loop corresponds to a node in a tree, and inner loops are represented as child nodes of an outer loop node. In contrast, our framework is based on a representation of loops in the so-called polyhedral program model [6].

3.1 Program Representation

A *statement* is a line of a program without control, typically an assignment with operations at the right hand side. The *depth* of a loop or a statement is the number of loops that surround it. The program top-level (depth 0) is a sequence of loops and statements which are numbered from 0 onwards (Fig. 4). Each loop in turn also contains a sequence of statements and loops that are numbered from 0 onwards. Each statement is uniquely identified by the vector composed of the numbers telling the position in each of the surrounding loops and the top-level.

This vector is called the *ordering vector*. It has dimension $D_S + 1$ with D_S the depth of the statement. An example is provided in Fig. 4.

A statement is executed for a set of values of the *iteration vector*, the vector containing the iterators of the surrounding loops (dimension D_S). A single execution of a statement is called a *statement instance*. The *iteration domain* is the set of values for which the statement is executed.

The *scheduling vector* of a statement is the vector with the elements of the ordering vector as odd elements and the iterators as even elements. The dimension is $2D_S + 1$.

The execution order of statement instances follows the lexicographical order of their scheduling vectors. The uniqueness of the ordering vectors ensures that the statement instances are strictly ordered.

We now restrict ourselves to programs where the loop bounds are linear expressions (affine functions) of the parameters and the iterators of the surrounding loops. In this case the iteration domains can be represented as parameterized integer polyhedra. Hence the name *polyhedral model*.

A **parameterized integer polyhedron** P_p is defined as

$$P_p = \{x \in \mathbb{Z}^n | Ax \geq Bp + b\}, p \in \mathbb{Z}^m$$

where A and B are constant integer matrices, b is a constant integer vector, and p is a vector of parameters. Consider the program in Fig. 1(a). The iteration domains for the two statements can be represented by polyhedra as follows

$$\mathcal{D}_{S1} = \{(i,j) \in \mathbb{Z}^2 | \begin{pmatrix} 1 & 0 \\ -1 & 0 \\ 0 & 1 \\ -1 & -1 \end{pmatrix} \begin{pmatrix} i \\ j \end{pmatrix} \geq \begin{pmatrix} 0 \\ -1 \\ 0 \\ -1 \end{pmatrix} (N) + \begin{pmatrix} 0 \\ 0 \\ 0 \\ 0 \end{pmatrix} \}$$

$$\mathcal{D}_{S2} = \{(k) \in \mathbb{Z}^1 | \begin{pmatrix} 1 \\ -1 \end{pmatrix} (k) \geq \begin{pmatrix} 0 \\ -1 \end{pmatrix} (N) + \begin{pmatrix} 0 \\ 1 \end{pmatrix} \}$$

or, using a more compact notation:

$$\mathcal{D}_{S1} = \{(i,j) \in \mathbb{Z}^2 | 0 \leq i \leq N \wedge 0 \leq j \leq N - i\}$$
$$\mathcal{D}_{S2} = \{(k) \in \mathbb{Z}^1 | 0 \leq k \leq N - 1\}$$

3.2 Describing Loop Transformations

As described above a loop nest is represented by a set of matrices and vectors. Loop transformations are described by matrix and vector operations. Therefore, transformations are easily combined by combining the corresponding operations. The exact representation of transformations, and their practical implementation in a tool called URUK, is presented in detail in [15] and [19]. Here, we only show how a sequence of transformations is applied to the running example.

Figure 5 (a)-(e) shows a graphical representation of the iteration domains of the two statements during a sequence of transformations to improve locality.

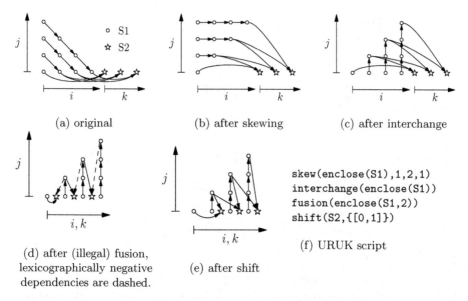

(a) original

(b) after skewing

(c) after interchange

(d) after (illegal) fusion,
lexicographically negative
dependencies are dashed.

(e) after shift

```
skew(enclose(S1),1,2,1)
interchange(enclose(S1))
fusion(enclose(S1,2))
shift(S2,{[0,1]})
```

(f) URUK script

Fig. 5. Example sequence of transformations on the code of Fig. 1(a) resulting in the code of Fig. 1(b)

The iterations of statement S1 are represented by circles, while the iterations of S2 are represented by stars. The data dependences between different iterations, are represented by arrows. Note that the scheduling vector of S1 is actually 5-dimensional and the scheduling vector of S2 is 3-dimensional. To make a graphical representation of both statements in a common space possible, they have been projected to a common 2-dimensional space in Fig. 5.

The locality analysis in Fig. 3 shows that two key transformations are necessary to improve locality. Firstly, a transformation of loop i is needed to reduce the distance between reuses of B occurring between different iterations of that loop. Secondly, loop i needs to be fused with loop k. In the first step (see (b)), the loop is skewed to make the data reuses in loop i aligned with the direction of the loop. Then (see (c)), loops i and j are interchanged, to make the reuses occur in the same iteration of the outermost i-loop. This implements the required tiling-like transformation indicated in Fig. 3.

The other required transformation is the fusion of loops i and k. This is performed in Fig. 5(d), resulting in an illegal schedule, since the three dependences indicated with dashed lines are lexicographically negative. To turn this into a legal schedule, the instances of S2 are shifted in (e). The resulting optimized code is shown in Fig. 1(b), where the corresponding reuse distance histogram shows that the locality has indeed been optimized. In (f), the specification of the above sequence of 4 transformations as an URUK script is illustrated. This example shows that it is easy to construct a legal schedule based on the transformations hinted by the analysis results shown in Fig. 3.

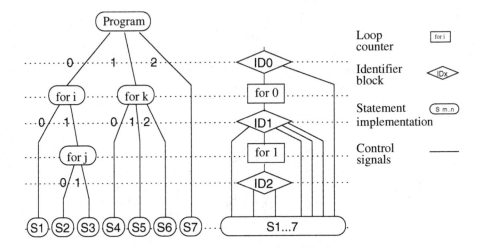

Fig. 6. Abstract syntax tree of the program in Fig. 4 and corresponding hardware architecture of the loop controller. A single hardware block implements all statements S1...7. The block *for 0* implements the loops at depth 0: *for i* and *for k*. Which of the two is executed depends on the value received from *ID0*.

4   Hardware Generation from the Polyhedral Model

In this section we propose a hardware architecture composed of two entities, one with the statements' implementation and one with a controller that drives the iterators and triggers the statements. A loop transformation only influences the controller entity and therefore the statements entity can be reused for several loop structures. On the other hand several variants of the statements, e.g., trading-off area and number of cycles, can be connected to the controller. The controller consists of a set of communicating automata, a so called factorized implementation [3].

4.1   Sequential Execution

We start with a sequential execution of the statement instances, equivalent to a software execution. For this case a loop controller can be generated automatically from a CLooG [5] input file. In the abstract syntax tree on Fig. 6 the numbers and iterators on the path between the top-node *program* and a statement node correspond to the elements of the scheduling vector of that statement in Fig. 4.

We propose a controller composed of automata, each corresponding with one dimension of the scheduling vector. This results in two types of automata. A first one with loop counters, e.g., *for 0* in Fig. 6, is responsible for the iterators. The other one, the identifier blocks, e.g., *ID 1* in Fig. 6, corresponds to the elements of the ordering vectors. The loop counter blocks calculate the loop bounds and stride in function of the parameters, the iterators of surrounding loops and the

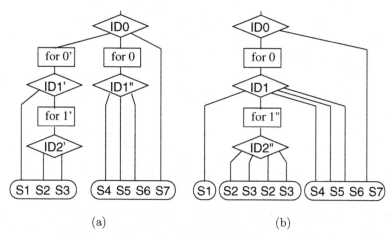

Fig. 7. Doubling hardware for reduction of complexity or introduction of parallelism

more significant elements of the ordering vector.[2] The identifier blocks count from zero onwards to enumerate the different statements and loops at the level below. All statements are implemented as a single VHDL process. This is only possible since no two statements operate at the same time. It allows the synthesis tools to "see" all statements during optimization and results in hardware being shared between statements.

This architecture has a.o. the following interesting properties. (1) Experiments showed that the proposed factorized implementation consumes less area and reaches a higher clock frequency than a monolithic control block. (2) The higher in the hierarchy, the lower the switching activity of the blocks. This allows clock gating [8] or other techniques for power reduction. (3) For deep and large loop nests some control blocks might become very complex as they implement different behavior for a lot of different identifier values (components of ordering vectors). In that case it may be beneficial to regard subtrees as programs in their own right and give them their own control hardware. This results in more, but smaller and faster automata and a trade-off between clock speed and area. E.g., in Fig. 7(a) the *for i* and *for k* loop get their own controllers. In principle the two loops can now also work in parallel.

4.2   Parallel Execution

By creating separate hardware for different loops and the statements they control it is possible to execute them in parallel. Dependence analysis using the polyhedral model allows to check which statement instances can run in parallel.

---

[2] The generated VHDL expressions for the loop bounds are equivalent to the expressions generated by CLooG. As a result operators as mod and div are synthesizable only for powers of 2. Techniques as those presented in [33] could extend this synthesizable subset.

$$\text{do } l = K\text{-}1,\, 0$$
$$S = R \,/\, 2^{l+1}$$
$$\text{do } j = 0,\, (C \,/\, 2^l)\text{-}1 \qquad\qquad \text{// Vertical filtering.}$$
$$\text{do } i = 0,\, (R \,/\, 2^{l+1})\text{-}1$$
$$B_{2i,j} =<\,A_{i-1...i+1,j}\,,\; H_o> + <A_{S+i-2...S+i+1,j}\,,\; G_o>$$
$$B_{2i+1,j} =<\,A_{i-1...i+2,j}\,,\; H_e> + <A_{S+i-2...S+i+2,j}\,,\; G_e>$$

$$S = C \,/\, 2^{l+1}$$
$$\text{do } i = 0,\, (R \,/\, 2^l)\text{-}1 \qquad\qquad \text{// Horizontal filtering.}$$
$$\text{do } j = 0,\, (C \,/\, 2^{l+1})\text{-}1$$
$$A_{i,2j} =<\,B_{i,j-1...j+1}\,,\; H_o> + <B_{i,S+j-2...S+j+1}\,,\; G_o>$$
$$A_{i,2j+1} =<\,B_{i,j-1...j+2}\,,\; H_e> + <B_{i,S+j-2...S+j+2}\,,\; G_e>$$

Fig. 8. Simplified representation of the IDWT basic algorithm. R and C are parameters representing the number of rows and columns of the image that is transformed over K levels. A and B are two-dimensional arrays and G_o, G_e, H_o and H_e are vectors containing the odd and even elements of the wavelet filters G and H (a 9/7 bi-orthogonal filter). $< x\,,\, y> = $ inproduct of x and y.

Thanks to the factorized implementation, parallelization, if legal, is made straightforward by duplication of subtrees or statements. E.g., in Fig. 7(b) duplication of S2 and S3 makes it possible to run several iterations of the j loop in parallel or in a pipeline.

5　Case Study: The 2-Dimensional Inverse Discrete Wavelet Transformation

We apply and evaluate the techniques explained in this article on a typical example of a multimedia application: the 2-Dimensional Inverse Discrete Wavelet Transformation (2D-IDWT). It is a typical DSP algorithm used for image processing or compression (e.g., JPEG-2000). A simplified description of the algorithm, using a 9/7 bi-orthogonal filter pair [24], is shown in Fig. 8.

After analysis of the required accuracy the data types were changed from floating to 18-bit fixed point.[3] This accuracy allows perfect image reconstruction, and corresponds to the embedded multipliers and memories on contemporary FPGAs, which have widths equal to multiples of 9-bit.

5.1　Design Trajectory

Finding Locality Optimizing Transformations. The techniques described in Sect. 2.2 are implemented in the SLO-tool [10,12] (Suggestions for Locality Optimization), which produces the analysis result shown in Fig. 9. The two most

---

[3] This conversion is essential for going to hardware but is also beneficial for a software implementation.

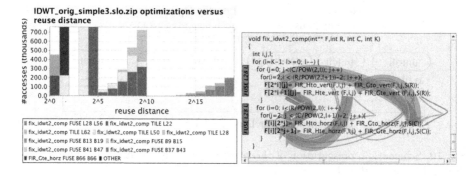

Fig. 9. Reuse distances for the 2D-IDWT as measured with SLO. The two most important transformations (see the bar chart at reuse distances larger than 2^{13}), are fusion of loops L28 and L56 and tiling of loop L22 in function `fix_idwt2_comp`, as shown in the legend. Loop L28 corresponds to the vertical filtering in Fig. 8. L56 is the horizontal filtering and loop L22 is the outer l-loop. The right hand side shows the visual highlighting of the required fusion in the source code by SLO. The loops are indicated by bars on the left. The array references and function calls that respectively generate the uses and the reuses that are optimized by the fusion are indicated by arrows. The thickness of the arrow is proportional to the number of reuses generated by the corresponding pair of references.

promising transformations proposed by SLO are fusion of the vertical filtering loop with the horizontal filtering loop and tiling of the outer l-loop (see Fig. 8).

The original algorithm (Fig. 8) consumes little on-chip memory but a lot of off-chip bandwidth. Loop fusion halves the bandwidth by buffering lines of the image. Tiling can further reduce the bandwidth to the theoretical minimum of $2RC$ (reading the input, writing the output).

The resulting code corresponds well with hardware solutions described in the literature [22,32],[4] what proves the strength of the analysis. The original version is known as a "row-column" version; the version after loop fusion is known as a "line-based" version and the version with subsequent tiling as a line-based one with interleaved (potentially parallel) execution of operations for the different transformation levels.

Preprocessing and Transformations. First, the code was converted to a dynamic single assignment form to eliminate false dependencies. Secondly, the outer loop was unrolled to remove the exponential expressions in the loop boundaries of the i and j loops of Fig. 8, so that the program could be represented in the polyhedral model. Next, we began by constructing a sequence of transformations containing the fusion and tiling indicated by the SLO tool. To render these optimizations legal, two enabling transformations are needed: stretch and interchange. The complete sequence of transformations is depicted in Fig. 10.

---

[4] We will not distinguish between the forward and the inverse transformation. The data access pattern of the former is the inverse of that of the latter which leads to similar locality optimizing transformations.

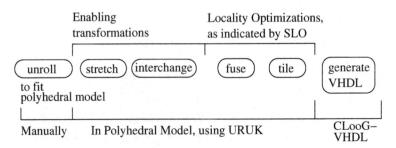

Fig. 10. Schematic representation of the sequence of transformations to optimize the locality for the 2D-IDWT

The four central transformations were automatically applied using the URUK-tool [15], by specifying them in a script. The *stretch* transformation, that scales the loop stride, was not yet present in URUK. It was easily incorporated into URUK by defining the corresponding matrix operations.

Down to Hardware. We implemented the translation to structural VHDL (Sect. 4.1) on top of the CLooG library [5], hence the name CLooGVHDL. CLooG translates a polyhedral representation into an AST.[5] The execution time of a statement instance does not have to be known at compile time and may vary during execution or between variants of the statement implementations. A simple handshake between controller and statements makes this possible *without losing clock cycles.*

In the current implementation the statements are driven sequentially. Future versions will introduce parallelism and pipelining of the execution. For comparison purposes three versions of the controllers for the IDWT were made: one without loop transformations, one after fusion and one after fusion and tiling.

The statement definitions are split into operations and array accesses. The former are translated into a VHDL-syntax and the latter are translated into memory transactions. An intermediate file shows the actions per cycle for each statement (e.g., Fig. 11(b)). In this file it is possible to do some scheduling optimizations by hand (Fig. 11(c)). From here the path to synthesizable VHDL is automated. Two variants of the statement block were made. One with and one without hand optimizations on the intermediate file. By combining controller and statement variants we get 6 designs. One extra design was generated to study the influence of the borders (Sect. 5.2).

The memory is assumed to be on-chip, having a short access time. To transform large images, off-chip memory is needed. In that case a hardware block for moving data between external RAM and on-chip buffers has to be built (Fig. 12), as was done for the manual design mentioned in Sect. 5.2. The execution speed will then depend on the bandwidth to the external memory.

---

[5] The existing control optimizations in CLooG [5] are also supported by CLooGVHDL. E.g., the stride option can eliminate if-expressions with modulos and save cycles by counting with strides larger than 1.

```
for(i=1;i<=N;i++){
  A[i]=
    (B[i]+B[i-1]+C[i])
    *B[i*2];
  // = S1(i)
}
```

(a) C Code

```
-- #define S1(i)
B_ad<=i;
B_ad<=i-1;
a0:=B_q;C_ad<=i;
a1:=B_q;B_ad<=i*2;
a2:=C_q;
a3:=B_q;
a4:=(a0+a1+a2)*a3;
A_ad<=i;A_we<='1';A_d<=a4;
```

(b) Statement execution steps

```
-- #define S1(i)
B_ad<=i;C_ad<=i;
a1:=a0;B_ad<=i*2;
a0:=B_q;a2:=C_q;
a3:=B_q;b0:=(a0+a1+a2);
a4:=b0*a3;
A_ad<=i;A_we<='1';A_d<=a4;
```

(c) After optimizations

Fig. 11. Example of optimizations on an intermediate file describing statement execution steps. Each line corresponds to one clock cycle. A data element (X_q) is read two cycles after the address (X_ad) assignment. Arrays B and C are put in a separate memory and can thus be read in parallel. B[i-1] is already loaded and can be reused (special case $i=1$ omitted for clarity). The calculation is split into 2 cycles, reducing the critical path. The number of cycles is reduced from 8 to 6.

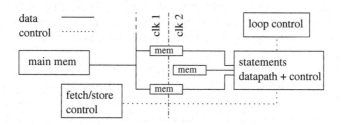

Fig. 12. Architecture with memory hierarchy. Fetching and storing data is done in parallel with the operations of the IDWT. Execution speed is determined by the slowest of these two processes. Multiple local buffers allow parallel memory accesses.

5.2 Results

Table 1 shows simulation and synthesis results for the different IDWT designs. Note that synthesis tools perform a lot of optimizations, e.g., removing unused signals, retiming, constant propagation. This frees the code generator from doing these tasks but makes the final result less predictable and dependent on the used tools and their settings.

Three designs were generated by ImpulseC [1], a commercial tool for automatic synthesis of stream-based applications. One design was made manually,[6] before we had access to the tools introduced in this article. The design trajectory went from C over SystemC to VHDL[17]. For a fair comparison, the blocks that communicate with the external memory are not counted in the synthesis results.

The IDWT uses mirroring at the edges of the input frames to have enough input samples for the filters. In four designs this was done in hardware. The other designs do not calculate the pixels near the border, leading to a large reduction in

---

[6] This design aimed at minimal area while transforming 45 CIF frames/s.

complexity. If a processor is available in the system it is probably more efficient to implement the borders in software and process only the non-border pixels on the FPGA.

ImpulseC has the worst synthesis results. It generates a single large automaton instead of a factorization into smaller automata. In some places 32 bit data types are used where smaller word lengths suffice, even if shorter data types are used in the source code. ImpulseC aims at compiling a larger class of C programs than those representable in the polyhedral model. Therefore it is more conservative in its approach to hardware generation, while CLooGVHDL has a more specialized implementation strategy.

When memory bandwidth is not considered, the hand-made design outperforms the others. We expect CLooGVHDL to gain a similar performance when it is extended to exploit parallelism. If the bandwidth is limited, the computational power is not fully exploited anymore. Figure 13 shows the frame rate for the different designs in function of the available bandwidth to the external memory. The horizontal part at the right corresponds to the calculation-limited area, the slope at the left to the bandwidth-limited area. At low bandwidths the fused versions have a throughput at least twice as large as the original versions. In fact the difference will be larger than indicated because the bandwidth depends on the burst mode usage, i.e., 50% of the transfers for the original algorithm and 100% for the transformed variants.

The manual design was tested on an Altera PCI Development Board with a Stratix EP1S25F1020C5 FPGA. First the IDWT was directly connected to an external DDR SDRAM memory running at 133MHz. A mean bandwidth between FPGA and memory of 35 MB/s was reached. Secondly an Avalon fabric (without burst mode[7]) was put on the FPGA to connect different hardware blocks to the memory, decreasing the bandwidth to only 12 MB/s. For low bandwidths the generated designs outperform the manually made design.

6   Related Work

6.1   Related Strategies to Improve Data Locality

The existing methods to increase the temporal data locality of a program can be categorized as either being fully-automatic, i.e., compiler-based, or user-driven, i.e., based on profiling to pinpoint areas of poor data locality. Basically, the compiler-based approaches, a.o. [29,26,7], look for specific code patterns that they know how to optimize legally. However, when the legality of the optimization cannot be guaranteed, as is often the case in the presence of data-dependent conditions or function calls, the compiler fails to optimize the locality. As such, for many programs, only a tiny fraction of the poor locality accesses are optimized automatically. In contrast, the profile-based methods, such as [9,14,25], do not search for patterns that they *can* optimize, but they search for the source code or data areas that generate poor locality, and consequently *needs* to be

---

[7] Introducing bursts will have little effect as only half of the accesses can profit of it.

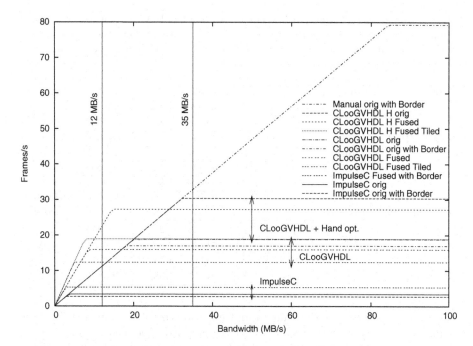

Fig. 13. Frame rate (CIF=288 × 352 pixels) in function of the available bandwidth to the external memory, using 2B/pixel. For non-loop-optimized versions the bandwidth is the harmonic mean of the bandwidth by horizontal and by vertical access. The vertical lines correspond with measured bandwidths. (H=hand-optimized statement).

optimized. The task of finding *how* to optimize the locality is left to the user. In this regard, the method presented here and implemented in the SLO tool, goes one step further in also suggesting an appropriate refactoring, that if it can be made legal, will improve the locality. A more detailed comparison with other tools is presented in [10,12].

6.2   Related Hardware Generation Strategies

Several projects aim at hardware generation from high-level languages. In MM-Alpha [20], loop nests are represented in a functional, dynamic single assignment language. The code is mapped onto a systolic array. The PICO project [27] also translates loop nests into systolic arrays and runs the left-over code on a specialized EPIC processor. PARO [21] maps Piecewise Regular Algorithms (PRA) onto a configurable processor array. These all handle a subset of the programs we can handle.

The User-Guided High-level synthesis tool (UGH) [4], takes C code and a Draft Data Path (DDP) of nodes in a Kahn Process Network (KPN) as input. After coarse and fine grain scheduling, a data path and FSM is generated. No loop transformations nor memory optimizations are performed. The techniques

Table 1. Comparison of different implementations of the IDWT. Synthesis results for the right side (clk 2) of Fig. 12 were obtained using Altera QuartusII v4.2 for the Stratix FPGA family. The frame rate is normalized to CIF frames (288 × 352) with borders. (* = Number of cycles for CIF resolution)

Tool	Transform	Borders	LE	DSP blocks (#Mul)	f_{max} (MHz)	Cycles (72×88)	Frames/s
CLooGVHDL	none	yes	3561	18(9)	46.72	214269	16.99
		no	1691	18(9)	52.16	187350	18.83
	fuse	no	1907	18(9)	47.22	200138	15.96
	fuse + tile	no	2533	18(9)	36.57	200158	12.36
CLooGVHDL + Manual opt.	none	no	1495	18(9)	58.16	129821	30.31
	fuse	no	1622	18(9)	57.32	142570	27.20
	fuse + tile	no	2155	18(9)	39.87	142590	18.92
ImpulseC	none	yes	37127	144(18)	24.13	697431	2.70
		no	13146	80(10)	30.27	605588	3.38
	fuse	yes	23283	144(18)	34.70	508116	5.32
Manually	none	yes	1738	10(5)	68.91	* 869530	79.25

could be used to automate the schedule optimizations mentioned in Sect. 5.1. The Compaan/Laura tool suite [28,33] translates polyhedral loop nests into KPNs, by eliminating global memory and global control. Laura translates the KPNs into VHDL.

The Cameron Project has created a high-level algorithmic language, named SA-C [13], for expressing image processing applications. Compilation to FPGAs is done using data flow graphs. Impulse-C [1] uses a subset of C extended with IO-macros. Translation is done by constructing one large finite automaton where the states relate to the control flow graph of the program.

These projects all focus more on exploiting parallelism than on improving bandwidth aspects. The inputs for the algorithms range from PRAs (MMAlpha, PICO, PARO), over polyhedral programs (Compaan, SA-C, this work), to more general constructs (Impulse-C). This results in different trade-offs between the set of algorithms handled and the efficiency of the resulting hardware.

7   Conclusion

It is known that often, long sequences of sometimes complex transformations are needed to improve data locality and parallelism. While these are key factors for generating fast software implementations, they are also the key factors for obtaining fast FPGA implementations. We proposed to reuse a state-of-the-art framework for composing long sequences of transformations targeted to software implementations. Our main original contributions consist of an analysis that pinpoints the key loop transformations to improve temporal data locality and a hardware architecture that allows to generate efficient VHDL code directly from the polyhedral model. By its factorized approach it offers efficient hardware usage. Furthermore it allows to easily explore parallelization strategies in future work. The methodology and associated tools introduced have been applied and evaluated on a 2D wavelet transformation, demonstrating their potential.

Acknowledgement. The authors would like to thank A. Cohen, S. Girbal and N. Vasilache for providing access to the URUK tool and giving support. This research is supported by I.W.T. grant 020174, F.W.O. grant G.0021.03 and by GOA project 12.51B.02 of Ghent University. Harald Devos is supported by the F.W.O. (Research Foundation - Flanders). We would like to thank Altera for donating FPGA boards and tools.

References

1. http://www.impulsec.com/.
2. A. V. Aho, R. Sethi, and J. D. Ullman. *Compilers: Principles, Techniques and Tools.* Addison-Wesley, 1986.
3. P. Ashar, S. Devadas, and A. R. Newton. *Sequential logic synthesis.* Kluwer Academic Publishers, 1992.
4. I. Augé, F. Pétrot, F. Donnet, and P. Gomez. Platform-based design from parallel C specifications. *IEEE Transactions on Computer-Aided Design of Integrated Circuits and Systems*, 24(12):1811–1826, December 2005.
5. C. Bastoul. Code generation in the polyhedral model is easier than you think. In *PACT*, pages 7–16, 2004.
6. C. Bastoul, A. Cohen, S. Girbal, S. Sharma, and O. Temam. Putting polyhedral loop transformations to work. In *LCPC*, volume 2958 of *Lecture Notes in Computer Science*, pages 209–225, 2003.
7. C. Bastoul and P. Feautrier. Improving data locality by chunking. In *Compiler Construction*, volume 2622 of *Lecture Notes in Computer Science*, pages 320–335, 2003.
8. L. Benini, P. Siegel, and G. De Micheli. Saving power by synthesizing gated clocks for sequential circuits. *IEEE Design & Test of Computers*, 11(4):32–41, 1994.
9. E. Berg and E. Hagersten. Fast data-locality profiling of native execution. In *SIGMETRICS*, pages 169–180, 2005.
10. K. Beyls and E. D'Hollander. Discovery of locality-improving refactorings by reuse path analysis. In *HPCC*, volume 4208 of *Lecture Notes in Computer Science*, pages 220–229, 2006.
11. K. Beyls and E. H. D'Hollander. Generating cache hints for improved program efficiency. *Journal of Systems Architecture*, 51(4):223–250, 2005.
12. K. Beyls and E. H. D'Hollander. Intermediately executed code is the key to find refactorings that improve temporal data locality. In *Proceedings of the 3rd conference on Computing Frontiers*, pages 373–382, 2006.
13. W. Bohm, J. Hammes, B. Draper, M. Chawathe, C. Ross, R. Rinker, and W. Najjar. Mapping a single assignment programming language to reconfigurable systems. *Journal of Supercomputing*, 21(2):117–130, February 2002.
14. J. Bormans, K. Denolf, S. Wuytack, L. Nachtergaele, and I. Bolsens. Integrating system-level low power methodologies into a real-life design flow. In *PATMOS*, pages 19–28, 1999.
15. A. Cohen, S. Girbal, D. Parello, M. Sigler, O. Temam, and N. Vasilache. Facilitating the search for compositions of program transformations. In *ICS*, pages 151–160, June 2005.

16. A. DeHon. The density advantage of configurable computing. *IEEE Computer*, 33(4):41–49, April 2000.

17. H. Devos, H. Eeckhaut, B. Schrauwen, M. Christiaens, and D. Stroobandt. Ever considered SystemC ? In *ProRISC Workshop*, pages 358–363, 2004.

18. G. Fursin. *Iterative Compilation and Performance Prediction for Numerical Applications*. PhD thesis, University of Edinburgh, 2004.

19. S. Girbal. *Optimisation d'applications - Composition de transformations de programme : modèle et outils*. PhD thesis, l'Université de Paris XI Orsay, 2005.

20. A. C. Guillou, P. Quinton, and T. Risset. Hardware synthesis for systems of recurrence equations with multi-dimensional schedule. *International Journal of Embedded Systems*, 2005. to appear.

21. F. Hannig, H. Dutta, and J. Teich. Mapping a class of dependence algorithms to coarse-grained reconfigurable arrays: Architectural parameters and methodology. *International Journal of Embedded Systems*, 2(1/2):114–127, 2006.

22. C.-T. Huang, P.-C. Tseng, and L.-G. Chen. Analysis and VLSI architecture for 1-D and 2-D discrete wavelet transform. *IEEE Transactions on Signal Processing*, 53(4):1575–1586, April 2005.

23. P. M. W. Knijnenburg, T. Kisuki, and M. F. P. O'Boyle. Iterative compilation. In *SAMOS*, volume 2268 of *Springer Lecture Notes in Computer Science*, pages 171–187, 2002.

24. S. G. Mallat. A theory for multiresolution signal decomposition: the wavelet representation. *IEEE Transactions on Pattern Analysis and Machine Intelligence*, 11(7):674–693, July 1989.

25. M. Martonosi, A. Gupta, and T. Anderson. Tuning memory performance of sequential and parallel programs. *IEEE Computer*, April 1995.

26. K. S. McKinley, S. Carr, and C.-W. Tseng. Improving data locality with loop transformations. *ACM Transactions on Programming Languages and Systems*, 18(4):424–453, 1996.

27. B. R. Rau and M. S. Schlansker. Embedded computer architecture and automation. *IEEE Computer*, 34(4):75–83, April 2001.

28. A. Turjan, B. Kienhuis, and E. Deprettere. Translating affine nested-loop programs to process networks. In *CASES*, 2004.

29. M. E. Wolf and M. S. Lam. A data locality optimizing algorithm. In *PLDI*, volume 26 of *SIGPLAN Notices*, pages 30–44, 1991.

30. M. Wolfe. Experiences with data dependence abstractions. In *ICS*, pages 321–329, 1991.

31. Y. Yu and E. H. D'Hollander. Loop parallelization using the 3D iteration space visualizer. *Journal of Visual Languages and Computing*, 12:163–181, 2001.

32. N. D. Zervas, G. P. Anagnostopoulos, V. Spiliotopoulos, Y. Andreopoulos, and C. E. Goutis. Evaluation of design alternatives for the 2D-discrete wavelet transform. *IEEE Transactions on Circuits and Systems for Video Technology*, 11(12):1246–1262, December 2001.

33. C. Zissulescu, B. Kienhuis, and E. Deprettere. Expression synthesis in process networks generated by LAURA. In *ASAP*, pages 15–21, July 2005.

Dynamic and On-Line Design Space Exploration for Reconfigurable Architectures

Fakhreddine Ghaffari[1,2], Michel Auguin[1], Mohamed Abid[2], and
Maher Ben Jemaa[2]

[1] I3S, University of Nice Sophia Antipolis, CNRS, les Algorithmes bat. Euclide, 2000,
route des Lucioles BP 121, 06903 Sophia-Antipolis
ghaffari, auguin@i3s.unice.fr
http://www.i3s.unice.fr/I3S/FR/
[2] Université de Sfax TUNISIA, Computer, Electronics and Smart engineering
systems design (CES),
ENIS, BPW 3038 Sfax, Tunisie
maher.benjemaa, mohamed.abid@enis.rnu.tn

Abstract. The implementation of complex embedded applications requires a mix of processor cores and HW accelerators on a single chip. When designing such complex and heterogeneous System on Chip (SoCs), the HW/SW partitioning needs to be made prior to refining the system description. Traditional system partitioning is generally done at the early stage of system architecture, by defining the tasks to be implemented on the embedded processor(s), and the tasks to be implemented on the hardware. We describe here a new approach of On-line Partitioning Algorithm (OPA) which consists of adapting dynamically the architecture to the processing requirements. A scheduling heuristic is associated to this partitioning approach. We consider soft real time data flow graph oriented applications for which the execution time is dependent on the content of input data. The target architecture is composed of a generic processor connected to a dynamically reconfigurable hardware accelerator. The dynamic reconfiguration allows the self adaptation of the architecture which avoids redesigning a new architecture according to variation of characteristics of applications algorithms. We compare our method with an Off-line static HW/SW partitioning approach. We present results of the OPA on an image processing application. Our experiments included simulation results with SystemC for on-line scheduling and partitioning approaches. An ILP solver is used to compare the experiment results with an off-line static HW/SW partitioning approach.

1 Introduction

Modern complex embedded real-time systems require significant computational power while guaranteeing latency and timing performance. Guaranteeing the performance of a multi-tasked system often requires a far more powerful processor if we minimize embedded resources as well. Hybrid hardware-software

P. Stenström (Ed.): Transactions on HiPEAC I, LNCS 4050, pp. 179–193, 2007.
© Springer-Verlag Berlin Heidelberg 2007

systems have a number of advantages over traditional microprocessor-based software systems or custom ASIC hardware solutions. The implementation of control-flow algorithms is difficult in hardware, while algorithms involving significant parallel arithmetic operations may be difficult to realize in a microprocessor-based software solution. Hybrid hardware software systems allow the parallelism to be exploited in hardware, while leaving control of the overall system in software. This may result in superior real-time performance, as argued in [1]. The aim is to adjust the computational power of current multimedia portable devices (such as embedded camera) while keeping their flexibility. Flexibility is required because different algorithms will run on the device, with different architecture requirements. Moreover, it enables upgrading and downloading of new applications. Reconfigurable hardware meets these two requirements and is therefore a valid solution for this problem. Hardware/Software partitioning is the process of dividing an application among software (running on microprocessors) and hardware units. Extensive research has shown that Hardware/ Software partitioning can result in overall software speedups [2, 3, and 4] as well as reducing system energy [14, 5 and 6]. Many applications, in particular in image processing (e.g. an intelligent embedded camera), have dependent data execution times according to the nature of the input to be processed. This kind of applications is often stressed by real time constraints, which demand adaptive computation capabilities. To partition data-dependent tasks on a heterogeneous architecture, new design approaches are necessary. Particularly for applications with soft real time constraints, we aim to minimize the embedded resources so as to avoid an architecture composed of the resources associated with the worst case execution times (WCET) of the functionalities. There is little work in the literature, which addresses this problem. The approach presented in [13] is based on an on-line HW/SW migration of tasks according to their execution times. This migration process is only applied locally to the most time consuming loop of the application program. The choice of dynamic re-allocation of the tasks presented in [13] is manual. The primary contribution of our work, though, is an extensive examination of the number of hardware resources savings as well as possible speedups through on line hardware/software partitioning. We have simulated our approach with a SystemC platform having a microprocessor coupled with a configurable logic on a real time image processing applications. The paper is organized as follows. Section 2 presents related works on HW/SW partitioning. Section 3 introduces the advances in dynamic reconfigurable systems. Section 4 presents the on-line partitioning algorithm. Section 5 shows the experimental results and finally we conclude in section 6.

2   Related Work

Recent works have introduced dynamic hardware/software partitioning [13]. During execution of an application, an on-chip profiling method detects critical regions of code for hardware implementation. An on-chip tool transparently re-implements those regions on FPGA (Field Programmable Gate Array). Researchers have explored other dynamic optimization approaches. For example, Dynamo performs dynamic software optimizations on the most frequently executed regions of code [1]. The ProfileMe approach [15] specialize subroutines for common inputs and determines by runtime profiling which configuration to call for the best performance. In [16] the performance is improved by re-mapping frequently executed regions of code to non-interfering cache locations. Value profiling [17] determines runtime invariant variables for constant propagation and code specialization for optimized performance, or even for reduced energy. The appearance of single-chip platforms incorporating a microprocessor and FPGA in a single chip [7, 8 and 9] has recently made the hardware/software partitioning problem even more attractive. Such platforms yield more efficient communication between the microprocessor and FPGA than using two chip designs, resulting in improved performance and reduced power. By considering the FPGA as a fast extension of the microprocessor, a designer can move critical software regions from the microprocessor onto the FPGA hardware, so as to improve performance whereas the physical architecture is unchanged.

3   Advances in Dynamic Reconfigurable Systems

In the literature, some reconfigurables architectures have been proposed to implement a dynamic partitioning approach. The architecture proposed in [11] is formed by a reconfigurable logic targeted by the dynamic HW/SW partitioning. During the design of this architecture, the main goal was to minimize the runtime of the on line reconfigurable placement and routing. In [12] an approach of tasks re-allocation between hardware and software units is presented. It details the communication after switching the implementation of a task from a unit to another. An embedded operating system has been used to manage the different communications, context saving, the placement/routing and memory management.

The target architecture in our approach is composed of a processor connected to a Reconfigurable Computing Unit (RCU) through an intelligent interface conceived by the CEA[1] and called ICURE [10]. This architecture is schematized in figure 1. The considered embedded processor can be of any type provided that it allows an efficient coupling with the RCU. The RCU reconfiguration is achieved by a dedicated unit situated in the ICURE interface. The reconfiguration data are stored in a structure called Contexts. This latter contains the bit-stream, the routing information and the object code necessary to the reconfiguration and execution of the hardwired mapped tasks. The CPU has access to ICURE functionalities through API (Application Programming Interface) allowing a transparent utilization of the reconfigurable resources.

---

[1] CEA: Commissariat lEnergie Atomique (Research Comitee on atomic energy).

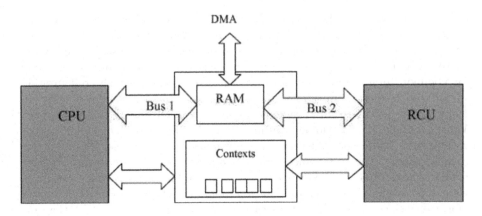

Fig. 1. The generic architecture

4   The On Line Partitioning Algorithm (OPA)

4.1   General Description

On-line HW/SW Partitioning has several important advantages over off-line approaches. OPA allows for a system to be optimized based on runtime behaviors and values, which may be hard to determine using off-line methods or costly simulations, and which also may change according to the environment with which the system interacts. Furthermore, on-line optimizations require no designer intervention and are applied transparently during runtime. In applications such as image processing, the execution of data dependent tasks consumes time accordingly to the characteristics of the incoming image. This time variation results from one or more Correlation Parameters (CP) in every processed image. An example of CP is the number of white pixels in an image or the number of moving objects. The goal of the On-line Partitioning Algorithm (OPA) is to dynamically allocate resources of the architecture to the tasks and schedule them such that the constraints are not violated. The OPA considers periodically the set of available embedded resources in the architecture.

The normal execution flow of the system on a sequence of input data In-1, In, In+1,... is illustrated in figure 2. During period In-1 the execution time of each task and of the whole application (Te) for the next period is estimated. While no violation of time constraints is estimated (Te ¡ Tmax), the current mapping and scheduling will be saved for the next period. Otherwise, a new partitioning/scheduling of the tasks is computed as depicted in period In in figure 2. The new mapping must deal with the available resources in the reconfigurable hardware unit and must provide a solution with an execution time less than the time constraint.

Partitioning is needed when violation of constraints are predicted. The basic idea consists to consider the current mapping and to carry out migrations of tasks between resources to satisfy the overall constraints (see period In+1 in

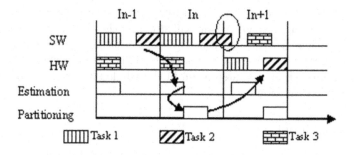

Fig. 2. Adaptation of partitioning to the processing need

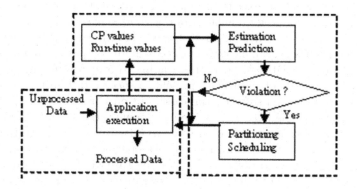

Fig. 3. Dynamic reconfigurable platform

figure 2). Assume that time constraint violation is predicted at period In and the task Ti is assigned to the processor. The current available area in the HW unit is Sn. A migration of Ti to the HW at the next period leads to a benefit of ?i on its execution time and the available area will be reduced to Sn+1 ¡ Sn. The On-line partitioning and scheduling are time consuming operations. Therefore the challenge is to develop fast efficient algorithms that can interact with the application functionalities and respect the time constraints of the application. Data flow-based applications are good candidates for this new approach. For example, while the system processes the image n, OPA performs the partitioning and the schedule of the estimations for image n+1. The figure 3 illustrates the functionalities embedded in an OPA system composed of two parts: the resources dedicated to the application itself and the OPA loop. The former is data flow oriented such as video, image, sound or any iterative data processing application with data dependent execution time. The application has its own internal data communications between dependant tasks, but only the exchanged data with the OPA loop subsystem is shown. The tasks of the application are executed according to the order given by the Scheduler. The execution time of each task and the associated CP value are collected in a database. At the end of each period, the OPA estimates the run time of each application task for the next period based on the measures in the database. If the estimated schedule respects the timing constraints, the OPA loop will stop and the system executes the next period. In the other case the algorithm runs the Partitioning function and tries to find a partition which respects the constraints. This global view of the algorithm leads to questions about its integration in the whole system, and how complex will be its implementation.

4.2 System Model

To model the application we consider a Data Flow Graph (DFG), where nodes are processing functions (tasks) and edges describe communication between tasks. The size of the DFG depends on the number of tasks and edges that have a great effect on the execution times of the partitioning and scheduling operations. A low processing granularity of the DFG makes the system easy to be predictable because data dependent task execution time can depend on a single CP. In opposite a low granularity DFG needs more computing to complete the algorithm loop on a DFG of great size, leading to overstep the image processing period. Each node of the DFG represents a specific task in the application, and it can run either on software (processor) or on hardware (RCU). The aim of using reconfigurable hardware is simply obtaining the same flexibility while executing an application task on hardware as on software. By migrating a task from software to hardware and conversely, we make a significant change on the execution time. Any migration of task to the software will free the reconfigurable area, but will consequently increase the task run time. In opposite, any migration of task to hardware will have the reverse effects. Thus, it is important to have the suitable choices of task migration, and the choices are made in the lap of time between two periods. If the video processing constraint is 40 ms for each image, then the application execution time and the OPA execution time should be under that limit. Another difficulty lies on having low resources OPA cost compared with the cost of the resources needed to execute the application tasks; else, it will not be beneficial to overload the system with the OPA approach. To resume, the On-line Partitioning Algorithm tries to update the partition of an application when it is running. The algorithm must make choices between all tasks migrations and schedule them. Its cost (run time and resources) must be small compared with the overall cost of the system. The following sections will explain clearly each OPA function in the figure 3.

4.3 Prediction Algorithm

The efficiency of the system depends on the estimation accuracy. With the estimated values, for the next period, the OPA decides if the partition has to be changed. To estimate the future execution time of a task (TEXE), we have considered a simple interpolation equation. The approach of estimating with an interpolated function considers tasks whose execution time depends only on one Correlation Parameter. The estimation of such task could be done by a polynomial equation, which is found in an off-line analysis or profiling of the task code.

The CP is the only unknown variable in the equation, consequently only the estimation of the CP is needed to know the estimated execution time. For each task, the equation could be different according to the implementation. Estimating the execution time with a polynomial equation is rather simple and efficient but an off-line analysis is required to deduce the coefficients of the polynomial equation.

4.4   Partitioning Algorithm

The partitioning is required when a violation of the constraints is predicted. The OPA performs migrations of tasks from SW to HW in order to decrease the execution time under the time constraint limit. Conversely, when the processing units remain idle before the end of execution of the current period, OPA performs a HW to SW migration in order to free resources from the RCU.

Up-speeding migration. The period (or iteration) time constraint includes the application execution time and the OPA execution time. For a video application, period takes 40ms; this should include the image processing and the OPA execution. If the OPA maximum run time is 1 ms, then the application is allowed to run for 39 ms. So if the application execution is predicted to run for more than 39 ms, then the partitioning must accelerate one or more tasks to reduce that time. In practice we consider a lower limit allowed to the application execution to avoid constraint violation due to errors in estimation and prediction. On line partitioning is performed in OPA by a migration process that changes the allocation of tasks, one task at once, until time constraints are met. Indeed, partitioning is not performed from scratch, it consist of an updating of the current mapping in order to take into account of local variations of execution times. The migration of a task consists of choosing a faster implementation among the set of contexts embedded in the system. The efficiency of the on-line partitioning depends on the right speed-up vs resources implementations selected in an offline profiling analysis and synthesis. For each potential migration the algorithm evaluates the parameter G defined as the product of the time benefit and the number of resources remaining free after migration. To examine the potential migration of the tasks we start by sorting the candidates' implementations by the decreasing order of G (Figure 4). If this up-speeding migration does not satisfy the time constraint then the next candidate migration is performed until the temporal constraint is satisfied or when the reconfigurable is fully exploited. Then we created a version of the application with all the critical tasks moved to the reconfigurable hardware.

Up-freeing migration. This type of migration is necessary to avoid the saturation of the reconfigurable caused by successive SW to HW migrations. The method is analogous to the up-speeding migration. We choose the task which has the minimum benefits of time on the Hardware and that make free the maximum of hardware resources. The partitioner will repeat this process until the total execution time is in between HL (High Level) and the LL (Low Level).

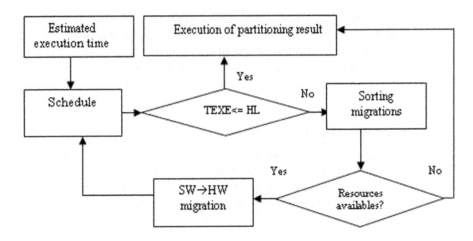

Fig. 4. Up-speeding Migration Approach

4.5 Scheduling Algorithm

To evaluate a partitioning solution, we must calculate the total execution time of the application on that partition. The objective is to find an execution order for the application. Due to the data dependencies in the DFG (described by the edges between tasks) and the sequential nature of the SW processor, the evaluation of the total execution time requires determining a schedule of the DFG. This schedule is based on the estimated execution times of the tasks according to the potential allocation provided after partitioning. Independent tasks allocated to hardware can run in parallel. The migration of task is considered only if there are enough free resources in the hardware. Scheduling decisions are thus related to tasks allocated to the processor. The task can have two states: waiting and scheduled. The waiting state remains until all the task predecessors are scheduled. If a task is to implement on hardware, then it goes in the scheduled state. If it is allocated to software, then the scheduler needs to check if the timing allows the task to be scheduled. There are three possible cases: 1. when the software resource is free and only one software task to be scheduled, 2. when the software resource is free and there is more than one software task to schedule, 3. when the processor is busy. In the first case, the task is scheduled because it is the only one that requires the processor. In the third case, all the tasks wait for the software resource to be free. All this tasks add a new sequencing dependency to their data dependencies. In the second case, the scheduler must choose the software task to be scheduled first. For this a priority table is constructed. The tasks priorities are affected according to the algorithm shown in figure 5. The value of a priority is only based on the successors of the task. The task with most critical successors has the highest priority. A task is critical if it has at least one hardware successor. The highest estimated execution time of all the hardware successors determines the first level of priority. If there is still more than one task having the same urgency then the second level of priority is the task which

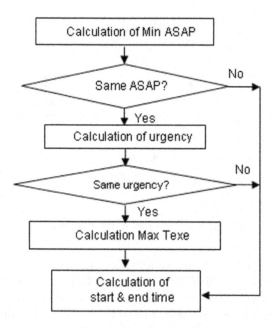

Fig. 5. New HW/SW scheduling approach

has the lowest execution time. In the DFG example shown in figure 6, there are two possible scheduling paths: after scheduling the task A on the processor, we can schedule B or C on the processor. This is because the computation of ASAP (As Soon As Possible) time and the urgency of tasks are as follows: The task B is more urgent than the task C because its successor is the more critical tasks in the DFG. The task D is a hardware task and its execution time is the highest one so its beneficial to schedule it as soon as possible. Given the complexity of the scheduling algorithm, we choose to implement it on hardware. Thus the computation time of the scheduling algorithm is neglected.

The scheduler architecture is fully synthesisable, and it was done with a XILINX Virtex II Pro FPGA tools. The size needed (number of CLB: Configurable Logic Bloc) depends upon the number of tasks, and the complexity of their interconnections. Moreover, the data bus size influences the whole synthesis process as much as the connections routing. To have a clear idea, the synthesis is done with the target core Virtex II Pro vp100: For the Data Bus Size of 10 bits the Whole Scheduler block takes:

- Number of Slices: 1677 out of 44096 3
- Number of Slice Flip Flops: 230 out of 88192 0
- Number of 4 input LUTs: 3088 out of 88192 3
- Minimum period: 11.336ns (Maximum Frequency: 88.211MHz)
- Minimum input arrival time before clock: 5.879ns
- Maximum output required time after clock: 23.875ns
- Maximum combinational path delay: 23.630ns

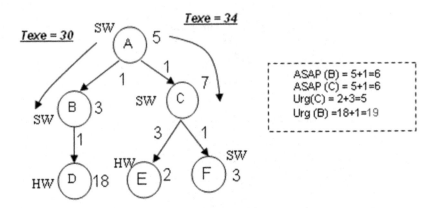

Fig. 6. Scheduling with urgency criteria

The idea of accelerating the scheduler makes the loop Partitioning-Scheduling more feasible in real application. By doing this, the gain of time is great and the cost of hardware is not excessive. All the results are obtained by simulating with Modelsim and Xilinx synthesis tools. The results satisfy the requirements for this OPA, which is minimising the cost of the Estimation-Scheduling-Partitioning time consumption.

5   Experimental Results

We have simulated our partitioning approach with SystemC on an image processing application. The motion object detection on fixed image background requires resources for data processing in order to process images in a real time. ICAM (Intelligent CAMera) is an algorithm developed by the C.E.A, used for embedded camera to detect objects motion (figure 7). Such application can be used for parking supervising, identification, and pieces selection according to the shape The choice of having ICAM as the test application for the OPA can be resumed to its complexity and its variable execution time. The algorithm of detection is based on the difference between the current input and a reference image. If there is an object on the image but not on the reference then ICAM considers it as object in motion. The given ICAM application is sequential on execution, thus we have modified its DFG. This later has been improved by adding virtual tasks running in parallel with the original ones. Each virtual task would simulate task behaviors with a time and resource consuming. Moreover, the new DFG permits to validate the scheduler algorithm and the behavior of the OPA against a complex system. The virtual tasks could have fixed or varying execution time. ICAM is considering as application with twenty tasks as depicted in the figure 7. Each of them could run on software as well as on hardware. The model in SystemC of this application must have the software and the hardware parts. On the software part, each task is a function which is called by the processor when needed. On the hardware side, each task is an independently hardware block

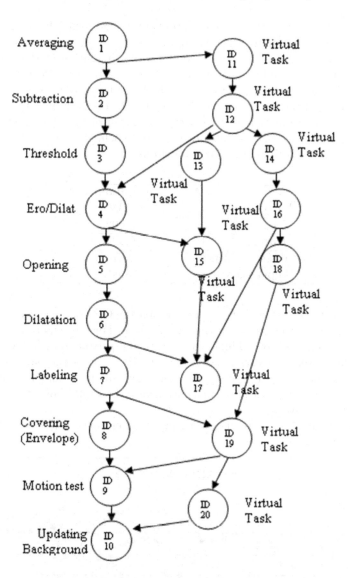

Fig. 7. DFG application

with inputs and outputs for data communications. The application running is
controlled by a kernel function, thus the software and hardware parts of the
ICAM have a direct communication with the Kernel function. Processed data
must circulate from task to task, and this is done by memory communications.
It has been considered that the ICAM tasks share the data through a dedicated
memory, and then there should have no direct data transmission from software
to hardware application tasks.

The communication with memories is only for image data. The communication with the Kernel function is control data: measured execution times and CP values. The execution time is measured with the simulating platform processor clock: the modeling and simulating have been done under a Pentium Centrino 1.5 GHz with MS Windows XP as O.S. The behavior of the system can change with the speed of the processor and the used O.S to run SystemC. Only software execution times are measured. The hardware execution times are deduced from the software by dividing this later over a fixed coefficient. The following table shows the execution time of all OPA functions:

Algorithm	Average execution time (ms)
Partitioning	0.330
Scheduling	0.002
Estimator	0.421
Database updating	0.010
Application	33.565

According to the table above, we notice that the OPA timing cost is neglected as compared with the execution time application. For our experiment the next CP value is computed by adding 5 percent to the precedent one. A comparison between measured and estimated execution time proves the efficiency of the estimator method. Figure 8 shows the execution time variation of the estimator algorithm on various iterations. As mentioned in the table above, this algorithm takes 0.421ms in average.

As depicted in figure 9, the Database management never exceeds the 0.012ms.

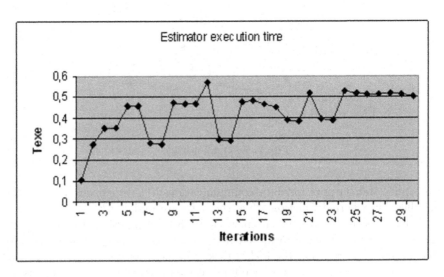

Fig. 8. Estimator computing time per iteration

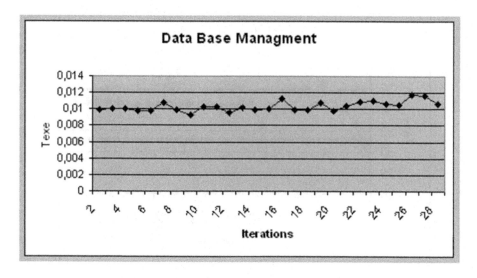

Fig. 9. Time computing of data management function

We remind that the OPA approach has for objective to adapt on-line the partitioning result with the processing requirements. This is shown clearly in the figure 10: the OPA limits always the application execution time between the high level time and the low level time by updating the HW/SW partitioning result.

We compare our partitioning approach with an optimal off-line partitioning method based on ILP (Integer Linear Programming) solver. The ILP based approach can solve the partitioning problem optimally. The partitioning problem is formulated as follows: The objective function is to minimize the number of hardware resources to be used by the application. The main constraint is that the total execution time must respect the real time constraint. The ILP is a static partitioning method based on the Worst Case Execution Times (WCETs) of the application tasks. As it is assumed in OPA, the communication delays between tasks are neglected. The table hereafter shows the differences between the two approaches results:

Approach	Resources used	Nbre Image lost	Off-line work	Resources added	flexible
ILP	852	0	Yes	No	No
OPA	300	0.35 percent	Limited	Yes	Yes

As depicted on the table above, ILP demands more resources for the application than OPA since it tries to reach the optimal solution. The OPA approach tries only to satisfy the constraints.

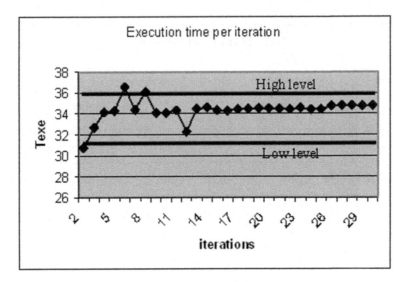

Fig. 10. Application total execution time per iteration

6   Conclusions

Results of our approach show the efficiency of the adaptation of partitioning to needs of treatment. The dynamics reconfiguration of the FPGA allows the architecture to accept several contexts of reconfiguration as results of HW/SW partitioning. A dynamic Hardware /software partitioning approach have many advantages over traditional partitioning approaches. Dynamic partitioning can adapt to an applications constraints dynamically at run time. We presented a HW/SW partitioning approach based on on-line reallocation tasks. We also presented our approach of scheduling based on a criticality parameter chosen on-line. Our future work consists in validating these approaches on real applications and industrial platform.

Acknowledgments. We thank the CEA for their donation of the ICAM application. This work was supported in part by the National Science Research Centre CNRS France.

References

1. Bala, V., Duesterwald, E., Banerjia. Dynamo: a transparent dynamic optimization system. Proceedings of the ACM SIGPLAN Conference on Programming Language Design and Implemenation, 2000.
2. Balboni, A., W. Fornaciari and D. Sciuto. Partitioning and Exploration in the TOSCA Co-Design Flow. International Workshop on Hardware/Software Codesign, pp. 62-69, 1996.
3. Eles, P., Z. Peng, K. Kuchchinski and A. Doboli. System Level Hardware/Software Partitioning Based on Simulated Annealing and Tabu Search. Kluwer's Design Automation for Embedded Systems, vol2, no 1, pp. 5-32, Jan 1997.

4. Ernst, R., J. Henkel, T. Benner. Hardware/Software Cosynthesis for Microcontrollers. IEEE Design and Test of Computers, pages 64-75, October/December 1993.
5. Dean, J., Hicks, J., Waldspurger, C.A., Weihl, W.E., Chrysos, G. ProfileMe: Hardware support for instruction level profiling on out-of-order processors, MICRO 1997.
6. Henkel, J., Y. Li. Energy-conscious HW/SW-partitioning of embedded systems: A Case Study on an MPEG-2 Encoder. Intl. Workshop on Hardware/Software Codesign, 1998.
7. Excalibur, Altera Corp., http://www.altera.com.
8. Triscend Corporation, http://www.triscend.com, 2003.
9. Virtex II Pro, Xilinx Corp., http://www.xilinx.com.
10. M. Auguin, K. Ben Chehida, J. P. Diguet, X. Fornari, A. M. Fouilliart, C. Gamrat, G. Gogniat, P. Kajfasz, and Y. Le Moullec, Partitioning and CoDesign tools and methodology for Reconfigurable Computing: the EPICURE philosophy, Proceeding of the third International Workshop on Systems, Architectures, Modeling Simulation (SAMOS03), July 2003, Samos, Greece.
11. Roman Lydecky, Frank Vahid A configurable Logic Architecture for Dynamic Hardware/Software Partitioning. In Proc. of the DATE 2004 Conference. Paris, February 2004.
12. J-Y. Mignolet, V. Nollet, P.Coene, D.Verkest, S.Vernalde, R. Lauwereins Infrastructure for Design and management of Relocatable Tasks in a Heterogeneous Reconfigurable System-on-chip. In Proc. of the DATE 2003 Conference. Messe Munich, Germany March 3-7, 2003.
13. Stitt, G., Lysecky, R., Vahid, F. Dyanmic hardware/software partitioning: a first approach. Proceedings of the 40th ACM/IEEE Conference on Design Automation (DAC), 2003.
14. Stitt, G. and F. Vahid. The Energy Advantages of Microprocessor Platforms with On-Chip Configurable Logic. IEEE Design and Test of Computers, Nov/Dec 2002.
15. Pettis, K., Hansen, R.C. Profile guided code positioning. ACM SIGPLAN Conference on Programming Language Design and Implementation (PLDI), June 1990.
16. Henkel, J. A low power hardware/software partitioning approach for core-based embedded systems. Design Automation Conference (DAC), 1999.
17. Calder, B., Feller, P., Eustace, A. Value profiling. MICRO pp. 259-267, 1997.

Automatic Discovery of Coarse-Grained Parallelism in Media Applications

Shane Ryoo, Sain-Zee Ueng, Christopher I. Rodrigues, Robert E. Kidd,
Matthew I. Frank, and Wen-mei W. Hwu

Center for Reliable and High-Performance Computing
Department of Electrical and Computer Engineering
University of Illinois at Urbana-Champaign
{sryoo, ueng, cirodrig, rkidd, mif, hwu}@crhc.uiuc.edu

Abstract. With the increasing use of multi-core microprocessors and hardware accelerators in embedded media processing systems, there is an increasing need to discover coarse-grained parallelism in media applications written in C and C++. Common versions of these codes use a pointer-heavy, sequential programming model to implement algorithms with high levels of inherent parallelism. The lack of automated tools capable of discovering this parallelism has hampered the productivity of parallel programmers and application-specific hardware designers, as well as inhibited the development of automatic parallelizing compilers. Automatic discovery is challenging due to shifts in the prevalent programming languages, scalability problems of analysis techniques, and the lack of experimental research in combining the numerous analyses necessary to achieve a clear view of the relations among memory accesses in complex programs. This paper is based on a coherent prototype system designed to automatically find multiple levels of coarse-grained parallelism. It visits several of the key analyses that are necessary to discover parallelism in contemporary media applications, distinguishing those that perform satisfactorily at this time from those that do not yet have practical, scalable solutions. We show that, contrary to common belief, a compiler with a strong, synergistic portfolio of modern analysis capabilities can automatically discover a very substantial amount of coarse-grained parallelism in complex media applications such as an MPEG-4 encoder. These results suggest that an automatic coarse-grained parallelism discovery tool can be built to greatly enhance the software and hardware development processes of future embedded media processing systems.

1 Introduction

In the past few years, several multicore microprocessors have been introduced for both general purpose and embedded systems computing [1,5,19,20,30]. Despite the parallelism many contemporary applications exhibit, compilers currently do not have the capability to automatically extract substantial coarse-grain, thread-level parallelism from them. Explicit parallel programming by human programmers also remains a major challenge. One of the primary reasons for this dilemma

P. Stenström (Ed.): Transactions on HiPEAC I, LNCS 4050, pp. 194–213, 2007.

is that multiple, sophisticated interprocedural analyses, performed by either a human or a compiler, must achieve a clear view of memory usage before safe and profitable transformations can be performed. There is also a lack of understanding in how one can build an analysis system to facilitate hand and automated parallelization of full-fledged, pointer-heavy modern applications. The goal of this work was to investigate the degree of coarse-grained parallelism that can be automatically discovered by an analysis system and determine the state of the analyses required to expose that parallelism in contemporary applications.

For this work we chose to focus on the media application domain, which has a high degree of inherent parallelism, a large user base desiring higher performance, and available reference codes from industry standards bodies. These applications are often implemented in C/C++, which have features that require sophisticated analysis to disambiguate memory accesses: pointers, indirect procedure calls, dynamically-allocated memory, and resizable data arrays. Some of the programs we have investigated are reference MPEG-4 encoders from standards bodies, jpegdec from MediaBench, and the LAME and mpg123 applications for MPEG Layer 3 audio encoding/decoding. These codes are often referenced when programmers write explicitly parallel versions or when hardware designers transfer algorithms into hardware description languages; thus, parallelism discovery is useful as a tool for these designers. It is worth noting that the target applications are much larger and more complex than benchmarks previously used for automatic parallelization research [3].

The remainder of this work begins with Section 2, which discusses the analyses we have found that expose coarse-grained parallelism in media applications. Section 3 will discuss the forms of coarse-grained parallelism we target. Section 4 goes into detail on one version of the MPEG-4 encoder, which had the richest parallelism among the applications. Section 5 will discuss previous efforts on these analyses with respect to parallelization, and Section 6 concludes with a summary of our contributions.

2   Analyses

A compiler uses its analyses to refine its picture of a program. For the purpose of discovering parallelism, data dependence is one of the most important characteristics of the program. Analyses clarify the picture either by finding precise data dependences or by removing spurious ones. Because analyses must be conservative when supporting optimizations and transformations, the compiler's picture of the program is often cluttered by spurious dependences. For example, accesses to two memory objects are marked as conflicting if the objects cannot be proved independent. A single spurious dependence can prevent multiple opportunities for parallel execution.

Many different analyses with different aspects or levels of sensitivity have been derived to remove these spurious dependences in different situations. In order for the compiler to recognize different forms of parallelism, such as those listed in Section 3, many different analyses must be combined or integrated. If critical analyses or specific options of an analysis are missing, existing parallelism will remain hidden.

The chief obstacle to discovering opportunities to parallelize a media application written in C/C++ is identifying dependences between pointer references (including references to arrays). A high-quality pointer analysis is essential in determining the relationship between pointer references. However, there are many coding constructs and programming practices that veil the true picture of memory usage from pointer analysis. For some of these cases, like recursive data structures and arrays, more specialized analyses such as shape analysis [8,32] and array analysis [9] can be very helpful in clarifying the picture.

In order to perform parallelization at the scale we are proposing, the analyses need to be scalable. The analyses can not be limited to only the parts of the program that are potentially parallelizable because those parts are coupled to the rest of the program by both pointer relationships and numeric values. Programs frequently possess diverse behaviors that are based upon input data, command-line flags, or defined constants. These settings are typically determined at the beginning of the program and propagate throughout the program code, and must be taken into account by the analyses.

It is certainly more expedient to rewrite a program to suit existing parallelizing analyses than to create new analyses sophisticated enough to understand existing programs. Nonetheless, there are practical benefits to be expected from an automated analysis framework. Programs may comprise many thousands or millions of lines of code and have multiple maintainers. Manually understanding and rewriting them is a tedious task that could benefit from automation. As programs become bigger and more complex, manual manipulation becomes even more difficult. More fundamentally, a more powerful set of analyses can be understood as granting the programmer more freedom to write flexible and modular code. For example, the IJG JPEG library stores all data related to the processing of a particular image in a dynamically allocated data structure. While many analyses would be more precise if the data were stored in global variables, to rewrite the library in such a manner would mean giving up reentrancy, which was designed into the library to make it usable in larger programs [18].

2.1   Pointer Analysis

Pointer analysis has been a subject of much research. At its core, pointer analysis determines what objects a memory reference can possibly access. The many extensions, like context-sensitivity, flow-sensitivity, and field-sensitivity, further specialize and clarify the picture pointer analysis presents by eliminating spurious dependences. Figuring out data dependence and data flow is very important for all of the different forms of parallelism in Section 3, and pointer analysis is essential to generate an accurate picture of the usage of memory objects. We will discuss the various features of pointer analysis we found indispensible for discovering parallelism. Implementing all of them in a single framework was a challenging task.

Pointer analysis needs to be scalable as well as precise. An important observation is that memory object allocation code and pointer assignments are often far from the usage of the objects, both in code location and execution time. Memory objects are frequently initialized towards the beginning of execution and used throughout the rest of the application. Of the two major options for pointer analysis, Andersen's-style (inclusion-based) and Steensgaard's-style (unification-based), Steensgaard's is generally cheaper and more scalable since it restrains the analysis' working set by merging the objects to which a pointer can reference. However, this can result in spurious dependences when any pointer, including those not in the parallel code region, can point to multiple objects. For this work, we used a scalable Andersen's-style analysis called FULCRA [26], which supports all options discussed in this section.

There are two pointer analysis options which have a highly synergistic effect and are generally necessary for adequate resolution of memory usage. First, the allocation function for a particular type of dynamically-allocated memory object is frequently reused to allocate multiple objects. A consequence of this code reuse is a need for the ability to distinguish certain objects that share a static allocation site, which we call *heap-sensitivity*. We specifically use heap specialization [27] enabled by a context-sensitive analysis to achieve heap-sensitivity. Context-sensitivity obtains a higher resolution in a pointer analysis by summarizing the pointer effects of procedures into their direct and indirect callers and obtaining information specific to the individual calling contexts. Heap specialization builds on top of this by versioning/cloning each heap object when pointer summaries are propagated to callers.

The other major analysis option is field sensitivity, which is needed because a non-field-sensitive pointer analysis will group together all of the objects pointed to by a structure. This prevents the compiler from distinguishing objects through those pointers. This case appears regularly since media programs commonly manipulate multiple data channels, and programmers use structures to organize data hierarchically. A natural way to organize channels of a single data set is to aggregate them as different fields of a larger structure.

As an example of the need for the multiple features of pointer analysis, consider the sample code in Figure 1. Without heap and context-sensitivity, the objects will be determined to be the same due to the similar calls to `AllocateBuffer`. Field-sensitivity is needed to distinguish `inphase` and `quadrature` as different fields of `signal`. Consequently field-sensitivity, context-sensitivity, and heap-sensitivity are all needed for the compiler to determine that the objects pointed to by the fields `inphase` and `quadrature` are independent.

The final pointer analysis option discussed here is flow-sensitivity. The default mode of operation for many pointer analyses is to not take into account the execution order of pointer assignments in programs, conflating the objects that the pointer references at different times. Flow-sensitivity instead includes ordering information into the analysis, but often at great cost to analysis working data size and runtime. The most common case where flow-sensitivity is useful is when a pointer is reused for different purposes or data at different program locations. Several pointer analyses in the past have attempted to make a tradeoff between flow-sensitive and non-flow-sensitive analysis, often using a derivative of the SSA form [13]. Partial flow-sensitivity of this nature is also supported in FULCRA [29].

```
/* AllocateBuffer() calls calloc() to allocate memory. */
signal->inphase = AllocateBuffer (length);
singal->quadrature = AllocateBuffer (length);
```

Fig. 1. Code example that requires numerous pointer analyses

2.2   Array Analysis

When two pointers are known to reference the same object, array analysis can indicate whether or not the pointers reference the same memory location. This form of analysis conveys information about which loop iterations carry a dependence. Iterations are independent and can be executed in parallel if there are no flow, output, or anti-dependences between them. Array analysis can also determine if different loops access disjoint subsets of a given object. Finally, array analysis can be used to derive the data correlation between iterations of separate loops.

The common situation for parallel loops in media applications is to read input data from a segment of an array or set of arrays, process the data, and write the output data to a segment of a separate set of arrays. Although pointer analysis will eliminate spurious flow and anti-dependences between the read and written memory objects, array analysis is necessary to eliminate the output dependences between stores of different iterations. There are also loops where the input and output array locations are the same for each iteration, due to reuse of data structures. These loops also require array analysis to eliminate flow and anti-dependences. To be scalable, a compiler should extract symbolic expressions and perform induction variable analysis [6] on a demand-driven basis.

One important aspect of media applications is that they often have a range of supported sample rates, sizes, or resolutions and use many symbolic variables in the interest of code reuse. When dimensions are known integers, array analyses only need to handle affine expressions, where at most one symbolic variable (the loop inductor) exists for each multiplicative term. Dimensions determined at runtime create non-affine expressions and variable loop bounds, which stymie many simple array disambiguation tests [3]. In these cases, value constraints can be obtained or computed to assist the array disambiguation analysis [12,21]. More on value constraints and relationships is discussed in Sections 2.3 and 2.4. We have incorporated the Omega Test [31] and an extension of the I-Test [24] that manipulates symbolic expressions into our analysis infrastructure.

An example containing non-affine array expressions and variable loop bounds is shown in Figure 2. Four writes to the array **large** are performed per inner loop iteration. A basic array analysis that only looks at affine expressions

```
for (j = 0; j < height - 1; j++) {
  for (i = 0; i < width - 1; i++) {
    item = small[j*width + i];
    large[2*j*width + 2*i] = item;
    large[2*j*width + 2*i + 1] = item;
    large[2*j*width + 2*(i+width)] = item;
    large[2*j*width + 2*(i+width) + 1] = item;
  }
}
```

Fig. 2. Non-affine array expressions in a variable-bounded loop

with constant loop bounds would be unable to address this code, since one address could be reproduced by numerous combinations of j, width, and i. More advanced analyses incorporate information about the value ranges of variables relative to constants and each other. In this case, all three variables are known to be non-negative and i is always less than width-1, due to inner loop iteration conditions, which removes spurious output dependences and identifies the loops as having parallel iterations.

Because of modularity and code reuse, it is not uncommon to have procedure calls in a loop that operate on a different segment of an array every iteration. We would like to preserve access summaries for procedure calls for the appropriate contexts, since inlining can greatly increase the code size of an application. Without summary information, the compiler must assume that the procedure can access all elements of an array, which prevents parallelism if elements are written to in the array. Prior work exists for the Fortran language [28], but efficient summaries for the C language are still under development.

2.3   Value Constraint Analysis

Many variables in a program have a relatively small set of values during the majority of program execution, restricted by control flow tests or written constants. Information about the possible range or other constraints on their values can be critical in evaluating symbolic tests, such as the array analyses mentioned in Section 2.2. Value constraint information can also eliminate "dead" error checks within loops that create early exits; multiple loop iterations cannot be run non-speculatively unless these checks are removed. Many of these checks serve to detect bugs during program development and cannot actually occur during error-free execution. The size of contemporary applications necessitates an interprocedural, demand-driven method for finding these value constraints.

As an example of the value constraint problem, consider the code in Figure 3. In the example, image->bits is a pointer to a linear array holding a two-dimensional greyscale image of dimensions width and height. The main processing phase in this simplified example consists of four nested loops. The body of the second loop generates one eight-by-eight block of data and writes it into the image. To determine whether parallelization of LOOP1, LOOP2, or

```
if (w <=) exit (1);
remainder = w % 8;
i->width = w + (8 - remainder);
i->block_width = i->width / 8;
```

Large amount of program control flow through multiple function calls and returns

```
        width = image->width;
LOOP1   for (j = 0; j < image->block_height; j++) {
LOOP2     for (i = 0; i < image->block_width; i++) {
            int block[8][8];
            int *base = image->bits + (8*j) * width + (8*i);
            .. /* write the contents of block */
LOOP3       for (y = 0; y < 8; y++)
LOOP4         for (x = 0; x < 8; x++)
                base[y * width + x] = block[y][x];
          }
        }
```

Fig. 3. Example of the value constraint and value relationship problems

LOOP3 is safe, an analysis needs to verify that there are no output dependences between the writes to `image->bits` in any iterations of those loops. If the absolute value of `width` is less than 8, then an output dependence exists between successive iterations of LOOP3, preventing independent execution of iterations of LOOP1, LOOP2, and LOOP3, as illustrated in Figure 4(a,b). If the compiler can locate the statement that generates the variable's value, it can determine that the alignment code restricts the value of `width` to a multiple of 8. It should be noted that contemporary applications often have this restricting code distant in code space and execution from the relevant uses, necessitating a whole-program analysis.

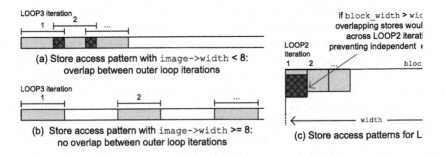

Fig. 4. Access patterns for the value constraint and relationship problems in Figure 3

Previous work on value constraint analysis has generally taken a dataflow approach to find valid ranges [12,21]. However, in contemporary C applications many values are loaded from dynamically-allocated memory, which require more sophisticated methods to be effective. We are currently experimenting with demand-driven backtracking methods through memory objects to find constraint information.

2.4 Value Relationship Inference

In addition to knowing the set of values that a variable may retain, symbolic array disambiguation analyses gain precision from knowing the relationship between the values of different variables. Often, one variable is used to compute the value of several other variables. When related variables appear in an index expression, symbolic analyses typically lose precision unless they know the relationship between the variables. The compiler can find these relationships by tracking values back through def-use relationships to find common terms [35]. This requires interprocedural expression computation through memory objects, often dynamically-allocated, to find the relationships between values. As with the value constraint problem, an analysis for value relationships should be performed in a demand-driven manner to be scalable.

Analyses have been constructed to infer the relationship of values in the absence of dynamically-allocated memory [2], but in the applications we have studied the relevant values are passed via fields of heap structures and require more sophisticated memory analysis to track its definitions and usage. These analyses are currently under development.

Operating on one data set at multiple granularities is a common characteristic of media codes. For example, signal processing often divides a signal into segments containing a small number of samples, and image processing often divides an image into square blocks of pixels. In such applications, we have a common coding practice of precalculating the dimensions of the data set at each level of granularity during initialization. To see how this may confuse array disambiguation tests, consider again the code example in Figure 3. The relationship between the bound of LOOP2, `block_width`, and the variable `width` used in indexing the image array, is established when the image's memory is allocated, during the program's initialization phase. If during the execution of LOOP2 i reaches `width/8`, then there will be an output dependence across the outer two loops. Without knowledge of the relationship between the loop bound `block_width` and the variable `width`, a compiler must be conservative and not parallelize LOOP2 or LOOP1. However, if the compiler can trace back to the initialization code, it can determine that LOOP2's bound value is `width/8`, that i can be at most `width/8 - 1`, and that no output dependence exists.

Figure 4(c) shows the effects on the target image. Each iteration of LOOP2 fills in an 8x8 pixel block in the image. By default, the compiler must assume that the subset of the image that is written in the inner loop can "wrap around" and overwrite data written in an earlier iteration (the hashed block), introducing an output dependence that precludes parallelization. Value relationship information can tell the compiler that this access is not possible.

3   Forms of Parallelism

There are multiple forms of coarse-grained parallelism that can be exploited in media programs. We have divided them roughly into three different categories. The first is *loop-iteration parallelism*, or simply iteration parallelism, where different iterations of the same loop can be executed independently. The second is *region parallelism*, where separate static code regions can be executed independently. The final category is *cross-loop parallelism*, where results of one loop feed another, but not all iterations of the first loop need to be completed for the second loop to begin. This section will present the different types of parallelism in detail and the conditions that must be asserted before parallelism can be leveraged via transformations [22]. In order for the compiler to automatically detect and check the the necessary conditions for parallelism, the compiler will need to leverage all of the analyses outlined in Section 2.

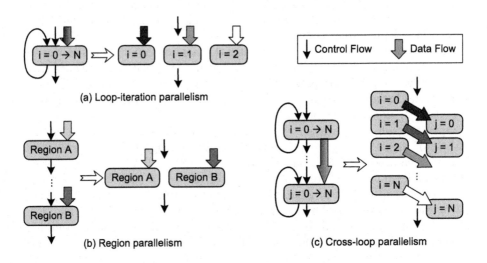

(a) Loop-iteration parallelism

(b) Region parallelism

(c) Cross-loop parallelism

Fig. 5. Forms of loop parallelism

When discussing compiler-detected coarse-grained parallelism, the first concept that comes to mind is often loop-iteration parallelism, as shown in Figure 5(a). When each iteration of a loop depends on different data, as indicated by the different colors of data flow, the iterations can be separated and executed in parallel via loop distribution. Much of the previous work in this area has been performed in the Fortran programming language. The move to C/C++ introduces new issues, some of which are covered in [22].

Before exploiting loop-iteration parallelism, the compiler must assert that the iterations are truly independent. The memory locations written by each iteration must be independent from those of other iterations, and no iteration can write to another iteration's input data. This assertion quickly becomes complicated due to the usage of pointers and dynamically-allocated memory objects in C/C++.

Large-scope or whole-program capable analyses are also needed: benefit from small inner loops is limited and the allocation of memory objects may be distant in execution and code. Finally, sophisticated pointer analysis features may be needed to successfully disambiguate memory objects.

Certain regions of static code can always be executed independently if they do not have any data dependences between them. Figure 5(b) illustrates this case of parallelism, which we term region parallelism. Although this form of parallelism may appear easier to determine than loop-iteration parallelism, the same assertions regarding data independence must be made. Furthermore, the determination of region boundaries when trying to detect this form of parallelism is not a trivial task [34]. For software engineering reasons, it may well be the case that function boundaries also define reasonable task boundaries, but this may not provide optimal parallelism in all cases.

Cross-loop parallelism arises when one loop produces data that is consumed by a following loop. If each iteration of the following loop only depends upon a limited and known number of iterations of the previous loop and does not over-write the first loop's input data, it is possible to execute part of the two loops in parallel as long as the real data dependences are respected. This parallelism is similar to that exploited in vector chaining, except at a much coarser granularity. Figure 5(c) shows an example of cross-loop parallelism, where each iteration of the second loop depends upon only the same iteration number of the first loop. The detection of cross-loop parallelism involves finding opportunities despite the presence of real dependences, rather than the absence of any dependence (as is the case for the previous two forms of parallelism). This necessitates the use of analyses to examine the data production/consumption patterns of different loops. Although this may be relatively trivial for some examples, more complicated situations exist that deal with data at different granularities and traversal order.

4   MPEG-4 Encoder Evaluation

To provide a greater understanding of the relative importance of various analyses, particularly in combination, we show the effects of these analyses on the degree of compiler-visible parallelism on an implementation of the MPEG-4 video encoder source code from the MPEG Industry Forum [25]. This implementation is specialized for MPEG-4 Simple Profile and optimized for execution on superscalar processors.

The size of the application is approximately 18 000 lines of code after removing comments and blank lines. There are 574 potentially called procedures with a total of 392 loops, and the maximum call depth is 10 procedures. Although the majority of execution time is spent in several dozen loops containing a few thousand lines of code, we emphasize that important and necessary information for analyses can be located anywhere in the application. Even so, our pointer analysis takes only 18 seconds to complete and uses 52 MB of memory on a 900 MHz Itanium 2 system. We will explain the basics of MPEG-4 encoding here; for further information on the MPEG standard, readers are directed to documentation from the MPEG Industry Forum.

4.1 MPEG-4 Overview

An MPEG-4 Simple Profile stream consists of a series of images, called *frames*, that are processed one at a time. The two types of frames supported by Simple Profile are *I-frames* and *P-frames*. I-frames are encoded similarly to JPEG images and used as starting references for P-frames. A JPEG image consists of three component images: one full-resolution *luminance* image and two quarter-resolution *chrominance* images.[1] These are subdivided into *macroblocks*, consisting of six 8x8 pel ("picture element", effectively pixel) blocks. Four of these form a 16x16 pel square of the luminance image, and the other two are the corresponding chrominance blocks for the same part of the total image.

In P-frame encoding, the input image is reproduced as closely as possible by copying similar macroblocks from nearby locations in the previous I- or P-frame. The difference between the input and newly reconstructed is calculated and encoded as an image. Because the difference is usually very small, difference images are simple and highly compressible. P-frames thus take advantage of both spatial and temporal locality and are responsible for the majority of MPEG-4's compression. Consequently, typical encoding configurations use a high ratio of P-frames to I-frames. P-frame encoding dominates the execution time of the MPEG-4 encoder because of the increased processing required over that of I-frames and their prevalence in the video stream.

Figure 6 shows a dataflow diagram of the processing that occurs on each macroblock during P-frame encoding. First, *Motion Estimation* finds a macroblock in the previous frame that closely approximates the current macroblock.[2] *Motion Compensation* reproduces the estimated image using vectors from motion estimation. *Frame Subtraction* calculates the difference/error between the input macroblock and the macroblock copied from the previous image. *Discrete Cosine Transform (DCT) and Quantization* perform a JPEG-style encoding on each 8x8 pel error block. *Dequantization and Inverse Discrete Cosine Transform (IDCT)* decode the encoded image for use as the reference image for the following P-frame. Finally, *Bitstream Encoding* performs variable-length encoding to produce the final video bitstream. Rate control, which adds additional data dependences between these stages, and the option for printing motion estimation debug information have been disabled.

The main point of interest in Figure 6 is that only a single set of data dependences exists between macroblocks, consisting of flow dependences within

---

[1] Rather than encode in the three colors red, green, and blue, luminance and chrominance are used because the human eye is more sensitive to changes in luminance than chrominance. The standard takes advantage of this by having a smaller/coarser resolution for the chrominance component images.

[2] There are a wide range of motion estimation algorithms published; we chose a version for which there are no data dependences between motion estimation computation for different macroblocks.

bitstream encoding. Otherwise, the processing of different macroblocks can be executed in parallel. Certain parts of the computation can be further subdivided into separate luminance and chrominance components. We have parallelized this code by hand into multi-threaded implementations to confirm the parallelism.

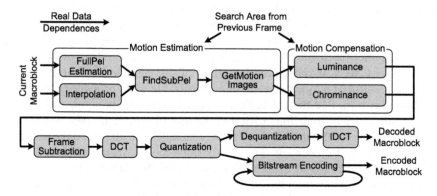

Fig. 6. A dataflow diagram of the processing of a single macroblock in the MPEG-4 encoder

Rather than perform all operations on a single macroblock at a time, as implied by Figure 6, the program performs subsets of the operations on the entire frame. It does not necessarily operate on a macroblock per loop iteration: for example, FrameSubtraction operates on single pixels. The pervasive use of pointers, differing traversal patterns, heap-allocated structures, and whole-program data and value flow make it difficult for the compiler to obtain a view of the application resembling Figure 6.

4.2 MPEG Analyses

The interaction and benefits of different analyses can be difficult to quantify in general, since individual analyses may fail to detect parallelism in isolation. Additionally, traditional metrics, such as points-to-sets, pairwise counts of independent memory operations, or weighted counts of parallelizable loops hold little meaning, as they may not indicate parallelization opportunity or represent parallelism of appropriate, practical granularity.

Because the purpose of this work is to identify parallelism rather than create a specific implementation, instead of a numeric metric we use a *loop-nest diagram* to express the parallelism visible to the compiler at different granularities. The specific example in Figure 7 is P-frame encoding. Each block in Figure 7 represents a loop or nested loops. Loop nesting is represented by blocks within blocks. The shading scheme represents the degree of iteration parallelism that the compiler can detect for each loop scope: black blocks cannot be safely parallelized without speculation, gray blocks can be parallelized if stores are ordered/serialized, and white blocks indicate completely iteration-parallel loops.

It is important to note that although the *iterations* of certain loops are not parallel, different *instances* of those loops may be parallel at a coarser granularity, such as an enclosing loop. The primary example of this are the loops within MotionEstimatePicture. Region parallelism is represented by blocks that are horizontally adjacent; horizontal lines passing through those blocks indicate spurious dependences that prevent safe parallel execution of those regions. For this example, cross-loop parallelism exists between every vertically neighboring pair of loops that exist at the same scope. This is often concealed by insufficient information about dependences or access patterns; the *blocked* opportunities are represented by an X at the shared boundary of the neighboring loops.

Only a handful of major loops are unparallelizable without algorithm changes in this application. SAD_Macroblock has an early exit in the loop, and is quite small in any case: 16 iterations with a maximum of approximately 100 instructions per iteration. MBMotionEstimation, FindSubPel, and BitstreamEncode have loops with data feedback. The non-parallel loops within SAD_Macroblock, MBMotionEstimation, and FindSubPel emphasize the importance of searching for parallelism at many loop levels. A system that only discovers inner-loop parallelism cannot parallelize the motion estimation code, one of the most compute-intensive regions of P-frame encoding execution, whereas Figure 7(i) shows that the loop-iteration parallelism of MotionEstimatePicture can be exposed to run multiple instances of MBMotionEstimation simultaneously.

Figure 7(a) shows the parallelism visible to the compiler with a context-insensitive, field-insensitive pointer analysis and array disambiguation analyses without non-affine expression or interprocedural support. The only loops that the compiler can identify as parallelizable are the small-granularity loops towards the bottom of the diagram. These loops are at most one to two hundred instructions per iteration, often much less, and are not well-suited for coarse-grained parallel execution. Figure 7(i) shows the parallelism that can be discovered if all of the analyses in Section 2 are used.

Figure 7(b,c,d,e) show the effects of adding a single feature to the analyses in (a), displaying the inability of isolated analysis features to expose the parallelism available in the application. Only a handful of opportunities are discovered, and these loops generally profit the least from parallelizing transformations since they do little data processing.

Figure 7(f,g,h,i) show one possible progression of combining analyses that expose more parallelism to the compiler (more white boxes and fewer lines and Xs). This does not imply that analyses should be run in this order: for example, all pointer analysis features would probably be run simultaneously, while interprocedural array disambiguation would be necessary only when a procedure boundary is encountered. For this application, the results of analyses do not exchange information and thus the ordering has no effect. The ordering was chosen solely to express the relative importance of particular analyses and options. The following subsections will discuss the effects of various analyses in greater detail.

Although our pointer analysis framework supports both inclusion-based pointer analysis and partial-flow sensitivity, this application does not manifest situations

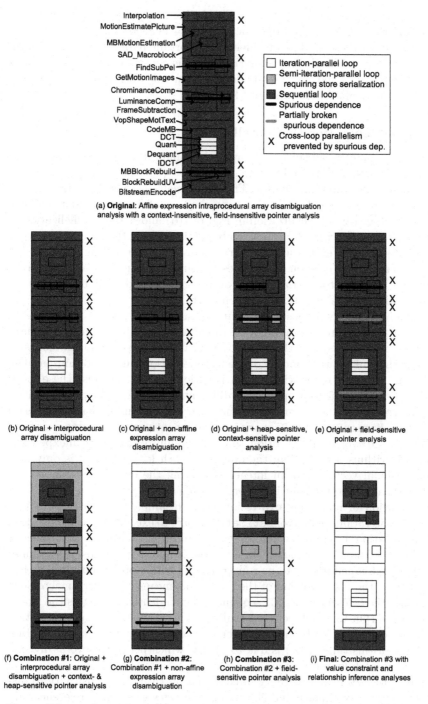

Fig. 7. Effects of various analyses on the compiler-visible parallelism in MPEG-4 P-frame encoding

where they add an appreciable benefit. This is due to the specialization for Simple Profile; the version of the reference MPEG-4 encoder that supports more features requires these analyses to identify important parallelism. As stated in Section 2, interprocedural array analysis and value constraints and relationships were computed by hand for this application, but all other analyses were performed automatically by the framework.

4.3   MPEG Loop Iteration Parallelism

Of the single analyses added to the original configuration in Figure 7(a), only interprocedural array disambiguation in Figure 7(b) exposes any reasonably coarse-grained iteration parallelism. This case occurs because the arrays being operated on are for a single macroblock, so they are of fixed dimension and statically allocated. Heap specialization in Figure 7(d) allows the parallelization of `Interpolation` and `FrameSubtraction` by distinguishing the input and output memory objects. However, these are very small loops and occupy less than 8% of the total execution time on a uniprocessor. Since the exposed parallelism is of a form that requires store serialization (ordering), it would likely be impractical to execute these loops' iterations independently.

Combining analyses exposes far more parallel loops to the compiler. In Figure 7(f), an interprocedural array disambiguation and heap-sensitive pointer analysis is able to discover that the loops that traverse over macroblocks in `MotionEstimatePicture` and motion compensation are iteration-parallel, despite the fact that loops within each iteration are not. Because these loops contain procedure calls that operate on different segments of an array each iteration, interprocedural array analysis is necessary to determine that the calls do not conflict. `MotionEstimatePicture` is a significant part of P-frame encoding, usually over 20% of total execution time on a uniprocessor with inexpensive, parallel algorithms. In addition, the output of each loop iteration is only four two-dimensional vectors and an integer indicating the encoding mode, so the store serialization requirement is not very significant.

The addition of non-affine expression array disambiguation in Figure 7(g) enables loop iterations in `MotionEstimatePicture` to execute in parallel without store serialization: it can determine that each iteration's output is to a different element of a variable-length array. In addition, it allows iterations of the upper portion of `VopShapeMotText` to be run in parallel with store serialization if they are split from the lower portion of the loop. This means that every macroblock can execute the `DCT` through `IDCT` sequence independently, as long as the writes back to the output frame object are serialized. This is another significant section of P-frame encoding, and can take over 50% of total uniprocessor execution time. Most of this time (70%) is due to `Quant`, which performs several division operations in each loop iteration.

Figure 7(h) uses field-sensitivity in combination with heap-sensitivity to distinguish different luminance and chrominance images when their references are stored into fields of a single structure. This allows complete parallelization of `FrameSubtraction`, although it is not a significant part of execution time. The combination is also necessary to fully parallelize the remaining gray loops which become white in Figure 7(i).

Figure 7(i) shows the results of value range and relationship inference, exposing the remaining parallelism in the program. GetMotionImages is made parallelizable by optimization: an early exit in the loop was removed by value range analysis proving that the exit cannot be taken. The motion compensation loops LuminanceComp and ChrominanceComp are fully iteration-independent because value range and relationship information allowed the parallelization of inner and outer loops. For similar reasons, iterations of MBBlockRebuild and BlockRebuildUV are also now identified as fully independent, which allows iterations of the upper portion of VopShapeMotText to be executed independently when split from the lower portion of the function.

4.4   MPEG Region Parallelism

The instances of region parallelism in the MPEG encoder involve operations on either separate, dynamically-allocated objects linked to a common structure, or separate regions of an array accessed by repeated calls to a function. Thus, single analysis options are incapable of removing the dependences that block region parallelism. Only in Figure 7(d) can the compiler separate one call to FindSubPel from the other four, as it writes to a different array.

The combination of non-affine expression array disambiguation and heap-sensitive pointer analysis enables the independent execution of the four "smaller" calls to FindSubPel in Figure 7(g). With the addition of field-sensitivity in Figure 7(h), the compiler can finally distinguish different luminance and chrominance images even when they are stored into fields of a single structure. This removes the two remaining horizontal black lines from the diagram and fully exposes the major instances of code region parallelism in the application.

4.5   MPEG Cross-Loop Parallelism

As shown by the absence of Xs in Figure 7(i), there is a high degree of cross-loop parallelism available in P-frame encoding. The two largest obstacles to discovering the producer-consumer relationships for cross-loop parallelism are the need to determine the independence of memory objects accessed by the loop and the ordering of processing (or lack thereof) allows an overlap in execution. The former issue is resolved by a full-featured pointer analysis. The latter is complicated by the use of procedures, non-affine expressions, and the fact that the granularities and order of processing can be different for different loops. For example, FrameSubtraction loops over pixels, while its neighboring loops operate on macroblocks. This does not translate into a direct ratio of iterations: macroblock processing will operate on an 16x16 block from the upper left corner of a luminance image, while pixel processing will go across the top row of pixels in the image before beginning the next row. Without significant transformation, FrameSubtraction would have to process 16 rows of data before VopShapeMotText could begin execution.

Little cross-loop parallelism is exposed by analysis until a heap-sensitive pointer analysis is combined with an interprocedural, non-affine expression array analysis, shown in Figure 7(g). The heap-sensitivity distinguishes the input and output data objects for many loops, while the full-featured array analysis permits a pattern analysis. Field-sensitivity in Figure 7(h) removes another blocked case by clarifying the multiple objects referenced in `FrameSubtraction`. The remaining blocked cases require value range and relationship inference to obtain clear data production and consumption pattern information.

5   Related Work

This paper covers a large range of compiler work, incorporating various compiler analysis techniques, the effects of integrating these techniques, the parallelism they expose for an automated parallelizing compiler, and further development and refinement of compiler techniques. This is in the same spirit as previous work by Hendren and Nicolau [15] and Ghiya et al. [7]. Our work differs in that our focus is on discovering available parallelism for consumption by multi-processing microprocessors. We currently limit ourselves to media applications, which are high in parallelism but are pointer-heavy serial implementations. In this section we address some of the major works that have been published in these areas.

Several existing analysis techniques form the foundation for our investigation. These include pointer analysis, induction variable recognition, symbolic scalar analysis, and array disambiguation. For an overview of previous work in pointer analysis, we refer to [16]. Another report by Hind [17] identifies, in a similar vein to our work, idioms and common patterns in C programs that can adversely affect the precision of different kinds of pointer analysis. The pointer analysis framework used for this work is described in detail in [26].

For an overview of several important array disambiguation techniques, we refer to [9]. The problem of disambiguating index expressions containing symbolic values has also been noted by Blume and Eigenmann, who propose the Range Test [3] to handle such expressions. The Access Region Test [28] also disambiguates symbolic expressions, with greater flexibility. While our choice of disambiguation tests is tuned to the problem domain, additional tests could easily be added.

A number of tools and techniques exist for symbolic numerical analysis. Existing value range propagation algorithms [12,21] work on an intraprocedural scope or on code without dynamic memory to infer the possible sets of values for some data, enabling refinement of control flow and index expressions. However, value range propagation has not been implemented in a scalable form that tracks value ranges both interprocedurally and through heap-allocated data structures for the C language. Value relationship inference has been implemented for program analysis and static error detection [2]. Again, to the best of our knowledge, no existing tools track values through heap-allocated data structures.

At present there is a shortage of work on coarse-grained parallelization of C programs. Several compiler projects, including Polaris [3], ParaScope [23], and

SUIF [10] have emphasized the interprocedural nature of parallelizing analysis and code transformation. These have primarily focused on Fortran programs. However, the disparity between C and Fortran semantics has resulted in automatic parallelization developed for Fortran not enjoying the same level of success when applied to C. Of these projects, only SUIF has published research on compilation of C programs. Their reported parallelization results are only for Fortran benchmarks [10,11].

There are other approaches to parallelization that are alternative or complementary to compile-time analysis. One alternative is to augment a programming language such as C to allow the programmer to communicate more information about pointer relationships to the compiler [14]. Another is to use run-time disambiguation or speculation when compile-time analysis fails [4,36]. Salamí and Valero [33] find that using a compiler-generated run-time disambiguation test to select between a parallel and non-parallel version of a loop produces speedups in multimedia applications comparable to the speedups garnered by interprocedural pointer disambiguation. While code versioning is useful as a fallback mechanism, it causes code growth due to multiple versioning and overhead due to runtime tests. Even in systems with run-time disambiguation support, success in static parallelization will increase the execution efficiency of applications.

6   Conclusions and Future Work

This paper discusses several forms of parallelism and studies the analyses required to expose them in media applications. We have shown the types of code sequences and practices that require the use of certain analysis options. Distinctions have been made between analyses that are already satisfactory for finding parallelism and those that currently do not have practical or scalable solutions.

Using a reference MPEG-4 encoder, we have shown the importance of combining analyses to obtain a much clearer view of the parallelism present in the application than when run individually. Our evaluation showed that an interprocedural, non-affine expression array analysis and a heap-sensitive pointer analysis are required to expose the majority of parallelism in the application. A field-sensitive pointer analysis and value range and relationship inference are necessary to find the remainder of the parallelism in the application.

For future work, we will continue work on developing practical and scalable analyses for those analyses that are not yet practical or scalable in the C language. Work is ongoing to apply the analyses to other applications. We are also developing software tools to assist programmers and developers in finding parallelism for use in their own designs.

Acknowledgments

We would like to thank Hillery Hunter at IBM and John Sias for their advice and feedback, and the reviewers for their comments. This work was partially supported by the MARCO Gigascale Systems Research Center (GSRC).

References

1. Advanced Micro Devices. AMD Athlon 64 X2 dual-core product data sheet, May 2005.
2. ASTRÉE Static Analyzer. http://www.astree.ens.fr/.
3. W. Blume, R. Eigenmann, K. Faigin, J. Grout, J. Hoeflinger, D. Padua, P. Petersen, W. Pottenger, L. Rauchwerger, P. Tu, and S. Weatherford. Polaris: The next generation in parallelizing compilers. Technical Report 1375, University of Illinois at Urbana-Champaign, 1994.
4. Mark Byler, James R. B. Davies, Christopher Huson, Bruce Leasure, and Michael Wolfe. Multiple version loops. In *Proceedings of the 1987 International Conference on Parallel Processing*, pages 312–318, 1987.
5. Cell Project at IBM Research. http://www.research.ibm.com/cell/.
6. Michael P. Gerlek, Eric Stoltz, and Michael Wolfe. Beyond induction variables: detecting and classifying sequences using a demand-driven SSA form. *ACM Transactions on Programming Languages and Systems*, 17(1):85–122, 1995.
7. R. Ghiya, D. M. Lavery, and D. C. Sehr. On the importance of points-to analysis and other memory disambiguation methods for C programs. In *Proceedings of the ACM SIGPLAN 2001 Conference on Programming Design and Implementation*, pages 47–58, 2001.
8. Rakesh Ghiya and Laurie J. Hendren. Is it a tree, a DAG, or a cyclic graph? A shape analysis for heap-directed pointers in c. In *Symposium on Principles of Programming Languages*, pages 1–15, 1996.
9. Rajiv Gupta, Santosh Pande, Kleanthis Psarris, and Vivek Sarkar. Compilation techniques for parallel systems. *Parallel Computing*, 25(13,14):1741–1783, 1999.
10. M. W. Hall, S. P. Amarasinghe, B. R. Murphy, S.-W. Liao, and M. S. Lam. Interprocedural parallelization analysis in SUIF. *ACM Transactions on Programming Languages and Systems*, 27:662–731, 2005.
11. M. W. Hall, J. M. Anderson, S. P. Amarasinghe, B. R. Murphy, S.-W. Liao, E. Bugnion, and M. S. Lam. Maximizing multiprocessor performance with the SUIF compiler. *IEEE Computer*, 29(12):84–89, 1996.
12. W. H. Harrison. Compiler analysis of the value ranges for variables. *IEEE Transactions on Software Engineering*, 3(3):243–250, May 1977.
13. R. Hasti and S. Horwitz. Using static single assignment form to improve flow-insensitive pointer analysis. In *Proceedings of the ACM SIGPLAN '98 Conference on Programming Language Design and Implementation*, pages 97–105, June 1998.
14. L. Hendren, J. Hummel, and A. Nicolau. Abstractions for recursive pointer data structures: Improving the analysis and transformation of imperative programs. In *Proceedings of the ACM SIGPLAN '92 Conference on Programming Language Design and Implementation*, pages 249–260, June 1992.
15. L. J. Hendren and A. Nicolau. Parallelizing programs with recursive data structures. *IEEE Transactions on Parallel and Distributed System*, 1(1):35–47, January 1990.
16. M. Hind. Pointer analysis: Haven't we solved this problem yet? In *Proceedings of the 2001 ACM SIGPLAN-SIGSOFT Workshop on Program Analysis for Software Tools and Engineering*, pages 54–61, 2001.
17. M. Hind and A. Pioli. Evaluating the effectiveness of pointer alias analyses. Technical Report RC21510, IBM T. J. Watson Research Center, March 1999.
18. Independent JPEG Group. coderules.doc. Text file in zipped archive, 1998. ftp://ftp.uu.net/graphics/jpeg/jpegsrc.v6b.tar.gz.

19. Intel Network Processors. http://www.intel.com/design/network/products/npfamily/.
20. Intel Pentium D Processor. http://www.intel.com/products/processor/pentium_D/ index.htm.
21. H. Johnson. Data flow analysis for 'intractable' imbedded system software. In *Proceedings of the 1986 SIGPLAN Symposium on Compiler Construction*, pages 109–117, 1986.
22. K. Kennedy and R. Allen. *Optimizing Compilers for Modern Architectures: A Dependence-based Approach*. Morgan Kaufmann Publishers, San Francisco, CA, 2002.
23. K. Kennedy, K. S. McKinley, and C. Tseng. Interactive parallel programming using the ParaScope editor. *IEEE Transactions on Parallel and Distributed Systems*, 2:329–341, 1991.
24. X. Kong, D. Klappholz, and K. Psarris. The I-Test: An improved dependence test for automatic parallelization and vectorization. *IEEE Transactions on Parallel and Distributed Systems, Special Issue on Parallel Languages and Compilers*, 2(3):342–349, July 1991.
25. MPEG Industry Forum. http://www.mpegif.org/.
26. E. M. Nystrom. *FULCRA Pointer Analysis Framework*. PhD thesis, University of Illinois at Urbana-Champaign, 2005.
27. E. M. Nystrom, H.-S. Kim, and W. W. Hwu. Importance of heap specialization in pointer analysis. In *Proceedings of ACM-SIGPLAN-SIGSOFT Workshop on Program Analysis for Software Tools and Engineering*, pages 43–48, June 2004.
28. Y. Paek, J. Hoeflinger, and D. Padua. Efficient and precise array access analysis. *ACM Transactions on Programming Languages and Systems*, 24(1):65–109, 2000.
29. James Player. An evaluation of low-overhead partial flow-sensitivity. Master's thesis, Department of Electrical and Computer Engineering, University of Illinois at Urbana-Champaign, 2005.
30. Power Mac G5. http://www.apple.com/powermac/.
31. W. Pugh. The Omega Test: A fast and practical integer programming algorithm for dependence analysis. In *Proceedings of Supercomputing 1991*, pages 4–13, November 1991.
32. M. Sagiv, T. Reps, and R. Wilhelm. Solving shape-analysis problems in languages with destructive updating. In *Proceedings of the ACM Symposium on Programming Languages*, pages 16–31, January 1996.
33. E. Salamí and M. Valero. Dynamic memory interval test vs. interprocedural pointer analysis in multimedia applications. *ACM Transactions on Architecture and Code Optimization*, 2(2):199–219, 2005.
34. V. Sarkar and J. Hennessy. Compile-time partitioning and scheduling of parallel programs. In *Proceedings of the ACM SIGPLAN 86 Symposium on Compiler Construction*, pages 17–26, June 1986.
35. Peng Tu and David Padua. Gated SSA-based demand-driven symbolic analysis for parallelizing compilers. In *Proceedings of the 1995 International Conference on Supercomputing*, pages 414–423, 1995.
36. M. Voss and R. Eigenmann. Dynamically adaptive parallel programs. In *Proceedings of the International Symposium on High Performance Computing*, pages 109–120, May 1999.

An Approach for Enhancing Inter-processor Data Locality on Chip Multiprocessors

Guilin Chen and Mahmut Kandemir

The Pennsylvania State University, USA
{guilchen,kandemir}@cse.psu.edu

Abstract. The tighter integration on chip multiprocessors exerts a higher pressure on off-chip accesses to the memory system. This makes minimizing the number of off-chip accesses a critical optimization goal. This paper discusses a compiler-based solution to this problem for the embedded applications that perform stencil computations. An important characteristic of this solution is that it distinguishes between the intra-processor data reuse and inter-processor data reuse. The first of these captures the data reuse that occurs across loop iterations assigned to the same processor, whereas the second one represents the data reuse that takes place across the loop iterations assigned to different processors. The proposed approach then optimizes inter-processor reuse by re-organizing the loop iterations of each processor carefully, considering how data elements are shared across processors. The goal is to ensure that the different processors access the shared data within a short period of time, so that the data can be captured in the on-chip memory space at the time of the reuse. This paper also presents an evaluation of the proposed optimization and compares it to an alternate scheme that optimizes data locality for each processor in isolation. The results obtained by applying our implementation to eight loop-intensive benchmark codes from the embedded computing domain show that our approach improves over the mentioned alternate scheme by 15.6% on average.

1 Introduction

The tighter integration on chip multiprocessors exerts a higher pressure on off-chip accesses to the memory system. This is because in chip multiprocessors there are several cores that need to access the off-chip memory system, and they may have to contend for the same buses/pins to get there. Therefore, it is critical to reduce the number of off-chip memory accesses as much as possible, even if this causes an increase in on-chip communication activities among parallel processors.

Since early nineties compiler researchers focused on optimizations for cache locality and proposed several techniques along this direction. In the context of data caches, the proposed techniques include both loop transformations (e.g., iteration space tiling [29,31] and loop permutation [2]) and data layout optimizations (e.g., dimension reindexing [17]). While one might think that these optimizations or some sort of combination of them can also be used in the context of chip multiprocessors, the problem is actually more complex than this simple view. This is because, optimizing the code assigned to each processor core for locality does not guarantee good data locality for

P. Stenström (Ed.): Transactions on HiPEAC I, LNCS 4050, pp. 214–233, 2007.

shared data. For example, if two accesses issued by two different processors for the same data element are far apart from each other, each of these accesses may need to go to the off-chip memory to fetch the same data. Therefore, it is important to re-organize data accesses in such a fashion that the shared data are accessed by the processors within a short period of time. This certainly increases chances for catching the data in on-chip memory at the time of its reuse.

This paper discusses and evaluates a new data reuse framework, specifically customized for embedded chip multiprocessors executing loop-intensive stencil applications. An important characteristic of this framework is that it distinguishes between *intra-processor data reuse* and *inter-processor data reuse*. The first of these captures the data reuse that occurs across the loop iterations assigned to the same processor, whereas the second one represents the data reuse that take place across the loop iterations assigned to different processors. The proposed approach then optimizes the inter-processor reuse by re-organizing loop iterations of each processor carefully, considering how data elements are shared across parallel processors. The goal is to ensure that the different processors access the shared data within a short period of time, so that the data can be captured in the on-chip memory space at the time of the reuse. We can summarize the main contributions of this work as follows:

• We show how inter-processor data reuse can be identified and represented, given a parallelized loop nest, and discuss how the compiler abstraction used to capture this reuse can be interpreted.

• We present a scheduling algorithm for stencil computations that re-organizes loop iterations assigned to processors such that inter-processor data reuse is improved, without degrading intra-processor data reuse. In this approach, the local iteration space of each processor is transformed using a different loop transformation.

• We present an evaluation of the proposed optimization and compare it to an alternate scheme that optimizes data locality for each processor in isolation The results obtained by applying our implementation to eight loop-intensive benchmark codes from the embedded computing domain show that the proposed approach improves over the mentioned alternate scheme by 15.6% on average.

The rest of this paper is structured as follows. Section 2 discusses the related work on stencil computations and chip multiprocessors. The mathematical theory behind our approach is discussed in Sect. 3. Section 4 presents an experimental evaluation of the approach and compares it to previous work. Section 5 gives our concluding remarks and outlines the future work.

2   Related Work

Stencil computation [6,7] is a common type of computation in embedded array-based application codes. In each iteration of a stencil computation, an array element, referred to as the *seed*, is updated based on the values of its *neighbor elements*. There are different types of stencils, e.g., 5-point stencil, 9-point stencil, etc., which use a different set of neighbors in updating a seed element. Figure 1 presents some example stencils.

Optimizing stencils is very important and some companies even built compilers customized for stencil computations [25]. Most of the previous work focused on optimizing

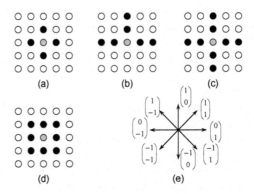

Fig. 1. Example stencils. The gray dots represent seed elements and the black dots represents neighbor elements. (a) 5-point stencil. (b) 7-point stencil. (c) 9-point cross stencil. (d) 9-point star stencil. (e) Eight possible directions for a two-dimensional stencil computation.

stencil computations targeting high-performance distributed memory based systems. Since communication costs are very high in such systems, reducing this cost is critical and has been studied extensively [5,6,7,8,16,25]. There is also prior work on improving intra-processor cache locality for stencil codes [11]. None of the prior efforts has studied the optimization of stencil computations in the context of embedded chip multiprocessors. Our work is targeting at chip multiprocessors where different on-chip processors can share data through an on-chip L2 cache and on-chip data communication could be much cheaper than off-chip memory accesses. Our goal is to utilize such characteristics and improve the performance of stencil computations by transforming the stencil codes for the best exploitation of inter-processor data reuse. In addition, our technique can be integrated with a general optimizing compiler framework that employs linear loop transformations. We specifically target at optimizing interprocessor data reuse, by transforming the local iteration space of each processor using a different transformation.

Chip multiprocessors are most promising in highly competitive and high volume markets, for example, embedded communication, multimedia, and networking. This imposes strict requirements on performance, power, reliability, and costs. They are becoming popular in both academic environments and industry [13,15,4,19,20,23]. Nayfeh et al [21] studied an important issue for MPSoC, that is, the ratio of processors to cache memory size to achieve the best cost/performance. They compared the trade-offs with different cache sizes and number of processors in an MPSoC system. The results showed that, for parallel applications, clustering via shared caches provides an effective mechanism for increasing the total number of processors in a system without increasing the number of invalidations. Hammond et al [14] evaluated three different microarchitectures, namely, superscalar, SMT, and MPSoC. They concluded that MPSoC architecture is favored over the others from the perspectives of both software and hardware trends. Wolf [28] review several commercial MPSoC designs and identified the unique challenges, from hardware to software, for MPSoCs in embedded domains.

Olukotun and Hammond [22] studied conventional uniprocessor and MPSoC. They discussed the major advantages of MPSoCs over conventional uniprocessors in several aspects: hardware design, performance, and power. They also showed that the transition to MPSoCs is inevitable. Richardson [24] studied the design issues in the MPOC project, a chip multiprocessor for embedded system. They found that four-stage pipeline and co-resident on-chip DRAM are very useful for improving performance. Gomma et al [12] utilizes the extra on-chip parallelism for improving MPSoC's reliability against hardware transient errors. Their proposed technique achieves fault tolerance by executing and comparing two copies of a given application. As chip multiprocessors post a new challenge for compiler researchers, they also provide new opportunities as compared to traditional architectures. Optimizing inter-processor data reuse is one such opportunity which is explored in this work.

3   Mathematical Theory

3.1   Background on Loop Representation and Loop Transformation

A loop nest of depth l defines an iteration space $\mathcal{I}$. Each iteration of the loop nest is identified by its index vector $\boldsymbol{I} = (i_1, i_2, \ldots, i_l)^T$. An array of dimension n defines an array space $\mathcal{A}$, and each element in the array is specified using an index vector $\boldsymbol{A} = (a_1, a_2, \ldots, a_n)^T$. We assume that multi-dimensional arrays are stored in memory in a row-major fashion (as in C and C++). We consider affine array access functions $f : \mathcal{I} \rightarrow \mathcal{A}, f(\boldsymbol{I}) = F\boldsymbol{I} + \boldsymbol{\zeta}$, where F is an $n \times l$ matrix and $\boldsymbol{\zeta}$ is a n-dimensional constant vector. As an example, the two array accesses $U[i][j]$ and $U[i-1][j-1]$ in Fig. 2 can be represented, respectively, as:

$$\begin{pmatrix} 1 & 0 \\ 0 & 1 \end{pmatrix} \begin{pmatrix} i \\ j \end{pmatrix} + \begin{pmatrix} 0 \\ 0 \end{pmatrix} \text{ and } \begin{pmatrix} 1 & 0 \\ 0 & 1 \end{pmatrix} \begin{pmatrix} i \\ j \end{pmatrix} + \begin{pmatrix} -1 \\ -1 \end{pmatrix}.$$

```
for (i=1; i<1024; i++)
  for (j=1; j<1024; j++)
    U[i][j]=U[i-1][j-1]+1;
```

Fig. 2. Example loop and array accesses

Linear loop transformations can be used to optimize a loop nest for various purposes, for example, improving cache locality. A linear loop transformation can be represented using an $l \times l$ non-singular matrix T for a loop nest with l loops [18,30]. As a result of the loop transformation, each iteration (index vector) in the original iteration space is mapped to a distinct iteration in the new iteration space. If $\boldsymbol{I}$ is an iteration in the original iteration space, and is mapped to $\boldsymbol{I}'$ after the transformation represented by T, then the following equations must be satisfied:

$$\boldsymbol{I}' = T\boldsymbol{I} \quad \text{and} \quad \boldsymbol{I} = T^{-1}\boldsymbol{I}'. \tag{1}$$

After the transformation, the new access function, $f'(I')$, and the original access function, $f(I)$, should access the same data element. That is: $f'(I') = f(I)$. Considering (1), we can obtain:

$$f'(I') = f(I) = f(T^{-1}I') = FT^{-1}I' + \zeta. \tag{2}$$

3.2   Algebraic Representation of Stencil Computations

A stencil can be represented by a *stencil matrix*, termed as S, in which the columns are the relative positions of its neighbors assuming that the position of the seed element is $(0 \quad 0 \cdots 0)^T$. S is an $n \times k$ matrix for an n-dimensional array and a stencil with k neighbors. For example, the 5-point stencil in Fig. 1(a) can be represented by a stencil 2×4 matrix S, where:

$$S = \begin{pmatrix} 1 & 0 & -1 & 0 \\ 0 & -1 & 0 & 1 \end{pmatrix}.$$

Similarly, the stencil matrix for the 7-point stencil in Fig. 1(b) is:

$$S = \begin{pmatrix} 0 & 0 & 1 & 2 & 0 & 0 \\ 1 & 2 & 0 & 0 & -1 & -2 \end{pmatrix}.$$

In a stencil, the neighbor elements can reside in different *directions* with respect to the seed element. For example, in Fig. 1(a), there are four directions that hold neighbor elements of the seed, whereas in Fig. 1(d) there are eight directions with neighbors. For a stencil on an n-dimensional array, there are a total of $3^{n+1} - 1$ possible directions, and each direction can be represented by an n-entry *direction vector*. A direction vector is defined as a non-zero vector in which each entry's absolute value is no more than one. A stencil can also be represented by a *stencil direction matrix*, termed as $\mathcal{D}$, in which the columns represents the directions that hold neighbors. For example, the stencil direction matrix of the stencil in Fig. 1(a) is

$$\mathcal{D} = \begin{pmatrix} 1 & 0 & -1 & 0 \\ 0 & -1 & 0 & 1 \end{pmatrix},$$

which is the same as its stencil matrix. The stencil direction matrix for the stencil in Fig. 1(b) is

$$\mathcal{D} = \begin{pmatrix} 0 & 1 & 0 \\ 1 & 0 & -1 \end{pmatrix}.$$

The stencil direction matrix of a stencil can be obtained by removing the identical columns of $||S||$, where S is the stencil matrix ($n \times k$), and $||S||$ is defined as:

$$\forall i, j, 0 \leq i < n, 0 \leq j < k, \quad ||S||(i,j) = \begin{cases} 1 \text{ if } S(i,j) > 0; \\ 0 \text{ if } S(i,j) = 0; \\ -1 \text{ if } S(i,j) < 0. \end{cases}$$

For example, by applying the $|| \ ||$ operator to the stencil matrix of the stencil given in Fig. 1(b), we obtain the following matrix:

$$\begin{pmatrix} 0 & 0 & 1 & 1 & 0 & 0 \\ 1 & 1 & 0 & 0 & -1 & -1 \end{pmatrix}.$$

After removing the identical columns from the above matrix, we obtain the corresponding stencil direction matrix:

$$\mathcal{D} = \begin{pmatrix} 0 & 1 & 0 \\ 1 & 0 & -1 \end{pmatrix}.$$

3.3   Processor Representation and Array Assignment

We focus on a block distribution of arrays on a multi-dimensional processor space. In such a distribution, each processor updates a distinct subset of the array elements. The position of each processor is specified using an n-entry vector for an n-dimensional array. Figure 3(a) presents a program segment performing 5-point stencil computation. In this program, the outermost t loop controls the number of times the stencil computation needs to be repeated so that the results converge. At the end of each round, the results in array $tempU$ are copied back to U. The $(i \quad j)^T$ loop nest implements the actual 5-point stencil computation, and is the focus of our approach. Therefore, we will omit the outermost t loop and the array copying part in the rest of our discussion. Figure 3(b) illustrates a 3×3 block distribution of the array across nine processors for a 5-point stencil. These processors are represented in our framework using nine vectors: $(0 \quad 0)^T$, $(0 \quad 1)^T, (0 \quad 2)^T, \cdots, (2 \quad 2)^T$.

After array-to-processor assignment, each processor executes a subset of the original loop iterations. The loops to execute these iterations are the same for different processors, except that they have different lower and upper bounds. This is illustrated in Fig. 3(c), which shows the part of the stencil computation in Fig. 3(a) assigned to the processor identified with $(p_1 \quad p_2)^T$, i.e., its local iteration space.

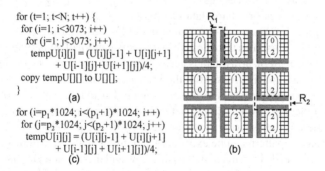

```
for (t=1; t<N; t++) {
  for (i=1; i<3073; i++)
    for (j=1; j<3073; j++)
      tempU[i][j] = (U[i][j-1] + U[i][j+1]
                   + U[i-1][j]+U[i+1][j])/4;
  copy tempU[][] to U[][];
}
            (a)
for (i=p₁*1024; i<(p₁+1)*1024; i++)
  for (j=p₂*1024; j<(p₂+1)*1024; j++)
    tempU[i][j] = (U[i][j-1] + U[i][j+1]
                 + U[i-1][j] + U[i+1][j])/4;
            (c)
```

Fig. 3. Example block distribution across a two-dimensional processor space. (a) A code segment that performs 5-point stencil computation over array U. (b) A 3×3 block distribution of the array across the processors. The nine processors are represented by the vectors written inside the blocks. Shaded areas represent the set of array elements that are shared by neighboring processors. For example, the array elements indicated by R_1 are shared by processor $(0 \quad 0)^T$ and processor $(0 \quad 1)^T$, and the array elements indicated by R_2 are shared between processor $(1 \quad 2)^T$ and processor $(2 \quad 2)^T$. (c) The code segment to be executed by processor $(p_1 \quad p_2)^T$ after data distribution.

We extend the $abs()$ function, which returns the absolute value of an integer, to the domain of vectors. That is:

$$V' = abs(V) \Rightarrow \forall j, 0 \leq j < n, V'(j) = abs(V(j)).$$

An n-entry vector is called a *unit vector* if it is one of the columns of an $n \times n$ identity matrix E. We use E_j ($0 \leq j < n$) to represent a unit vector that has a '1' in its jth entry, and all '0's in other entries. For example, we have $E_0 = (1 \quad 0 \cdots 0)^T$ and $E_{n-1} = (0 \quad 0 \cdots 1)^T$. Two processors P_1 and P_2 are said to be neighbors to each other if and only if $abs(P_1 - P_2)$ is a unit vector. The vector $abs(P_2 - P_1)$ is called the *neighboring direction* between P_1 and P_2. For example, in Fig. 3, processors $(1 \quad 1)^T$ and $(1 \quad 2)^T$ are neighbors because $abs((1 \quad 1)^T - (1 \quad 2)^T)$ is $(0 \quad 1)^T$, which is a unit vector. In comparison, processors $(1 \quad 1)^T$ and $(2 \quad 2)^T$ are not neighbors because $abs((1 \quad 1)^T - (2 \quad 2)^T)$ is $(1 \quad 1)^T$, which is not a unit vector.

3.4 Inter-processor Data Reuse

In stencil computations, neighboring processors share data at their boundaries. Figure 3(b) illustrates such data sharing. The shaded areas in Fig. 3(b) represent the array elements that are shared by neighboring processors. For example, R_1 captures the array elements shared by processors $(0 \quad 0)^T$ and $(0 \quad 1)^T$, and R_2 indicates the array elements shared by processors $(1 \quad 2)^T$ and $(2 \quad 2)^T$. For processors that are not neighbors, they either do not share data (e.g., processor $(0 \quad 0)^T$ and processor $(0 \quad 2)^T$), or they share a very small amount of data (e.g., processor $(0 \quad 0)^T$ and processor $(1 \quad 1)^T$ in a 9-point star stencil). Consequently, in our approach, we consider data sharing only between the neighboring processors.

While all neighboring processors share data in Fig. 3(b), in the general case, whether two neighboring processors share data or not depends on the stencil direction matrix $\mathcal{D}$ as well. Figure 4(a) gives a 3-point stencil and Fig. 4(b) shows its stencil direction matrix. Figure 4(c) illustrates the original data access pattern of an individual processor. In this data access pattern, array data is accessed row by row in the increasing order and the data within each row is accessed in the increasing order. Figure 4(d) highlights the data sharing between processors in a 3×3 block distribution. We can observe from this figure that there is no data sharing between the neighboring processors in the same column, but there is data sharing between the neighboring processors in the same row. Such a data sharing pattern can be expected from this stencil, since in this stencil, both the neighbors of a seed element are in the same row and there is no data sharing between two neighboring processors if they access different rows of the array. Therefore, for two neighboring processors P_1 and P_2 to share data, the direction from P_1 to P_2, captured by $P_2 - P_1$, needs to be compatible with some direction vector in the stencil direction matrix $\mathcal{D}$. In mathematical terms, such a compatibility can be formulated as follows:

$$(P_2 - P_1)^T \mathcal{D} \neq 0. \tag{3}$$

In the above formulation, 0 represents a vector with all entries being zero. For example, processors $(0 \quad 0)^T$ and $(0 \quad 1)^T$ share data, since:

$$\left(\begin{pmatrix} 0 \\ 1 \end{pmatrix} - \begin{pmatrix} 0 \\ 0 \end{pmatrix} \right)^T \begin{pmatrix} 0 & 0 \\ 1 & -1 \end{pmatrix} = (1 \; -1) \neq 0$$

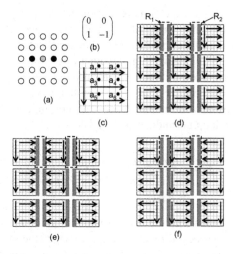

Fig. 4. Data sharing and data reuse in a 3-point stencil. (a) 3-point stencil. (b) Stencil direction matrix. (c) Access pattern of an individual processor. Array data are accessed row by row. In each row, the data are accessed in the increasing order (from left to right). The rows are accessed in the increasing order (from top to bottom). The six array elements, represented by black dots, are accessed in the order of $a_1, a_2, a_3, a_4, a_5, a_6$. (d) 3×3 block distribution across nine processors. The shaded areas highlights the data sharing between processors. (e) Access pattern that exploits inter-processor data reuse. (f) Another access pattern that exploits inter-processor data reuse.

On the other hand, there is no data sharing between processors $(0 \quad 0)^T$ and $(1 \quad 0)^T$. This is because, we have:

$$\left(\begin{pmatrix} 1 \\ 0 \end{pmatrix} - \begin{pmatrix} 0 \\ 0 \end{pmatrix} \right)^T \begin{pmatrix} 0 & 0 \\ 1 & -1 \end{pmatrix} = \begin{pmatrix} 0 & 0 \end{pmatrix} = \mathbf{0}.$$

It is important to note that data sharing between processors does not necessarily lead to inter-processor data locality. Let us consider Fig. 4(d) as an example. When processor $(0 \quad 0)^T$ accesses the data in the region indicated by R_1, processor $(0 \quad 1)^T$ is accessing the data in the region indicated by R_2. Since they do not access their shared data together, there is little data locality in this access pattern. fully exploited). On the other hand, in the data access patterns shown in Fig. 4(e) and Fig. 4(f), neighboring processors access their shared data together, and thus there is good inter-processor data locality in these two scenarios. Our objective is to transform the local iteration spaces of the processors so that their new data access pattern is similar to the ones shown in Fig. 4(e) or Fig. 4(f). We observe that the common characteristic between the access patterns of Fig. 4(e) and Fig. 4(f) is that the neighboring processors that share data proceed in the opposite directions when accessing each row and they proceed in the same direction when accessing each column. For example, in Fig. 4(e), processor $(0 \quad 0)^T$ accesses each row from left to right, while processor $(0 \quad 1)^T$ accesses each row from right to left. Also, both these two processors access each column from top to bottom. Note that in this case, accessing each row means accessing along the direction identified by $abs((0 \quad 1)^T - (0 \quad 0)^T)$, i.e., their neighboring direction. In general, for two neighboring processors to access their shared data together, they need to have *opposite* access directions when accessing data along their neighboring direction, and have the same access direction when accessing data along any other directions.

Let us now define the access directions in different dimensions for a given array access function $f(I)$. We assume that each loop iterator is increased by one as we move from one iteration to another. The loops with non-unit steps can be transformed to unit-step loops using loop normalization [1]. The access direction vector Q_k for the kth loop can be defined as:

$$Q_k = f(I + E_k) - f(I)$$
$$= F(I + E_k) + \zeta - F(I) - \zeta$$
$$= FE_k.$$

That is, Q_k is the kth column of the access matrix F of $f(I)$. Therefore, the access matrix of $f(I)$ is also the access direction matrix, in which the kth column is the access direction vector at the kth loop. From (2), we can see that the new access direction matrix after the loop transformation represented by matrix T is $T^{-1}F$.

Our approach is to find a suitable loop transformation for each processor so that we can have data reuse between the processors that share data. Our approach proceeds as follows. First, we identify all the neighboring processor pairs. After that, for each processor pair, we determine whether they share data or not using (3). As has been discussed earlier, for two neighboring processors P_1 and P_2 that share data, they should have the opposite access directions along their neighboring direction $abs(P_1 - P_2)$, and they should have the same access directions in other directions. To formulate this requirement, we define a function $Expand() : n \times 1 \rightarrow n \times n$, which expands a direction vector into a matrix. Mathematically, we can define $Expand()$ as follows:

$$X = Expand(V) \Rightarrow \forall i, j, 0 \leq i < n, 0 \leq j < n,$$
$$X(i, j) = \begin{cases} 1 \text{ if } i = j \text{ and } V(i) = 0 \\ -1 \text{ if } i = j \text{ and } V(i) \neq 0 \\ 0 \text{ if } i \neq j \end{cases} \quad (4)$$

It is easy to see that:

$$Expand(V)^{-1} = Expand(V); \quad Expand(abs(V)) = Expand(V).$$

The function $Expand()$ can be used to express the requirement of the access directions of two neighboring processors that share data. The transformation matrices T_1 (for processor P_1) and T_2 (for processor P_2) should satisfy the following condition:

$$FT_1^{-1} = Expand(P_2 - P_1)FT_2^{-1}. \quad (5)$$

Since $Expand(V)^{-1} = Expand(V)$, the above equation is equivalent to:

$$FT_2^{-1} = Expand(P_1 - P_2)FT_1^{-1}. \quad (6)$$

Equation (5) captures the requirement that, after these transformations, P_1 and P_2 should have opposite access directions along the neighboring direction between P_1 and P_2, and have the same access direction in all others.

Assume that there are V processors and W processor pairs that share data. Therefore, we have W equations in the form of (5), and V unknowns in these equations. After solving this set of equations, we can obtain the transformation matrices needed to transform the local iteration space of each processor so that the inter-processor data reuse can be exploited. Figure 5 gives a sketch of our compiler algorithm. Note that if one of the transformation matrix is known in (5), this equation can be simplified as follows:

$$AT = B, \tag{7}$$

where A and B are known, and T is the unknown matrix. There exist several algorithms [3,9] that can be used for solving $AT = B$, and we can use any of these algorithms in our approach. In the algorithm shown in Fig. 5, we maintain two sets of equations. The set $\mathcal{L}$ contains all the equations that have two unknown matrices in them, while the set $\mathcal{C}$ contains all the equations that have exactly one unknown matrix. At each step, we try to solve an equation which has only one unknown matrix. Once we obtain a solution for this equation, all the equations in which both the transformation matrices are known are removed from $\mathcal{C}$, and all the equations with exactly one unknown matrix are moved from $\mathcal{L}$ to $\mathcal{C}$. When $\mathcal{C}$ becomes empty and $\mathcal{L}$ is not empty, we randomly select an equation from $\mathcal{L}$, and set one of the unknown matrices to identity matrix E (i.e., the loop of the corresponding processor is not transformed). If an equation has no solution, we simply ignore that equation, in which case the inter-processor data reuse represented by this equation cannot be exploited. Assuming that the complexity of solving (7) is Y and the number of equations is W, the complexity of our algorithm in Fig. 5 is WY.

3.5   Impact on Intra-processor Data Reuse

There are two types of intra-processor data reuses: *self-reuse* and *group-reuse* [29]. Self-reuse refers to the situation where the same array reference accesses adjacent data in successive loop iterations. Group-reuse refers to the situation where two array references access adjacent data in successive loop iterations. In this section, our goal is to show that transformation matrices obtained from our algorithm preserve all self-reuse in the original program and preserve the group-reuse in the most frequent cases.

Mathematically, self-reuse of an access function $f(\boldsymbol{I}) = F\boldsymbol{I} + \zeta$ can be defined as:

$$f(\boldsymbol{I} + (0\ 0\ \cdots\ 1)^T) - f(\boldsymbol{I}) = (0\ 0\ \cdots\ \delta)^T, \tag{8}$$

where $abs(\delta)$ is a small integer number. The above equation can be represented in matrix/vector form as follows:

$$F(0\ 0\ \cdots\ 1)^T = (0\ 0\ \cdots\ \delta)^T. \tag{9}$$

The group-reuse between two access functions, $f(\boldsymbol{I}) = F\boldsymbol{I} + \zeta$ and $f'(\boldsymbol{I}) = F'\boldsymbol{I} + \zeta'$, can be defined as:

$$f'(\boldsymbol{I} + (0\ 0\ \cdots\ 1)^T) - f(\boldsymbol{I}) = (0\ 0\ \cdots\ \delta)^T, \tag{10}$$

```
1:    L =the set of equations;
2:    C = ∅;
3:    while (L ≠ ∅) {
4:        randomly select an equation e₀ from L;
5:        T₀ is one of the unknown matrices in e₀;
6:        T₀ = E;
7:        move e₀ from L to C;
8:        while (C ≠ ∅) {
9:            randomly select an equation e from C;
10:           T is the only unknown matrix in e;
11:           solve e;
12:           if (there is solution for e) {
13:               T = the solution for e;
14:               remove from C all equations with T;
15:               move all equations in L with T to C;
16:           }
17:           else
18:               remove e from C;
19:       }
20: }
```

Fig. 5. The algorithm for solving a set of equations in the form of (5). Each equation in L has two unknowns, and each equation in C has exactly one unknown matrix. E is the identity matrix.

where $abs(\delta)$ is a small integer number. The different access functions in a stencil computation have the same access matrix (i.e., $F' = F$). Therefore, the above equation can be represented in a matrix/vector form as follows:

$$F(0\ 0\ \cdots\ 1)^T = (0\ 0\ \cdots\ \delta)^T + (\zeta - \zeta'). \tag{11}$$

Lemma 1: In (5), if processor P_2 exhibits self-reuse after loop transformation T_2, then processor P_1 also exhibits self-reuse after loop transformation T_1.

Sketch of the proof: After the transformations, the new access matrix of P_1 is FT_1^{-1} and the new access matrix of P_2 is FT_2^{-1}. Mathematically, Lemma 1 is equivalent to:

$$FT_2^{-1}(0\ 0\ \cdots\ 1)^T = (0\ 0\ \cdots\ \delta_2)^T \quad \Rightarrow \quad FT_1^{-1}((0\ 0\ \cdots\ 1)^T) = (0\ 0\ \cdots\ \delta_1)^T,$$

where both $abs(\delta_1)$ and $abs(\delta_2)$ are small integer numbers. Let $X = Expand(P_2 - P_1)$, we obtain:

$$\begin{aligned} FT_1^{-1}(0\ 0\ \cdots\ 1)^T &= XFT_2^{-1}(0\ 0\ \cdots\ 1)^T \\ &= X(0\ 0\ \cdots\ \delta_2)^T \\ &= (0\ 0\ \cdots\ \pm\delta_2)^T. \end{aligned}$$

The last step can be inferred from the definition of $Expand()$ given by (4). □

A processor P obtains its transformation T in two possible ways. One way is through line 6 in the algorithm in Fig. 5. In this scenario, since the transformation matrix is the identity matrix E, which means no transformation, self-reuse is clearly preserved. The other way is through line 13, in which T obtains its value by solving an equation in the form of (5). By using induction, we can easily prove from Lemma 1 that the transformation matrices obtained from our algorithm preserve the self-reuses in the original program.

Lemma 2: In (5), if the last column of F has only one non-zero entry and processor P_2 preserves group-reuse after loop transformation T_2, then processor P_1 also preserves group-reuse after transformation loop T_1.

Sketch of the proof: In mathematical terms, Lemma 2 is equivalent to:

> **Condition 1:** The last column of F has only one non-zero entry and
> **Condition 2:** $F(0\ 0\ \cdots\ 1)^T = (0\ 0\ \cdots\ \delta_0)^T + (\zeta - \zeta')$ and
> **Condition 3:** $FT_2^{-1}(0\ 0\ \cdots\ 1)^T = (0\ 0\ \cdots\ \delta_2)^T + (\zeta - \zeta')$
> $\Rightarrow FT_1^{-1}(0\ 0\ \cdots\ 1)^T = (0\ 0\ \cdots\ \delta_1)^T + (\zeta - \zeta')$,

where $abs(\delta_0)$, $abs(\delta_1)$ and $abs(\delta_2)$ are small integer numbers. Since $F(0\ 0\ \cdots\ 1)^T$ is the last column of F, we can infer from the first two conditions that:

$$F(0\ 0\ \cdots\ 1)^T = (0\ 0\ \cdots\ \Delta)^T, \text{ and}$$
$$(\zeta - \zeta') = (0\ 0\ \cdots\ \theta)^T.$$

Therefore, the third condition can also be expressed as:

$$FT_2^{-1}(0\ 0\ \cdots\ 1)^T = (0\ 0\ \cdots\ (\delta_2 + \theta))^T. \tag{12}$$

Letting $X = Expand(P_2 - P_1)$, we obtain:

$$\begin{aligned} FT_1^{-1}(0\ 0\ \cdots\ 1)^T &= XFT_2^{-1}(0\ 0\ \cdots\ 1)^T \\ &= X(0\ 0\ \cdots\ (\delta_2 + \theta))^T \\ &= (0\ 0\ \cdots\ \pm(\delta_2 + \theta))^T. \end{aligned}$$

The last vector above can be expressed as:

$$\begin{cases} (0\ 0\ \cdots\ \delta_2)^T + (0\ 0\ \cdots\ \theta)^T & \text{for the '+' case;} \\ (0\ 0\ \cdots\ (-\delta_2 - 2\theta))^T + (0\ 0\ \cdots\ \theta)^T & \text{for the '-' case.} \end{cases}$$

Since the distance between the data elements accessed by successive iterations in a stencil computation is small, the value of $abs(\theta)$ is small. Therefore, $abs(-\delta_2 - 2\theta)$ is also a small number. Considering that $(\zeta - \zeta') = ((0\ 0\ \cdots\ \theta)^T$, we see that the transformation T_1 preserves the group-reuse. □

Similarly, we can prove from Lemma 2 that the transformation matrices obtained from our algorithm preserve the group-reuse in the original program if the last column of F has only one non-zero entry. Having only one non-zero entry in the last column of F requires that the index variable of the innermost loop appears in the access function only once. Although this seems restrictive, almost all the known stencil computations satisfy this requirement. Therefore, our algorithm preserves group-reuse in the most common cases.

3.6 Examples

In this section, we use two examples to illustrate how to use the mathematical framework in Sect. 3.4 to transform the local iteration space of each processor for exploiting inter-processor data reuse.

Example 1. Let us consider the stencil computation presented in Fig. 3. The stencil direction matrix $\mathcal{D}$ and the access direction matrix F for this stencil are:

$$\mathcal{D} = \begin{pmatrix} 1 & 0 & -1 & 0 \\ 0 & -1 & 0 & 1 \end{pmatrix} \text{ and } F = \begin{pmatrix} 1 & 0 \\ 0 & 1 \end{pmatrix}.$$

In this figure, there are twelve neighboring processor pairs. For each processor pair, we use (3) to determine whether they share any data or not. There are two types of neighboring directions between the neighboring processors: row-wise and column-wise. These two types of directions correspond to two direction vectors: $(0 \quad 1)^T$ and $(1 \quad 0)^T$. Applying (3) to these two directions vectors, we obtain:

$$(0 \quad 1) \begin{pmatrix} 1 & 0 & -1 & 0 \\ 0 & -1 & 0 & 1 \end{pmatrix} = (0 \quad -1 \quad 0 \quad 1) \neq \mathbf{0};$$

$$(1 \quad 0) \begin{pmatrix} 1 & 0 & -1 & 0 \\ 0 & -1 & 0 & 1 \end{pmatrix} = (1 \quad 0 \quad -1 \quad 0) \neq \mathbf{0}.$$

This means that, all the neighboring processors share data. Figure 3(b) illustrates the data sharing patterns exhibited by the processors.

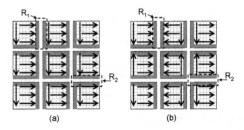

(a)   (b)

Fig. 6. (a) The original access pattern. (b) The new access pattern after the loop transformations.

Figure 6(a) shows the original access pattern for each processor. Since the neighboring processors do not access the shared data at the same time, such an access pattern is not good as far as exploiting inter-processor data reuse is concerned. In the next step, we transform the program code for each processor so that the inter-processor data reuse can be exploited; i.e., the data reuse can be converted to data locality. We use $T_{p1,p2}$ to represent the transformation matrix for processor $(p1 \quad p2)^T$. First, we apply $Expand()$ to the direction vectors, namely, $(0 \quad 1)^T$ and $(1 \quad 0)^T$:

$$X_1 = Expand((0 \quad 1)^T) = \begin{pmatrix} 1 & 0 \\ 0 & -1 \end{pmatrix}; \quad X_2 = Expand((1 \quad 0)^T) = \begin{pmatrix} -1 & 0 \\ 0 & 1 \end{pmatrix}.$$

After that, we build a set of equations containing twelve equations for the twelve neighboring processor pairs.

$$FT_{0,0}^{-1} = X_1 FT_{0,1}^{-1}; \ FT_{0,1}^{-1} = X_1 FT_{0,2}^{-1}; \ FT_{1,0}^{-1} = X_1 FT_{1,1}^{-1}; \ FT_{1,1}^{-1} = X_1 FT_{1,2}^{-1};$$
$$FT_{2,0}^{-1} = X_1 FT_{2,1}^{-1}; \ FT_{2,1}^{-1} = X_1 FT_{2,2}^{-1}; \ FT_{0,0}^{-1} = X_2 FT_{1,0}^{-1}; \ FT_{1,0}^{-1} = X_2 FT_{2,0}^{-1};$$
$$FT_{0,1}^{-1} = X_2 FT_{1,1}^{-1}; \ FT_{1,1}^{-1} = X_2 FT_{2,1}^{-1}; \ FT_{0,2}^{-1} = X_2 FT_{1,2}^{-1}; \ FT_{1,2}^{-1} = X_2 FT_{2,2}^{-1}.$$

```
for (i=1024; i<2048; i++)              for (i=-2047; i<=-1024; i++)
  for (j=1024; j<2048; j++)              for (j=-2047; j<=-1024; j++)
    tempU[i][j]=(U[i][j-1]+U[i][j+1]       tempU[-i][-j]=(U[-i][-j-1]+U[-i][-j+1]
    +U[i-1][j]+U[i+1][j])/4;               +U[-i-1][-j]+U[-i+1][-j])/4;
           (a)                                     (b)
```

Fig. 7. (a) The original code for processor $(1 \quad 1)^T$. (b) The transformed code for processor $(1 \quad 1)^T$.

For example, for processors $(0 \quad 0)^T$ and $(0 \quad 1)^T$, the open form of the equation is:

$$\begin{pmatrix} 1 & 0 \\ 0 & 1 \end{pmatrix} T_{0,0}^{-1} = \begin{pmatrix} 1 & 0 \\ 0 & -1 \end{pmatrix} \begin{pmatrix} 1 & 0 \\ 0 & 1 \end{pmatrix} T_{0,1}^{-1}.$$

Using the algorithm given in Fig. 5, we obtain a solution to the above set of equations:

$$T_{0,0} = T_{0,2} = T_{2,0} = T_{2,2} = \begin{pmatrix} 1 & 0 \\ 0 & 1 \end{pmatrix};$$

$$T_{0,1} = T_{2,1} = \begin{pmatrix} 1 & 0 \\ 0 & -1 \end{pmatrix}; \quad T_{1,0} = T_{1,2} = \begin{pmatrix} -1 & 0 \\ 0 & 1 \end{pmatrix}; \quad T_{1,1} = \begin{pmatrix} -1 & 0 \\ 0 & -1 \end{pmatrix}.$$

These transformation matrices can be used to transform the local iteration spaces of processors. As an example, Fig. 7(a) presents the original program code for processor $(1 \quad 1)^T$, and it is transformed, using $T_{1,1}$, to the code given in Fig. 7(b). After the transformations, we obtain the new data access pattern shown in Fig. 6(b). Obviously, this new access pattern exploits inter-processor data reuse much better than the one shown in Fig. 6(a). For example, in Fig. 6(a), processors $(0 \quad 0)^T$ and $(0 \quad 1)^T$ do not access the shared array elements in R_1 together, while in Fig. 6(b) the array elements in R_1 are accessed together by these two processors, in which case inter-processor data reuse is converted to inter-processor data locality. Similar observations can be made for all the other data regions shared by the neighboring processors.

Example 2. The code segment shown in Fig. 8(a) is obtained by applying loop-tiling to the code segment given in Fig. 3(a). This stencil computation is parallelized over four processors, and the default data access pattern is shown in Fig. 8(b). The corresponding stencil direction matrix $\mathcal{D}$ and the access direction matrix F are:

$$\mathcal{D} = \begin{pmatrix} 1 & 0 & -1 & 0 \\ 0 & -1 & 0 & 1 \end{pmatrix} \text{ and } F = \begin{pmatrix} 8 & 0 & 1 & 0 \\ 0 & 8 & 0 & 1 \end{pmatrix}.$$

There are three neighboring processor pairs, and all the neighboring direction vectors between them are of the form $(0 \quad 1)^T$. Consequently, applying (3) to this directions vector, we obtain:

$$(0 \quad 1) \begin{pmatrix} 1 & 0 & -1 & 0 \\ 0 & -1 & 0 & 1 \end{pmatrix} = (0 \quad -1 \quad 0 \quad 1) \neq \mathbf{0}.$$

```
for (i=1; i<384; i++)
  for (j=1; j<384; j++)
    for (x=1; x<8; x++)
      for (y=1; y<8; y++)
        tempU[8*i+x][8*j+y] = (U[8*i+x][8*j+y-1] +
          + U[8*i+x][8*j+y+1] + U[8*i+x-1][8*j+y]
          + U[8*i+x+1][8*i+y])/4;
```
(a)

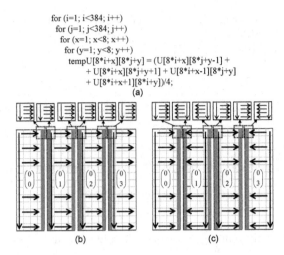

(b)   (c)

Fig. 8. (a) The original stencil code for Example 2. (b) Distribution across four processors and the default data access pattern. The shaded (gray) areas indicate the shared data, and the arrows represent access pattern. Captured in small squares are the access patterns used for visiting the elements inside each tile. (c) The new data access pattern after the loop transformations.

This means that all the neighboring processors share data. Figure 3(b) illustrates the data sharing patterns exhibited by the processors. As before, we use $T_{p1,p2}$ to represent the transformation matrix for processor identified by $(p1 \quad p2)^T$. First, we apply $Expand()$ to the direction vector $(0 \quad 1)^T$:

$$X = Expand((0 \quad 1)^T) = \begin{pmatrix} 1 & 0 \\ 0 & -1 \end{pmatrix}.$$

We then build a system of three equations for the three neighboring processor pairs. That is:

$$FT_{0,0}^{-1} = XFT_{0,1}^{-1}; \quad FT_{0,1}^{-1} = XFT_{0,2}^{-1}; \quad FT_{0,2}^{-1} = XFT_{0,3}^{-1};$$

Finally, using the algorithm in Fig. 5, we obtain a solution to the above set of equations:

$$T_{0,0} = T_{0,2} = \begin{pmatrix} 1 & 0 & 0 & 0 \\ 0 & 1 & 0 & 0 \\ 0 & 0 & 1 & 0 \\ 0 & 0 & 0 & 1 \end{pmatrix}; \quad T_{0,1} = T_{0,3} = \begin{pmatrix} 1 & 0 & 0 & 0 \\ 0 & -1 & 0 & 0 \\ 0 & 0 & 1 & 0 \\ 0 & 0 & 0 & -1 \end{pmatrix}.$$

Figure 8(c) gives the new access pattern after applying these transformations to the local iteration spaces of our four processors. Again, the new (transformed) access patterns exploit the inter-processor data reuse much better than the original patterns given in Fig. 8(b). These two examples show that one can exploit inter-processor data reuse by employing a customized loop transformation matrix for each processor in the system.

4 Experimental Results

To perform our experimental evaluation, we used the Simics tool-set [26]. Simics is an instruction set simulator and operating system emulator. It allows simulation of multiple processors connected through an on-chip memory space, which can have multiple layers. We modified Simics to keep track of the behavior of shared and non-shared data separately. The default values of the important simulation parameters we used in our experiments are listed in Table 1. The code modifications required by our approach are automated within the SUIF infrastructure [27].

Table 1. Important simulation parameters used in our experiments and their default values. Each processor has its own L1 cache and all processors share an L2 cache.

Parameter	Default Value
Number of Processors	8
L1 Size	8KB
L1 Line Size	32 bytes
L1 Associativity	4-way
L1 Latency	1 cycle
L2 Size	2MB
L2 Associativity	4-way
L2 Line Size	64 bytes
L2 Latency	10 cycles
Memory Access Latency	120 cycles
Bus Arbitration Delay	5 cycles
Replacement Policy	Strict LRU

The benchmark codes used in this study are given in Table 2. The common characteristic of these codes is that they all perform some sort of stencil computation. The second column gives a description of each benchmark and the next one shows the amount of input data used for executing the benchmark. The fourth column gives the number of execution cycles for each benchmark when no locality optimization is applied. The goal of our approach is to reduce the execution cycles by minimizing the number of off-chip

Table 2. Stencil applications used in our experiments

Benchmark Name	Brief Description	Input Size (KB)	Execution Cycles (M)
Gauss-Seidel	Gauss-Seidel Computation	3731.4	386.9
Weather	Weather Prediction	5982.2	901.1
Edge	Edge Detection Algorithm	5418.5	513.2
Jacobi	Jacobi Iterative Solver	1545.0	155.7
VB 2.0	Vertex Blending	7816.4	995.1
Map 1.1	Cube Mapping	2998.9	372.3
RB-SOR	Red-Black Successive-Over-Relaxation	4115.6	664.8
TDer	Terrain Detection	6695.1	756.9

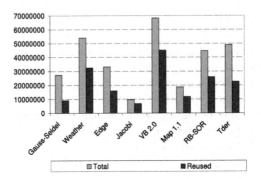

Fig. 9. Number of off-chip memory references

references. The execution cycle reductions given in the remainder of this section are normalized values with respect to the last column of Table 2.

Figure 9 gives the number of off-chip memory references for our benchmarks. The bar marked "Reused" correspond to the number of visits to the off-chip memory for a data element that has previously been on the on-chip memory space. In other words, it captures the number of references to the off-chip memory due to not being able to exploit inter-processor data reuse while the data is in the on-chip memory space. The bar marked "Total", on the other hand, gives the total number of off-chip memory references. We observe that, on an average, nearly 56% of the off-chip references are due to not being able to exploit the inter-processor data reuse, which indicates an approach that can convert these misses in the on-chip memory space to hits can be very effective in practice.

Figure 10 summarizes the savings achieved by our approach in three groups. Note that, before applying our approach that optimizes inter-processor reuse, we optimized intra-processor reuse for each processor independently. The first bar for each benchmark gives the percentage savings (reductions) in the off-chip memory references that belong to the "Reused" category. The second bar gives the percentage savings when all the off-chip references are considered. We see that the average saving in the "Reused" and "Total" categories are 77.6% and 42.4%, respectively. The last bar shows the reductions in execution cycles. We observe that our approach reduces the overall execution cycles by 22.6% on the average. Figure 11 gives similar results for the alternate scheme that optimizes locality for each processor in isolation (i.e., that optimizes for intra-processor locality only). The most striking observation from this figure is that the reductions in the "Reused" category is very low compared to our approach, and amounts to 27.1% when averaged over all benchmark codes in our experimental suite. This is mainly because this alternate approach does not consider the reuse of the data shared by multiple processors. However, when we look at the second bar for each benchmark (marked "Total"), we see that the average savings is about 32.2% when all benchmarks are considered. That is, although it is not very effective for the shared data, this approach is successful in converting the remaining misses into hits in the on-chip memory space. We also see from Fig. 11 that the average reduction in execution cycles with this approach is around 8.2%. To sum up, by comparing Fig.s 10 and 11, one can see that exploiting locality for the shared data is very important for stencil type of applications.

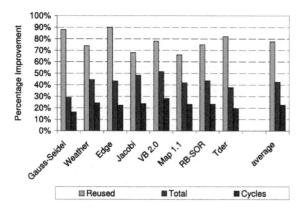

Fig. 10. Savings in the off-chip memory references and execution cycles with our approach

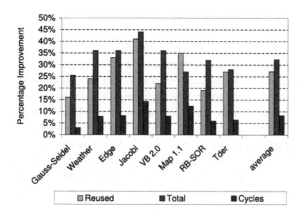

Fig. 11. Savings in the off-chip memory references and execution cycles with the alternate approach that optimizes data locality for each processor in isolation

We now change the default number of processors used in our experiments so far, and conduct a sensitivity analysis. Figure 12 plots the percentage improvements in execution cycles when our approach is used. For each application in this graph, each bar corresponds to a processor count (from 2 to 64). Recall that the default values used so far was 8. Maybe the most important conclusion one might draw from these results is that the effectiveness of our approach increases as we increase the number of processors (without changing the data set size). For example, while the average saving with 4 processors is around 14.2%, that with 32 processors is about 34.3%. This is because when the number of processors is increased, interprocessor communication (i.e., data sharing) also increases (i.e., some of the intra-processor computation – before we increase the processor count – needs nonlocal data after we increase the processor count). This in turn increases the importance of optimizing the locality behavior of the shared data. We do not present the results with the alternate scheme here in detail, but want to say that our approach consistently generated better results than the alternate scheme.

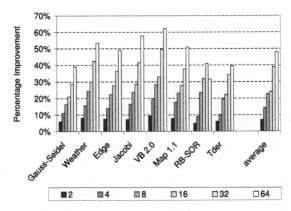

Fig. 12. Reduction in execution cycles with different processor counts

5   Conclusions and Future Work

Minimizing the number of off-chip memory references is very important in embedded chip multiprocessors from both the performance and power perspectives. This paper proposes and evaluates a compiler-based solution to this problem. It primarily focuses on data shared across processors, and re-organizes loop iterations assigned to processors in a coordinated fashion so that the reuse distance to shared data is minimized. Our experiments with eight benchmark codes from the embedded computing domain indicate significant reductions in off-chip memory accesses. We are in the process of evaluating the impact of other locality oriented optimizations on our inter-processor reuse representation. We are also working on developing a new code parallelization strategy that leads to better inter-processor reuse (in terms of both volume and sharing pattern).

Acknowledgement

This work was supported in part by NSF Career Award #0093082 and by GSRC.

References

1. R. Allen and K. Kennedy. Automatic translation of FORTRAN programs to vector form. *ACM Transactions on Programming Languages and Systems.* 9(4):491-542, 1987.
2. U. Banerjee. A theory of loop permutations. In Proc. *2nd Workshop on Languages and Compilers for Parallel Computing.* August 1989.
3. E. H. Bareiss. Sylvester's Identity and Multistep Integer-Preserving Gaussian Elimination. *Mathematics of Computation,* 22(103):565-578, July 1968.
4. L. A. Barroso, K. Gharachorloo, R. McNamara, A. Nowatzyk, S. Qadeer, B. Sano, S. Smith, R. Stets, and B. Verghese. Piranha: A Scalable Architecture Based on Single-Chip Multiprocessing. In *Proceedings of International Symposium on Computer Architecture,* 2000.
5. R. Bordawekar, A. Choudhary, and J. Ramanujam. Automatic optimization of communication in compiling out-of-core stencil codes. In *Proc. ACM International Conference on Supercomputing,* May 1996.

6. R. G. Brickner, W. George, S. L. Johnsson, and A. Ruttenberg. A stencil compiler for the connection machine models CM-2/200. *Technical Report TR-22-93,* Center for Research in Computing Technology, Harvard University, December 1993.
7. R. G. Brickner, K. Holian, B. Thiagarajan, and S. L. Johnsson. A stencil compiler for the Connection Machine model CM-5. *Technical Report CRPC-TR94457,* Center for Research on Parallel Computation, Rice University, June 1994.
8. M. Bromley, S. Heller, T. McNerney, and G. L. Steele Jr. Fortran at ten gigaflops: the connection machine convolution compiler. In *Proc. ACM Conference on Programming Language Design and Implementation,* June 1991.
9. S. Cabay. Exact solution of linear equations. In *Proc. ACM Symposium on Symbolic and Algebraic Manipulation,* pp. 392-398, 1971.
10. D. Culler, J. P. Singh, and A. Gupta. *Parallel Computer Architecture: A Hardware/Software Approach.* Morgan Kaufmann, 1998.
11. K. Davis and F. Bassetti. Exploiting temporal locality in stencil based applications. In *Proc. International Conference on Information Systems Analysis and Synthesis,* 1999.
12. M. Gomaa, C. Scarbrough, T. N. Vijaykumar, and I. Pomeranz. Transient-fault recovery for chip multiprocessors. In *Proc. International Symposium on Computer Architecture,* 2003.
13. M. Gschwind, P. Hofstee, B. Flachs, M. Hopkins, Y. Watanabe, and T. Yamazaki. A novel SIMD architecture for the Cell heterogeneous chip-multiprocessor. *Hot Chips 17,* 2005.
14. L. Hammond, B. A. Nayfeh, and K. Olukotun. A single-chip multiprocessor. *IEEE Computer Special Issue on "Billion-Transistor Processors",* September 1997.
15. R. Hetheringtonh. The UltraSPARC T1 Processor - Power Efficient Throughput Computing. *Sun White Paper,* December 2005.
16. F. F. Lee. Partitioning of regular computation on multiprocessor systems. *Journal of Parallel and Distributed Computing,* 9:312-317, July 1990.
17. S.-T. Leung and J. Zahorjan. Optimizing data locality by array restructuring. *Technical Report 95-09-01,* University of Washington, September 1995.
18. W. Li and K. Pingali. A singular loop transformation framework based on non-singular matrices. In Proc. *5th Workshop on Languages and Compilers for Parallel Computing,* Yale University, August 1992.
19. MAJC-5200. http://www.sun.com/microelectronics/ MAJC/5200wp.html
20. MP98: A Mobile Processor. http://www.labs.nec.co.jp/MP98/top-e.htm.
21. B. A. Nayfeh and K. Olukotun. Exploring the design space for a shared-cache multiprocessor. In Proc. *International Symposium on Computer Architecture,* 1994.
22. K. Olukotun and L. Hammond. The future of microprocessors. *ACM QUEUE Magazine,* September 2005.
23. POWER4 System Microarchitecture, *White Paper,* http://www-1.ibm.com/servers/eserver/pseries/hardware/whitepapers/power4.html.
24. S. Richardson. MPOC: A chip multiprocessor for embedded systems. Technical Report HPL-2002-186, HP Labs, 2002.
25. G. Roth, J. Mellor-Crummey, K. Kennedy, and R. G. Brickner. Compiling stencils in high performance Fortran. In Proc. *ACM/IEEE conference on Supercomputing,* 1997.
26. SIMICS Toolset. http://www.virtutech.com.
27. SUIF Compiler Infrastructure. http://suif.stanford.edu/
28. W. Wolf. The future of multiprocessor systems-on-chips. In *Proc. ACM Design Automation Conference,* 2004.
29. M. E. Wolf and M. S. Lam. A data locality optimizing algorithm. In *Proc. ACM Conference on Programming Language Design and Implementation,* pp. 30-44, June 1991.
30. M. E. Wolf and M. S. Lam. A loop transformation theory and an algorithm to maximize parallelism. *IEEE Transactions on Parallel and Distributed Systems,* 2(4):452-471, July, 1991.
31. M. J. Wolfe. *Optimizing Supercompilers for Supercomputers.* Cambridge, MIT Press, 1989.

Part 3

ACM International Conference on Computing Frontiers 2006 Best Papers

Introduction to Part 3

I am very pleased to welcome you to this special section highlighting the embedded-systems oriented papers from Computing Frontiers 2006. The papers in this section of the volume demonstrate current topics in embedded computing, attempting to strike a balance between design and use. The authors are from both industry and academia. We strove to provide a panorama of some of the most interesting, novel systems in recent study or development. I hope you find these papers interesting in their insights, and informative in the details provided.

The first paper in the issue, "Hardware/Software Architecture for Real-Time ECG Monitoring and Analysis Leveraging MPSoC Technology", describes a system-on-a-chip (SOC) solution to real-time heart-rate monitoring: the solution parallelizes computation of the ECG kernel to enable real-time analyses. The result is more accurate diagnoses and more prompt responses to abnormal heart activity.

The next paper, "Using Application Bisection Bandwidth to Guide Tile Size Selection for the Synchroscalar Tile-Based Architecture", describes a tile-based architecture, Synchroscalar, a reduced-power architecture that potentially represents the chip-multiprocessor organizations that will soon appear in many embedded systems. Tiled architectures are gaining influence in many arenas, and thus we examine them here. The tile size selection work herein can be used to evaluate tile size when considering multiple applications simultaneously (a probable scenario for embedded systems), providing a convenient platform for hardware-software co-design.

The third paper, "Static Cache Partitioning Robustness Analysis for Embedded On-Chip Multi-Processors", describes metrics for quantifying the quality of partitioning of L2 caches on CMPs when running different tasks per processor. The configurations investigated match how CMPs are likely to be used in embedded systems, as opposed to in supercomputing systems. The combination of analysis and experimentation makes this a particularly interesting research paper.

The next paper, "Selective Code Compression Scheme for Embedded Systems", describes a software-based code compression scheme that reduces program storage requirements, reducing off-chip access time in SoC (System-on-a-chip) embedded architectures. Efficient usage of memory resources becomes even more important in embedded systems, and so schemes such as those described in this paper have substantial potential to have enormous impact on a variety of systems.

The paper "A Prefetching Algorithm for Multispeed Disks" describes a power-saving scheme for data-intensive applications using disk-resident datasets. This paper provides a compelling argument for commercial multispeed disk drives.

Finally, we return to the frontiers of current systems with "Exploration of Reconfiguration Strategies for Environmentally Powered Devices", which exploits environmental energy in a multiphased approach. The first phase profiles many aspects of energy utilization, and the second uses this information in a reconfiguration manager to configure applications to run most efficiently.

P. Stenström (Ed.): Transactions on HiPEAC I, LNCS 4050, pp. 237–238, 2007.

These papers represent the diversity of work being done in the embedded systems arena; I hope you enjoy reading them, and that you learn something from each, as I have. Thanks go to Per Stenström, the Editor-in-Chief of these transactions and the person who made this special issue possible. I also thank Monica Alderighi and Valentina Salapura, the co-general chairs of 2006 ACM Computing Frontiers Conference, along with all the members of the organizing and steering committees. Their dedication made the conference a success and helped yield the papers you see here. Special thanks also go to Stamatis Vassiliadis, from TU Delft. He served as General Chair of the first Computing Frontiers Conference in 2004, and has steadfastly served as a steering committee member and program committee member in following conferences. His passions for research, food, and life have helped make Computing Frontiers unique among ACM conferences: it is a venue for exchanging research ideas, discussing ideologies, speculating and debating about the future technologies of our field, turning colleagues into friends, and turning friends into old friends. His contributions cannot be overestimated.

Sally A. McKee
Cornell University
Guest Editor
Transactions on HiPEAC

Hardware/Software Architecture for Real-Time ECG Monitoring and Analysis Leveraging MPSoC Technology

Iyad Al Khatib[1], Davide Bertozzi[2], Francesco Poletti[3], Luca Benini[3], Axel Jantsch[1], Mohamed Bechara[4], Hasan Khalifeh[4], Mazen Hajjar[4], Rustam Nabiev[5], and Sven Jonsson[5]

[1] ECS, ICT, Royal Institute of Technology (KTH), Stockholm, Sweden
{iyad, axel}@imit.kth.se
[2] Engineering Department, University of Ferrara, Ferrara, Italy
dbertozzi@ing.unife.it
[3] DEIS, University of Bologna, Bologna, Italy
{fpoletti, lbenini}@deis.unibo.it
[4] ECE, FEA, American University of Beirut, Beirut, Lebanon
{mfb05, hik05, mah39}@aub.edu.lb
[5] Biomedical Engineering Department, Karolinska University Hospital
Huddinge, Stockholm, Sweden
{rustam.nabiev, sven.jonssoni}@karolinska.se

Abstract. The interest in high performance chip architectures for biomedical applications is gaining a lot of research and market interest. Heart diseases remain by far the main cause of death and a challenging problem for biomedical engineers to monitor and analyze. Electrocardiography (ECG) is an essential practice in heart medicine. However, ECG analysis still faces computational challenges, especially when 12 lead signals are to be analyzed in parallel, in real time, and under increasing sampling frequencies. Another challenge is the analysis of huge amounts of data that may grow to days of recordings. Nowadays, doctors use eyeball monitoring of the 12-lead ECG paper readout, which may seriously impair analysis accuracy. Our solution leverages the advance in multi-processor system-on-chip architectures, and it is centered on the parallelization of the ECG computation kernel. Our Hardware-Software (HW/SW) Multi-Processor System-on-Chip (MPSoC) design improves upon state-of-the-art mostly for its capability to perform real-time analysis of input data, leveraging the computation horsepower provided by many concurrent DSPs, more accurate diagnosis of cardiac diseases, and prompter reaction to abnormal heart alterations. The design methodology to go from the 12-lead ECG application specification to the final HW/SW architecture is the focus of this paper. We explore the design space by considering a number of hardware and software architectural variants, and deploy industrial components to build up the system.

Keywords: Multiprocessor System-on-Chip, embedded system design, HW/SW, electrocardiogram algorithms, real-time analysis, hardware space exploration.

P. Stenström (Ed.): Transactions on HiPEAC I, LNCS 4050, pp. 239–258, 2007.
© Springer-Verlag Berlin Heidelberg 2007

1 Introduction

Despite the ongoing advances in heart treatment, in the United States [1] and Canada [2] as well as in many other countries, the various forms of cardiovascular disease (CVD) and stroke remain by far the number one cause of death for both men and women regardless of ethnic backgrounds. According to the World Health Organization (WHO) Report in 2003, 29.2% of total global deaths are due to CVD, many of which are preventable by action on the major primary risk factors and with proper monitoring [1]. It is estimated that by 2010, CVD will be the leading cause of death in developing countries. Since the rate of hospitalization increases with age for all cardiac diseases [3], a periodic cardiac examination is recommended. Hence, more efficient methods of cardiac diagnosis are desired to meet the great demand on heart examinations. However, state-of-the-art biomedical equipment for heartbeat sensing and monitoring lacks the ability of providing large-scale analysis and remote, real-time computation at the patient's location (point of need). The intention of this work is to use MPSoC microelectronic technology to meet the growing demand for telemedicine services, especially in the mobile environment. The project attempts to address the existing problem of reducing the costs for hospitals/medical-centers through using MPSoC-based designs that may replace biomedical machines and have higher quality, reduce the nurse's and doctor's work-load, and improve the quality of healthcare for patients suffering from heart diseases by exploring one potential solution. From the hospital side, deploying this solution will further reduce the costs of rehabilitating and following up on patients "primary care" since it allows better home-care. Home-care ensures continuity of care, reduces hospitalization costs, and enables patients to have a quicker return to their normal life styles. From a technical viewpoint, real-time processing of ECG data would allow a finer-granularity analysis with respect to the traditional eyeball monitoring of the paper ECG readout. Eventually, warning or alarm signals could be generated by the monitoring device and transmitted to the healthcare center via telemedicine links, thus allowing for a prompter reaction of the medical staff. In contrast, heartbeat monitoring and data processing are traditionally performed at the hospital, and for long monitoring periods a huge amount of collected data must be processed offline by networks of parallel computers. New models of healthcare delivery [2] are therefore required, improving productivity and access to care, controlling costs, and improving clinical outcomes. This poses new technical challenges to the design of biomedical ECG equipment, calling for the development of new integrated circuits featuring increased energy efficiency while providing higher computation capabilities.

The fast evolution of biomedical sensors and the trend in embedded computing are progressively making this new scenario technically feasible. Sensors today exhibit smaller size, increased energy efficiency and therefore prolonged lifetimes (up to 24 hours) [4], higher sampling frequencies (up to 10 kHz for ECG) and often provide for wireless connectivity. Unfortunately, a mismatch exists between advances in sensor technology and the capabilities of state-of-the-art heart analyzers [5][6][7]. They cannot usually keep up with the data acquisition rate, and are usually wall-plugged, thus preventing for mobile monitoring. On the contrary, the deployment of wearable devices such as SoC devices has to cope with the tight power budgets of such devices, potentially cutting down on the maximum achievable monitoring period. In this paper we propose a wearable multi-processor biomedical-chip for electrocardiogram (MPSoC ECG biochip) paving the way for portable real-time electrocardiography applications targeting heart disorders. The biochip leverages the computation horsepower provided by many (up to twelve) concurrent DSPs and is able to operate in real-time while performing the finest granularity analysis as specified by the ECG application. Moreover, in case of heart failure emergency aid should arrive in a period of few minutes from the time when the heart failed, otherwise brain damage may occur. Hence, real time analysis must be done in few seconds to allow the alarm signal to reach the emergency aid team, which should act immediately. The biochip system builds upon some of the most advanced industrial components for MPSoC design (multi-issue VLIW DSPs, high-throughput system interconnect and commercial off-the-shelf biomedical sensors), which have been composed in a scalable and flexible platform. Therefore, we have ensured its reusability for future generations of ECG analysis algorithms and its suitability for porting of other biomedical applications, in particular those collecting input data from wired/wireless sensor networks [8].

This article builds upon the results of a paper from the ACM International Conference on Computing Frontiers 2006 [9]. We present our investigation that goes through all the steps of the design process, from application functional specification to hardware modeling and optimization. System performance has been validated through functional, timing accurate simulation on a virtual platform. We point out the need for simulation abstractions matching the application domain. A 0.13µm technology-homogeneous power estimation framework leveraging industrial power models is used for power management considerations [10][11]. The paper presents the process of software functional specification, optimization and parallelization, as well as the results of the hardware design space exploration, which leads to the final performance- and energy-optimized solution.

2 Biomedical Background

The electrocardiogram (ECG) is an electrical recording of the heart activity that is used as a diagnosis tool by physicians and doctors to check the status of the heart. The most commonly used way to detect the heart status is the 12-lead ECG technique. This technique uses nine sensors on the patient's body (Fig. 1). The three main sensors are distributed by: placing one sensor on the left arm (LA), a second sensor on the right arm (RA), and a third sensor on the left leg (LL). The right leg (RL) is connected by only a wire to be used as ground for the interconnected sensors. By only having these three sensors physicians can use a method known as the 3-lead ECG, which suffers from the lack of information about some parts of the heart but is useful for some emergency cases to have quick analysis. In this respect, medical doctors require more sensors (i.e., more leads). Hence, six more sensors (V1-V6) are added on the chest (Fig. 1). The voltages V1-V6 are measured with respect to *Ground* (G) on the right leg (RL). In some cases, physicians use these six chest-placed sensors to analyze the heart. Using all the nine sensors and interconnecting them for the 12-lead ECG gives twelve signals known in biomedical terms as: Lead I, Lead II, Lead III, aVR, aVL, aVF, V1, V2, V3, V4, V5, and V6 (Fig. 1). The 12-lead ECG produces huge amounts of data especially when used for a long number of hours. Physicians use the 12-lead ECG method, because it allows them to view the heart in its three dimensional form; thus, enabling detection of any abnormality that may not be apparent in the 3-lead or 6-lead ECG technique. Fig. 2 shows an explanatory example of a typical ECG signal. The most important points on the ECG signal are the peaks: P, Q, R, S, T, and U. Each of these peaks is related to a heart action that is of importance to the medical analysis. Figure 3 shows real recorded signals from 12-leads, which are printed on the eyeballing paper.

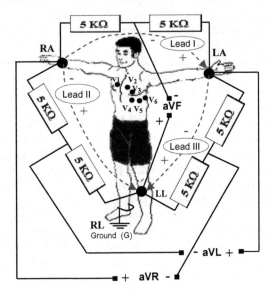

Fig. 1. 12-lead ECG: RA, LA, LL, & RL are the right arm, left arm, left leg, and right leg sensors; RL is grounded (G)

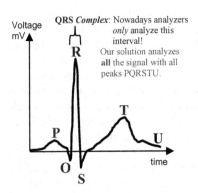

Fig. 2. Ideal ECG Signal for lead I

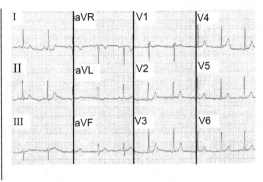

Fig. 3. Complete paper readout, which is not accurate to see peaks nor easy to read for long recordings

This paper printout is the classical medical technique used for looking at ECG signals, and it is still used. However, the eyeballing paper print makes the check of the different heart peaks and rhythms difficult and inaccurate due to its dependence on the physician's eyes. On the other hand, when using digital recording and filtering we can determine the peaks more accurately. Consequently, we can use digital computing to process the sensed data and analyze the heart beat. In addition, there are normal medical ranges for the inter-peak time intervals, and every combination of different inter-peak intervals proves a type of heart illness. The most important of the peaks is the R peak, which refers to the largest heart blood pump.

3   Previous Work

Electrocardiogram methods for heart analyses have been one of the most important medical practices, hence, the monitoring and analyses of ECG signals have not only gone through a lot of research work, but also many companies have investigated and worked on commercial solutions.

However, we are not aware of any solution in the research or the commercial markets that is composed of a single-chip real-time analysis solution for full 12-lead ECG, and that is able to estimate the heart period independent of the peak signals and, at the same time diagnose all the peaks: P, Q, R, S, T and U and their inter-peak intervals to result in disease diagnosis. Most of the work done involves only recording huge amounts of data in large storage media and then analyzing the stored data, but not allowing the ease of patient mobility. Most of the time, the patient has to be confined to a bed for a number of hours (could be for a whole day). Some commercial solutions are only capable of concluding if the heart beat is normal or abnormal but can not specify the period nor could they diagnose the disease. Other real time solutions available in the market, in healthcare institutes, and in research organizations, are *only* capable of sensing and transmitting ECG data [12] to: either a local machine [13] or to a distant healthcare center [14]. In both cases, the work that is executed involves checking if the heart beat is healthy or unhealthy without analyzing the disease and not in real-time. Moreover, the commercial solutions under study [15] do not look into the parallelization of the ECG analysis into multiple cores, so to speed up processing.

4   Sensing and Filtering Stage

ECG analysis requires three main phases: (i) acquiring the signals from the leads, (ii) filtering the lead-signals (each alone), and (iii) analysis (Fig. 4). Firstly, the sensing phase requires an A/D converter in order to be able to have digital data for our digital filter. We use 16 bit A/D converters, because our analysis algorithm and ECG biochip are designed based on having 16-bit filtered data as input. We briefly discuss the filtering method we use as an essential part of our proposed solution, and then we discuss the biochip design that depends on this filtering step.

The high investment in sensor technology and biomedical research in general gave the birth to biomedical sensors that have more advanced features than the commercial available ones just a few years ago. For instance, the nowadays sensors are characterized by prolonged lifetimes (up to 24 hours), and higher sampling frequencies (up to 10 kHz for ECG). Some sensor companies have produced wireless biomedical sensors in order to aid patient mobility [4]. This advance in biomedical sensors faces a mismatch with biomedical heartbeat analyzers that still lack behind to cope with the huge amounts of data, the high rates, and the wireless features that modern sensors can provide [6]. In our work, many sensors may be chosen, and for the moment we choose the sensors that can serve our real-time aim and that have reasonable prices for the market success of the solution, hence we choose the state of the art commercial sensor from Ambu Inc. silver/silver chloride "Blue Sensor R" [4] shown in Fig. 4. It is characterized by: 24 hour lifetime, superior adhesion, optimal signal measuring during stress tests. It is small to carry (57mm x 48mm), and it is easily wearable.

On the other hand, even the state of the art sensors suffer from the usual problems that most biomedical sensors suffer from. For instance, data provided by biomedical sensors suffers from several types of noise: physiological variability of *QRS complexes* (The *QRS Complex* is shown in Fig. 2), baseline wander, muscle noise, artifacts due to electrode motion, power-line interference [16]. The presence of several noise sources might impair ECG analysis accuracy, as showed in the R-Peak detection marked by circled areas in Fig. 5. Two peaks may be detected where there should be only one. In order to deal with noisy input signals, we designed an IIR filter with order 3 that outputs its results in 16-bit binary format (Fig. 4).

However, we need to be aware of the fact that we want to look in our solution at high sampling frequencies (250Hz, 1000Hz and above), because we want to: (a) make use of the available accuracy of the state of the art sensors, (b) have finer granularity of data, and (c) get more accurate analysis since in some cases more data samples are needed to discover a disease; like, for instance, the medical case known as the R on T phenomena [17], where the R and the T peaks are very near in time so we need a very high number of samples and an intelligent algorithm to discover them. Moreover, it is extremely important to choose a sampling frequency that minimizes the risk of aliasing. The highest frequency needed for the ECG signal is 90Hz (due to the medical frequencies of the heart), which implies that the lowest sampling frequency that can be used is equal to the Nyquist rate (180Hz). However, in order to sample at such a frequency, the analogue signal has to be band limited to 90Hz, which can be achieved by the use of a complex analogue bandpass filter with a very sharp frequency response. This solution, although advantageous on limiting the amount of data to be stored, has a disadvantage on the analogue side, since the bandpass filter, being complex in order to meet the sharpness requirement, will probably have a considerable power consumption. An alternative solution would be to sample at a frequency much higher than the Nyquist rate, such that the analogue bandpass filter can have a relaxed frequency response, while still effectively filtering out the frequencies that would cause aliasing during sampling. For instance, by choosing a sampling frequency of 5kHz, all frequencies beyond 2.5kHz would have to be filtered out before sampling, but that task is simpler than before, since all frequencies between

90Hz and 2.5kHz can be attenuated without affecting the data needed for analysis. After sampling, band limitation to 90Hz can be implemented using a digital filter. This approach has the advantage of using a lower-complexity bandpass filter, and reducing considerably the risk of aliasing and folding. Moreover, increasing the number of samples increases the accuracy of the sample, and makes the overall filtered signal smoother when used for analysis.

Our IIR filter is built to deal with these problems. Another main advantage of using the IIR filter is to eliminate the noise that is directly proportional to the DC offset of the sensed ECG [16], which is around 0.1mv. The two plots in Fig. 5 clearly show how the filtering algorithm remedies this problem. In our implementation, the filter is implemented in hardware on a dedicated chip feeding the external SDRAM memory of our biochip. Our filter is the convolution of the noisy signal with the filter impulse response given in (1):

$$y[n] = \sum_{k} h[k] \times x[n-k].$$
(1)

where, $x[n]$ is the noisy signal, $h[n]$ is the filter impulse response, and n is the sample index. This filter in (1) is also an infinite impulse response (IIR, Chebyschev filter), so it can be written as (2):

$$y[n] = \sum_{k} x[n-l] \times b[l] - \sum_{m=1} y[n-m] \times a[m].$$
(2)

where, y is the output of the filter and x is the input, b is the vector that contains the filter coefficients for signal x, and a is the vector that contains the filter coefficients for output y.

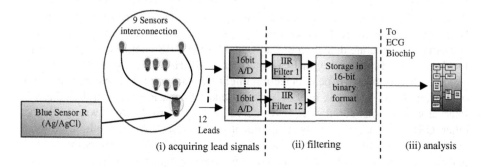

Fig. 4. The System for sensing and filtering of ECG lead signals before sending data to the ECG Biochip for analysis. Blue Sensor R is from Ambu Inc. [4].

The upper limits of the coefficients are dependent on the order of the filter being used. Our IIR filter is of order 3, because our ECG data does not require higher orders. We

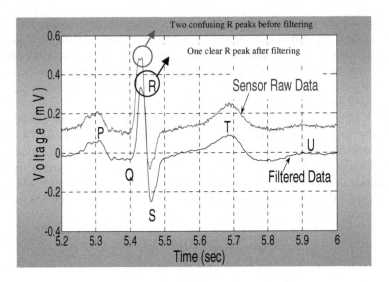

Fig. 5. ECG raw and filtered data (lead I)

can improve our filter (when needed) by simply knowing the needed values of the coefficients in vectors $a[.]$ and $b[.]$.

5 ECG Algorithm

Most ECG systems make use of the Pan-Tompkins analysis algorithm [18], which targets QRS complexes (Fig. 2) detection and consists of the cascade of four filters: (i) band pass, (ii) differentiator, (iii) squaring operation, and (iv) a moving window integrator. In principle, traditional ECG analysis starts from a reference point in the heart cycle (the R-peak is commonly used as the reference point). As a consequence, accurate detection of the R-peak of the QRS complex is a prerequisite for the reliable functionality of ECG analyzers [18]. However, as an effect of ECG signal high variability, R-peak detection might be inaccurate. For instance, in the R on T phenomena, a T peak may be wrongly taken for an R peak, and then the R-T interval will be considered as an R-R interval, and the period will be wrong. Hence, other QRS parameters will be consequently inaccurate. As a result, traditional techniques may fail in detecting some serious heart disorders such as the R-on-T phenomenon (associated with premature ventricular complexes) [17].

Our approach takes a different perspective: instead of looking for the R-peaks and then detecting the period, we detect the period first (via autocorrelation) and then look for the peaks. We use an autocorrelation function (ACF) to calculate the heartbeat period without looking for peaks. Then, we can restrict our analysis to a time window equal to the period and detect all peaks. Although potentially more accurate, our algorithm incurs a higher computational complexity: 3.5 million multiplications, which have been reduced to 1.75 million through a number of code

(SW) optimizations. The single-chip multiprocessor architecture that will be selected for the practical implementation of the algorithm will provide the scalable computation horsepower needed for the highly accurate ECG analysis that we are targeting. The autocorrelation we use, as shown in (3), has a certain number of Lags (L) to minimize the computation for our specific application as discussed below. We validated our algorithm over several medical traces [19][20].

$$R_y[k] = \sum_{n=-\infty}^{n=\infty} y[n] \times y[n-k] \tag{3}$$

where Ry is the autocorrelation function, y is the filtered signal under study, n is the index of the signal y, and k is the number of lags of the autocorrelation (L has an effect on the performance due to the high number of multiplications).

We run the experiments for $n = 1250$, 5000 and 50,000 relative to the sampling frequencies of 250, 1000, and 10,000Hz, respectively. In order to minimize errors and execution time we use the derivative of the ECG filtered signal since if a function is periodic then its derivative is periodic. Hence the autocorrelation function of the derivative can give the period as shown in Fig. 6. In order to be able to analyze ECG data in real-time and to be reactive in transmitting alarm signals to healthcare centers (in less than 1 minute), a minimum amount of acquired data has to be processed at a time without losing the validity of the results. For the heart beat period, we need at least 4 seconds of ECG data in order for the ACF to give correct results.

The autocorrelation function is deployed within the algorithm shown in Fig. 7, which computes the required medical parameters: heart period, peaks P, Q, R, S, T, and U, and inter-peak time spans. Peak heights and inter-peak time ranging outside normal values, which indicates different kinds of diseases, are detected with our algorithm. From a functional viewpoint, the algorithm consists of two separate execution flows: one that finds the period using the autocorrelation function (process 1 in Fig. 7), and another one that finds the number, amplitude and time interval of the peaks in the given 4-second ECG data (process 2 in Fig. 7). In process 1, we firstly find the discrete derivative of the ECG signal.

This will not affect the analysis since the derivative of a periodic signal is periodic with the same period. The advantage of taking the derivative, and thus adding some overhead to the code, is that the fluctuations taking place in the signal and especially those around the peaks would be reduced to a near-zero-value. Moreover, performance overhead associated with derivative calculation of the ECG signal is negligible compared to the rest of the algorithm, especially the autocorrelation part. Finally, if the original signal is periodic, then the autocorrelation of the derivative of the signal is periodic by definition, with the same period as that of the original signal under test. In process 2, a threshold is used to find the peaks. This threshold was experimentally set to 60% of the highest peak in the given search interval.

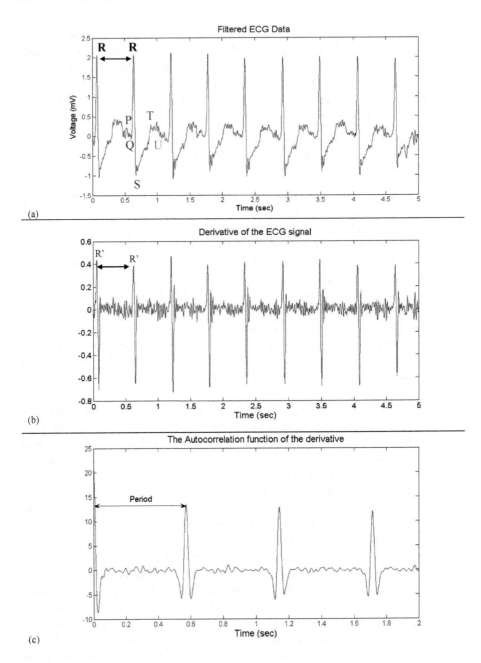

Fig. 6. Heart period analysis: (a) ECG signal peaks P, Q, R, S, T, and U; (b) derivative amplifying R peaks; (c) autocorrelation of the derivative characterized by significant periodic peaks having the same value as the period of the ECG signal in *(b)* and thus *(a)*

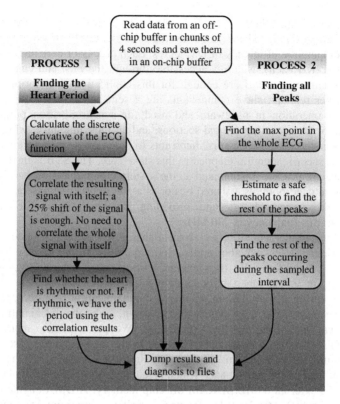

Fig. 7. The Autocorrelation function-based methodology for ECG analysis

Our proposed ECG-analysis algorithm was conceived to be parallel and hence scalable from the ground up. Since each lead senses and analyzes data independently, each lead can then be assigned to a different processor. So, to extend ECG analysis to 15-lead ECG or more, then what is required is to change the number of processing elements in the system. Alternatively, more leads can be processed by the same processor core provided the real-time requirements are achieved.

6 MPSoC Architecture

In order to process filtered ECG data in real-time, we chose to deploy a parallel Multi-Processor System-on-Chip architecture. The key point of these systems is to break up functions into parallel operations, thus speeding up execution and allowing individual cores to run at a lower frequency with respect to traditional monolithic processor cores.

Technology today allows the integration of tens of cores onto the same silicon die, and we therefore designed a parallel system with up to 13 masters and 16 slaves (see Fig. 8). Since we are targeting a platform of practical interest, we chose advanced industrial components [21]. The processing elements are multi-issue VLIW DSP cores from STMicroelectronics, featuring 32KB instruction and data caches.

Processor speed can achieve 400 MHz, although 200 MHz can be preferred in more power-aware solutions. These cores leverage the flexibility of programmable cores and the computation efficiency of DSP cores. Each processor core has its own private memory (512KB each), which is accessible through the bus, and can access an on-chip shared memory (8KB are enough for this application) for storing computation results. Other relevant slave components are a semaphore slave, implementing the test-and-set operation in hardware and used for synchronization purposes by the processors or for accessing critical sections, and an interrupt slave, which distributes interrupt signals to the processors. Interrupts to a certain processor are generated by writing to a specific location mapped to this slave core. The STBus interconnect from STMicroelectronics was instantiated as the system communication backbone. STBus can be instantiated both: as a shared bus or as a partial or full crossbar, thus allowing efficient interconnect design and providing flexible support for design space exploration. Bus frequency is 200 MHz.

In our first implementation, we target a shared bus to reduce system complexity (see Fig. 8) and assess whether application requirements can already be met or not with this configuration. We then explore also a crossbar-based system, which is sketched in Fig. 9. The inherent increased parallelism exposed by a crossbar topology allows decreasing the contention on shared communication resources, thus reducing overall execution time. In our implementation, only the instantiation of a 3x6 crossbar was interesting for the experiments. We put a private memory on each branch of the crossbar, which can be accessed by the associated processor core or by a DMA engine for off-chip to on-chip data transfers. Finally, we have a critical component for system performance which is the memory controller. It allows efficient access to the external 64MB SDRAM off-chip memory. A DMA engine is embedded in the memory controller tile, featuring multiple programming channels. The controller tile has two ports on the system interconnect: one slave port for control and one master port for data transfers. The overall controller is optimized to perform long DMA-driven data transfers. Embedding the DMA engine in the controller has the additional benefit of minimizing overall bus traffic with respect to traditional standalone solutions. Our implementation is particularly suitable for I/O intensive applications such as the one we are targeting in this work.

In the above description, we have reported the worst case system configurations. In fact, fewer cores can be easily instantiated if needed. In contrast, this architectural template is very scalable and allows for further future increase in the number of processors. This will allow to run in real time even more accurate ECG analyses for the highest sampling frequency available in sensors (10,000Hz, and 15 leads, for instance), since this platform is able to provide scalable computational power. The entire system has been simulated by means of the MPSIM simulation environment [21], which provides for cycle-accurate functional simulation of complete MPSoCs at a maximum simulation speed of about 200Kcycles/second (running on a P4 at 3.5GHz). The simulator provides also a power characterization framework leveraging 0.13μm technology-homogeneous industrial power models from STMicroelectronics [10][11]. We believe that for life-critical applications such as ECG real-time analysis, it is important to conduct low-level accurate simulations in order to perfectly understand system level behavior and have a predictable system with minimum degrees of uncertainty.

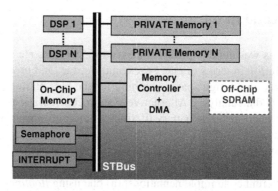

Fig. 8. Single bus architecture with STBus interconnect

Each processor core programs the DMA engine to periodically transfer input data chunks onto their private on-chip memories. Moved data typically corresponds to 4 seconds of data acquisition at the sensors: 10KB at 1000Hz sampling frequency, transferred on average in 319279 clock cycles (DMA programming plus actual data transfer) on a shared bus with 12 processors. The consumed bus bandwidth is about 6MBytes/sec, which is negligible for an STBus interconnect, whose maximum theoretical bandwidth with 1 wait state memories exceeds 400Mbyte/sec. Then each processor performs computation independently, and accesses its own private memory for cache line refills. Different solutions can be explored, such as processing more leads onto the same processor, thus impacting the final execution time. Output data, amounting to 64 bytes, are written to the on-chip shared memory, but their contribution to the consumed bus bandwidth is negligible. In principle, when the shared memory is filled beyond a certain level, its content can be swapped by the DMA engine to the off-chip SDRAM, where the history of 8 hours of computation can be stored. Data can also be remotely transmitted via a telemedicine link.

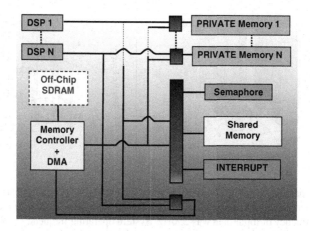

Fig. 9. Crossbar architecture with STBus interconnect. Low-bandwidth slaves have been grouped to the same crossbar branch (partial crossbar concept).

7 Experimental Results

The first analysis was done to profile the execution of the code and to determine the best coding solution in terms of energy, execution time, and precision. Furthermore, we have explored the design space searching for the best platform configuration for the 12-lead ECG data analysis. Alternative system configurations have been devised for different levels of residual battery lifetime, trading off power with accuracy.

7.1 Floating Point vs. Fixed Point Code

We ran two different code implementations: (a) one using *floating point* variables and (b) one using *fixed point integers* [22] with an exponent of 22. Fig. 10 shows the results for the two different code implementations from *time (execution time)* and *energy (relative)* points of view. The ST220 processor core runs at 200MHz. We have performed the analysis for 3, 6 and 12 leads; furthermore we process each lead on a separate core.

We found that the precision of the results obtained with fixed point code, by using 64 bit integer data types representation, almost matches the results obtained with floating point code for a large number of input data traces. On the contrary, the time needed to process data, and also the energy required, decreases up to 5 times. This is mainly due to the fact that, like many commercial DSPs, our processor cores do not have a dedicated floating point unit. Therefore, floating point computations are emulated by means of a C software library linked at compile time. Fig. 10 also shows that even with 12 concurrent processors, the bus is not saturated, since we observe negligible effects on the stretching of task execution times. In contrast, adding more processors determines a linear increase in energy dissipation.

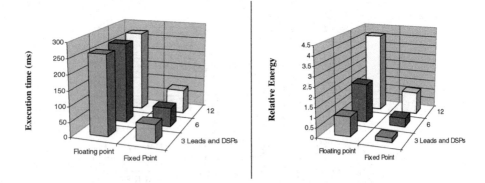

Fig. 10. Comparison between different code implementations for the analysis of the 3-lead, 6-lead and 12-lead ECG. Data analysis for each lead is computed on a separate processor core. Sampling frequency of input data was 250Hz. System operating frequency was 200 MHz.

7.2 Comparison Between Processor Cores

We then compared the performance of an ARM7TDMI with the ST220 DSP core, in order to assess the relative performance of the chosen VLIW DSP core with respect to a reference and popular architecture for general purpose computing, when put at work to process the computation kernel of our specific application. In order to have a safe comparison, we set similar dimensions of the cache memory (32KB) for the two solutions, and we run two simulations for the processing of one ECG-Lead at 250Hz sampling frequency. We count execution cycles to make up for the different clock frequencies.

We adopt this single-core solution, since our first aim is to investigate the computation efficiency of the two cores for our specific biomedical application, and de-emphasize system level interaction effects such as synchronization mismatches or contention latency for bus access. In Fig. 11, we can observe that the ST220 DSP proves more effective both in execution time and energy consumption, as expected. In detail, the ARM core is 9 times slower than the ST220 in terms of execution time, and it consumes more than twice the energy incurred by the DSP. These results can be explained based on three considerations:

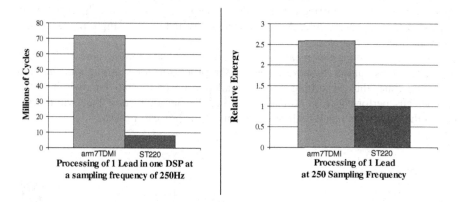

Fig. 11. Comparing ARM7TDMI with ST200 DSP performances, when processing 1 Lead at 250Hz sampling frequency

- The ST220 has better software development tools, which result in a smaller executable code. The size of the executable code for the ARM is 1.7 times larger than that of the ST220.
- The ST220 is a VLIW DSP core, therefore it is able to theoretically achieve the maximum performance of 4 instructions per cycle (i.e., 1 bundle).
- A metric which is related to both previous considerations is the static instructions per-cycle, which depends on the compiler efficiency and on the multi-pipeline execution path of the ST220. For our application, this metric turns out to be 2.9 instructions-per-bundle for ST220.

7.3 Allocation of Computation Resources

Based on previous findings (Sect. 7.1 and Sect. 7.2), we will adopt a HW/SW architecture consisting of the ST220 DSP core and a fixed point coding implementation of the algorithm for the experiments that follow. The ST220 will be operated at its typical frequency of 400MHz, while the rest of the system will run at 200 MHz. We now want to optimally configure the system to satisfy the application requirements at the minimum hardware cost. We therefore measure the execution time and the energy dissipation for an increasing number of DSP cores in order to find the optimal configuration of the system. Since commercially available ECG solutions target sampling frequencies ranging from 250 to 1000Hz, we performed the exploration for these two extreme cases for the 12-lead ECG signal. We analyze a chunk of 4secs of input data, which provides a reasonable margin for safe detection of heartbeat disorders.

Figure 12 shows that if we increase the number of processors, the execution time scales almost linearly, at least up to 6 processors. After that, we observe diminishing returns in increasing system parallelism. Since the real-time requirement of 4 seconds for the overall computation is largely met, we conclude that in the range of interest (up to 6 processors) second order effects typical of multi-processor systems (e.g., bus contention reducing the offered bandwidth to the processor cores with respect to the requested one) are negligible. A single shared bus and even a single processor core are well suited for this case.

However, this does not mean that the amount of data moved across the bus is negligible. This data is, however, read by the processor cores throughout the entire execution time, thus absorbing only a small portion of the bus bandwidth. In this regime, bus performance is still additive, i.e. the bus delivers a bandwidth which equals the sum of the bandwidth requirements of the processor cores.

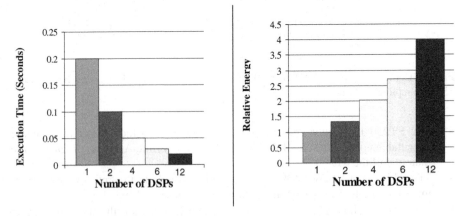

Fig. 12. Execution Time and relative energy of the system with an increasing number of DSPs and input data sampled at 250Hz sampling frequency. System interconnect is a shared bus.

Moreover, the good scalability of the application is also due to memory controller performance. In fact, at the beginning of the computation each processor loads processing data from the off-chip to the on-chip memory, hence, requiring peak memory controller bandwidth. The architecture of the memory controller proves capable of providing the required bandwidth in an additive fashion.

By looking at the 1000Hz plot (Fig. 13), we observe that for the single processor case, the time it takes for a DSP to process 12 leads increases by more than 15 times with respect to the 250Hz case. Energy has increased as well by 90%. We still have about 1 second margin before the deadline (4 seconds), which is enough to perform additional analysis of the results of the individual lead-computations and converge to a diagnosis based on computed heartbeat parameters.

In case a larger margin is needed, the increased workload can be effectively tackled by activating a larger number of processor cores. This comes at smoother energy degradation than the 250 Hz case, as showed in Fig. 13 (for the 1kHz sampling frequency). The larger number of energy consuming cores is better amortized by the savings on application execution.

Although even for the 1kHz case, 1 DSP already meets the real-time requirements, the inherent parallelism of our architecture is useful in many senses. Firstly, when the margin to the deadline is too tight to run a complex diagnosis algorithm, the execution time can be reduced by using more processors. Secondly, working with a large number of processors allows sustaining higher sampling frequencies than 1kHz and more complex algorithms for high accuracy analysis. Thirdly, more processors can help save power, since instead of running one processor at full-speed, we may want to run more processors at reduced speeds thus cutting down on overall system energy.

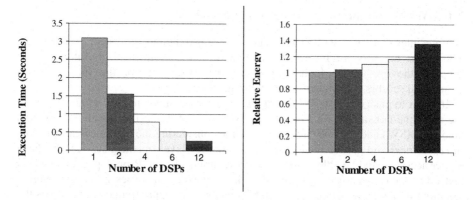

Fig. 13. Execution Time and relative energy of the system with an increasing number of DSPs and input data sampled at 1000Hz sampling frequency. System interconnect is a shared bus.

An overview of the performance and energy overhead that is incurred when moving from 250Hz to 1000kHz sampling frequencies of input data is reported in Fig. 14. Interestingly, the performance plot shows a constant 15x increase in computation time up to 4 processors. In the 6 processor case, the larger amount of data which needs to be transferred on the bus by each processor (due to data over-sampling) determines an increase of bus access times and therefore a longer execution time. As we push system parallelism to the limit, we observe (see the 12 DSPs case) that the computation workload is fully parallelized, and a huge but unique peak bandwidth is requested to the bus. Moving from 1 DSP to 12 DSPs, we move from 12 null contention bandwidth peaks to a single, heavy contention peak. This traffic profile shapes the execution time ratio curve as showed in Fig. 14.

The energy-ratios plot confirms that the overhead for introducing more processors is worth in the 1000Hz case, while is not fully justified for the 250Hz case due to the different computation complexities to be tackled.

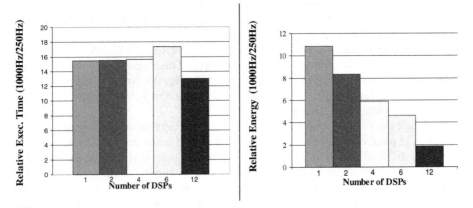

Fig. 14. Relative Execution Time and Energy Ratios between the 1000Hz and the 250Hz sampling frequency experiments

7.4 HW/SW Optimization for Aggressive Scalability

We are interested in assessing the achievable upper bound in system performance. This paves the way for further improvements of the biomedical algorithm, and it supports the use of the high data acquisition capabilities of the state-of-the-art biomedical sensors (i.e. higher sampling frequencies).

In order to push our HW/SW design to suit more accurate analysis while respecting the real-time constraint, we look at how we can push both: the specific-application algorithm (SW) and the HW architecture while considering the high medical demands of *correctness* and *accuracy* of results at the service level (medical service). To have higher accuracy and be able to diagnose arrhythmias like the R-on-T phenomena [17] and other medical cases, we found that the biomedical analyses necessitate higher sampling frequencies as input. The need for analysis at higher frequencies delivers the reality that: not only do we need to look at HW issues, but we also have to look at the algorithm parameters. In previous experiments, we used a 4-second input chunk to leave a safety margin for the input signals, and we used the number of Lags (L) variable to compensate for the data chunk size. We found that in the case of higher frequencies we can change some parameters so that the input data chunk can be optimized while still keeping good service (medical) level results. The solution is that we restrict the analysis chunk-size of our biomedical algorithm to 3.5 seconds (instead of 4 seconds), which also effects the number of multiplications that are needed. From the HW viewpoint, we simulated a 12 processor system performing the 12-lead ECG analysis with increasing sampling frequencies to determine the threshold value beyond which the system does not converge to a solution in real-time. We found that the limit for the input sampling frequency to be 2200Hz (maximum). We verified that in this operating condition, system performance is communication-limited, i.e. the shared bus architecture is not able to keep up with the increase in communication bandwidth requirements any more. Therefore, we face the need to push the hardware as the algorithm was pushed to the maximum. By further performing hardware optimization, we were able to replace the shared bus with a full crossbar, and observed that 12 leads could be processed then in slightly more than 1 second, i.e. well below the 3.5 seconds deadline. Such an optimized HW/SW architecture was proved to work in real-time up to a sampling frequency of 4000Hz. In this condition, the system turns out to be computation-dominated, hence the communication architecture is not the bottleneck.

The flexibility of our system interconnect allows to achieve the same performance with less hardware resources. In fact, a partial crossbar design was experimented, consisting of grouping low bandwidth cores on the same crossbar branch. We observed that performance with the partial crossbar closely matches that of a full-crossbar (less than 2% average difference) but with almost 3 times less hardware resources. We found the optimal crossbar configuration (5x5 instead of 13x13) by accurate characterization of shared bus performance. On a shared bus, we increased the number of processors and observed when the execution time started deviating as an effect of bus contention. With up to 4 cores connected to the same communication resource, this latter is still able to work in an additive regime. Hence, it is not necessary to use full crossbars, but partial crossbars can be equally effective with less hardware resources.

8   Conclusion and Future Work

We present an application-specific MPSoC architecture for real-time ECG analysis, which paves the way for novel healthcare delivery scenarios (e.g., mobility) and for accurate diagnosis of heart-related diseases in real-time. Although a single DSP architecture proves capable of meeting the real-time requirements of our biomedical applications for lower than the maximum (10kHz) that state-of-the-art biomedical-sensors can deliver, the inherent parallelism we provide prevents the architecture from being the bottleneck for further advances in the field of ECG analysis. Our biochip solution can support the increasing sampling frequencies of biomedical sensors and the increased computation efficiency of analysis algorithms optimized for accuracy. We propose a case of such algorithms, leveraging auto-correlation function as a better performing alternative to the traditional and commonly-used Pan-Tompkins algorithm. An in-depth comparison of these algorithms goes beyond the scope of this paper, and is left for future work. The hardware architecture was built based on industrial components, and its performance upper bounds were clearly identified. The optimized HW/SW platform proves capable of dealing with up to 4000Hz sampling frequencies, when system performance becomes computation-limited.

Acknowledgments. We would like to thank Mr. Rabih Salibah, Mr. Fadi Bitar, Ms. Sandra Al Hattab, and Mohammad AbdelHak from the American University of Beirut (AUB), Beirut, Lebanon, for their discussions and work on the filters and validations.

References

1. Fuster V.: Epidemic of Cardiovascular Disease and Stroke: The Three Main Challenges, Circulation, Vol. 99, Issue 9, (March 1999) 1132-1137
2. Heart and Stroke Foundation of Canada: The Changing Face of Heart Disease and Stroke in Canada 2000, Annal report (1999)
3. Chan, C., Han, J., Ramjeet, D.: LabVIEWTM Design of a Vectorcardiograph and 12-Lead ECG Monitor: Final Year Project for the Bachelor of Science Degree in the University of Manitoba (March 2003)
4. Ambu, Inc. biomedical devices company: www.ambuusa.com
5. Harland, C., Clark, T., Prance, R.: Electric Potential Probes– New Directions in the remote sensing of the human body, Measurement Science and Technology, Vol. 13, (2002) 163-169
6. Harland, C., Clark, T., Prance, R.: High resolution ambulatory electrocardiographic monitoring using wrist-mounted electric potential sensors, Measurement Science and Technology, Vol. 14 (2003) 923-928
7. Malmivuo, J., Plonsey, R.: Bioelectromagnetism: Principles and Applications of Bioelectric and Biomagnetic Fields, Oxford University Press (1995)
8. Chevrollier, N., Golmie, N.: On the Use of Wireless Network Technologies in Healthcare Environments, Proceedings of the fifth IEEE workshop on Applications and Services in Wireless Networks, ASWN2005 (June 2005) 147-152
9. Khatib, I. A., Bertozzi, D., Poletti, F., Benini, L., Jantsch, A., Bechara, M., Khalifeh, H., Hajjar, M., Nabiev, R., Jonsson, S.: MPSoC ECG Biochip: A Multiprocessor System-on-Chip for Real-Time Human Heart Monitoring and Analysis, ACM SIGMICRO International Conference on Computing Frontiers (May 2006)
10. Loghi, M., Poncino, M., Benini, L.: Cycle-Accurate Power Analysis for Multiprocessor Systems-on-a-Chip,' GLSVLSI04, Great Lake Symposium on VLSI (April 2004) 401-406
11. Bona, A., Zaccaria, V., Zafalon, R.: System level power modeling and simulation of high-end industrial network-on-chip, Design and Test in Europe Conference-DATE (February 2004) 318-323
12. Lo, B., Thiemjarus, S., King, R., Yang, G.: Body Sensor Network–A Wireless Sensor Platform for Pervasive Healthcare Monitoring, Adjunct Proceedings of the 3rd International Conference on Pervasive Computing-PERVASIVE'05 (May 2005) 77-80
13. Association of Cardiac Technology in Victoria-ACTIV: http://www.activinc.org.au/
14. Code Blue- Wireless Sensor Networks for Medical Care: http://www.eecs.harvard.edu/~mdw/proj/codeblue/
15. BIOPAC Systems Inc.: http://biopac.com/
16. Company-Bosch, E., Hartmann, E.: ECG Front-End Design is Simplified with MicroConverter, Journal of Analog Dialogue, Vol. 37 (November 2003)
17. Aaron Segal: EKG tutorial, EMT-P (1997): http://www.drsegal.com/medstud/ecg/
18. Pan, J. and Tompkins, W.: A Real-Time QRS Detection Algorithm, IEEE Transactions on Biomedical Engineering, Vol. BME-32, No. 3 (March 1985)
19. PhysioBank, physiologic signal archives, for biomedical research: http://www.physionet.org/physiobank/database/ptbdb/
20. MIT-BIH arrhythmia database- Tape directory and format specification: Document BMEC TR00, Mass. Inst. Tech. Cambridge (1980)
21. Loghi, M., Angiolini, F., Bertozzi, D., Benini, L., Zafalon, R.: Analyzing On-Chip Communication in an {MPSoC} Environment, Design and Test in Europe Conference-DATE (February 2004) 752-757
22. ARM DAI 0033A Note 33: Fixed Point Arithmetic on the ARM (September 1996)

Using Application Bisection Bandwidth to Guide Tile Size Selection for the Synchroscalar Tile-Based Architecture

John Oliver[1], Diana Franklin[2], Frederic T. Chong[3], and Venkatesh Akella[1]

[1] University of California, Davis
[2] Cal Poly State University, San Luis Obispo
[3] University of California, Santa Barbara

Abstract. This paper investigates the impact of proper tile size selection on the power the power consumption for tile-based processors. We refer to this investigation as a tile *granularity* study. This is accomplished by distilling the architectural cost of tiles with different computational widths into a system metric we call the *Granularity Indicator* (GI). The GI is then compared against the bisection bandwith of algorithms when partitioned across multiple tiles. From this comparison, the tile granularity that best fits a given set of algorithms can be determined, reducing the system power for that set of algorithms. When the GI analysis is applied to the Synchroscalar tile architecture [1], we find that Synchroscalar's already low power consumption can be further reduced by 14% when customized for execution of the 802.11a reciever. In addition, the GI can also be a used to evaluate tile size when considering multiple applications simultaneously, providing a convenient platform for hardware-software co-design.

1 Introduction

As power and complexity have become increasingly problematic in modern microprocessors, tile-based architectures have become increasingly attractive (ie. [2] [3] [4]). In essence, these systems trade architectural complexity for communications, spreading work across a number of sparsely-connected small tiles rather than among richly-connected functional units of a monolithic, wide core.

However, the choice of tile size for tile-based architectures has been largely an ad-hoc, qualitative process. While this may be because of practical reasons (such as availability of cores), this may not yield an efficient design.

In this paper, we find that in systems where low power operation is critical, proper tile size selection is important. How does an architect find the best tile size for low-power operation? To investigate this we first generate cores with different amounts of computational power. We note that the larger, more richly interconnected tiles have higher average switching capacitance per operation, but also have a larger locality of data available to them. Then, we tile these cores until a fixed amount of total computational parallelism is reached, providing us with a set of tile architectures with different computational *granularity* but with the same amount of total computational power. By mapping the power efficiency per operation, we then generate a power efficiency curve that we call the Granularity Indicator (GI).

P. Stenström (Ed.): Transactions on HiPEAC I, LNCS 4050, pp. 259–278, 2007.

Once we find the GI for a tile architecture with different granularities, we then partition and map different algorithms to the different granularities of the tile architecture and execute them. This process yields the computation cost and the communications cost required for the algorithms to execute across multiple tiles for a tile architecture of differing granularities.

Finally, we can then compare the cost of partitioning an algorithm against the energy efficiency of the tile architecture which is embodied within the GI. If large amounts communications are exposed by partitioning the algorithm, larger tiles that invest more heavily in connectivity are favored, as they are more apt to hide communications. This is despite the fact that the extra connectivity within larger tiles contribute to higher average switching capacitance. On the other hand, if little communications is exposed when partitioning an algorithm, then smaller, more power efficient tiles are favorable. The result of this comparison is to find the the granularity of tile that has the best power consumption for a given algorithm.

To drive this exploration, we use Synchroscalar [1] architecture as a basis, but other tile-based architectures could be used with a similar methodology. We use the GI framework on the Synchroscalar architecture to investigate how the computation power of the Synchroscalar tiles can be tailored to execute a the 802.11a PHY layer application at low power. We then weigh the cost of this customization against other applications that Synchroscalar may execute. We find that by tailoring the tile granularity to a given application may significantly negatively impact the power consumption of other algorithms, making tile granularity an important decision for low-power tile architectures.

The rest of this paper is structured as follows. First, we develop a set of cores with different amounts of computational parallelism. With these cores, we populate a tile architecture similar to Synchroscalar and generate multiple variants of Synchroscalar with different tile granularities. Using these Synchroscalar-like processor-variants, we can find the GI. Next, we describe the methodology used to partition, map and execute different algorithms on our tile architectures with differing tile granularities. This process yields the computation time required to execute and algorithm and the number of cycles required for inter-tile communication that are required to maintain data coherency across multiple tiles. These cycle results then allows us to compare the communications requirements against the GI. This, we will demonstrate, can tell us which granularity of tile executes a given algorithm at the lowest power. Finally, we use the GI as a guide and we re-design the Synchroscalar architecture for low power 802.11a PHY layer execution. We will show how much power can be saved through the choice of proper tile granularity and also investigate the implications of this optimization on other applications executed on Synchroscalar. We finish this paper with related works and then conclude.

2   Tile Scaling Models

In this section, we develop tiles with different amounts of computational parallelism with which to create a tile-based architecture. While the models presented here could be developed in a number of different ways, it is important to remember that the central message of the GI arises from non-linear scaling as issue-width grows wider. We argue that this is a valid assumption for any set of tile sizes, since linear scaling would, in essence, reduce a large tile to a collection of small tiles.

To connect the tiles of our tile architecture, we develop models for a bus, statically scheduled mesh, and dynamically scheduled mesh interconnects. These interconnect topologies are intended to be general and cover a wide range of interconnect topologies. Other interconnect networks, such as Raw's Scalar Operand Network [5], could be employed in a similar study.

2.1 Tile Area

The goal of our tile model is to capture the first-order scaling effects of computational width on area and power. We define the computational width of a tile as the maximum number of arithmetic operations that can be completed per clock cycle, where the operands are in the local register file. The smallest tile we consider in this study can compute a single operation in every cycle, while the largest tile we consider can compute 32 operations in parallel every cycle. We assume a VLIW-based architecture, which can be efficiently scheduled for data-parallel applications like media applications. The register file of our model is assumed to provide one write and two read ports for each operation.

We first developed a tile based on the Blackfin Digital Signal Processor (DSP) [6], which can be viewed as having a computational width of two. In order to get a power and area estimate for this processor, we modeled the control logic of this processor in VHDL and synthesized it using the Synopsys Design compiler. The data-path units, i.e. multipliers, register file and memory, were estimated using published numbers [7,8,9]. Parameters used to develop a model of the Blackfin DSP are shown in Table 1.

Table 1. Technology Parameters

Parameter	Value	Source
Technology	130 nm	
Minimum Voltage	0.7V	Blackfin DSP [6]
Maximum Voltage	1.65 V	Estimated [10]
Threshold Voltage	0.332 V	[10]
Temperature	40 C	Assumed
Oxide Thickness	3.3 nm	[10]
Dielectric Strength of Oxide	5e6 V/cm	[10]
Max Frequency	600 MHz	SPICE using [10]
Tile Power	0.1mW/MHz	See estimate above
Tile Size	1.82 mm^2	Synthesis
Wire Cap.	387 fF/μm	Semi global [11]
Wire pitch	16 λ	Semi global wiring [11]

Using the width-2 Blackfin DSP as a basis, we extrapolate the tile area for tiles with a computational width of one, four, eight, sixteen and thirty-two. We assume that the area of control logic scales linearly with computational width as well as the area contributions of the ALU, shifter, accumulator and multiplier. Memory capacity is assumed to grow linearly with computational width at 32 KB of instruction and 32 KB of data memory per computational width.

For the register file, we assume that the number of ports in the register file, as well as the capacity, grows linearly with the computational width. This produces a quadratic increase in both power and area in the register file. Finally, the on-chip wiring/data-forwarding paths are also assumed to grow quadratically, in a similar manner as the register file.

Figure 1 shows the area results of our tile model. We hold the total computation width constant at 32 computational widths, so when we halve the computational width of a tile, we double the number of tiles we are using. The left most bar in Fig. 1 shows the area breakdown for a single tile with a computational width of 32. The next bar to the right shows a tile model with two tiles with width 16. The column furthest on the right shows the area of 32 tile each with a single computational width. The single large tile with a width of 32 has a 93% area growth over the array of 32 tiles with computational widths of one. Note that if processor area is a design constraint, this will need to be weighed in conjunction with any power saving we present in this paper. However, for this study, we concentrate only on saving power.

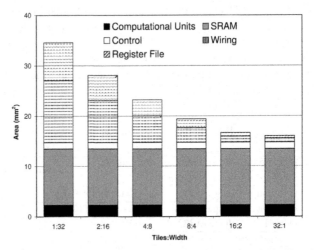

Fig. 1. Tile area scaling for one 32-wide tile (1:32) to 32 1-wide tiles (32:1)

2.2 Tile Power

The tile power of our tile model is composed of two portions, the active power and the leakage power. To find the active power, we use power numbers based upon synthesis of the Blackfin core, as described in the previous section. This yielded a power estimate of 0.1 mA/MHz at 1 V, on average.

For the other granularity of tiles the average current for each of tiles is assumed to be proportional to the area relative to our Blackfin core. This is a decent approximation if two conditions are met. First, the activity factor of the tiles must be constant.

Since the partitioning of data parallel multimedia applications used in this study are done in a load-balanced manner, this should hold approximately true. Second, for those micro-architectural structures that have non-linear area growth, their power consumptions must track the growth in area. This is true for the register file to a first approximation, as register files have been shown to have active power consumption that is linearly proportional to area [9].

For our leakage model, we assume that leakage power is proportional to the number of transistors. Using an average of 830 pA of leakage per transistor [12], we approximate that the Blackfin DSP leaks 1.5mA. This provides a range where the smallest, single-width tile leaks 0.74 mA of current, and the largest, width-32 tile leaks 23.68 mA of current.

Having established the assumptions for our tile power scaling, we find that this provides a range of currents consumed for different sized tiles. A single computational width tile uses 0.05 mA/MHz on average, while the largest 32-width tile consumes 4.87 mA/MHz on average. For a total of 32 computation ways, this yields a tile architecture that has current requirements as shown in Fig. 2.

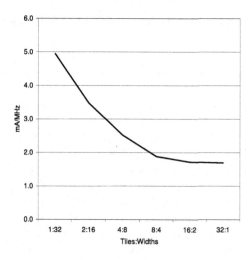

Fig. 2. Current required for our tile architecture model with 32 computational widths of differing granularities

2.3 Tile Power Model Correlation

Although the GI metric and analysis methodology can be applied to a wide array of tile power scalings, in order to demonstrate the usefulness of the GI, our tile model needs to reflect the scaling trends that real processors will observe. In order to see if our tile power model scales as industrial processors do, we have plotted published power results from similar processors from industry. We expect our power models to lie below the curve of the realistic processors for two reasons. First, we model only the core components, not the I/O devices and special purpose circuits. In addition, often commercial projects scale not only the width, but also the functionality, adding specialized units and other functions while we are only looking at computational cores. Figure 3 shows commercial processors, normalized for process technology. Next to Fig. 3, we show Table 2 which contains the references for the processors used in Fig. 3. We can see that, as expected, our scaling model shows a similar trend but has lower absolute power than the published results.

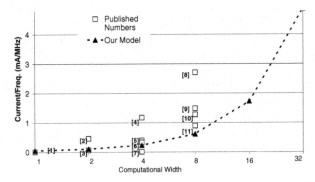

Fig. 3. Current required for our tile architecture model with 32 computational widths of differing granularities

Table 2. Published numbers for similar VLIW-based processors

Plot #	Processor	Citation
1	Analog Devices ADSP-2191	[13]
2	TI TMS320C2810	[14]
3	NEC SPXK5	[15]
4	Hitachi SH-Mobile3	[16]
5	Infineon Tricore 2	[17]
6	Analog Devices TS-101	[18]
7	Transmeta Crusoe TM5700	[19]
8	Transmeta Efficeon TM8820	[20]
9	TI TMS320C62x	[21]
10	TI TMS320C64x	[22]
11	TI TMS320DM643	[23]

2.4   Inter-tile Interconnect

To properly account for the power due to inter-tile communication, we need two values - the delay caused by the interconnect (and thus the idle cycles of the tiles) and the power required by the interconnect to perform communication. In this study, we evaluate both a single bus and a generalized mesh interconnect topologies. We also assume that data is communicated between tiles using explicit message passing. A similar study could be done with a shared memory system with a hardware-enforced coherence protocol.

Interconnect Delay. In order to calculate communications delay, we must know how much communication occurs and how long each transmission takes. Details on how we find the amount of communication required by an algorithm are described later in Section 4. For a shared bus, the delay for each communication is a single cycle, regardless of the source and destination. Since the distance of the bus is small and operational frequencies are limited in the Synchroscalar architecture, single cycle communications is possible using a bus. The delay of a mesh is a function of the contention on the mesh. This requires a traffic simulator to accurately find contention on the mesh. Mesh simulations were completed using the FlexSim mesh simulator from USC [24]. FlexSim was configured in a 2-D space for up to 32 switches, where each switch is attached to an end-node with one injection channel to the switch. FlexSim was modified in two ways. First, the default latencies were reduced to allow low-overhead flit-level routing as expected for an on-chip network. Also, an optional mode was introduced in which only the link overhead was counted, and the routing overhead was discounted, in order to simulate the delay for a statically-scheduled mesh. This allows us to more closely emulate the statically scheduled nature of the Synchroscalar inter-tile interconnect.

Interconnect Power. For our inter-tile interconnect power model, we employ power costs as abstracted from the Orion interconnect power model [25] from Princeton University. We find that our wires are using in the neighborhood or 10 pJ/bit for a 10mm trace, similar to Stanford's Smart Memories [26].

As observed in previous studies by the RAW project [27] and the Synchroscalar project [1], interconnect switching power can be a small portion of the overall power consumption. The reason for this is two-fold. First, the number and size of tiles used in this study are relatively small, thus not requiring an abundance of interconnect resources. Second, the frequencies of operation of the tiles in this study is relatively low compared to high-speed processors, resulting is low frequency communications as well.

3   The Granularity Indicator (GI)

Now that the tile area and power model used in this study has been introduced, we will encapsulate the power of different granularities of tiles into a metric we call the Granularity Indicator (GI).

The GI expresses the *architectural power characteristics* of a tile architecture that is comprised of tiles with different computational granularities. At it's simplest form, the GI is a measure of the relative energy efficiency per operation of different granularities of tile architectures, similar to Fig. 2 except with a simple added transformation. The additional energy saved on every operation by a finer granularity tile architecture is reinvested into a communications budget. So, for every pJ of energy a smaller tile saves in energy consumption versus a larger tile, it can re-invest that energy into communications. This has the effect of changing the vertical axis of Fig. 2 from power consumption to allowable communications overhead while maintaining iso-power consumption.

For our tile model, with an power consumption curve as shown in Fig. 2, this transformation creates the GI which is shown in Fig. 4. On the left of Fig. 4, we see a single large tile with 32 computational widths. As we move to the right on Fig. 4, we double

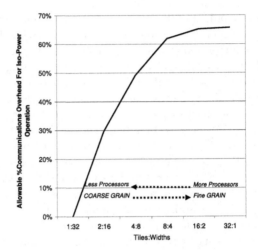

Fig. 4. The GI for tile model. A single 32-width tile is shown on the left and thirty-two 1-width tiles is shown on the right. Smaller tiles have less average switching capacitance, which can be re-invested into communications.

the number of tiles but halve the widths. By moving to finer-grain tiles, we know that the average energy consumption per operation is reduced, as shown in Fig. 2. However, this is shown as allowable communications given iso-power consumption in Fig. 4. This change in axis is convenient for comparing the energy efficiency of a tile architecture with a given granularity for a given communications requirements for a given algorithm because the communications overhead allowed can be easily matched against the communications requirements of a partitioned algorithm.

Alternatively, to find the system power of an architecture executing a given algorithm, extensive simulation is typically involved. This transformation to the GI allows us to decouple the architectural contributions to power consumption from the algorithm's demands for computation and communications cycles. This decoupling allows an architect to make architectural-based decisions to minimize power while quickly evaluating the effectiveness of those architectural decisions for a given set of algorithms. In Sect. 3.1 we look at the impact of voltage scaling on the GI. In Section 3.2 we describe how a mode that puts tiles into a low-power mode when completing inter-tile communications can affect the GI. In Section 5, it will be clear how these shifts can lead to understanding of the effectiveness of certain architectural features for a given algorithm or application.

3.1 Tile Voltage-Frequency Scaling

As we can see from the GI in Fig. 4, a tile architecture comprised of smaller tiles has a higher allowable communications overhead than a tile architecture made of larger tiles and still have the same power consumption. However, to support this communications overhead, additional cycles are required which will result in a higher operational frequency for a given throughput. Additionally, this higher frequency requires a higher op-

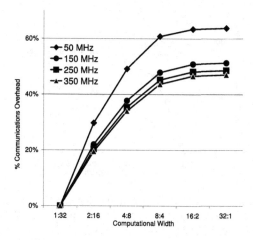

Fig. 5. Finer grain tiles require more cycles to execute a given algorithm, because of added communications costs. Added cycles require higher frequency of operation, thus higher supply voltages.

erational voltage, which also will increase the power consumption of a tile architecture comprised of smaller tiles. Therefore, in the presence of voltage scaling, a tile architecture with many small, higher frequency tiles will consume relatively more power than a tile architecture with fewer, lower frequency tiles.

Figure 5 shows four GI curves, corresponding to four different base frequencies. The base frequency is defined as the frequency of operation of a single tile with a computational width of 32. We see that the GI is shifted down-wards at higher frequencies. So the impact of voltage scaling is to reduce the amounts of allowable communications for a finer grain tile architecture for the same amount of power consumption as a coarser grain tile architecture.

3.2   Low Power Idle Tiles for Low Power Communication

The GI can also show how using an idle communication mode in the tiles impacts the power consumption. The Blackfin DSP requires a total of two cycles to enter two cycles to exit from idle mode. While in idle mode, the core consumes approximately a fifth of the active power consumption. For communications that cannot be overlapped with computation, this mode can be used to reduce the overall system power.

Figure 6 shows the impact on the GI when using tiles with this idle mode fornon-overlappable communications. Intuitively, communication with the addition of this mode now costs relatively less. The result is that fine-grain tiles should become more attractive since fine-grain tiles require more communication than coarse grain tiles for a fixed amount of aggregate parallelism. Likewise, we would expect the power consumption of an application mapped onto fine grain tiles to decrease. This effect is shown on the GI in Fig. 6. We see that this can make a dramatic difference in the communication supported by smaller tiles. Not surprisingly, as more tiles (requiring more communication) are used, more power is saved by the implementation of the idle mode.

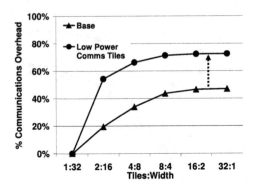

Fig. 6. An idle mode used to limit the energy consumption of tiles when idle. Since finer grain tiles expose more communications, features that reduce the power cost of communications favor finer grain tiles. The result is that the GI shifts up-wards.

Now that we have introduced the GI and presented a pair of features that may impact the GI, we will now talk about how we find the communications overhead required by partitioned algorithms.

4   Algorithm and Applications Partitioning Methodology

The goal of our algorithm partitioning and mapping analysis is to find out, for each granularity of tile architecture, the amount of communication and computation that needs to occur for completion of that algorithm and to minimize this communication requirement.

We use several typical media algorithms in this study. All of the algorithms evaluated in this paper are statically schedulable media algorithms. We assume that these algorithms are partitioned in a latency sensitive manner, so algorithms such as FFT and FIR can be used in applications such as the IEEE 802.11a wireless protocol.

FIR filter evaluated is a 64 TAP, 16 sample block FIR filter.

FFT used a radix-2 64 point transform.

Viterbi decoder implemented is a constraint length = 7, 208b block 1/2 rate decoder.

LDPC decoder is a block error decoder. From a computer architect's standpoint, this can be viewed as a huge message-passing algorithm that requires over 61000 messages to be passed between the nodes of a bipartite graph.

Software Radio is a benchmark by the MIT Raw project. Each sample is read in, filtered, demodulated and equalized with the previous inputs.

802.11a 54 Mbps wireless receiver. The four major components in the 802.11a receiver are the FFT, demodulation, de-Interleaving and the Viterbi decoder. The FFT is a 64-point FFT, demodulator and de-Interleaver is implemented by a look-up table and filtering. The Viterbi Decoder is a K=7 one half rate decoder.

MPEG-4 encoder. We implement Motion Estimation (to remove temporal redundancy between successive frames), DCT and Quantization, which constitute about 90% of the computation of the video encoder [28].

The algorithms we chose to evaluate are those that can be executed on the Synchroscalar tile architecture, namely static media-based applications. Due to the static nature of these algorithms, we adopted a graph-oriented approach using the best-known graph partitioning algorithms to obtain the best parallelization possible for each granularity. For dynamic workloads, other partitioning methods may be used in conjunction with the GI to find the optimal power consumption of those workloads.

The first step is to express the algorithms as data flow graphs (DFGs). Next, an algorithm is then partitioned onto multiple tiles. To partition and map the DFGs, we iteratively employ Chaco [29], which is a graph partitioning tool that is used in the scientific computing community for high-performance multiprocessors. In particular, Chaco uses recursive spectral bisection (which performs minimum cuts through eigenvalues of an adjacency matrix) with a Kernighan-Lin heuristic to improve the partition resolution. The result is load balanced partitions with minimal N-section bandwidth.

To find the execution time of the algorithms, we can first use the Blackfin simulator to find the execution time of the computational nodes in the graph. Then we use the FlexSim cycle accurate network simulator [24] to simulate the communications cycles required. This process is repeated for each tile granularity and each algorithm, yielding the number of computational and communications cycles required for each algorithm on each granularity of tile architecture.

5   Partitioning Results and Granularity Analysis

We now show the partitioning results of several algorithms and compare these results against the GI. This will allow us to see which algorithms execute most efficiently on a given granularity of tile architecture.

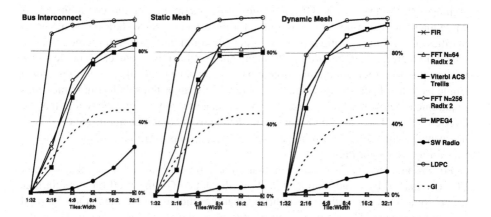

Fig. 7. The communication overhead of our algorithms on three interconnection networks. The left chart shows results for a bus interconnect, the middle for a statically scheduled mesh, and the right for a dynamically scheduled mesh.

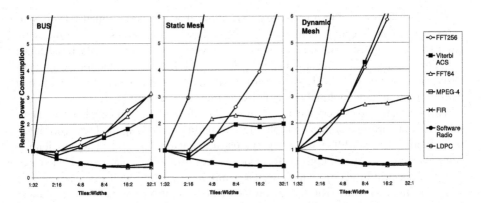

Fig. 8. The relative power consumptions of our algorithms on three interconnection networks. Note that these are relative to the difference between the communications requirements of an algorithm and the GI.

Figure 7 shows the amount of inter-tile communication overhead of the different algorithms on three different interconnects - bus, statically routed mesh, and dynamically routed mesh. We assume that the interconnect wire-widths is 32b for each of the topologies. We can see in Fig. 7 that LDPC requires the most communication, and both trellis-based algorithms, the FFT and Viterbi ACS, have high degrees of communication. For an FIR block filter, our partitioning was able to hide most of the required communications. Likewise, MPEG4 encoding and Software Radio do not expose large amounts of communications when partitions cross multiple tiles.

Now, lets compare the communications requirements of these algorithms against the GI. The dotted line in Fig. 7 is the GI for our tile scaling model for the Synchroscalar architecture. Remember, the GI curve shows the maximum amount communications while maintaining iso-power consumption for tile architectures with different tile granularities. Therefore, algorithms that have inter-tile communications requirements above the GI for a given tile granularity will execute more efficiently a coarser-grain tile architecture. If the exposed communications curve is above the GI at all granularities, then a single large tile the most efficient choice. Conversely, algorithms with communications requirement below the GI will execute most efficiently at the granularity that has the largest distance between the GI curve and the exposed communications curve. It is in this way that the GI exposes relative power consumptions for different granularities of tiles for a given algorithm.

For instance, in Fig. 7, we can see that on a static mesh interconnect, the 64 point FFT (as marked by white triangles) is above the dotted GI line at all tile granularities except for a single large tile. This indicates that the amount of communication exposed by partitioning the FFT is greater than what is allowed by the GI to maintain iso-power execution. Therefore, a single large tile is the most efficient granularity for a 64 point FFT that requires 32 widths of total performance. Likewise, we can see that the Viterbi ACS trellis (as marked by black squares), dips below the GI when executed on a static mesh for two tiles with a computational width of 16. Since the Viterbi ACS exposed communications curve is above the GI at all other granularities, the Viterbi ACS trellis will execute at lowest power on two tiles with a computational width of 16.

To show that the relative location of the communications curve compared with the GI is a good indicator of minimal power consumption, we also show in Fig. 8 the power consumption of these algorithms on Synchroscalar-based tile architecture. In Fig. 8, for a static mesh, we can see that FFT (again marked by white triangles) has a higher power consumption for all partitionings, so a single large tile is best. For Viterbi ACS, the power consumption is lowest for the 2:16 case for the statically scheduled mesh, just as indicated by the GI analysis.

Finally, to summarize, Fig. 9, we show the power consumption of six different applications, the Viterbi ACS, MPEG4, Software Radio, 64 point FFT, a 64 TAP FIR filter, and the 802.11a application at 6 Mbps. The granularity of tile with the lowest power consumption is circled for each application or algorithm.

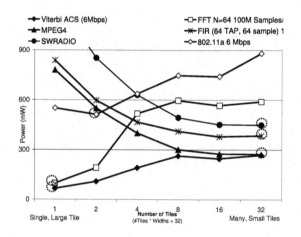

Fig. 9. Power Consumption of different algorithms for different tile granularities

5.1   Using the GI

Thus far, we have developed the GI to describe the best-fit granularity of tiles for a given application. However, the GI can also be used to direct architectural design.

Suppose an architect is interested in building a media processor to run FFTs. Furthermore, the architect has flexibility to choose what size of tile to use as well as the width of the mesh-based interconnect, but is constrained to a total of 32 computational widths. The GI can be used to guide the architect to these decisions.

Figure 10 shows the communication overheads for a 64 point FFT, mapped with the base-line GI. From this figure, we can see that the FFT requires more communication than a 64b mesh can support at any granularity, except for a single large tile. Therefore, for a tile architecture with a 64b mesh, running on a single tile is the best option. However, as we increase the bandwidth of the mesh, the inter-tile communication overhead is reduced. This has the effect of making large tiles that have high amounts of local

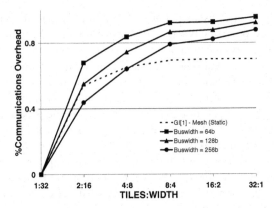

Fig. 10. The GI and the communication requirements for a 64 point FFT for different mesh bandwidths

on-tile interconnect relatively less powerful than smaller tiles. Indeed, for a 256b mesh, we see that the FFTs communication overhead curve has dipped below the GI for 2:16 and 4:8 points. This indicates the large 32-wide tile is no long the most power efficient. Furthermore, by utilizing the GI for the FFT with our tile model, we can make trade-offs between tile granularity and inter-tile interconnect. These trade-offs are shown in Fig. 11. For instance, we can see that 32 width-1 tiles using a 128b mesh has a lower GI number than eight width-4 tiles using a 64b mesh. The GI Number gives the architect the ability to weigh the added (predominantly) area cost of the larger interconnect with the power saved by using a larger mesh.

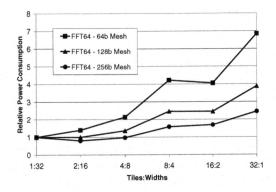

Fig. 11. Relative power for FFT plotted for different mesh bandwidths. We can see that the bandwidth of the inter-tile interconnect impacts the best granularity of tile for low-power execution. For a 256b Mesh two 16-width tiles is most efficient, while for a 64b mesh, a single 32-width tile is most efficient.

Likewise, we can see the power consumption of a few end-to-end applications. Figure 12 shows the power consumption of the 802.11a application on different granularities of tiles with different bandwidth interconnects. As expected, for a communications intensive application like 802.11a (and thus an application who's bisection

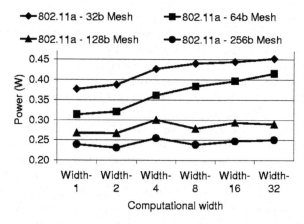

Fig. 12. The power consumption of the 802.11a application on different granularity of tiles with different bandwidth interconnects

bandwidth is above the GI), adding more interconnect bandwidth significantly improves the power consumption of the system. From Fig. 12, we see that moving from 64b to 128b interconnects, marked by squares and triangles respectively, decreases the power consumption greatly. The impact is much larger for the coarse granularity tiles because communication stall cycles are much more expensive for coarse-grain tiles than fine-grain tiles. Figure 13 shows a similar result for the software radio application.

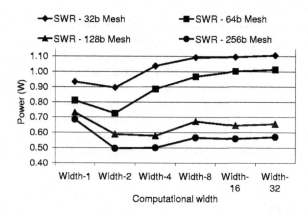

Fig. 13. The power consumption of the software radio application on different granularity of tiles with different bandwidth interconnects

6   Application of the GI to Improve Synchroscalar

Using the GI, we can revisit the design of the Synchroscalar architecture. Synchroscalar was designed as a system based on 2-wide Blackfin tiles. We will attempt to use the GI and customize the tile granularity for efficient execution of 802.11a PHY layer baseband processing.

We will assume the same tile scaling model as presented in Section 2. First we need to compute the GI for our tile model. We will also assume that this version of Synchroscalar uses a generalized, statically scheduled mesh as an inter-tile interconnect. The GI for this model is shown in Fig. 14 as a dotted line.

Next, we need to find the communications overhead of 802.11a when it is partitioned across 2, 4, 8, 16 and 32 tiles. This is shown in Fig. 14 as a solid black line.

Now, to find the most efficient granularity, all we need to do is find the place where the communications exposed by partitioning 802.11a is lowest relative to the GI. From Fig. 14, we can clearly see that this occurs with two tiles with a computation width of 16. Again, for validation, the power consumption of 802.11a on differing granularities of Synchroscalar has also been plotted in Fig. 14, as marked by triangles. Indeed, we can see that two 16-width tiles is the lowest power consuming granularity, saving Synchroscalar 14% power over Synchroscalar's already very low power consumption.

Before moving on, in Sect. 3.1 and 3.2 we discussed how architectural features can shift the GI up or down. We can now see how this is useful information. A downward shift in the GI would likely mean that for the Viterbi decoder on a static mesh, two 16-width tiles would no longer be the most efficient operating point. This is because if the GI shifted down-wards (perhaps by implementing dynamic voltage-frequency scaling on the tiles), the Viterbi decoder's communications requirements would likely be above the GI curve. So, if the GI shifted down-wards, this indicates that a single large tile would be the most efficient for executing the Viterbi decoder. A similar result can be seen here in the case of 802.11a. Conversely, if tile idle modes were implemented, the GI would shift up-wards. This would perhaps allow some more algorithms to execute more power efficiently on finer grain tiles.

Now that we have found the tile granularity that most efficiently executes for 802.11a, lets investigate the impact of this on the other applications that Synchroscalar supports. In Fig. 15, the power consumptions of four different applications are shown, both for the original width-2 tile Synchroscalar array and the width-16 tile Synchroscalar array. The changes in power consumption are shown numerically on top of each pair of bars. We see that 802.11a saves about 14% power over the orginal Synchroscalar array, but this comes at a cost of a 65% increase in power consumption for MPEG4. The architect can then easily find the best trade-off of tile granularity and power consumption for all the applications of interest by using the GI as a guide. This makes the GI a useful hardware/software co-design tool.

7   Related Work

Our work attempts to build intuitive understanding of a design space occupied many diverse projects. The MIT SCALE project [30] is developing a tile-based power efficient architecture based on their Vector-Thread paradigm. In their prototype SCALE processor, they are able to develop a simple micro-architecture that attains high performance and low power execution by avoiding complex control structures and utilizing spatial locality. The EnyAC group at Carnegie Mellon [31] is investigating globally asynchronous, locally synchronous designs to allow for dynamic voltage and frequency scaling for low power consumption.

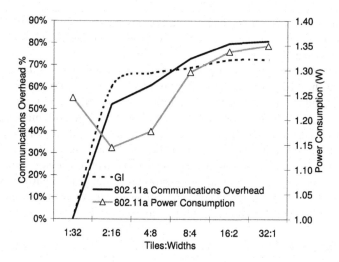

Fig. 14. The dotted line is the GI and the solid Line is the communications overhead exposed when partitioning the 802.11a signal chain on up to 32 tiles. The Power Consumption of 802.11a tracks the relative distance between the GI and communications overhead.

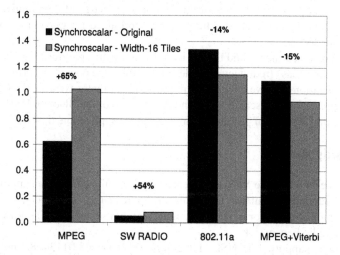

Fig. 15. Four different applications are plotted for the original width-2 Synchroscalar array and the width-16 Synchroscalar array. Added power consumption percentages are shown above each set of bars.

On the processor-power efficiency front, Zyuban [32] has developed an architectural based power-performance efficiency metric for a single microprocessor which allows efficiency to be evaluated during the development of the ISA. In a complementary study, Hartstein and Puzak [33] develop an power efficiency metric and investigate the power efficiency of deep pipelines on a processor. While these studies are concerned with the power efficiency of a single tile, our study extends the study of power efficient processors to multiple-processors on a single chip. In the paper, Custom Fit Processor [34], a VLIW tile model is developed and performance is weighed against area cost, but not against power. A study similar to ours for energy efficient interconnects [35] has been published by Heo and Asanovic.

Finally, it is because of the many different tile based architectures that are being researched that this study was developed. The RAW project [2] [36] uses MIPS-based cores as tiles and shows performance scalability through their robust, three-level inter tile communication structure. Also, in a similar effort is the Smart Memories project cite smart-memories. Smart Memories uses finer-grain tiles than the RAW processor. The TRIPS architecture [3] also attacks wire-scalability by utilizing multiple cores. Additionally, TRIPS is a malleable architecture that can adapt to different types of workloads to gain performance, yet maintain performance for general purpose workloads. One study that looks at a heterogeneous tile structure was done at Technion [37] and allows the core with the best power efficiency to execute.

8 Conclusions

The Granularity Indicator (GI) provides a novel way to encapsulate power scaling factors when trying to meet performance targets with parallelism. The GI can be used to discover which algorithms can be executed in a power efficient manner on small or large tiles. Additionally, through the use of the GI and knowledge of communication overheads from algorithms, tile architectures can be optimized for granularity of targeted application mixes.

We have presented the GI and used it to show many different forms of analysis. We have explored how base frequency and idle-modes affect the power-performance scaling and how applications behave with different tile widths. Finally, we used the GI to revisit tile granularity in Synchroscalar. We found that the use of the Blackfin DSP as our tile, was non-optimal in terms of power for our centerpiece application, the 802.11a receiver.

Acknowledgments

We would like to thank the SMART Interconnects group at USC for support with the FlexSim interconnect simulator, the Orion group at Princeton University for support with the Orion power-performance interconnect simulator and the MIT Raw group for the software radio benchmark.

This work is supported by NSF ITR grants 0312837 and 0113418, and NSF CAREER and UC Davis Chancellor's fellowship awards to Fred Chong.

Diana Franklin's faculty position is funded by a Forbes Endowment.

References

1. Oliver, J., Rao, R., Sultatna, P., Crandall, J., Czernikowski, E., Jones, L.W., Franklin, D., Akella, V., Chong, F.T.: Synchroscalar: A multiple clock domain, power-aware, tile-based embedded processor. In: 31th Annual International Symposium on Computer Architecture (31th ISCA-2004) Computer Architecture News, ACM SIGARCH / IEEE (2004)
2. Taylor, M.B., et al.: The Raw microprocessor: A computational fabric for software circuits and general-purpose programs. IEEE Micro 22(2) (2002) 25–35

3. Sankaralingam, K., Nagarajan, R., Liu, H., Kim, C., Huh, J., Ranganathan, N., Burger, D., Keckler, S.W., McDonald, R.G., Moore, C.R.: Trips: A polymorphous architecture for exploiting ilp, tlp, and dlp. ACM Trans. Archit. Code Optim. 1(1) (2004) 62–93

4. Mai, K., Paaske, T., Jayasena, N., Ho, R., Dally, W.J., Horowitz, M.: Smart memories: A modular reconfigurable architecture. In: 27th Annual International Symposium on Computer Architecture (27th ISCA-2000) Computer Architecture News, Vancouver, British Columbia, Canada, ACM SIGARCH / IEEE (2000) Published as 27th Annual International Symposium on Computer Architecture (27th ISCA-2000) Computer Architecture News, volume 28.

5. Taylor, M.B., Lee, W., Miller, J., Wentzlaff, D., Bratt, I., Greenwald, B., Hoffmann, H., Johnson, P., Kim, J., Psota, J., Saraf, A., Shnidman, N., Strumpen, V., Frank, M., Amarasinghe, S.P., Agarwal, A.: Evaluation of the raw microprocessor: An exposed-wire-delay architecture for ilp and streams. In: ISCA. (2004) 2–13

6. Kolagotla, R., Fridman, J., Aldrich, B., Hoffman, M., Anderson, W., Allen, M., Witt, D., Dunton, R., Booth, L.: High Performance Dual-MAC DSP Architecture. IEEE Signal Processing Magazine (2002)

7. Gupta, S., Keckler, S., Burger, D.: Technology independent area and delay estimates for microprocessor building blocks. In: Technical Report TR2000-05, Department of Computer Science, University of Texas. (2000)

8. Wolfe, A., Fritts, J., Dutta, S., Fernandes, E.S.T.: Datapath design for a vliw video signal processor. In: HPCA. (1997) 24–

9. Rixner, S., Dally, W., Khailany, B., Mattson, P., Kapasi, U., Owens, J.: Register organization for media processing. In: International Symposium on High Performance Computer Architecture (HPCA), Toulouse, France (2000)

10. Hu, C.: Berkeley predictive technology model (2004)

11. Ho, R., Mai, K., Horowitz, M.: The future of wires. In: Proceedings of the IEEE. Volume 89. (2001) 490–504

12. Thompson, S., Alavi, M., Hussein, M., Jacob, P., Kenyon, C., Moon, P., Prince, M., Sivakumar, S., Tyagi, S., Bohr, M.: 130nm logic technology featuring 60nm transistors, low-k dielectrics, and cu interconnects. Intel Technology Journal 6(2) (2002) 5–13

13. AnalogDevices: ADSP-2191 Processor Data Sheet. (2002)

14. TexasInstruments: TMS320C28x Processor Manual. (2001)

15. T. Kumura, M. Ikekawa, M.Y., Kuroda, I.: VLIW DSP for Mobile Applications. IEEE Signal Processing Magazine (2002)

16. Mizuno, H., Irie, N., Uchiyama, K., Yanagisawa, Y., Yoshioka, S., Kawasaki, I., Hattori, T.: SH-Mobile3: Application Processor for 3G Cellular Phones on a Low-Power SoC Design Platform. Hot Chips 16 (2004)

17. Norden, E., Leteinturier, P., Barrenscheen, J., Scheibert, K., Hellwig, F.: A Fast Powertrain Microcontroller. (2004)

18. AnalogDevices: TS-101 Data Sheet. (2002)

19. Transmeta: Transmeta Crusoe TM5700/5900 Processors. (2003)

20. Transmeta: Transmeta Crusoe TM8300/8600 Processors. (2004)

21. TexasInstruments: TMS320C62x Processor Manual. (2001)

22. Agarwala, S., Anderson, T., Hill, A., Ales, M.D., Damodaran, R., Wiley, P., Mullinnix, S., Leach, J., A., L., Gill, M., Rajagopal, A., Chachad, A., Agarwala, M., Apostol, J., Krishnan, M., Bui, D., An, Q., Nagaraj, N.S., Wolf, T., Elappuparackal, T.T.: A 600MHz VLIW DSP. (2002)

23. TexasInstruments: TMS320DM642 Data Sheet. (2005)

24. SMART Interconnect Group, U.: Flexsim 1.2 flit level simulator (2005)

25. Chen, X., Peh, L.S.: Leakage power modeling and optimization in interconnection networks. In: ISLPED '03: Proceedings of the 2003 international symposium on Low power electronics and design, ACM Press (2003) 90–95

26. Ho, R., Mai, K., Horowitz, M.: Efficient on-chip global interconnects. In: IEEE Symposium on VLSI Circuits. (2003) Stanford Univeristy.
27. Kim, J.S., Taylor, M.B., Miller, J., Wentzlaff, D.: Energy characterization of a tiled architecture processor with on-chip networks. In: ISLPED '03: Proceedings of the 2003 international symposium on Low power electronics and design, ACM Press (2003) 424–427
28. Stechele, W.: Algorithmic complexity, motion estimation and a vlsi architecture for mpeg-4 core profile video codecs. In: International Symposium on VLSI Technology, Systems and Applications. (2001)
29. Hendrickson, B., Leland, R.: The chaco user's guide, version 2.0, technical report sand94-2692 (1994) http://www.ti.com/ corp/docs/press/backgrounder/omap.shtml.
30. Krashinsky, R., Batten, C., Hampton, M., Gerding, S., Pharris, B., Casper, J., Asanovic, K.: The vector-thread architecture. SIGARCH Comput. Archit. News **32**(2) (2004) 52
31. Marculescu, D.: Application adaptive energy efficient clustered architectures. In: ISLPED '04: Proceedings of the 2004 international symposium on Low power electronics and design, ACM Press (2004) 344–349
32. Zyuban, V.: Unified architecture level energy-efficiency metric. In: GLSVLSI '02: Proceedings of the 12th ACM Great Lakes symposium on VLSI, ACM Press (2002) 24–29
33. Hartstein, A., Puzak, T.R.: The optimum pipeline depth considering both power and performance. ACM Trans. Archit. Code Optim. **1**(4) (2004) 369–388
34. Fisher, J.A., Faraboschi, P., Desoli, G.: Custom-fit processors: letting applications define architectures. In: MICRO 29: Proceedings of the 29th annual ACM/IEEE international symposium on Microarchitecture, IEEE Computer Society (1996) 324–335
35. Heo, S., Asanovic;, K.: Replacing global wires with an on-chip network: a power analysis. In: ISLPED '05: Proceedings of the 2005 international symposium on Low power electronics and design, New York, NY, USA, ACM Press (2005) 369–374
36. Taylor, M., Kim, J., Miller, J., Wentzlaff, D., Ghodrat, F., Greenwald, B., Ho, H., m Lee, Johnson, P., Lee, W., Ma, A., Saraf, A., Seneski, M., Shnidman, N., Frank, V., Amarasinghe, S., Agarwal, A.: The raw microprocessor: A computational fabric for software circuits and general purpose programs (2002)
37. Morad, T.Y., Weiser, U.C., Kolodny, A., Valero, M., Ayguade, E.: Performance, power efficiency and scalability fo asymmetric cluster chip multiprocessors. In: CCIT Technical Report 514, Technion (2005)

Static Cache Partitioning Robustness Analysis for Embedded On-Chip Multi-processors

Anca M. Molnos[1], Sorin D. Cotofana[2],
Marc J.M. Heijligers[1], and Jos T.J. van Eijndhoven[1]

[1] NXP Semiconductors, HTC 31, Eindhoven, The Netherlands
[2] Technical University of Delft, Mekelweg 4, Delft, The Netherlands

Abstract. In this paper we propose a method to analyze the robustness of multi-tasking media applications when mapped on an on-chip multi-processor platform. We assume a multiprocessor structure which embeds a cache hierarchy with two levels: an L1 that each processor may have and an L2 shared among the processors. To enable compositionality, i.e, to be able to evaluate the system performance out of the individual tasks performance, this shared L2 is partitioned per task basis. In this paper we first introduce two metrics to quantify the robustness. The internal robustness is estimated by a sensitivity function which measures the performance variations induced by the inter-task cache interference. The external robustness is quantified by a stability function which reflects the variations induced by different input data on the partitioned L2 behavior. Subsequently, we exercise our method on a set of multimedia applications running on a CAKE multi-processor platform. Our experiments indicate that, if the cache is partitioned, the sensitivity is on average 4%. whereas for the shared cache it is 25%. Over the investigated workloads the stability is at least 90% therefore, for the those applications, we can conclude that the static cache partitioning is quite robust to input stimuli.

1   Introduction

State-of-the-art media applications are characterized by high requirements with respect to computation and memory bandwidth. On the computation side, the embedded domain low power and low cost demands make the use of general purpose architectures with clock frequencies in the order of several GHz inappropriate. Instead, on-chip multi-processor architectures are preferred. On the memory side, media applications process large amounts of data residing off-chip. The availability of these data at the right moments in time is critical for the application performance, therefore a common practice is to buffer parts of the data on an on-chip memory.

A possible organization of the on-chip memory which alleviates the data availability problem is based on hierarchical caches. In such a context each and every processor core has associated its private cache memory (called L1 cache in this paper). As these L1 caches cannot provide the required application bandwidth

P. Stenström (Ed.): Transactions on HiPEAC I, LNCS 4050, pp. 279–297, 2007.

[1], shared level two (L2) caches are used [9], [10]. The advantage of an L2 is that large part of the data is kept on chip, where the access is at least 10 times faster than an off chip access [12]. The disadvantage of such a shared L2 cache is that different tasks may flush each others data out of the cache, leading to an unpredictable number of L2 misses. As a consequence, the system performance cannot any longer be derived from the individual tasks performance (property addressed as compositionality).

For media applications guaranteeing the completions of tasks before their deadlines is of crucial importance. Therefore, predictability and robustness are among the main required properties in this domain. A solution for the predictability problem is to use static partitioning of the cache as proposed in [14]. In this approach, the compositionality is induced by allocating parts of the L2 cache, exclusively, to each individual task in the application. However, the compositionality is not 100% ensured because the L1 cache is assumed to be private to each and every task during its execution and only the L2 is partitioned. Thus, in order to guarantee performance, one should be able to estimate the variations induced by the L1 inter-task sharing.

Moreover, static cache partitioning is utilized, thus the application may use only one partitioning ratio during its entire execution. This cache partitioning ratio is computed utilizing the application's statistics for a given input data set [13]. However, during the application execution different other input data might have to be processed. It is quite probable that for these new data sets the partitioning ratio for which the application has its best performance is different than the one which is in use. To be able to guarantee performance, the designer should be able to estimate these deviations too.

In the view of previously mentioned phenomena two *robustness* aspects are relevant in our context: (1) the variations introduced by the inter-task L1 interference (2) the variations induced in the L2 behavior by various input data sets. The first robustness type is addressed as "intern" because instabilities are caused by the tasks comprising the application. The second robustness type is addressed as "extern" because variations in performance are caused by the extern input stimuli.

In this paper we propose an approach to assess the robustness of an application running on a multi-processor system with statically partitioned L2. The present article is an extension of the work in [17]. As previously mentioned, for this type of systems the internal robustness is determined by inter-task interference in the L1 cache. This interference strongly depends on the task switching rate. To estimate the internal robustness we introduce a sensitivity metric which reflects the variation in L2 misses number for different task switching rates. To assess the external robustness, we introduce the stability metric. It measures the performance deviations for the case when the application processes another input data set than the one utilized to determine the static partitioning ratio. An application is considered to be stable if its number of misses obtained with a certain input data is close to the least number of misses possible for that input data.

To demonstrate our approach we analyze two types of parallel applications: (1) applications consisting of communicating tasks and (2) applications consisting of independent tasks. From the first category we exercise two applications: a picture-in-picture (PiPTV) video decoder and an H.264 decoder. From the second category we analyzed six applications composed by different multimedia tasks. We utilize a CAKE multi-processor instance [10] as simulation platform. For these applications, we evaluate the sensitivity function (internal robustness) and the stability function (external robustness). Our experiments indicate that, if the cache is partitioned, the sensitivity is on average 4% whereas if the cache is shared the sensitivity is 6 times larger. Thus, as expected, cache partitioning drastically reduces the inter-tasks conflicts. Most important, for our applications, this small percentage of variations suggests that partitioning the L2 is enough to achieve compositionality in a large degree. The variations induced in the L2 behavior by various input data sets are at most 10% over all the application range that we tried. This accounts for an average stability of 92%, therefore, for the investigated applications, we can conclude that the static cache partitioning is quite robust with respect to input stimuli variations.

The remainder of the paper is organized as follows. Background information over the considered multi-processor platform and the cache partitioning method is introduced in Sect. 2. The robustness evaluation method is described in Sect. 3. Sect. 4 presents practical experiments and results, and Sect. 5 concludes the paper.

2   Background

This section introduces briefly the targeted system and the application model, and then details our task centric cache management scheme.

2.1   Target Architecture

The envisaged multi-processor architecture consists of a homogeneous network of computing tiles on a chip [10]. Each tile contains a number of CPUs, a router (for out of tile communication), and memory banks. The processors are connected to memory by a fast, high-bandwidth interconnection network. Each of the processor cores has its own L1 cache. The on-tile memory is actually used as a large, unified L2 cache, shared between processors, facilitating a fast access to the main memory which resides outside the chip. In case a task doesn't find its required data in the corresponding L1, a coherence protocol is executed to determine if the data are located in another processor L1 cache. If the data are not present in none of the L1 caches, the L2 is accessed. In this paper we use one tile of the multi-processor like the one depicted in Fig. 1.

An application executed on this architecture consists of multiple tasks. These tasks may exchange data among each other, or they may be independent. If inter-task communication is present, we assume that it is performed through the memory hierarchy, thus through the shared L2.

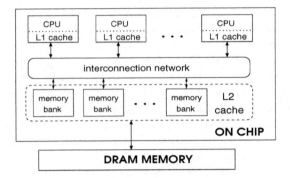

Fig. 1. Multi-processor target architecture

Each task can be regarded as a process consuming input data and producing output data. For an application formed by communicating tasks, these tasks are naturally synchronized based on data availability. In this case a task temporarily stops its execution (is swapped out) in two cases: (1) when task's input data buffers are empty or its output buffers are full, (2) when an interrupt occurs. In the case an application is formed by independent tasks, these tasks may stop their execution when the task scheduler policy dictates. Between two executions of the same task, a processor can execute other tasks. Moreover, in order to support a natural load balancing, the tasks may freely migrate from one processor to another, depending on the processors availability.

2.2   Cache Partitioning

We assume a conventional cache to be a rectangular array of memory elements arranged in "sets" (rows) and "ways" (columns). The accessed address is logically split in three fields: *tag*, *index*, and *offset*. The *offset* part of the address identifies the required data word inside a cache line. The set where a data item can be placed is uniquely identified by the *index* part of the address. Inside that set, the data may reside in one of the ways. In case some data item is required, all the ways are searched to determine if and in which one of them it is cached. In a traditional cache, neither the index addressing, nor the replacement policy are aware of the internal, task-based, structure of the application. This unawareness may cause unpredictable inter-task misses which should be avoided in order to ensure compositionality.

We assume that in a CAKE-like organization, the L2 is likely to be largely affected by inter-task cache conflicts, as it is shared among the processors. Although the L1s are also shared among task, this sharing is different than the L2 sharing. Tasks can successively execute on the same processor, but on a given moment in time only one task can evict data out of the processor L1. Thus we assume the L1 as private to each task during its execution. As a results, our we focus on isolating tasks in the L2 (assign a L2 part to each one of them), such that their number of misses are independent of each other. For this we utilize a cache partitioning scheme.

Based on the conventional cache organization, there are two main natural partitioning manners: (1) based on associativity and (2) based on sets. In the remainder of this subsection we describe in detail these main options, their potential implementation in the context of the CAKE multiprocessor architecture and in the end of this section we detail the manner we use them to enhance compositionality.

Associativity Based Partitioning. The associativity based partitioning scheme is depicted in Figure 2. As one can observe, each and every task gets a number of ways from every set of the cache. In case the required data item is present in the cache, it is accessed, just like in a conventional cache. However, in case of a miss, when a cache line has to be replaced, one task can flush out only its own cache ways. In this manner, different tasks do not interfere unpredictably.

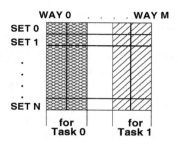

Fig. 2. Associativity based cache partitioning (logic organization)

This type of partitioning is implemented by changing the cache replacement policy as suggested in [2]. This require a small table that specifies which task owns which cache ways, and some extra logic to restrict the victim lines that can be flushed. This logic is not on the critical path, as the line to be victimize does not have to be known before the data are actually loaded from a lower memory level. On our CAKE platform, loading an L2 line from the main memory takes at least 90 cycles, thus we can consider that there is no time penalty involved in associativity based partitioning. From the area point of view, all the necessary hardware represents a negligible fraction of the size of a L2 cache. This negligible penalty, together with the fact that the implementation doesn't require modifications in the structure of the cache or in the addressing mode [2], leads to a common use of variations of this partitioning type [7] [11] [15] for the purpose of reducing the number of misses and speeding up the application.

In the context of compositionality, the main shortcoming of associativity based partitioning is that the number of allocable resources is restricted to the number of ways in a set (cache organization). A state-of-the art L2 cache typically has only up to 16 ways. Every extra way present in a cache requires and extra comparator on the critical path [12]. Thus the reason for supporting just few ways is that extra circuitry involved in implementing associativity slows down the cache and burns a lot of power at each lookup. In media applications there is a trend in

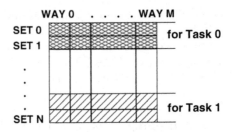

Fig. 3. Set based cache partitioning (logic organization)

adding new features, so increasing the number of tasks. Consequently, for such an application there might be not enough ways for every task, therefore multiple tasks would share the same way, leading to unforeseeable cache interference.

Set Based Partitioning. The set based partitioning scheme is illustrated in Figure 3. In this case, each and every task gets a different amount of sets from the cache. As already mentioned, in a conventional set associative cache organization the address splits into three parts: tag, index, and offset. Set based partitioning implies that the addresses a task accesses may have only some restricted indexes, pointing to the task's cache sets. This is equivalent with an address space partitioning. To our knowledge, there are two previous approaches to implement this address space partitioning. One implements the partitioning at compiler and linker level [8] and the other at operating system level [4]. In the scheme proposed in [8] the compiler and the linker allocate variables and instructions addresses such that the cache partitioning is achieved. In our case the platforms may contain standard processor cores, thus the compilers are developed by external parties. A platform specific change of the compiler would be costly or time consuming. The cache partitioning method controlled by the operating system proposed in [4] has also drawbacks as it is limited to physically indexed caches and requires a virtual memory model. In our approach, we would like to support all types of caches on platforms with or without memory paging. Consequently, none of the existing method are suitable for our purpose, thus in the following we propose a new technique to implement set based cache partitioning.

We achieve the cache partitioning through a level of indirection, without interfering with the memory space. This is somewhat similar with the mechanism in [4], but the address translation is not at memory page level, but directly at cache level. In this manner there is no restriction in the type of cache supported, nor in the underlying memory model. Our scheme modifies the index bits of an address into new index bits, before cache lookup (Fig. 4), taking into account who initiates the access. The purpose of the index translation is to send all the access of a task T_i, and only the accesses of task T_i, in a cache region decided at design time.

To avoid expensive index calculation, the partition sizes are limited to power of two number or sets. We propose to use a table (indexed by the *task id*) that provides the information needed for the index translation (*MASK* and *BASE*

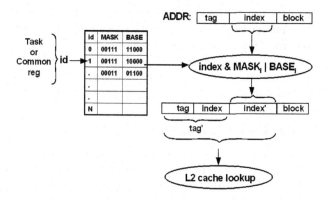

Fig. 4. Set based cache partitioning (implementation)

bits). To clarify the mechanism, let us assume that an access to data A belonging to task T_i has the index idx_A, in a conventional cache case. We denote by 2^k the size of the partition for T_i and by 2^C the size of the total cache (both size values are considered in number of sets). The $MASK_A$ bits actually select the k least representative bits of idx_A (instead of doing modulo with the cache size 2^C we do only modulo with the partition size 2^k). $BASE_A$ fills the rest of the $C - k$ index bits such that different tasks accesses are routed in disjoint parts of the cache.

After index translation, two addresses that didn't have the same old index might end up having the same new index. In this case the system is not able to distinguishes among such two addresses, leading to data corruption. To prevent data corruption, the index bits changed by the translation process still have to identify somehow the associated memory access. The easiest way to achieve this is to augment the tag part of the address with those changed index bits. For our example, task T_i has 2^k cache sets thus the $C - k$ most representative are changed, and have to be included in the tag. Because it is not beneficial to have a tag with variable length (k varies with the task's allocated cache size) we choose to augment the tag with all index bits. In this case, for instance, for 2MBytes L2, 8 ways associative, 512Bytes block size, the tag has 9 extra bits, representing less that 0.5% of the total L2 area, so the implied area penalty can be considered negligible.

In this work we assume a multiprocessor platform with cache coherence among the L1 caches of each processor core, as described in the beginning of this section. In case a task doesn't find its data in the corresponding L1, a coherence protocol is executed to determine if the data are located in another processor L1 cache. The execution of the coherence protocol is always launched before of an L2 access, and takes few cycles. Consequently, the index translation for L2 accesses can be performed in parallel with the cache coherence resulting in no additional delay penalty associated to the extra index translation.

As one could see, the implementation of set base partitioning is more "intrusive" into the cache organization than associativity based partitioning, in the sense that it requires the alteration of addressing scheme. However, the advantage of this partitioning type comes form the fact that typically, a cache like the L2 we target, may have thousands of sets and only few ways. The number of resources (cache sets in this case) is large, thus set based partitioning permits every task to have its own exclusive part, hence it is a good candidate for achieving compositionality.

2.3   Task Centric Cache Management

As aforementioned, we consider that an application can be formed by communicating or independent tasks. In the following we briefly present our cache management strategy for both these types of applications.

In the case of independent tasks compositionality is realized by assigning a part of cache to each task. The experiments in [6] suggest that for static partitioning, the set based strategy performs better that the associativity based one. The reason for this is that associativity based cache partitioning is decreasing the number of ways a task can use. It is known that, having a fixed cache size, a cache organization with a large associativity (and a small number of sets) performs most of the times better than one with less associativity (but more sets) [12,?]. In addition, as we already mentioned, the set based method offers, for the same cache dimensions, more allocable cache units than the associativity based one, as in a state-of-the-art cache the number of sets is few orders of magnitude larger than the number of ways. Therefore, in the case of independent task we opt for set based partitioning.

In the case of application consisting of communicating tasks, the problem that arise is where to cache the shared data. To solve this problem we proposed in [14] a mixed set and associativity based partitioning. First, each task and each inter-task communication buffer gets an exclusive part of the cache sets. Second, inside the cache sets of a communication buffer each task accessing it gets a number of ways. In this manner tasks may compositionally share data or instructions. As there is no principal difference between sharing data or instructions, we use the term "common region" to denote both these shared parts.

The partitioning ratio is determined such that the overall application number of misses is minimized. Let us assume that in the general case an application A is composed out of N tasks, $T = \{T_i\}_{(i=1,N)}$, and M common regions $CR = \{CR_j\}_{(j=1,M)}$ (for the particular case of an application composed out of independent tasks $M = 0$). The process of finding this optimized ratio requires first an information gathering phase during which every task T_i is individually simulated having different amounts of cache. Subsequently, the best partitioning ratio is computed such that the sum of all task misses is minimized, under the constraint that all allocated cache cannot be larger than the available cache. This best partitioning ratio BPR is a set of cache sizes $\{c_i\}_{(i=1,N+M)}$, where c_i is the cache allocated to task T_i, or to common region CR_j (we consider that the indexes j of the common regions actually run from $N+1$ to $N+M$). Using these notation, in the following section we introduce the two metrics for assessing the application robustness.

3   Robustness Evaluation Method

This section presents the proposed approach to assess the robustness of an application running on a multi-processor as the one described in Subsection 2.1. We consider two aspects of robustness: (1) internal robustness defined as the sensitivity of the L2 misses of a task on the other tasks' behavior, (2) external robustness defined as the variations induced in the L2 behavior by various input data sets.

3.1   Internal Robustness

In a memory organization like the one we consider, the internal variations in task performance are due to the fact that task switching pollutes the L1 caches. When, on a processor P_k, a task T_i is swapped out by a task T_j, T_i's data are gradually flushed out of P_k's L1 by T_j memory accesses. The amount of data that T_i might still find in the cache on its next execution on P_k depends on how long T_j was executed and on whether other tasks were executed in the mean time on P_k. High task switch rates are likely to pollute L1 caches less at a time, but for many times. Low task switch rates are likely to pollute the L1 cache more at a time, but rarely. The exact amount of L1 pollution depends on the application. For a picture-in-picture video decoder our experiments indicate that when the average task switching rate almost doubles (from 24K times/second to 41K times/second) the number of accesses to the L2 cache increase with 60%. Under these conditions, if a certain off-chip bandwidth has to be guaranteed, the robustness of the system to task switching rate has to be investigated.

For internal robustness analysis we propose to use the L2 sensitivity function. In order to define it, let us assume that the application is composed out of N tasks, $T = \{T_i\}_{(i=1,N)}$ and that $SWR = \{swr_r\}_{(r=1,R)}$ is the set of investigated task switching rates. The number of L2 misses of task T_i depends on T_i's allocated cache size c_i, and on the task switching rate swr_r. We denote these T_i's misses with $miss_i(c_i, swr_r)$. The L2 sensitivity corresponding to a task T_i is defined as being the maximum difference in the number of L2 misses among the investigated task switching rates, when a given L2 cache size c_i is allocated to T_i. To give an idea about the impact of this variation on the application performance, we define the task sensitivity relative to the number of misses obtained when the tasks switch at a reference rate, swr:

$$sens_i(c_i) = \frac{\left|\max_{SWR}\{miss_i(c_i, swr_r)\} - \min_{SWR}\{miss_i(c_i, swr_r)\}\right|}{\sum_{i=1}^{N} miss_i(c_i, swr)} \times 100\%. \quad (1)$$

For a relevant estimation, the reference task switching rate swr should be the most probable, real life task switching rate. If this value is not know or it is variable, the designer might choose to relate to the application misses obtained for one of the swr_r, or to an average over them.

In the same way as the task's sensitivity, we define the application's sensitivity $sens_A$ as being the relative maximum difference in overall number of misses over the investigated task switching rates, when a certain L2 partitioning ratio is applied:

$$sens_A = \max_{T_i \in T}\{sens_i(c_i)\}. \tag{2}$$

The smaller $sens_A$ the more robust is the application. Ideally, we would like to get $sens_A = 0$, but this cannot be achieved for the case when only L2 is partitioned. The platform we target has also a level of L1 caches which are not considered subject to inter-task interference. In reality this is not the case, but, due to typical small sizes, L1 is unsuited for static partitioning. In a multi-processor system, if L1 is statically partitioned the application's tasks should be statically assigned to processors (it makes no sense to allocate cache for a task on a processor where that task might never run). This is not a preferred option because it restricts the run-time processors' load balancing options. For example in a video decoder where all tasks concur for processing frames at a certain rate, restricting run-time load balancing can diminish the performance. Even in the case that L1 is dynamically partitioned, the application's sensitivity $sens_A$ still cannot be zero because the variation may occur due to repartitioning.

3.2   External Robustness

This subsection presents a method to determine the performance deviations for the case when the application processes another input data set than the one utilized to determine the static cache partitioning ratio. First we illustrate the analysis of external robustness by using a small example, and after that we present the general formulation of this analysis.

Let us assume that the investigated application has three tasks ($N = 3$) and two relevant sets of input data in_1 and in_2 are considered in the cache partitioning process. Let us assume that when the application uses in_1 (in_2) as input data its best performance is achieved if tasks have as partitioning ratio $BPR_1 = \{c_1^1, c_2^1, c_3^1\}$ ($BPR_2 = \{c_1^2, c_2^2, c_3^2\}$), as depicted in Fig. 5. BPR_1 and BPR_2 are calculated such that the application's L2 misses is minimum, under the constraint that the allocated cache is smaller that the available cache (14 units in our case).

It can be observed that the best partitioning ratio BPR_1 and BPR_2 are different. When using static cache partitioning the application may use just one single partitioning ratio, $BPR = \{c_1, c_2, c_3\}$. This ratio can be BPR_1, BPR_2, or any compromise between those two. For instance any partition with $c_1 \in [\min(c_1^1, c_1^2), \max(c_1^1, c_1^2)]$, $c_2 \in [\min(c_2^1, c_2^2), \max(c_2^1, c_2^2)]$, and $c_3 = c_3^1 = c_3^2$ can be utilized.

If, for example, BPR_1 is not used as the partitioning ratio, in case the application is processing in_1 as input data, its performance is deviating from the best achievable one. In this case it is of interest to estimate an upper bound of the potential performance degradation. For this purpose, we calculate the worst partitioning ratio, $\overline{BPR_1} = \{\overline{c_1^1}, \overline{c_2^1}, \overline{c_3^1}\}$, with $\overline{c_1^1}, \overline{c_2^1}$, and $\overline{c_3^1}$) bounded by

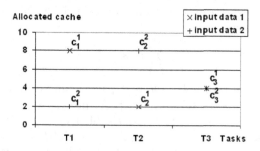

Fig. 5. Example: Partitioning ratios corresponding to two input data

BPR_1 and BPR_2. $\overline{BPR_1}$ is determined utilizing the same optimization method as for BPR_1, but with the constraints that $\overline{c_1^1} \in [\min(c_1^1, c_1^2),\ \max(c_1^1, c_1^2)]$, $\overline{c_2^1} \in [\min(c_2^1, c_2^2), \max(c_2^1, c_2^2)]$, and $\overline{c_3^1} = c_3^1 = c_3^2$. Because we want to estimate the worst performance, the number of misses is maximized instead of minimized.

Let us assume that, for example, for input data in_1 the application minimum number of misses is denoted by M_1 and it is given by the following:

$$M_1 = miss_1(c_1^1, in_1) + miss_2(c_2^1, in_1) + miss_3(c_3^1, in_1). \tag{3}$$

where $miss_{1,2,3}$ are the number of misses experienced by the three tasks of the application, when processing data in_1. Thus for input in_1 and any valid partition BPR the largest number of misses is given by the following:

$$\overline{M_1} = miss_1(\overline{c_1^1}, in_1) + miss_2(\overline{c_2^1}, in_1) + miss_3(\overline{c_3^1}, in_1). \tag{4}$$

The same type of investigation can be done for in_2 also and the values $\frac{\overline{M_1}}{M_1}$ and $\frac{\overline{M_2}}{M_2}$ reflect the robustness of the system to input data.

In media applications, time deadlines are imposed for processing a number of data units, for example a video decoder might have to decode 25 frames in a second. Therefore, it is also interesting to evaluate the variations in L2 behavior caused by different data units belonging to the same input stream. This means that, for instance, input data in_1 may be the first frame of a video stream and in_2 may be the next frame of the same video stream. Such a stability evaluation is useful because it gives a bound of the dynamic behavior inside the same input stream.

For a general application having N tasks $T = \{T_i\}_{(i=1,N)}$ and M common regions $CR = \{CR_j\}_{j=1,M}$, let $IN = \{in_l\}_{(l=1,L)}$ be the set of relevant input data sets. To express the allocated cache size c, we use the same index i to refer to tasks as well as to common regions. For the sake of simplicity we can consider that the first N values of c_i correspond to the application tasks and the next M (from $N + 1$ to $N + M$) correspond to the application common regions. A task T_i's or a common region CR_j's number of misses $miss_i(c_i, in_l)$ depends on task's allocated L2 size c_i and on the input data in_l. When the application processes the input data in_l, its number of misses, is denoted with M_l and it is given by the following:

$$M_l = \sum_{i=1}^{N} miss_i(c_i^l, in_l).\qquad(5)$$

For every input data $in_l \in IN$ the best partitioning ratio BPR_l is the set of tasks' allocated cache sizes $\{c_1^l, c_2^l, ..., c_N^l\}$. As previously mentioned, it is possible that the best partitioning ratio BPR_l differ among each other. The final partitioning ratio, $BPR = \{c_1, c_2, ..., c_N\}$ can be BPR_1, BPR_2, ... , BPR_L or any compromise among them, that respects the following condition:

$$c_i \in \left[\min_{IN}\{c_i^l\}, \max_{IN}\{c_i^l\}\right].\qquad(6)$$

In order to estimate an upper bound of the potential performance degradation in the case of in_l we calculate the worst partitioning ratio that respects the previous condition. We denote this ratio as being $\overline{BPR_l} = (\overline{c_1^l}, \overline{c_2^l}, ..., \overline{c_N^l})$. To determine $\overline{BPR_l}$ we use the same calculation method as for BPR_l, with the constraints that $\overline{c_i^l} \in \left[\min_{IN}\{c_i^l\}, \max_{IN}\{c_i^l\}\right]$ and instead of minimizing the number of misses, we maximize it (we are looking for the worst behavior). The application largest number of L2 misses under the previous conditions is denoted with $\overline{M_l}$, and it is given by the following formula:

$$\overline{M_l} = \sum_{i=1}^{N} miss_i(\overline{c_i^l}, in_l).\qquad(7)$$

We define the application's stability $stab_l$ to in_l as being the relative variation between M_l and $\overline{M_l}$:

$$stab_l = \frac{M_l}{\overline{M_l}} \times 100\%.\qquad(8)$$

The overall application stability is defined as the worst stability over the set of input data IN:

$$stab_A = \min_{IN}\{stab_l\}.\qquad(9)$$

If the stability is close to 100% the application behaves good for all its representative input data, so it is externally robust. If the difference between $\overline{M_l}$ and M_l are large, the static cache partitioning is not robust to input data variations and for better performance a dynamic repartitioning should be considered. In the next subsection we briefly discuss a number of dynamic cache repartitioning options.

3.3   Robustness Considerations for Dynamic Cache Repartitioning

An good overview of dynamic cache repartitioning schemes is given in [11]. Similar to the static partitioning case, there are mainly two types of dynamic cache repartitioning. The first is the associativity based repartitioning. The number of cache ways (cache organization) limits the granularity of this partitioning type. Repartitioning is cheap because data correctness can be preserved without flushing the cache. The second is the "set based" repartitioning. Typically in a cache there are more sets than ways, thus this method can potentially offer finer partitioning granularity. However, at repartitioning data correctness cannot be preserved without flushing parts of the cache. This makes this second type of cache repartitioning more expensive than the first type.

The existing dynamic cache repartitioning scheme are associativity based [15] [16]. In these schemes the task that have either high priority [16] or large cache needs [15] dynamically "steals" cache ways from the other tasks. The purpose is to increase the performance of high priority tasks [16] or to improve the overall hit rate [15].

An allocation scheme in which a task will be granted all the requested cache can lead to cache "starvation" of some of the tasks. For example, a repartitioning strategy that attempts to improve the overall hit rate will eventually give a large part of cache to an erroneous task asking for it. Given this fact, the system will fail. Therefore, in a robust system, the cache repartitioning cannot be done fully at tasks requests, like in the existing approaches. The cache manager should have a global view on the application's tasks and their allocated cache, to prevent starvation and system failures. Our future work will include robust dynamic cache repartitioning strategies.

4   Experimental Results

For our experiments we use a CAKE multi-processor platform [10] with 4 Trimedia processor cores and a 4 ways associative L2 cache of various sizes, depending on the application. Each and every Trimedia processor core has separate instructions and data L1 caches. The shared L2 cache is unified (it contains both data and instructions). To enhance compositionality, we use the mixed L2 partitioning previously presented in Sect. 2.3. The experimental workload consists of two application types: (1) applications composed out of communicating tasks and (2) application composed out of independent tasks. In the following we introduce these applications.

From the first category the applications we consider are two video decoders (an H.264 decoder and a picture-in-picture-TV decoder), each of which consisting of several communicating tasks. The H.264 decoder consists of 15 tasks [18], as follows: first an entropy decoder task processes the input stream and passes the data via a data scheduler to a set of transform decoders and loop filters tasks doing inverse quantization, transformation, prediction and deblocking on different parts of the image. The PiPTV application decodes two different video streams and outputs a raw pictures stream containing both video stream images, scaled with a given factor. This application consists of the following tasks: video demultiplexing of transport stream, two MPEG2 decoders (every one having multiple tasks [19]), two video scalers, video multiplexing the two images, and output. Both these applications are described in YAPI [20].

In order to build applications formed by independent tasks, we use various multimedia programs, some of which derive from the MediaBench benchmark

[5]. From this collection of programs we pruned out the ones that are relatively small and not memory intensive. Moreover, in order to make the benchmark more representative for emerging technologies, we augmented the MediaBench suite with two H.264 video processing programs, an encoder and a decoder. For clarity sake, we emphasize the fact that all these programs are sequential and different than the H.264 decoder or the MPEG2 decoders introduced in the previous paragraph. In the experimental framework, an application is formed by a collection four such programs, each of which representing a task. Table 1 presents the set of 9 tasks exercised. All of these are reasonably memory intensive workloads. Using different combinations of these 9 tasks, we build 6 different applications $(A_1, A_2, ..., A_6)$.

Table 1. Media workloads

H.264	A very low bit-rate video coder (h264enc) and decoder (h264dec) based on the H.264 standard.
MPEG2	A motion video compression coder (mpeg2enc) and decoder (mpeg2dec) for high-quality video transmission, based on the MPEG-2 standard.
EPIC	An image compression coder (epic) and decoder (unepic) based on wavelets and including run-length/Huffman entropy coding.
Audio	MPEG-1 Layer III (MP3) audio decoder and encoder.
JPEG	A lossy image compression coder for color and gray-scale images, based on the JPEG standard.

In the remainder of this section the robustness assessment methods we introduced in Sect. 3 are applied. The results obtained for the case of the partitioned cache are compared with the ones for the shared cache. To our knowledge, no cache related robustness investigation method exists in the literature, therefore we cannot compare our proposal with previous work.

4.1 Internal Robustness

As aforementioned, the applications consisting of communicating tasks are described in YAPI, thus the data exchange and synchronization among the tasks is done through blocking FIFOs. A task is blocked (and consequently its processor switches to other task) when it has no available input data or output buffer space. On our experimental platform, for the purpose of our investigations, we induce higher task switching rate by shrinking the FIFOs sizes. For FIFOs larger than a certain size the task switching rate does not decrease anymore because a value intrinsic to the application is reached. We consider this lowest value as the reference task switching rate, as defined in the Sect. 3.1. In our case, both applications have the least number of misses for the lowest task switching rate. The internal robustness is relative to this number of misses, therefore the presented results reflect the largest deviations.

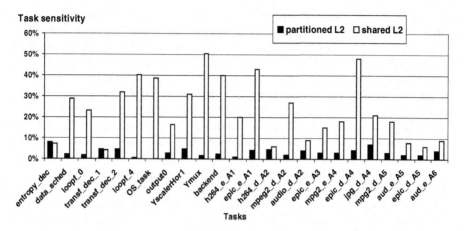

Fig. 6. Tasks sensitivity: shared vs. partitioned cache

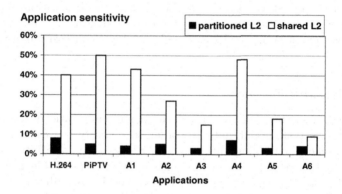

Fig. 7. Application sensitivity: shared vs. partitioned cache

For the communicating tasks, the investigated average task switching rate values start at 41K and 24K times per second, corresponding to 4KB FIFOs and 2KB FIFOs for the H.264 and PiPTV, respectively. The task switching rate range ends at 74K and 41K times per second, corresponding to 0.5KB FIFOs and 0.4KB FIFOs for the H.264 and PiPTV, respectively. For FIFOs larger than 4KB and 2KB, for the H.264 and PiPTV respectively, the average task switching rate does not decrease anymore because the value intrinsic to the application is reached. For FIFOs smaller than 0.5KB for H.264 and 0.4KB for PiPTV, the applications deadlock, so the average task switching rate cannot be increased anymore. These task switching variation account for 30% respectively 66% difference in the number of L2 accesses for the H.264 and PiPTV.

In the case of applications composed from independent tasks, the task switching rate depends on the task scheduler policy. We enforced a policy that pre-empts tasks with a rate ranging from 40K times per second to 400 times per second. This range is chosen to cover a large variety of possibilities. We consider the reference task switching rate as being the lowest one, therefore the internal robustness is relative to the number of misses encountered on that case.

For both application types, the L2 sensitivity of tasks is compared for the partitioned and the shared cache case (Fig. 6). In Fig. 6 are depicted only the tasks that have the sensitivity larger than 2% in the partitioned cache case or larger than 20% in the shared cache case. In this figure it can be observed that, in general, the shared L2 is more sensitive than the partitioned one or their sensitivities are pretty close. Among the tasks that are not depicted in Fig. 6, there are few for which the sensitivity of the partitioned L2 cache is larger than the one of the shared cache. However, for those few tasks, the sensitivity is smaller than 0.5%, so they do not influence the general observed trend i.e. the shared cache is more sensitive that the partitioned one. Fig. 7 presents the application sensitivity for our eight case. Over all the applications, the shared cache is on average 6 times more sensitive to task switching than the partitioned one. The largest sensitivity was observed at the applications $H.264$ and $PiPTV$ for the case of partitioned and shared cache, respectively. For a partitioned cache, over the investigated task switching range, the application sensitivity as defined in Sect. 3.1 is at most 8%. These results suggest that, for the analyzed applications, partitioning the L2 is enough to achieve compositionality to a large extent.

4.2   External Robustness

As detailed in section 3.2, the best cache partitioning ratio of an application varies with its tasks input data. In order to quantify the differences among the best cache partitioning ratio, we use the maximum variation of the L2 size allocated to a task, across different input streams. Table 2 depicts (for each application) the maximum variation of the L2 size allocated to a task, across different input streams. The values in Table 2 are relative to the total cache size available to each application. In general we found that the differences among the best partitioned ratio corresponding to different input data are relatively small. As one can see in Table 2, over the 8 applications that we exercised, the cache of a task varies at maximum with 20% from the total cache size.

Table 2. Maximum variation in the L2 size allocated to a task

application	H.264	PiPTV	A_1	A_2	A_3	A_4	A_5	A_6
max L2 variation	2%	7%	16%	9%	16%	12%	20%	12%

For some input data, the partitioning ratio is non-optimal and this induces a performance degradation. To quantify this degradation, in Sect. 3.2 we introduced the stability metric. In Table 3 the stabilities corresponding to each application are illustrated. For all the eight applications we investigated four different input data streams (these streams are the one required by each application task, as some tasks decode video, some process audio, etc.). We would like to mention that the set of input data corresponding to a task has the same size and the same "quality" level for each experiment. In this section we do not investigate the effects of things like enlarging the resolution or the scaling factor of a video stream, or changing the encoding quality of an image. These issues are subject to future work.

Table 3. Application stability for different input data

input data	in_1	in_2	in_3	in_4
H.264	96%	96%	100%	98%
PiPTV	92%	100%	93%	98%
A_1	100%	93%	93%	96%
A_2	90%	100%	91%	97%
A_3	97%	93x%	100%	90%
A_4	95%	91%	100%	95%
A_5	100%	95%	98%	96%
A_6	92%	91%	93%	100%

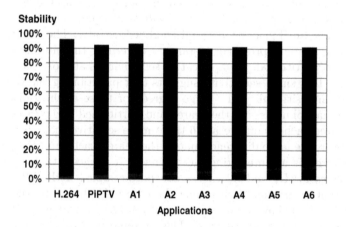

Fig. 8. Minimum application stability

Fig. 8 presents, for each of the eight applications, the minimum stability over the set of four input streams. We observe that the minimum stability of each application is pretty high, ranging over the eight applications from 90% to 96%, with an average of 92%. Taking these facts into account, we can conclude that all the eight applications are quite robust to input stimuli in the presence of static cache partitioning. A stability comparison between the shared and the partitioned cache is not possible because the stability, as defined in Sect. 3.2, is linked to the partitioned ratio, thus it cannot be computed for the shared cache scenario.

5   Conclusions

In this paper we proposed a method to analyze the static cache partitioning robustness of an application mapped on an on-chip embedded multi-processor. In
this context we considered a memory organization which has two levels of cache:
(1) L1, private to every processor and (2) L2, shared between the processors, but
partitionable per task basis. For applications executed on this multi-processor,
two types of robustness are discussed: internal (determined by inter-task interference in the not-partitioned L1 cache) and external (determined by the variations
of the L2 behavior due to various input data sets). For both types of robustness we introduced quantification metrics. For internal robustness we defined
the sensitivity function which measures the deviation of L2 misses caused by
the L1 variations over a spectrum of task switching rates. To assess external
robustness we introduced the stability function which measures the performance
deviation for the case the application processes another input data set than the
one utilized to determine the static L2 partitioning ratio.

To demonstrate our approach we analyzed two types of parallel applications:
(1) applications consisting of communicating tasks and (2) applications consisting of independent tasks. In the first category we analyzed two applications: a
picture-in-picture video decoder and an H.264 decoder. In the second category
we analyzed six applications each of which composed by different multimedia
tasks. These tasks were chosen from the MediaBench suite, augmented with two
more programs, an H.264 encoder and an H.264 decoder. The simulation platform is a CAKE multi-processor instance. Concerning the internal robustness,
if the cache is partitioned, the application sensitivity is at most 8% with an average of 4%. This small sensitivity suggests that partitioning the L2 is enough
to achieve compositionality in a large degree, for these applications. Comparing the internal robustness of the shared and partitioned cache cases, we found
that the shared cache is on average 6 times more sensitive than the partitioned
one. Moreover, the large difference among the shared cache and the partitioned
cache sensitivity is an interesting fact on itself. It suggests that the optimizations processes for L1 and L2 caches can be decoupled if the L2 is managed
on a task centric manner. Concerning the external robustness, the variations
induced in the L2 behavior by various input data sets are at most 10% over all
the application range that we tried. This accounts for an average stability of
92%, therefore, for the investigated applications, we can conclude that the static
cache partitioning is quite robust with respect to input stimuli variations.

References

1. A. Stevens, "Level 2 Cache for High-performance ARM Core-based SoC Systems",
   ARM white paper, 2004
2. D. T. Chiou, "Extending the Reach of Microprocessors: Column and Curious
   Caching", PhD thesis Department of EECS, MIT, Cambridge, MA, 1999
3. Allan Hartstein, Viji Srinivasan, Thomas R. Puzak, Philip G. Emma, "Cache miss
   behavior: is it sqrt(2)?", Conf. Computing Frontiers, pages 313-320, 2006

4. Jochen Liedtke, Hermann Härtig, Michael Hohmuth, "OS-Controlled Cache PRedictability for Real-Time Systems", 3rd IEEE Real-Time Technology and Applications Symposium, 1997
5. L. Chunho, M. Potkonjak, W.H. Mangione-Smith. "MediaBench: A Tool for Evaluating and Synthesizing Multimedia and Communicatons Systems" In *International Symposium on Microarchitecture*, 1997.
6. A. M. Molnos, Marc J.M. Heijligers, Sorin D. Cotofana, Jos T.J. van Eijndhoven, "Compositional Memory Systems for Data Intensive Applications", Proceedings, Design, Automation and Test in Europe, 2004
7. Harald S. Stone, John Truek, Joel L. Wolf, "Optimal Partitioning of Cache Memory", IEEE Transactions on computers, volume 41, number 9, pages 1054-1068, 1992
8. F. Mueller, "Compiler Support for Software-Based Cache Partitioning", In *ACM SIGPLAN Notice*, 1995.
9. B.A. Nayfeh and K. Olukotun, "Exploring the Design Space for a Shared-Cache Multiprocessor", In Proceedings, ISCA, pages 166-175, 1994
10. J.T.J. van Eijndhoven, J. Hoogerbrugge, M.N. Jayram, P. Stravers, and A. Terechko, "Cache-Coherent Heterogeneous Multiprocessing as Basis for Streaming Applications", In "Dynamic and robust streaming between connected CE-devices", Kluwer Academic Publishers, 2005
11. P. Ranganathan, S. Adve, and N.P. Jouppi, "Reconfigurable caches and their application to media processing", In Proceedings, 27th Annual International Symposium on Computer Architecture, pages 214-224, 2000
12. J.L. Hennesy and D.A. Patterson, "Computer Architecture: A Quantitative Approach", Morgan Kaufmann Publishers, 2003
13. A.M. Molnos, M.J.M. Heijligers, S.D. Cotofana, and J.T.J. van Eijndhoven, "Compositional memory systems for multimedia communicating tasks", In Proceedings, Design, Automation and Test in Europe, pages 932-937, 2005
14. A.M. Molnos, M.J.M. Heijligers, S.D. Cotofana, and J.T.J. van Eijndhoven, "Compositional, efficient caches for a chip multi-processor", In Proceedings, Design, Automation and Test in Europe, to appear in 2006
15. G.E. Suh, L. Rudolph, and S. Devadas, "Dynamic Partitioning of Shared Cache Memory", The Journal of Supercomputing, volume 28, number 1, pages 7-26, 2004
16. Y. Tan and V.J. Mooney, "A Prioritized Cache for Multi-tasking Real-Time Systems", In Proceedings of the 11th Workshop on Synthesis And System Integration of Mixed Information Technologies, pages 168-175, 2003
17. A.M. Molnos, S.D. Cotofana, M.J.M. Heijligers, and J.T.J. van Eijndhoven, "Static cache partitioning robustness analysis for embedded on-chip multi-processors", In Proceeding of the ACM International Conference on Computing Frontiers, 2006
18. E.B. van der Tol, E.G. Jaspers, and R.H. Gelderblom, "Mapping of H.264 decoding on a multiprocessor architecture", In Proceedings, SPIE Conference on Image and Video Communications and Processing, 2003
19. P. van der Wolf, P. Lieverse, M. Goel, D. La Hei, K.A. Vissers "An MPEG-2 Decoder Case Study as a Driver for a System Level Design Methodology", In Proceedings, 7th International Workshop on Hardware/Software Co-Design, pages 33-37, 1999
20. E. A. de Kock, W. J. M. Smits, P. van der Wolf, J.-Y. Brunel, W. M. Kruijtzer, P. Lieverse, K. A. Vissers, and G. Essink "YAPI: application modeling for signal processing systems", In Proceedings, 37th conference on Design Automation, pages 402-405, 2000

Selective Code Compression Scheme for Embedded Systems*

Shlomit S. Pinter[1] and Israel Waldman[2]

[1] IBM, Haifa Research Laboratory
[2] CS Department, Haifa University

Abstract. The extensive usage of embedded systems involves running complex applications that require tightly limited resources such as memory and storage. One efficient way to satisfy the resource requirements is to reduce the code size through code compression. Our work describes a software-based code compression scheme that reduces the storage space of a program, which in turn induces a reduction of access time to off-chip memory in SoC (System-on-a-chip) embedded architectures. To select those sections of code that are most advantageous for compression, our scheme utilizes profiling information to evaluate and trade off storage space reduction for future run-time overhead. During run-time, the compressed parts are decompressed as necessary into a run-time buffer for execution. Experimental results on the SPEC CPU2000 and Media-Bench suites show reduction in code size averaging 18.5%, along with reasonable memory consumption overhead averaging 3.8%, and a reasonable run-time overhead averaging 7.8%.

Keywords: Code compression, run-time decompression, code size reduction.

1 Introduction

Memory space, storage space, and power consumption are important design constraints for embedded systems. These systems are beginning to integrate more sophisticated applications, such as image and speech applications, where demands for extended memory and storage space have grown tremendously. In embedded systems such as SoCs, binary code is stored in external off-chip storage (e.g., FLASH), which has high latency access compared to the on-chip memory [16]. Moreover, in embedded memory systems, significant amount of energy is consumed when data is moved between the memory and the CPU, and the energy consumption increases as the memory hierarchy level is higher [4]. Thus, minimizing the amount of data fetched from external storage can save execution time and power in embedded architectures.

Code compression is one way to overcome the increasing demand storage space. Code compression can reduce the size of binaries in storage, thus cutting down on the storage space requirements. Furthermore, fewer fetches are needed to load a

---

* This paper extends the Computing Frontiers 2006 paper [24] with new performance results comparing different compression techniques, and additional discussions.

P. Stenström (Ed.): Transactions on HiPEAC I, LNCS 4050, pp. 298–316, 2007.

compressed binary from off-chip storage as compared to an uncompressed binary. This can, in turn, reduce the power consumption and eliminate the performance impact of the storage's high latency access. For code compression to be feasible for embedded systems, it should not dramatically affect the system's performance and memory consumption.

There are two basic kinds of compression schemes, hardware-based schemes [1, 2 6, 8, 10, 11, 12, 15, 24, 25, 26] and software-based schemes [5, 7, 9 20]. Hardware-based schemes employ special hardware to execute the compressed code. Software-based schemes allow the selection of different compression algorithms for different architectures and can be implemented without increasing the complexity of the hardware.

The main issues that differentiate the various software compression schemes are the analysis methods for selecting the code to compress, the granularity and characteristics of the fragments selected for compression, the methods for integrating the compressed code with the non-compressed fragments, and the time and method used to integrate the decompressed fragments prior to execution.

In this paper, we present a new software-based code compression scheme that reduces the size of binaries in storage, yet keep them in executable form, while maintaining reasonable overheads for run-time and memory consumption. The scheme uses profiling information to generate binaries that contain compressed code. The main idea is to select and compress code regions that reduce the overall code size, while yielding a potentially small run-time overhead. During run-time, if necessary, these compressed parts are decompressed into a run-time buffer for execution.

Experimental results on SPEC CPU2000 [21] and MediaBench suites [17] show a 7.2% to 31.7% (average of 18.5%) reduction in code size, along with reasonable memory consumption overhead (-16.3% to 22.1%, with an average of 3.8%), and reasonable run-time overhead (-1.6% to 16.2%, with an average of 7.8%). The negative overheads can be explained by the rearrangement of the binaries due to compression and the partition of the binaries into small files that are loaded only on demand. In SoC embedded systems we can expect further reduction in run-time overhead due to the decrease in the amount of data (code) fetched from storage.

The paper is organized as follows: Section 2 presents our code compression scheme. Section 3 describes the experiments and the results obtained on different benchmarks. Section 4 presents related work. Finally, in Section 5 we discuss our conclusions and future work.

2 The Code Compression Scheme

Our code compression scheme has three main components: analysis of input based on profiling information, preparation of compressed code, and dynamic decompression with execution at run-time. During the input analysis phase, the input code is analyzed and fragments of the code are selected for compression. In the preparation phase, these fragments are actually compressed and integrated into the compiled code. At run-time, when the compressed code is first called, it is decompressed into a *run-time buffer* and is executed from there. When possible, further calls to this compressed code are directed to the buffer, thus, bypassing the decompression phase.

The assembly code produced by the compiler may include labels that serve as entry points or jump targets. A *compressible region* is a fragment of the assembly code that has a single entry point and a single exit point for code outside the region. The region may include function calls that are not considered exit points. Basic blocks and whole functions are examples of compressible regions. Our scheme finds large compressible regions and evaluates the future impact of compressing them in terms of storage space reduction and run-time overhead. The scheme compresses and embeds the regions in the code together with code that invokes a run-time library; this library is referred to as a *decompression engine*.

In order to select the best compressible regions, we evaluated the strength of the compression and decompression algorithms, employed by our scheme, on different input sizes. The evaluation produced two graphs that describe the size reduction and the run-time for different input sizes. In addition, we collected data, which is architecture dependent, on the overhead added by the decompression scheme:

1. The time overhead for invoking the decompression engine on compressed code.
2. The time overhead incurred by invoking the decompression engine to direct the execution to the run-time buffer for executing a decompressed code region.

2.1 Input Analysis Phase

The input for the system includes source files and a makefile. The source files are compiled into assembly (.s) files. This stage also generates profiling information, which includes control flow graphs annotated with statistics.

Finding Maximal Compressible Regions. The algorithm is applied separately on each single source file function in order to find its maximal compressible region. We compute two potentials for each compressible region B: the potential of code size reduction, R_B, measured in bytes; and performance overhead potential, T_B, measured in seconds. R_B is defined as follows: $R_B = CS_B - RS_B$, where CS_B is the original code size of B and RS_B is the reduced code size after compression. Both sizes are measured in bytes. The estimate of RS_B is based on the size of the region, the quality of the compression, and the code overhead incurred by our scheme (discussed later in more detail). The time overhead T_B of a compressible region B is defined as follows: $T_B = DT_B + BPT_B$, where DT_B is the decompression time during the first call to B at run-time. This value is estimated based on the graphs obtained from the compression scheme. The time overhead during calls to B that avoid decompression phase, is BPT_B; these calls direct the execution to the run-time buffer when the code is still there. This value is estimated based on the execution frequency of the compressible region generated by the profiler and the overhead incurred by the code for the redirection.

The percentage of the performance overhead potential, O_B, is computed from T_B by comparing the overhead relative to the native run-time of the entire program. $O_B = (T_B / E_P) * \varDelta_B$, where E_P, measured in seconds, is the execution time of the program; it is obtained from the profiler and is used for normalization. $\varDelta_B$ is a weight factor (between 0 and 1) for the compressible region B, calculated from the profiling information (on the training dataset). The need for the weight factor arises from the differences in the size of the train vs. real datasets. On one hand, real datasets are often larger than the training datasets and thus have longer execution times (i.e., large E_P). On the other hand, larger inputs may increase the number of times the decompression is bypassed during run-time, resulting in a higher BPT_B. Consequently, the expected ratio (T_B / E_P) for real datasets is probably smaller than for training datasets; thus, when using real datasets, we need to adjust the measurement (T_B / E_P) to achieve a better estimate of the performance overhead potential. When we estimate, based on a large BPT_B, that the region may cause a significant execution overhead on real datasets due to many bypasses of the decompression phase, we assign a high value to Δ_B.

We define our problem as an optimization problem:

Given a source file, the different characteristics of our compression engine, the code overhead incurred by our scheme, find for each source file function a maximal compressible region that has the highest code size reduction potential, subject to performance overhead potential that is bounded by a threshold value.

The input is the control flow graph $G = (V, E)$ of a single source file function, in which each vertex represents a basic block in this function and each edge represents a control transfer from one basic block to another. The output is a subset B of V, such that the following conditions are met:

1. B is a compressible region
2. R_B is maximized
3. $O_B \leq \theta_O$

The threshold θ_O represents the performance overhead potential that is acceptable for the application. Since in some cases the code size reduction obtained from compressing a code region can be small, in our heuristics algorithm we use a second threshold θ_R to indicate a lower bound on the code size reduction potential. The thresholds were selected to reflect the desired size reduction and time overhead tradeoffs.

Algorithm for Finding a Maximal Compressible Region. Initially, R_B is computed for each basic block, based on its size and the compression values measured for the compression algorithm. The performance overhead for a basic block, O_B, is computed based on timing and execution frequencies measured for the block by the profiler and the overhead incurred by our additional code (measured once). In the next step, basic blocks are accumulated to generate a larger compressible region and the values are combined.

We denote the largest basic block in V by b_{max} and use it to initialize B ($B = \{b_{max}\}$). Significant savings are obtained only when the region is large enough; thus, we first accumulate blocks as follows:

*   Until $R_B \geq \theta_R$ or B cannot be enlarged, the algorithm checks the expansion possibilities for B (which preserve the condition of a single entry, single exit region), and chooses in a greedy manner to enlarge B towards the direction that increases R_B as much as possible. When checking the profitability of an expanding possibility, the new R_B is estimated using the following calculations:

1. The code size CS_B is calculated by summing over the combined regions.
2. The reduced size RS_B is found based on the values computed for the compression scheme and the code addition incurred by our scheme, based on the instructions in the additional regions.

-   If $R_B \geq \theta_R$ the algorithm considers θ_O as follows:
    Further expansions of B are performed only if R_B increases, yet $O_B \leq \theta_O$. For estimating O_B, the following calculations are carried out:
    1. The decompression time DT_B is based on the code size of B as derived from the sum of all the combined regions along with the additional code incurred by our scheme. The time is estimated based on the decompression time of our scheme for different input sizes.
    2. The time overhead BPT_B is estimated by calculating the execution frequency of B as the maximum on all its parts.

Figure 1 illustrates the algorithm for finding a maximal compressible region. This source file function has six basic blocks in its control flow graph, denoted *bb1* to *bb6*. Figure 1(a) shows the beginning of the algorithm, in which B was initialized to {*bb4*}, since *bb4* is the largest basic block among all six basic blocks. Figure 1(b) shows the first iteration of the algorithm. In this iteration, the two expanding possibilities expand towards *bb2* or expand towards *bb5*. In order to maintain the property defining a compressible region, namely single entry and single exit, these two possibilities are reduced to one possibility, which is to expand B such that $B' = B \cup \{bb2, bb3, bb5\}$. The next two expansion possibilities (*bb1* and *bb6*) are checked in the subsequent iteration and *bb1* is selected (see Figure 1(c)). Expanding B to include *bb6* was found

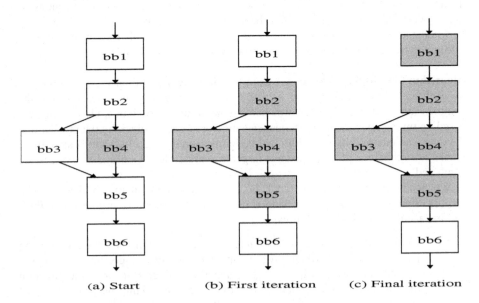

(a) Start   (b) First iteration   (c) Final iteration

Fig. 1. Finding a maximal compressible region

to be non-profitable. At this point, no possibilities to expand or improve B are left, and the algorithm stops. Applying the algorithm resulted in at most one maximal compressible region for each source file function; such a region is referred to as a *compressed region* and will be compressed by our scheme.

2.2 Compressed Code Preparation Phase

Following the analysis phase, the compressed code is prepared using five major steps, which involve two compilations.

Step 1 – First Compilation. The function call instructions within the compressed regions are handled as follows:

- A file that does not contain a compressed region is compiled directly into an object file.
- A file containing a compressed region is first compiled into an assembly file (.s file). A compressible region may have function calls represented by 'bl' (brunch and link) or 'bla' (brunch and link absolute) instructions in the IBM Power architecture. Since such a function will reside on a different segment[1], we insert 'nop' instructions as space holders that will be replaced by the proper reference (instructions) to the code of the called function. The 'nop' instructions keep the correctness of the offsets in the compressed region (jumping offsets) during the compilations in the preparation phase. The difficulty in enabling function calls from the run-time buffer is discussed later in this section. The assembly file (latter used in Step 2.d) is then compiled into an object file.
- All the object files created in this step are linked together into one executable file.

Step 2 – Creating New Assembly Files and Binary Units - First Versions. The executable file produced in Step 1 for the modified assembly code is disassembled, and the first version of each binary unit is created as follows:

a. For each compressed region we generate a *function list*, which includes a list of its called functions. The logical address of each of the called functions may need update following the changes in the executable file.
b. The code of each compressed region that appears in the disassembled executable file is used in the compression step. To each such unit of code, referred to as a *binary unit*, we add prolog and epilog instructions that are part of the registers store/restore process; these enable the binary unit to return from the run-time buffer to the decompression engine, when it finishes its execution.
c. Each compressed region is assigned a unique identifier, which is used by the decompression engine to identify the corresponding binary unit.

---

[1] In our implementation, the run-time buffer is located in a different segment from the executable's code segment. We discuss this in the Run-time Phase section.

d. In every assembly file that corresponds to a compressed region, and was modified in Step 1, the assembly code of the compressed region is replaced by a few assembly instructions that invoke the decompression engine with the compressed region's identifier. At run-time, the decompression engine will eventually transfer the control to the suitable binary unit's instructions representing this region.

Step 3 – Second Compilation. The new assembly files that were produced in Step 2 are compiled into object files. These object files along with the unchanged object files obtained in Step 1 are linked together into one executable file; this file is dynamically linked to the decompression engine.

Step 4 – Creating the Binary Units - Final Versions. The executable file produced in Step 3 is disassembled in order to locate the new logical addresses of the functions being called from the binary units.

- The new logical address of each function in the function list of each binary unit is found in the disassembled file.
- The machine instructions that perform these function calls in every binary unit (from Step 1), along with the 'nop' instructions (installed in Step 1), are now replaced by new machine instructions that include the new logical addresses, thus enabling function calls from the run-time buffer to the needed targets.

Figure 2 illustrates Steps 1 to 4 of the preparation phase. Figure 2(a) shows a source file function (my_function) containing a compressed region. The region includes a function call instruction (bl .printf{PR}). Figure 2(b) shows the region following the insertion of the 'nop' instructions (oril r0,r0,0x0000) in Step 1. The final executable produced in Step 1 is shown in Figure 2(c) for 'printf' with a logical address of 0x10002912 in this executable. Figure 2(d) presents the instructions in the binary unit (first version) produced in Step 2. The function list produced for the unit in Step 2 is shown in Figure 2(e). The final executable produced in Step 3 is shown in Figure 2(f) for 'printf' with a new logical address of 0x10002800 in this executable.

Figure 2(g) presents the modified function call instructions in the binary unit (final version) produced in Step 4.

Step 5 – Compressing the Binary Units. In order to choose the most suitable compression technique for our scheme, we evaluated different compression techniques from [19] and compared their compression ratios on different sized binary units. We selected a data compressor from the PPM family [22] to compress and decompress each of the binary units. This technique uses an unbounded context-length PPM model, implemented with a sliding window suffix tree. It yields the highest compression ratios when compressing PowerPC machine instructions (even short sequences) and decompresses binary units with reasonable performance slowdown.

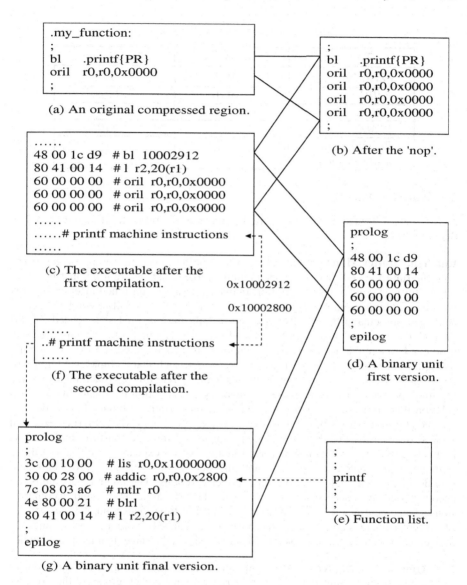

(a) An original compressed region.

(b) After the 'nop'.

(c) The executable after the first compilation.

(d) A binary unit first version.

(f) The executable after the second compilation.

(e) Function list.

(g) A binary unit final version.

Fig. 2. Enable function calls from the run-time buffer

Table 1 presents some of the different compression techniques that were evaluated. The second and third columns list the compressed size of 1500 and 2788 Bytes binary files that contains PowerPC machine instructions, respectively. These values represent common sizes of binary units that are compressed by our scheme.

To summarize, the final output of the preparation phase has two components: a reduced size executable file and a collection of compressed binary units.

Table 1. Compression techniques evaluation

Technique	Binary File 1	Binary File 2
LZRW3-A	953	1275
BZIP2	931	1168
GZIP	817	979
PPMZ2	754	870
BICOM (the selected technique)	720	848

2.3 Run-Time Phase

At run-time, if needed, binary units are decompressed into the run-time buffer, before their execution.

Run-Time Buffer Management. The run-time buffer management approach impacts both the run-time and memory consumption overhead. There are a number of possibilities for managing a run-time buffer. In one approach, a run-time buffer can hold at most one decompressed binary unit at a given time, where the buffer can be allocated and freed on demand or initially allocated to hold the maximal size needed. In this method, the memory consumption overhead is relatively small, yet, the run-time overhead can be large due to repeating decompressions of the same code [5]. An alternative approach is to use a very large run-time buffer, such that a compressed unit will be decompressed at most once, upon its first call. While this approach decreases the run-time overhead, it may increase the memory consumption overhead. We chose a solution that combines the two approaches. In our system, a binary unit is decompressed at most twice. A binary unit that was found cold or nearly cold, (i.e., executed at most once in the profiling stage) is decompressed into the run-time buffer on its first call, and is evicted from the buffer when it finishes executing. This is useful, for example, with initialization or error handling code. Upon a second call to such a unit, it is decompressed again, without any further evictions. The other binary units are decompressed only once upon their first call. This dynamic on-demand decompression management has several advantages. First, run-time management tasks such as cache replacement algorithms (of the buffer) are reduced. In addition, it handles infrequently executed code such as initialization code, in the same manner as cold code.

Run-Time Buffer Implementation. At run-time, we must be able to both write to and execute from the run-time buffer. In our system, the code segment of the executable produced in the preparation phase is 'write protected' at run-time. Hence, we use the Unix IPC (Inter Process Communication) mechanism to implement the run-time buffer on a shared memory segment.

A binary unit may contain function calls that need special treatment, since the buffer lies in a different logical segment than the called functions. Direct subroutine linkage, through assembly instructions such as 'bl' and 'bla', are limited to targets located in the same logical segment address space boundaries. Hence, executing a function call from the run-time buffer to the executable's code segment requires more assembly instructions. The additional instructions (as opcodes) guarantee that the call will return to the correct calling code. These instructions are installed in the binary units during Step 4 of the preparation phase.

Decompression Engine. The decompression engine is invoked with one parameter, a binary unit identifier. The engine maintains a *units table* in which it keeps track of each binary unit. When the engine is invoked with a certain binary unit identifier, it stores all the registers it will use. Then, if the binary unit has already been decompressed and is in the buffer, the engine retrieves (from the units table) the unit's start address in the run-time buffer. If it is not in the buffer, the engine proceeds as follows:

1. Allocates buffer space, decompresses the binary unit, and for cold/nearly-cold unit it sets the decompressed 'once' or 'twice' flags based on their previous values.
2. Flushes the data cache to ensure that the instructions of the binary unit are written into the run-time buffer.

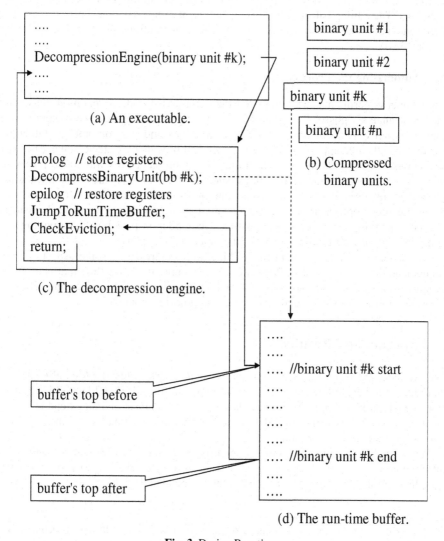

Fig. 3. During Run-time

At this point, the engine restores all the registers that were saved and jumps unconditionally to the unit's decompressed instructions (for execution).

Upon return from the buffer, if the unit is cold/nearly-cold and the decompressed twice flag is not set the engine evicts the unit's decompressed instructions and frees the buffer space. The engine then immediately returns to its caller code.

Figure 3 illustrates the decompression operation at run-time. Figures 3(a) and 2.3(b) show an executable created in the preparation phase along with n binary units. This executable contains one function call to the decompression engine to decompress a non-cold/nearly-cold binary unit number k (DecompressionEngine(binary unit #k);). Figure 3(c) shows how this function call evolves at run-time; the sub-routine 'DecompressBinaryUnit' does the actual code decompression. The 'buffer's top before' and 'buffer's top after' represent the buffer's top value before and after the unit's decompression. The 'JumpToRunTimeBuffer' represents the machine instructions that jump unconditionally to the unit's decompressed instructions in the run-time buffer (Figure 3(d)).

2.4 Automating the Process

To conduct experiments, we automated the compressed code preparation phase and the input analysis phase. The analysis algorithm for finding maximal compressible regions is not dependent on the type of instructions and the computer architecture. Recursive calls are supported, since each such call uses its own stack frame. Still, our scheme uses two words in the stack frame for saving data. This was found problematic when aggressive optimization flags (such as –O3 and –O4) are used, since some of these optimizations break linkage conventions of the functions' stack frames. Thus, to enable more optimizations, re-implementation of this data saving mechanism is needed. Integration of our scheme within a compiler is possible by providing the compiler with profiling information for the input analysis phase.

Our scheme is general for most machine architectures, yet, some aspects of our implementation are specific to PowerPC. One example is a procedure that is used for jumping to the decompressed code and back to the program. This procedure relies on information used for saving and restoring the appropriate context.

3 Experimental Results

We evaluated the proposed scheme using two benchmark suites: the MediaBench [17] suite built for benchmarking embedded systems and the SPEC CPU2000 [21] suite. Each benchmark is supplied with two datasets, a train dataset and an extended (reference) dataset. We used the train dataset to profile our benchmarks and the extended dataset to evaluate our technique[2].

While the SPEC CPU2000 suite is primarily used to measure workstation performance, some of its applications, such as 181.mcf (vehicle scheduling) and 177.messa (graphics library), are likely to be merged into embedded devices.

---

[2] For the *pegwit* benchmark, we used the GNU libc text manual and for the *epic* benchmark, we used the baboon.tif image.

Table 2 lists the benchmarks and the datasets used. Some of the MediaBench suite benchmarks are composed of two different executables, an encoder and a decoder. We present each MediaBench suite benchmark as such.

Table 2. Benchmarks and datasets

Benchmark	Train input	Reference input
adpcm_dec	clinton.adpcm	S_16_44.adpcm
adpcm_enc	clinton.pcm	S_16_44.pcm
epic_dec	test_image.pgm.E	baboon.tif.E
epic_enc	test_image.pgm	baboon.tif
gsm_dec	clinton.pcm.gsm	S_16_44.pcm.gsm
gsm_enc	clinton.pcm	S_16_44.pcm
pegwit_dec	pegwit.dec	libc.txt.enc
pegwit_enc	pegwit.enc	libc.txt
181.mcf	train	Ref
177.messa	train	Ref

The benchmarks were compiled for a Power604 processor (in 32 bit mode) using the IBM xlc v5.0 compiler. The source files of each benchmark were compiled with the '-O2' optimization flag. The optimizations invoked by this flag do not break linkage conventions. An additional compilation flag, '-S', was used to generate the assembly files. The executable file produced in Step 3 of the preparation phase, was stripped using the 'strip' shell command, in order to reduce its size as much as possible. Each reference (native) benchmark was compiled and stripped as the corresponding compressed version. Profile information was collected using an IBM profiling tool, called FDPR [18]. The control flow graphs were generated from the FDPR output. The code of every compressed region in the executable file (Step 2 of the preparation phase) was obtained using the 'objdump' shell command. Execution times and memory usage data were measured on a 200 MHz Power604 processor machine (RISC architecture), in 32 bit mode (that is similar to many modern embedded processors), running AIX version 5.1, with 512 MB of main memory, 32KB primary data cache and 32KB primary instruction cache.

The thresholds were set as follows: θ_R was set to 400 bytes and θ_O to 2%; namely, a region selected for compression must reduce at least 400 bytes of its native size and must not slowdown the whole program's execution time (on real datasets) by more than 2%. These threshold values were chosen following preliminary experiments and analysis of the tradeoff between the size reduction and the run-time overhead yielded by our decompression engine on different input sizes. We found that relatively large compressible regions can significantly contribute to the overall size reduction, whereas their impact on the overall run-time overhead may be small. Small regions can hardly contribute to the overall size reduction, whereas their impact on the overall run-time overhead may be quite significant. Often, for a relatively small source file function, the potential of code reduction was less than θ_R, and hence, no compressible region was selected for compression.

Execution time of each benchmark was calculated as the average of 10 consecutive runs. The code size of each benchmark generated by our scheme includes the executable file produced in Step 3 of the preparation phase along with its compressed binary units.

3.1 Storage Consumption

Table 3 lists the size reductions (in bytes) and the compression rates achieved by our scheme. The second column lists the size of each benchmark used as input to the

Table 3. Benchmarks and sizes of binary units

Benchmark	Code Size	Binary Units Size	Binary Units Compressed Size	Compression Ratio
adpcm_dec	4041	596	296	0.50
adpcm_enc	4049	788	348	0.56
epic_dec	25132	9700	1395	0.86
epic_enc	30588	8172	2019	0.75
gsm_dec	64801	16988	4304	0.75
gsm_enc	64801	16988	4304	0.75
pegwit_dec	65779	22336	2965	0.87
pegwit_enc	65779	22336	2965	0.87
181.mcf	16375	5608	2086	0.63
177.messa	675084	68112	14214	0.79

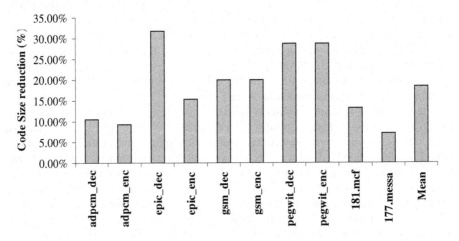

Fig. 4. Code size reduction

analysis phase. The third column lists the total size of the binary units before compression (after Step 4 of the preparation phase). The fourth column lists the total size of the compressed binary units. The fifth column lists the compression ratio achieved. The compression ratios emphasize the efficiency of the compression technique used in the scheme and the potential for saving storage space.

Figure 4 shows the percentage of code size reduction. The reduction ranges from 7.2% (177.messa) to 31.7% (epic_dec), with an average of 18.5%.

3.2 Run-Time Performance

Figure 5 shows the run-time overhead incurred by our proposed scheme. The range of the run-time overhead is from -1.6% (177.messa) to 16.2% (pegwit_dec), with an average of 7.8% slowdown. In 177.messa the same code regions were executed both in the training and the real datasets. Thus, the acceleration in 177.messa can be explained by the reorganization of the final executable, as created by our scheme; this is reflected in better cache utilization and less page faults at run- time. Note that in SoC embedded architectures [16], fetch time is reduced due to the reduction in size of the compressed binary units on storage space.

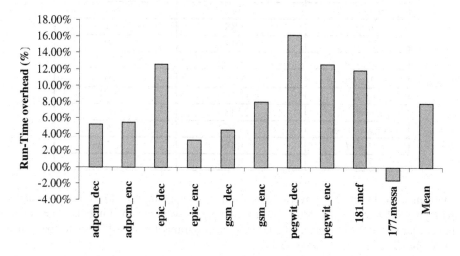

Fig. 5. Run-time overhead

3.3 Memory Requirement

In other software schemes [5], [7], all the compressed code fragments are combined together or are combined with the uncompressed code; whereas, in our scheme, each compressed unit is a stand-alone binary file known only to the decompression engine. As a result, there is an opportunity to cut down on memory usage at run-time. This can happen when a single compressed unit is loaded into memory only when needed, and not because of a load of another compressed unit or some uncompressed code. Widened memory architectures [4] may implement such a loading model. Following this observation, and since the run-time buffer can be allocated and grow dynamically, we compute the memory requirements of a program at runtime to include: (i) the sum (in bytes) of the program's uncompressed instructions; (ii) the size of the dynamic buffer that it needs for execution (decompressed code), and (iii) the total size of the compressed binary units it executes (these are loaded into memory prior to decompression). The decompression engine can be part of the system's OS or the system's run-time environment. Thus, the decompression engine is not considered in the memory consumption calculation. Still, we add to the calculation the memory used for tracing the program's binary units, e.g., the units table entries.

Table 4 lists the memory usage overhead incurred by our scheme. The second column lists the dynamic buffer size (in bytes) needed for execution. The third column lists the memory usage overhead (percentage) incurred by our scheme relative to the memory usage of the native benchmark.

Table 4. Benchmarks and sizes of dynamic run-time buffer

Benchmark	Dynamic Run-Time Buffer Size	Memory Usage Overhead
adpcm_dec	596	4.2
adpcm_enc	788	10.2
epic_dec	9700	6.9
epic_enc	8172	11.2
gsm_dec	5472	-16.3
gsm_enc	16580	4.7
pegwit_dec	22336	5.2
pegwit_enc	17752	-2.5
181.mcf	5608	22.1
177.messa	9032	-7.6

The range of the memory overhead is from -16.3% (gsm_dec) to 22.1% (181.mcf), with an average of 3.8%. Memory usage reductions were obtained in benchmarks that have a large number of binary units. In such programs the possibilities to load only the required binary unites are greater.

4 Related Work

Compression techniques using hardware methods have been proposed to reduce the size of executable programs. A MIPS processor, "Code Compressed RISC Processor," has been developed [2], [8], [25] to decompress Huffman encoded instruction cache lines. Some simple compression methods based on dictionaries [1], in which instructions are replaced by indexes into a table have been proposed [27]. More complex dictionary methods, such as arithmetic coding, have been examined [11], [12]. IBM uses a Huffman based dictionary compression scheme in PowerPC microprocessors [6]. Other dictionary methods are based on mini-subroutines [9], [15]. Profile driven code compression in combination with Pre-cache architecture is presented in [26].

Software-based code compression techniques are not new [5], [7], [10], [20]. Lefurgy et al., [10] proposed using the instruction cache as a decompression buffer. Their scheme works at the granularity of cache lines. On a cache miss, compressed instructions are read from the main memory, decompressed, and placed in the cache. Although their compression scheme is software-based, it requires two modifications to the instruction set architecture: changing the instructions to raise an exception on a cache miss and adding an instruction to modify the contents of the cache. In their scheme, only instructions that are likely to be executed are decompressed, yet the high interrupt latency resulting from invoking the decompression per cache miss may significantly slow down the system's performance. Shogan et al., [20] proposed combining code compression as part of a Software Dynamic Translation (SDT) system. Their technique is targeted at SDT systems and thus operates on the same granularity as SDT systems. Debray et al. [5] proposed the use of profiling to identify cold regions to be packed and compressed into single units. As opposed to our scheme, these units have multiple entry and exit points that may incur additional overhead, yet, they enable additional compression options. Their compressed units are decompressed at run-time through a function call into a run-time buffer that can hold no more than one unit at any given time. Thus, a compressed unit may be decompressed many times. Consequently, non-cold code can eventually increase the execution time dramatically. Kirovski et al [7] proposed a software-managed scheme, in which whole procedures are compressed individually and decompressed procedures are cached in a dedicated portion of the RAM as complete units. This procedure cache must be large enough to hold the largest procedure and support defragmentation if there is not enough space for a new decompressed procedure, or invoke procedure eviction if necessary. They use LZRW1 [23], an adaptive Ziv-Lempel algorithm for compression. In contrast to the latter two approaches, our scheme considers the code size reduction and the time overhead that can be obtained prior to selecting a code for compression. In this way, our scheme maximizes the code size reduction obtained, while at the same time maintaining a reasonable run-time overhead. Our scheme also does not incur significant run-time buffer management overhead, since most of the compressed units are decompressed once, except for extreme cases. Moreover, in our experiments, none of the compressed units were decompressed more than once.

Power Consumption. Some factors may influence the power consumption in embedded systems. Benini et al. [3] proposed a method for compressing code in order to decrease the power requirements of memory access code. This causes reduction in the power consumption resulting from accessing external (either a ROM or a FLASH) memory chip. The reduction is carried out by encoding the most frequently executed instructions of a program with 8-bit patterns (and store them in memory), instead of the original (32-bit) instructions; in this way, the utilization of the width of the instruction bus is improved, and so is the power required to execute the program.

The authors of [13] proposed an approximate arithmetic coding and a fast table-based decoding. Since the power consumed on the bus is proportional to the number of bit toggles on the bus, this coding scheme minimizes the number of bit toggles in external buses, in order to reduce the power consumption. The formulas for estimating the power costs of the system are based on bus capacitances, voltage differences, and the bit toggle count. They explore the trade-offs between compression ratios and bus-related power consumption and show that high compression ratios do not necessarily result in lowest power consumption.

Lekatsas et al. [14] proposed to use a code compression scheme as an efficient method for reducing power consumption on embedded systems with complete SOC, which consists of a CPU, separate instruction and data caches, and a main memory along with data and address buses. The main contribution of the scheme is a new architecture for decompressing instructions, which places the decompressor between the cache and the CPU, rather than between the memory and cache (the usual approach). By doing so, both of the data-buses, before and after the cache, profit from the compressed instruction code, since the instructions are only decompressed before they are fed into the CPU. They measured the overall power savings, and showed that the contribution depends on various system parameters (e.g., I-cache size) as well as on the characteristics of the tested applications.

When introducing a compression scheme the number of executed instructions increases and so is the power consumption. As a result, it is important to trade off this overhead with the power saved by reducing bus access to external memory (saved by the compression). Such a tradeoff can be integrated with our scheme if the profiler would have additional data on memory access (bus utilization) and an embedded system would be used for running the experiments.

5   Conclusions and Future Work

We have presented a software-based scheme that, without any special hardware, uses profiling for directing code compression. We proposed a unique scheme for selecting code regions that may significantly reduce the code size, when compressed, and yet incur a reasonable run-time overhead when decompressed.

We have shown the benefit of the scheme for compressing cold and non-cold code. Experimental results show that our scheme significantly reduces the footprint of binaries in storage, along with reasonable run-time and memory usage overheads. Moreover, our scheme can improve performance when main memory latency is high, thus it may reduce energy consumption in architectures that utilize flash main memory.

Our work can be enhanced further by adding an empirical power model into the constraint set and trading off time, space, and energy consumption when exploring the different compression options.

References

1. Bell T., Cleary J. and Witten I. (1990) 'Text compression', *Prentice Hall*.
2. Benes M., Nowick S.M. and Wolfe A. (1998) 'A Fast Asynchronous Huffman Decoder for Compressed-Code Embedded Processors', *Proceedings of the International Symposium on Advanced Research in Asynchronous Circuits and System*, March, pp. 43-57.

3. Benini L., Macii, A., Macii, E. and Poncino M. (1999) 'Selective instruction compression for memory energy reduction in embedded systems', *Proceedings of the International Symposium on Low Power Electronics and Design*, August, pp. 206–211.

4. Benini L., Macii A. and Poncino M. (2003) 'Energy-Aware Design of Embedded Memories: A Survey of Technologies, Architectures, and Optimization Techniques', *ACM Transactions on Embedded Computing Systems (TECS)*, Volume 2, Issue 1, February, pp. 5 – 32.

5. Debray S. and Evans W. (2002) 'Profile-Guided Code Compression', *Proceedings of the conference on Programming Language Design and Implementation*, June, pp. 95-105.

6. Game M. and Booker A. (1999) 'CodePack: Code Compression for PowerPC Processors', *MicroNews 5(1)*, IBM.

7. Kirovski D., Kin J. and Mangion-Smith W.H. (1997) 'Procedure Based Program Compression', *Proceedings of the International Symposium on Microarchitecture*, December, pp. 204-217.

8. Kozuch M. and Wolfe A. (1994) 'Compression of Embedded Systems Programs', *Proceedings of the IEEE International Conference on Computer Design: VLSI in Computer & Processors*, October, pp. 270-277.

9. Lefurgy C., Bird P., Chen I.-C. and Mudge T. (1997) 'Improving Code Density Using Compression Techniques', *Proceedings of the International Symposium on Microarchitecture*, December, pp. 194-203.

10. Lefurgy C., Piccininni E. and Mudge T. (2000) 'Reducing Code Size with Run-time Decompression', *Proceedings of the International Symposium on High Performance Computer Architecture*, January, pp. 218.

11. Lekatsas H. and Wolf W. (1998) 'Code Compression for embedded Systems', *Proceedings of the Conference on Design Automation*, June, pp. 516-521.

12. Lekatsas H. and Wolf W. (1999) 'Random Access Decompression using Binary Arithmetic Coding', *Proceedings of IEEE Data Compression Conference*, March, pp. 306-315.

13. Lekatsas H., Henkel J. and Wolf W. (2000) 'Arithmetic coding for low power embedded system design', *Proceedings of the Conference on Data Compression*, March, p. 430.

14. Lekatsas H., Henkel J. and Wolf W. (2000a) 'Code compression for low power embedded system design', *Proceedings of Design Automation Conference*, June, pp. 294-299.

15. Liao S., Devadas S. and Keutzer K. (1995) 'Code Density Optimization for Embedded DSP Processors Using Data Compression Techniques', *Proceedings of the Conference on Advanced Research in VLSI*, March, pp. 272-285.

16. Lyons W. (2005) 'Meeting the Embedded Design Needs of Automotive Applications', *Proceedings of the conference on Design, Automation and Test in Europe*, March, pp. 142-147.

17. MediaBench (1997), http://cares.icsl.ucla.edu/mediabench.

18. Nahshon I. and Bernstein D. (1996) 'FDPR - A Post-Pass Object Code Optimization Tool', *Proceedings of the Poster Session of the International Conference on Compiler Construction*, April, pp. 97-104.

19. Nelson M. (2004) 'DataCompression.info', http://datacompression.info/.

20. Shogan S. and Childers B.R. (2004) 'Compact Binaries with Code Compression in a Software Dynamic Translator', *Proceedings of the conference on Design, Automation and Test in Europe*, February, pp. 1052-1057.

21. SPEC CPU2000 (2000), http://www.spec.org/cpu2000/.

22. Timmermans M. (2000) 'BICOM BIjective COMpressor', http://www3.sympatico.ca/mt0000/bicom/.

23. Williams R.N. (1991) 'An Extremely Fast Ziv-Lempel Data Compression Algorithm', *Proceedings of the IEEE Data Compression Conference*, April, pp. 362-371.

24. Waldman I., Pinter S. (2006) 'Profile-driven Compression Scheme for Embedded Systems', *Proceedings of the Conference on Computing Frontiers,* May, pp. 95-103.

25. Wolfe A. and Chanin A. (1992) 'Executing Compressed Programs on an Embedded RISC Architecture', *Proceedings of the International Symposium on Microarchitecture*, December, pp. 81-91.

26. Xie Y., Wolf W. and Lekatsas H. (2003) 'Profile-Driven Selective Code Compression', *Proceedings of the conf. on Design, Automation and Test in Europe*, March, pp. 462-467.

27. Yoshida Y., Song B.-Y., Okuhata H., Onoye T. and Shirakawa I. (1997) 'An Object Code Compression Approach to Embedded Processors', *International Symposium on Low-Power Electronics and Design*, August, pp. 265-268.

A Prefetching Algorithm for Multi-speed Disks[*]

Seung Woo Son and Mahmut Kandemir

Department of Computer Science and Engineering
The Pennsylvania State University, University Park, PA 16802, USA
{sson,kandemir}@cse.psu.edu

Abstract. Power consumption of disk based storage systems is becoming an increasingly pressing issue for both the commercial and the scientific application domains. Prior work proposed several hardware based approaches to reducing disk power consumption by making use of techniques such as spinning down idle disks and rotating them at lower speeds than the maximum speed possible. While such techniques are certainly very important, it is also critical to consider the influence the software can exercise in shaping the power consumption of disk-intensive application programs. Motivated by this observation, the main goal of this work is to study whether an optimizing compiler can be used for increasing the power benefits that could be obtained from multi-speed disks. Specifically, we propose and experimentally evaluate a compiler-directed energy-aware data prefetching scheme for scientific applications that process disk-resident data sets. This scheme automatically determines the prefetch distances for all disk access instructions, the disk speeds to be employed, and the associated disk layouts (striping parameters) in a unified setting. We implemented the proposed approach within an optimizing compiler framework and conducted experiments with several disk-intensive applications. Our experimental evaluation shows that the proposed approach brings significant reductions in disk energy consumption over a state-of-the-art software-based I/O prefetching mechanism that does not take into account energy consumption explicitly. Our results also show that the energy-aware prefetching scheme does not bring any extra performance penalties and the energy reductions achieved are consistent across a wide spectrum of values of the simulation parameters. We also show that our scheme can be extended to multiple application scenarios using a hierarchical disk layout determination.

1 Introduction

High power consumption is one of the most pressing issues for computing platforms that target large-scale data-intensive applications [7,6,12,13]. While most of the recent research efforts on minimizing power consumption have been performed in the CPU, network, and memory domains, the research on disk power

---

[*] This work is supported in part by NSF grants #0444158 and #0406340, and a grant from the GSRC. This paper extends the Computing Frontiers 2006 paper [26], by explaining how our approach can be extended to handle multiple application scenario and evaluating it.

P. Stenström (Ed.): Transactions on HiPEAC I, LNCS 4050, pp. 317–340, 2007.

optimization is still in its infancy. A couple of recent papers (e.g., providing multi-speed setting for server disks [5,14], power-aware storage cache management schemes [33,34], and compiler-guided disk power management schemes [25]) have focused exclusively on disk power consumption and proposed hardware and software based solutions to the problem. Most of these papers estimate and/or control disk power consumption or present static/dynamic code/data reorganizations for maximizing power savings that could be obtained from the low-power operating modes supported by the disk system.

While conventional disk power optimization approach [11,10,18] based on spinning down idle disks has been successful in the past in the context of laptop disks, it is not the best option for server disks and scientific workloads that exhibit very short idle disk periods. Therefore, one of the prior proposals [5,14] to disk power saving in high-performance systems has been to employ disks with the capability of changing their rotational speeds dynamically. Since such multi-speed disks (e.g., those from [19] and [31]) can serve requests even under low rotational speeds, they can potentially exploit short idle periods as well and, at the same time, save power (due to reduced speed). However, the question of whether one can increase the power savings that could be achieved through such multi-speed disks remains important and largely unexplored. In particular, the role of the software-level optimizations for utilizing such multi-speed disks in the most effective way needs to be investigated.

The main goal of this paper is to demonstrate that compiler-directed rescheduling of disk access instructions in scientific applications can be very effective in practice and can increase power savings obtained from multi-speed disks significantly. The specific strategy proposed and evaluated in this work *hoists* the disk access instructions in the program code to increase the time-gap between the issue of the instruction and the actual access to the disk. In this way, the hoisted instruction can use a disk that operates with a lower speed than the maximum available one. More specifically, the approach proposed in this paper determines the most suitable prefetch distance for each array reference in the application code, the disk speeds (RPM levels) for all the disks in the storage system, and the data layouts for the disk-resident arrays in a unified setting. Note that since our goal is to issue prefetches to the disks that rotate at lower speeds, our prefetch distances are larger than those normally used in conventional I/O prefetching.

We implemented the proposed approach within a research compiler [15] and conducted experiments with four different data-intensive applications that process disk-resident datasets. The results from our experiments indicate that the proposed energy-aware I/O prefetching approach reduces disk energy consumption over a state-of-the-art, energy-agnostic I/O prefetching scheme by 19.6% on average, without hurting the performance of the latter. Our experimental results also show that the achieved disk energy savings are consistent across a wide range of values of the major simulation parameters, and that our approach introduces very little (less than 1%) performance overhead, as compared to the conventional I/O prefetching. We also show that our scheme can be applied to multiple application execution scenarios using a hierarchical disk layout determination.

The remainder of this paper is structured as follows. The next section discusses the related work on disk power optimization. Sect. 3 gives a high level view of the storage system under consideration and defines the technical concepts frequently used in this paper. Sect. 4 gives an example to demonstrate the benefits of the proposed approach. Sect. 5 explains the technical details of our approach. An experimental evaluation of our approach and its quantitative comparison against the prior work are presented in Sect. 6. Sect. 7 presents an experimental evaluation under the multiple application scenario. Finally, the paper is concluded by a summary and a brief discussion of the planned future work in Sect. 8.

2   Related Work

Most of the prior studies on reducing disk power/energy consumption make use of observed idle times during program execution. To exploit disk idle periods, the disk drive itself needs to provide a low-power operating mode, either in the form of completely stopping disk rotation (spinning down) or in the form of dynamically adjusting the rotational speed. Providing low-power modes is important, because even if a disk is idle it consumes almost as much energy as it would consume in the active (fully operational) mode [14,17]. For the laptop/desktop domain where the applications typically exhibit long idle periods, several studies have already considered techniques such as spinning down idle disks by using a fixed threshold period (i.e., the time to wait before spinning down a disk) or by estimating the threshold period adaptively [10,11,18].

Once the disk is equipped with some sort of low-power operating mode, we can make use of these modes within an operating system (OS) or at an application level by increasing the duration of idle periods so that a given disk can be placed into low-power modes for longer durations of time. Among the efforts focusing on the OS layer, Zhu et al. [33] and Papathanasiou et al. [20] consider power-aware caching and prefetching strategies. The rationale behind both these studies is that conventional I/O caching and I/O prefetching techniques, which mainly focus on the performance angle, can hardly produce any long idle periods. Rather than spreading disk accesses across the entire execution period, energy-efficient prefetching generates burst disk access patterns, which is preferable from the energy perspective. The enlarged idle periods in turn allow a disk to be placed into one of the supported low-power operating modes.

Zhu et al. [33] also study a power-aware cache replacement algorithm, called PA-LRU, in the context of large storage systems, which are typically equipped with several GBs of aggregated cache memory. The main idea behind their approach is to selectively maintain cache blocks from certain disks, so that the remaining disks can stay in low-power modes for a longer period of time. In another paper, Zhu et al. [34] propose a different approach, called PB-LRU (Partition-Based LRU), to the same problem. PB-LRU explores various cache replacement techniques in the context of disk arrays equipped with multi-speed disks. Lastly, Zhu et al. [32] recently proposed a holistic disk power management technique, called Hibernator, that combines three major techniques: dynamic disk speed setting, multi-tier data layout, and data reorganization. Since frequent modulations of disk speeds might decrease disk reliability, their idea is to adjust disk speed at a coarse granularity. To guarantee the specified response time limit, Hibernator keeps track of average response time dynamically. If the specified response time guarantee is at risk, Hibernator restores the speeds of all disks to full speed.

Several studies investigated the problem of disk power management at the application/compiler level. For example, Heath et al. [16] studied an application code transformation technique for energy-aware device management by generating I/O burstiness in laptop disks. More recently, Son et al. proposed several compiler-based code transformation techniques to conserve disk energy consumption. First, they studied a compiler technique that inserts explicit disk power management calls in sources codes of scientific applications [25]. The idea is that a compiler can extract information on how disks are traversed during execution time using the application source code along with the file level striping information. By inserting explicit power management calls, e.g., spin_up and spin_down, in the application code, one can eliminate (to a large extent) the performance penalty that would normally be incurred by reactive disk power management schemes. Second, they revisited conventional loop distribution and iteration space tiling techniques from an energy perspective. To achieve the best energy savings without slowing down performance much, they showed that both code and underlying disk layout must be considered at the same time. In another paper [24], the same authors described a compiler approach to reducing disk power consumption in the presence of parallel disk systems. To increase disk idleness, the proposed technique schedules the code fragments assigned to a number of processors according to the disk access patterns extracted by an optimizing compiler, which captures both intra- and inter-processor disk reuses.

Since large data centers host huge amounts of data for several application domains, they typically exhibit locality at a disk partition level or a file level. This means that, in a given time period, not all the disks participate in servicing I/O requests. Observing this, MAID (Massive Arrays of Idle Disks) [9] was proposed to reduce disk energy consumption using a small number of disks as cache drives, thereby potentially reducing the number of spin-ups for disks. While cache drives service the requests to the disk array, other unused disk drives can be placed into the low-power modes. Pinheiro et al. [21], on the other hand, proposed a data migration technique called PDC (Popular Data Concentration). The main idea behind this scheme is to dynamically move the most frequently-accessed disk data to a subset of the disks in the array, thereby increasing the idle periods for the remaining disks in the system. PDC is a feasible solution for network servers because workloads processed by such systems are heavily skewed towards a small set of files. Techniques such as MAID and PDC manipulate data at a file system granularity, therefore, at least one day is required to collect the file access patterns and adjust the file layouts according to the gathered information.

The approach proposed in this paper is different from all pure hardware based disk power management schemes since it is compiler based. It is also different from the prior compiler based studies in that, it minimizes disk energy consumption through code hoisting (energy-aware prefetching), instead of linear code transformations. In addition, as against studies such as [33], our approach determines the prefetching distance, disk speeds, and data layouts in a unified setting. However, we also want to mention that the approach proposed in this paper can also be used in conjunction with prior compiler-directed code modification schemes such as [24] for reducing disk power consumption even further. Finally, in contrast to the previous studies that target multi-speed disks, our approach determines disk speeds statically for each application at compile-time. Therefore, it has practically no impact on reliability due to the frequent modulation in disk speed at run-time.

3   High Level View of Storage System

The storage system considered in this work is shown in Fig. 1 at a high level. Our focus is on large, data-intensive scientific applications that manipulate disk-resident, multi-dimensional arrays. The disk requests in this architecture are directed to I/O nodes over which the array files are striped. Within each I/O node, a stripe assigned to that I/O node is further striped at the RAID level (depending on the specific RAID implementation [8] adopted). Therefore, as depicted in Fig. 1, each data array in our storage architecture is striped at *two different levels* (I/O node level and RAID level). While the RAID level striping is

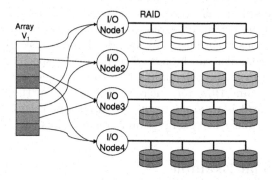

Fig. 1. Two-level striping of array data across disks

hidden from the software, the I/O node level striping is visible to the software (to the compiler in our case) and can be controlled through calls from the underlying I/O library and/or the parallel file system used. For example, in PVFS [4,23], one can manipulate the I/O node level striping information of files by changing the pvfs_filestat structure, which includes the stripe unit and the number of disks used for striping.

In this paper, we determine rotational speeds of disks and data layouts of arrays at an I/O node granularity. That is, when we set the speed of a particular

I/O node, it means setting the speed of all the disks controlled by that I/O node. However, for the ease of discussion, we use the term "disk" instead of "I/O node" when we explain our approach below. The "disk layout" concept used in the rest of this paper refers to the I/O node level striping; i.e., when we mention "striping", we mean the striping at the I/O node level. In our experimental evaluation, we assume a one-to-one mapping between data arrays and files. In other words, we assume that each data array is stored in a single file and a file contains only a single array. Under this assumption, one can talk about "striping an array over the I/O nodes." While we can easily relax this assumption by allowing one-to-many and many-to-one mappings between the disk files and the data arrays, we do not evaluate these options in this paper.

The proposed compiler-directed approach operates under two assumptions. The first assumption is that the I/O node level striping can be accessed and controlled by the compiler. This is possible because current parallel file systems and run-time libraries (e.g., PVFS [4,23]) provide API calls that enable this. Our second assumption is that the disk system is exercised by a single application at a time or multiple applications simultaneously but, in the latter, each application runs in a different machine (of course, the different applications can use the same system at different times). In our approach, the compiler can manage/control the disk power consumption by inserting prefetching instructions to array data, which are stored in multi-speed disks. Since storing array data in a low-speed disk does *not* destroy the data itself, our approach will *not* create a correctness issue if the second assumption fails. However, if the disk speeds determined when considering one application are not appropriate for the other concurrently-executing applications, our energy savings might be reduced and we can incur I/O performance degradations unless we tune the disk speed for the other applications accordingly. We believe that the disk usage information extracted by our compiler can be passed to the OS at specific program points, and the OS in turn can use this information to implement a global disk power management algorithm. However, such extensions are not the focus of this paper. Our goal instead is to evaluate the potential power savings from a single application's viewpoint when energy-aware prefetching is employed.

4   Motivational Example

In this section, we demonstrate how our approach can reduce disk energy consumption by hiding latencies of low-speed disks using the example code fragment shown in Fig. 2(a). The code fragment given in this figure accesses a two-dimensional disk-resident array, named V_1, using a loop nest constructed from two loops. For illustrative purposes, V_1 is assumed to be striped over 4 disks with a stripe size of S (see Fig. 2(b)) and all four disks in question are assumed to be running at 12,000 RPMs. As depicted in Fig. 3(a), if we do not apply any prefetching, every access to the first data element in each block incurs an access (R_i) to the disk system. In this example, we assume that it takes T_d cycles to complete a disk access when the rotational speed of disks is 12,000

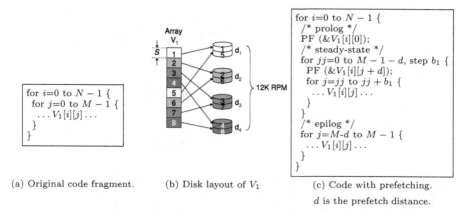

(a) Original code fragment.   (b) Disk layout of V_1 (c) Code with prefetching.

d is the prefetch distance.

Fig. 2. An example application of prefetching

RPM. After T_d cycles elapse, the requested data block is ready (D_i) and thus the computation on that block can proceed.

Since our approach targets at scientific benchmarks whose access patterns can be extracted and reshaped by an optimizing compiler, we can use the software prefetching algorithm proposed by Brown et al. [2] to hide disk I/O stall time and reduce overall execution latency. The code fragment after applying I/O prefetching is given in Fig. 2(c). Software prefetching generates a prolog, a steady-state, and an epilog from each original loop nest. The prefetch distance (d), i.e., the number of iterations ahead of which the disk I/O needs to be initiated to hide I/O latency, can be calculated as:

$$d = \lceil \frac{T_d}{s + T_{pf}} \rceil, \tag{1}$$

where T_d is the estimated I/O latency (in cycles) to prefetch one block, T_{pf} is the overhead (again in terms of cycles) of executing a prefetch instruction, and s is the number of cycles in the shortest path through the loop body. Once the prefetch distance, d, is calculated, we then stripe-mine the loop nest to make explicit the point at which the prefetch instruction is to be inserted. The result of this transformation for our example is given in Fig. 2(c). In this example, d iterations of j loop are assumed to be required to hide I/O latency and $b1$ is the strip size used for strip-mining.

Up to this point, we have discussed software prefetching as a technique that can be used to hide disk I/O latency, specifically hiding T_d, as proposed in the literature. However, if we examine the components of disk I/O time, we can see that T_d is composed of seek time, rotational latency, transfer time, and controller overhead. Since in modern disk drives the controller overhead is negligible compared to other three values, we can see that T_d is almost directly proportional to the disk rotation speed. However, it has been shown by prior research that the disk power consumption is quadratically proportional to the disk rotational speed [14]. This suggests that one can take an approach to conserve disk energy

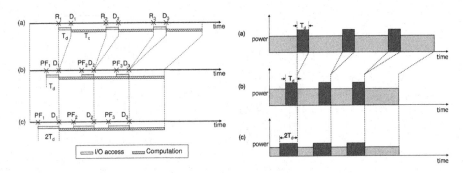

Fig. 3. Comparison of I/O timings. (a) Original code without prefetching. (b) Prefetching to high-speed disks. (c) Prefetching to low-speed disks. T_d is the disk I/O time for a single block data.

Fig. 4. Comparison of disk power states. (a) Original code without prefetching. (b) Prefetching to high-speed disks. (c) Prefetching to low-speed disks. T_d is the disk I/O time for a single block data.

by storing array data in low-speed disks, e.g., a disk running at lower than 12,000 RPM (in this example), and by eliminating the increased I/O latency using software prefetching with an increased prefetch distance. That is, one can save disk energy by increasing prefetch distance and reducing disk speed at the same time.

Fig. 3 and Fig. 4 show how prefetching to high-speed disks and low-speed disks affects I/O timing and disk power consumption. In this example, the rotational speed of the low-speed disks is assumed to be 6,000 RPM (i.e., half of the maximum speed possible). Consequently, the time it takes to complete a disk access is doubled, i.e., it is now $2T_d$. One can see from Figs. 3(b) and (c) that we can hide the latency of low-speed disks by issuing the prefetch early enough. Specifically, since the I/O latency is doubled from T_d to $2T_d$, the prefetch distance (d) is also doubled based on (1) given above. On the other hand, the energy consumption profiles after applying prefetching with different prefetch distances are depicted in Fig. 4. Fig. 4(a) shows the power profile throughout the program execution time when no prefetching is employed. Note that we assume the disk drive can be placed in either active mode when servicing I/O request or idle mode when the disk is not used. Therefore, the disk is in the active mode during T_d when there is a request being processed. For the remaining time, the disk is placed into the idle mode. Figs. 4(b) and (c) show how the prefetching affects the power consumption profile of a disk. If we apply prefetching using high-speed disks, we can conserve disk energy consumption by the amount of reduced execution time. In this case, the energy savings come from the reductions in the total disk idle time. In comparison, as shown in Fig. 4(c), if the data is stored in low-speed disks and we apply prefetching, we can reduce disk energy consumption further by cutting the energy consumption in the active and idle periods as well.

It should be noted that we may not be able to take advantage of low-speed disks for all disk-resident arrays due to following reasons: As mentioned earlier in this section, using low-speed disks entails longer prefetch distances, which may not be very appropriate for a loop nest whose iteration count is not sufficient for hiding such a long I/O latency. Therefore, one needs to be careful when selecting the disk speeds to employ. Furthermore, since we focus on large scientific programs that consist of multiple loop nests, it is possible that the determined disk speed for a particular array in one loop nest may not be appropriate for another loop nest that manipulates the same array (by accessing the same set of disks). Consequently, selecting prefetching distance and disk speeds depends on the disk layout of data as well as the data access patterns exhibited by the application code being optimized. Because of this, these parameters should be considered together.

5   Compiler Algorithm

In this section, we discuss the details of our compiler algorithm for energy-aware prefetching that determines prefetch distance, disk speeds, and data layouts on disks (I/O nodes).

5.1   Basics

Before describing the algorithm, let us first define a few important mathematical concepts. In our framework, an array based, loop-intensive program $\mathcal{P}$ that consists of s loop nests is represented as:

$$\mathcal{P} = (\mathcal{L}_1, \mathcal{L}_2, \ldots, \mathcal{L}_s),$$

where $\mathcal{L}_i (i = 1, 2, \ldots, s)$ is the ith loop nest in program $\mathcal{P}$. We further assume that a loop nest $\mathcal{L}_i$ of the following form:[1]

$$\mathcal{L}_i: \text{for } i_1 = l_1 \text{ to } u_1, \text{ step } b_1$$
$$\text{for } i_2 = l_2 \text{ to } u_2, \text{ step } b_2$$
$$\cdots$$
$$\text{for } i_k = l_k \text{ to } u_k, \text{ step } b_k$$
$$\{\text{loop body}\}$$

can be represented as:

$$\mathcal{L}_i = \text{for } \boldsymbol{I} \in [\boldsymbol{L}_i, \boldsymbol{U}_i], \text{ step } \boldsymbol{b} \ \langle a_1(\boldsymbol{I}), a_2(\boldsymbol{I}), \ldots, a_m(\boldsymbol{I}) \rangle,$$

where $\boldsymbol{I}$ is the iteration vector, and $\boldsymbol{L} = (l_1, l_2, \ldots, l_k)^T$ and $\boldsymbol{U} = (u_1, u_2, \ldots, u_k)^T$ are the lower and upper bound vectors, $\boldsymbol{b} = (b_1, b_2, \ldots, b_k)^T$ is the loop step vector, and $a_j(\boldsymbol{I})$ $(j = 1, 2, \ldots, m)$ is the jth array reference in the body of loop nest $\mathcal{L}_i$. While executing, loop nest $\mathcal{L}_i$ is assumed to access n arrays, V_1, V_2, $\ldots$, V_n. We use $\mathcal{V}$ to represent a set comprised of these n arrays. The array element accessed by $a_j(\boldsymbol{I})$ $(j = 1, 2, \ldots, m)$ can be represented as $V_i[\boldsymbol{F}(\boldsymbol{I})]$ $(i =$

---

[1] If $\mathcal{L}_i$ is not perfectly nested, one can use techniques such as code sinking [30] to make it perfectly nested.

$1, 2, \ldots, n$, $j = 1, 2, \ldots, m$), where V_i is the name of the array and function $\boldsymbol{F}$ maps iteration vector $\boldsymbol{I}$ to a vector of subscripts for array V_i. Specifically, $\boldsymbol{F}(\boldsymbol{I})$, which maps k loop iterators into d array indices, where k is the depth of the loop nest and d is the dimensionality of the array, can be defined as:

$$\boldsymbol{F}(\boldsymbol{I}) = M\boldsymbol{I} + \boldsymbol{o},$$

where M is a $d \times k$ matrix (called the access matrix), $\boldsymbol{I}$ is a k-element iteration vector, and $\boldsymbol{o}$ is an offset vector [29].

We also assume that the multi-speed disks considered in this work provide l different rotational speeds: $RPM = (1, 2, \ldots, l)$, where 1 represents the lowest disk speed and l corresponds to the highest disk speed available.

Lastly, we define the disk-layout for each array (V_i) using a triplet of the following form:

$$(start\_disk, stripe\_factor, stripe\_size),$$

where start_disk is the first disk where the file striping starts from, stripe_factor is the number of disks being used for striping, and stripe_size is the unit size of each file stripe residing on each disk. For example, the layout of array V_1 in Fig. 2(b) can be represented as (d1, 4, S). The compiler approach described in the next section determines a prefetch distance for each array access in the application code, a rotational speed for each disk in the storage system, and a data layout for each disk-resident array manipulated by the application.

5.2 Energy-Aware Prefetching

To exploit low-speed disks using prefetching in order to save energy, our prefetching algorithm needs to analyze the data locality exhibited by each loop nest $\mathcal{L}_i$ in program $\mathcal{P}$. Given the mathematical representation discussed in Sect. 5.1, temporal reuse is said to occur between two loop iterations $\boldsymbol{I}_1$ and $\boldsymbol{I}_2$ whenever $\boldsymbol{F}(\boldsymbol{I}_1) - \boldsymbol{F}(\boldsymbol{I}_2) = \boldsymbol{0}$. That is, temporal reuse occurs whenever the difference between the two loop iterations lies in the nullspace of $M(\boldsymbol{r}) = \boldsymbol{0}$, i.e., $span(M)$. Spatial reuse, on the other hand, is said to occur when two different loop iterations access the same row (in a given array) [29]. To extract the spatial reuse vector space, we simply replace the last row in M with zeros to create a reduced access matrix, M_S, and solve for nullspace of M_S, which gives us $span(M_S)$. After determining the temporal/spatial reuse vector spaces, we next choose the set of innermost loop iterators that can exploit reuse. This is called *localized iteration space* [29]. This space captures only those loops for which data reuse can result in data locality. In our context, to translate the obtained reuses to locality, we need to take into account the loop iteration count and available memory capacity. Since the loop bounds are assumed to be known at the compile time (if not, we make use of available profile data), one can determine the set of innermost loops whose accessed data fit in the main memory capacity. Data locality is then captured by intersecting the reuse vector space with the localized iteration space, where both are represented by vector space notation. These steps to analyze reuse and data locality exhibited in the given programs are fundamentally unaltered from those developed in the context of conventional I/O prefetching [2]. However, to support prefetching to multi-speed disks for reducing disk power consumption, we need to be careful in selecting prefetch distance for every disk-resident array references, as will be discussed in detail below.

Using the obtained vector space representation of data locality exhibited by each loop $\mathcal{L}_i$, our approach next determines prefetch distance (The value of d in (1)) for each array reference $(V_i[\boldsymbol{F}(\boldsymbol{I})]$ made by the loop body of nest $\mathcal{L}_i$. Note that, once d is calculated and reference $V_i[\boldsymbol{F}(\boldsymbol{I})]$ is found to have spatial locality on i^{th} loop, the ith loop is strip-mined, where $1 \leq i \leq k$ and k is the depth of loop nest. Generally, prefetches are software pipelined around this i^{th} loop that changes the value of the array-indexing function $(V_i[\boldsymbol{F}(\boldsymbol{I})])$. This chosen loop is called the *pipeline loop*. As mentioned in the previous section, if we put the data in low-speed disks, the prefetch distance linearly increases with respect to disk I/O time (i.e., the value of T_d in (1)), while power consumption is quadratically reduced by the amount of disk speed scaling [14]. Therefore, we need to tune the prefetch distance based on the disk speed, and in fact, our approach determines them together, as explained below.

In the first step of our energy-aware prefetching algorithm, we determine the disk speeds that will provide the maximum energy savings for each array in the application code. To do this, we process array references in the code one

```
INPUT:
    Input program, P = (L₁, L₂, ..., Lₛ);
    Available disk speeds, RPM = (1, 2, ..., l);
OUTPUT:
    Determined RPM-group(i), where 1 ≤ i ≤ l;

Tₚf = the number of cycles for PF instruction;
for each Vₖ ∈ V // for each array;
    G[Vₖ] = ∅; // possible disk speeds for each array;

// repeat for each loop nest Lᵢ.
for each Lᵢ ∈ P {
    sᵢ = number of cycles need to execute
            the loop body of Lᵢ;
    for j = 1 to l { // for each RPM available
        // repeat for all array reference in Lᵢ
        // assume aᵢ(I) accesses array element Vₖ[F(I)].
        for each array reference aᵢ(I) {
            calculate I/O latency, Td(j), when RPM is j;
            // determine prefetch distance, dⱼ, at jth RPM.
            dⱼ = ⌈ Td(j) / (sᵢ+Tₚf) ⌉;
            if (dⱼ > total number of iterations for the pipeline loop)
                G[Vₖ] = G[Vₖ] ∪ {j};
        }
    }
}

// RPM-group(l) generated by adding
//    maximum value from set G[Vᵢ].
for each array Vᵢ {
    l = {x|x ∈ G[Vᵢ] and MAX(G[Vᵢ])};
    RPM-group(l) = RPM-group(l) ∪ {Vᵢ};
}
```

Fig. 5. Disk speed detection algorithm

by one. In processing an array reference, we consider all possible disk speeds (RPM levels) and select the one that brings the maximum energy savings without performance penalty. It needs to be noted that we may not always select the minimum RPM level for a given array access because there may not be sufficient number of iterations in the loop nest where this array reference appears[2]. Therefore, at the end of this first step of our approach, we determine the preferable disk speed for each array reference. However, if a disk-resident array can be accessed from within multiple loop nests, we set the disk speed for that array to the highest speed among all the preferable speeds for all the references to that array. The algorithm that selects the most suitable disk speeds to be used for each array is given in Fig. 5. The for-each loop in this algorithm goes over the loop nests in the application and the references in them and determines the required disk speed. The for-loop at the end of the algorithm, on the other hand, selects the required RPM level for each array (each V_i). Note that, at the end of this first step, our approach also determines the prefetch distances for all array references, in addition to determining the preferable disk speeds for disk-resident arrays, using the approach explained in the first two paragraphs of this section. To summarize, in the first step, we determine both prefetch distances and preferable disk speeds for arrays.

In the next step of our approach, we determine the disk layouts of the arrays in the application. In order to do this, we first form what we call the *RPM-groups*. An RPM group holds the arrays that require the same RPM level. Each RPM-group is also attached a *weight*, which captures the sum of the number of accesses to the elements of the arrays in that RPM-group. Our approach next determines the number of disks that will be assigned to each RPM-group. We currently perform this by distributing the available disks (actually I/O nodes as mentioned in Sect. 3) across the RPM-groups based on their weights in a proportional manner. More specifically, an RPM-group with a larger weight gets assigned more disks than an RPM-group with a lower weight. The reason is that, by assigning more disks to the RPM-group with larger weight, one can exploit the aggregated bandwidth and parallelism presented by multiple disks better. In other words, assigning more disks to the heavy-weighted RPM-group tends to buy more performance benefits. After an RPM-group is assigned its disks, the arrays in that group are striped over those disks using conventional striping. Note that, at the end of this second step of our approach, we fix the disk layout of all disk-resident arrays in the application. The algorithm for determining the disk layouts of arrays is given in Fig. 6.

The last step of our approach is to restructure the application code in order to insert prefetch instructions. Since the prefetch distances for all array references have already been determined by the first step explained above, the third step uses this information and restructures the application code accordingly

---

[2] An alternate approach would be inserting the prefetch call for a given loop nest in one of the preceding loop nests; but, this makes code generation extremely difficult; so, we did not explore this option further.

```
INPUT:
    Input program, P = (L₁, L₂, ..., Lₛ);
    Determined RPM-group(i), where 1 ≤ i ≤ l;
OUTPUT:
    Determined data layout for each array;

tot_disks = total number of disks available;
init_disk = 0;
weight[Vᵢ]: the number of accesses made to Vᵢ within P;
weight[V]: the number of accesses made to all arrays within P;

// determine stripe_factor for Vᵢ with same disk speed
// based on the sum of weight[Vᵢ] in RPM-group(i).
for i = 1 to l { // for each RPM-group
    for all Vᵢ ∈ RPM-group(i)
        sum += weight[Vᵢ];
    stripe_factor(Vᵢ) = tot_disks × ⌈ sum/weight[V] ⌉;
    tot_disks -= stripe_factor(Vᵢ);
}

// determine start_disk for each array Vᵢ
// based on the determined stripe_factor for each array.
for i = 1 to l {
    start_disk (Vᵢ) = init_disk;
    init_disk += stripe_factor (Vᵢ);
}
```

Fig. 6. Data layout detection algorithm

based on the strip-mining based approach proposed by Brown et al. [2]. Fig. 7 shows the pseudo-code for the algorithm that modifies the application code. The overall view of our approach to energy-aware prefetching is depicted in Fig. 8.

As explained above, our approach determines prefetch distances, data layouts and disk speeds in a unified setting. However, it can also be modified to work with given data layouts and disk speeds. If the data (array) layout and disk speeds are fixed, our hoisting algorithm determines prefetch distance based on existing information and then modifies the code accordingly.

5.3 Example

We now give a more detailed example to show how our algorithm described in Sect. 5.2 works in practice. The original code fragment shown in Fig. 9(a) has three loop nests, $\mathcal{L}_1$, $\mathcal{L}_2$, and $\mathcal{L}_3$ and it manipulates three different disk-resident arrays, namely V_1, V_2, and V_3, using different indexing functions in each loop nest. For illustrative purposes, let us assume that all the arrays are of the same size, $N \times N$. Let us further assume that we have four possible RPM levels, namely, 15K, 12K, 9K, and 6K RPMs, for each disk in the system. Originally, all disks are assumed to be run at 15K RPM. Based on the locality analysis, we can obtain the temporal/spatial locality information of $\mathcal{P}$, as shown in Fig. 9(b). This locality information indicates that, in the first loop nest ($\mathcal{L}_1$), all three array references have spatial locality in the j loop. Since j is chosen as the pipeline loop, we subsequently calculate the prefetch distance (d_i) for every possible disk

```
INPUT:
    A loop nest L: for I ∈ [L, U], step b ⟨a₁(I), ..., aₘ(I)⟩
        L = (l₁, l₂, ..., lₙ)ᵀ
        U = (u₁, u₂, ..., uₙ)ᵀ
OUTPUT:
    Transformed loop nest L'; for I' ∈ [L', U']⟨a₁(I'), ..., aₘ(I')⟩

// assume that Iₚ ∈ (I₁, I₂, ..., Iₖ)ᵀ is the selected pipeline loop
for each Iₚ selected for Vᵢ {
    add a new controlling loop denoted by IIₚ (=[l'ₚ, u'ₚ]) to the loop nest I
        such that I' = (I₁, ..., IIₚ, Iₚ, ..., Iₖ)ᵀ;
    // calculate new loop bounds for IIₚ and Iₚ.
    [l'ₚ, u'ₚ] = [lₚ, uₚ];
    b'ₚ = loop step needed to strip-mine Iₚ loop;
    add b'ₚ into the loop step vector, b
        such that b' = (b₁, ..., b'ₚ, bₚ, ..., bₙ);
    [lₚ, uₚ] = [l'ₚ, l'ₚ + b'ₚ];
}
emit "for I' ∈ [L', U'], step b' ⟨";
// insert prefetch instruction.
for all array references being prefetched
    emit "PF(Vᵢ[F[I']])";
// copy loop body from original loop body.
emit "a₁(I'), ..., aₘ(I')⟩";
emit ")";
```

Fig. 7. Code restructuring algorithm

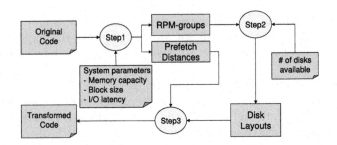

Fig. 8. The three steps of our approach to energy-aware data prefetching

speeds, i.e., 15K, 12K, 9K, and 6K (using the algorithm in Fig. 5). For ease of illustration, let us assume that the determined d_i values for disk speeds 15K, 12K, 9K, and 6K are $(N/8)j$, $(N/4)j$, Nj, and $2Nj$ loop iterations, respectively. This implies that, when considering $\mathcal{L}_1$ alone, we can store all arrays (V_1, V_2, and V_3) in 6K RPM disks, which require $2Nj$ loop iterations to schedule-ahead the disk access since the latency incurred by 6K RPM disks can be eliminated by choosing next surrounding loop nest, i.e., loop i as the pipeline loop. However, since both arrays V_1 and V_2 are accessed again in nests $\mathcal{L}_2$ and $\mathcal{L}_3$ respectively, possible disk speeds for V_1 and V_2 arrays are also dependent on the $\mathcal{L}_2$ and $\mathcal{L}_3$ nests. After processing all the three loop nests, we obtain the possible RPMs for each array, i.e., we have $G[V_1] = \{6K, 12K\}$, $G[V_2] = \{6K, 15K\}$, and $G[V_3] = \{6K\}$. The RPM-groups can be obtained by aggregating the maximum possible RPM from each $G[V_i]$, and they are listed in Fig. 9(c). This indicates that, for the array V_1

```
L₁: for i = 1 to N − 2 {
      for j = 1 to N − 2 {
        ...V₁[i][j]...
        ...V₂[i][j]...
        ...V₃[i][j]...
      }
    }
L₂: for j = 0 to N − 1 {
      ...V₁[N][j]...
    }
L₃: for i = 0 to N − 1 {
      ...V2[i][N]...
    }
```

(a) Original loop nests.

Reference	Locality	
$V_1[i][j]$, $V_2[i][j]$, $V_3[i][j]$	$\begin{matrix}i\\j\end{matrix} =$	none spatial
$V_1[N][j]$	$j =$	spatial
$V_2[i][N]$	$i =$	none

(b) Locality analysis for each array reference.

RPM-group	arrays
15K	V_2
12K	V_1
6K	V_3

(c) Determined RPM-groups.

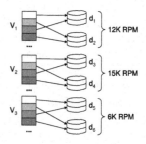

(d) Determined disk speeds and data layouts for arrays.

```
L₁′: for ii = 1 to N − 4, step b₁ {
       PF (&V₃[i + 2][j]);
       for jj = 1 to N − 2 − (N/4), step b₂ {
         PF (&V₁[i][j + (N/4)]);
         for i = ii to ii+b₁ {
           for j = jj to jj+b₂ {
             ...V₁[i][j]...
             ...V₂[i][j]...
             ...V₃[i][j]...
           }
         }
       }
     }
```

```
L₂′: for jj = 0 to (N − 1) − (N/4), step b₃ {
       PF (&V₁[N][j + (N/4)]);
       for j = jj to jj+b₃ {
         ...V₁[N][j]...
       }
     }


L₃: for i = 0 to N − 1 {
      ...V2[i][N]...
    }
```

(e) Transformed loop nests. Both L_1' and L_2' show only the steady state of the pipelined loops.

Fig. 9. An example application of our hoisting algorithm

accessed by both L_1 and L_2, we can assign 12K RPM because the j loop in L_2 is sufficient for hiding latency with a $(N/4)j$ prefetch distance. The disk speed originally assigned to V_2 remains in 15K RPM since the obtained reuse vector for array reference in L_3 indicates that there is no inherent spatial locality. Based on these disk speeds determined, the resulting data layouts (determined using the algorithm in Fig. 6) and the transformed code fragment (obtained using the algorithm in Fig. 7) are given in Figs. 9(d) and (e), respectively. In this example, since all three arrays are of the same size, we assign two disks (out of six disks) per each array (and per RPM-group in this case), and the speed of each disk is set to the RPM level as determined by our algorithm. As we can see from Fig. 9(d), we can save disk energy consumption by running four disks (out of a total of six disks) at lower speeds. Further, it is important to note that the performance of this transformed code is not expected to be any worse than an alternate code that uses compiler-based I/O prefetching, such as [2], that does not care about energy consumption.

6   Experimental Evaluation

6.1   Simulation Platform

To evaluate the effectiveness of our approach in reducing disk energy consumption, we implemented a simulation platform using DiskSim [3]. We assumed that each I/O node has one disk; that is, no further striping is applied within any I/O node. DiskSim is driven by externally-provided disk I/O traces, which are generated by our trace generator. The trace generator generates disk I/O traces, extracted from the disk layout information and the disk access pattern, the latter of which can be obtained either through profiling or static analysis. We modeled an IBM Ultrastar 36Z15 disk [17] and its relevant power and performance characteristics are shown in Table 1. Since we use multi-speed disks running at different RPM levels, we model the performance and energy values at every possible disk speed used. Based on the data from a conventional IBM36Z15 disk, whose rotational speed is 15K RPM, we obtained the performance and energy consumption values at idle and active state by using the quadratic disk power model described in [14]. The energy and performance values for these multi-speed disks are also given in Table 1. The default disk layout for disk-resident array is (1, 64KB, 16).

Table 1. Major simulation parameters and their default values

Disk Parameters		Disk Performance and Energy Model	
Parameter	Value	Parameter	Value
Disk Model	IBM Ultrastar 36Z15	Rotation speed	15K/12K/9K/6K RPM
Interface	SCSI	Average seek time	3.4/3.76/7.0/10.83 ms
Storage Capacity	18.4 GB	Average rotational latency	2.0/2.5/3.33/5.0 ms
Disk Cache Size	4 MB	Power (active)	13.5/11.3/9.1/6.9 W
Internal Transfer Rate	55 MB/sec	Power (idle)	10.2/8.66/7.12/5.58 W

For each application in our experimental suite, we performed experiments with three different schemes:

- Base:This is the baseline version that does not employ any prefetching scheme. It executes benchmark programs on a disk subsystem where all disks run at the highest available speed, i.e, 15K RPM. All the reported disk energy and performance numbers presented later in this section are given as normalized values with respect to the corresponding numbers obtained using this version (which are given in the last two columns of Table 2).
- PF: This scheme corresponds to the conventional I/O prefetching approach, as explained in [2]. The underlying disk speed is fixed at the default RPM level (15K) and the data layouts are exposed to the compiler. As in the base version, we striped all arrays across all disks in the system. Given the disk speeds and data layout of arrays, this scheme restructures the loop nests in the application code to hide I/O latency incurred by accessing high-speed disks.

Table 2. Benchmarks and their characteristics

Name	Description	Data Size (GB)	Base Energy (J)	Exec Time (sec)
171.swim	Shallow Water Modeling	115.2	50648.1	301.9
172.mgrid	Multi-grid Solver: 3D Potential Field	95.5	175470.3	1066.1
173.applu	Parabolic/Elliptic Partial Differential Equations	99.2	121798.5	736.9
301.apsi	Meteorology: Pollutant Distribution	107.9	456479.1	2786.7

– PF+: This scheme corresponds to our energy-aware data prefetching approach, as has been discussed in detail in Sect. 5. As discussed earlier, it determines the disk speeds for all disks in the system and the data layout for each disk-resident array. Based on these determined parameters, it also restructures loop nests.

In our experiments, we used four SPEC2000 float-point benchmark programs [27]. The important characteristics of these benchmark programs are given in Table 2. We made the array data manipulated by these benchmark programs disk-resident; so, accessing an array data during execution results in a disk I/O of a block size (default block size is 8KB), unless the access is captured in the cache. To be fair in evaluating our approach, however, we also optimized these benchmark codes (even the base version) so that the number and volume of I/O accesses are minimized as much as possible. That is, our benchmarks are highly optimized as far as their I/O behavior is concerned. Also, to complete our simulations within a reasonable amount of time, we focused only on the loop nests whose cumulative I/O times account for more than 90% of the total I/O time of each benchmark. Using the default simulation parameters given in Table 1, the baseline energy and performance results are given in the last two columns of Table 2. These baseline results are obtained by executing our benchmark programs on a disk subsystem where all disks run at the highest RPM level (15K). As mentioned earlier, the results which will be given in the next subsection, are normalized with respect to the values in these last two columns.

6.2   Results

The bar-chart shown in Fig. 10 gives the normalized energy consumptions of the benchmark programs in our experimental suite. One can make several observations from these results. First, PF brings an average disk energy savings of 39.6% across all four benchmarks compared to the Base version. These savings are due to the reductions in disk idle times. The second observation one can make from this bar-char is that the PF+ version (our approach) achieves additional energy savings, 19.6% on average when all benchmarks are considered. This indicates that our approach successfully determines the lowest possible rotational speed for each disk and the corresponding disk layouts. As opposed to the PF version, our approach is able to reduce the energy spent in active periods.

We now present the performance results. The normalized execution times for our benchmarks are presented in Fig. 11. One can see from this graph that the

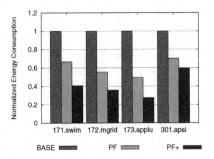

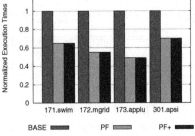

Fig. 10. Normalized energy consumptions

Fig. 11. Normalized execution times

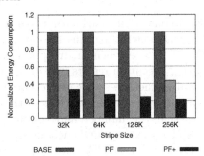

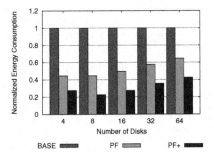

Fig. 12. Normalized energy consumptions with the different stripe sizes

Fig. 13. Normalized energy consumptions with the different stripe factors

PF scheme reduces execution time by 41.3% compared to the Base scheme. This result shows that prefetching is beneficial in enhancing performance by hiding the latency incurred by I/O requests. One can also see that the performance of the PF+ scheme is almost same as that of the PF scheme (the execution time difference between PF and PF+ is negligible, i.e., below 1%). This suggests that our approach can achieve a significant amount of disk energy savings with little impact on the performance improvement achieved by the PF scheme.

6.3   Sensitivity Analysis

In our next set of experiments, we perform a sensitivity analysis, varying simulation parameters pertinent to disk striping. Specifically, we vary the stripe size and stripe factor (the number of disks used for striping) to see how our approach gets affected. For illustrative purposes, we choose one benchmark, *173.applu*, and conduct all sensitivity analysis using that benchmark. However, the results we observed extend to other three benchmarks as well. Fig. 12 gives the normalized energy consumptions with the different stripe sizes (ranging from 32KB to 256KB). Recall from Table 1 that the default stripe size was 64KB. The values of the all other simulation parameters are fixed at the values given in Table 1. We see from these results that the energy savings achieved by our scheme are slightly increasing as we increase the stripe size. This can be explained as follows. When the stripe size increases, a given disk tends to service I/O requests for a longer period of time. This in turn leads to fewer disks being involved in processing the I/O requests, thereby increasing the idle periods of other disks. Consequently, these longer idle periods contribute to reduction in disk energy consumption.

In our next sensitivity experiment, we measured the impact of the different stripe factors (i.e., the total number of disks used for striping). Fig. 13 gives the normalized energy consumption with the different stripe factors (ranging from 8 to 64 disks). We observe from these results that the energy savings our approach achieve decrease slightly decreasing as the number of disks increases. This is because, as we increase the number of disks used in striping, this increases the overall idleness of disks. And, since a disk in the idle state consumes almost same amount of energy as it would consume in the active state, this in turn increases the overall energy consumption. Still, the experimental results given in Figs. 12 and 13 clearly show that our approach is successful across a range of values for stripe sizes and the number of disks.

7   Multiple Application Execution

While our prefetching scheme explained so far generates a significant energy savings for a single application execution, running several applications simultaneously may not lead to the same results due to at least several reasons. First, the applications running in parallel compete for the shared I/O resources, which in turn increases I/O response times. Second, due to the increase in I/O response times, the prefetch predictions made in an application basis can be inaccurate when we execute multiple applications at the same time. However, it is also likely that several applications running on different machines will share the large arrays of disks. In the rest of this section, we present the impact of energy-aware prefetching on the cases where multiple applications run in parallel.

We extend our energy-aware prefetching scheme to address the multiple application execution scenario. Recall that our energy-aware prefetching scheme is composed of three steps: disk speed detection, layout detection, and code restructuring. For the multiple application scenario, we repeat the same sequences of these steps used in the single application scenario (see Fig. 8). However, we now need to make some changes on it to remove the interference between the different applications. We start by determining the disk speed that can be assigned to each array in each program. For this purpose, we use the same algorithm in Fig. 5 except that we apply it to every application that will be executed in parallel. The first step that selects the most suitable disk speed for a given application is described in the first phase of Fig. 14. As a result of phase 1, each RPM-group contains all arrays that can be stored in the same set of disks spinning with the same speed, which are from all the applications under consideration.

In the next phase of our approach for the multiple application scenario, we determine the disk layouts for each array in the determined RPM-groups. In

```
INPUT:
    Set of applications, A = (P₁, P₂, ..., Pₙ);
OUTPUT:
    Transformed applications A' = (P'₁, P'₂, ..., P'ₙ);

weight[Pᵢ]: the number of disk accesses made by each Pᵢ;
weight[A]: the number of disk accesses made by A;

// Phase 1
for each application Pᵢ ∈ A {
    for each loop nest Lⱼ ∈ L {
        Determine RPM-Group for all available RPM level l;
    }
}
// Phase 2
for each program Pᵢ ∈ A {
    Determine the disk layout for Pᵢ based on weight fraction, weight[Pᵢ]/weight[A];
    for each RPM-group {
        Determine disk layouts for each Vᵢ ∈ V within Pᵢ;
    }
}
// Phase 3
for each application Pᵢ ∈ A {
    Follow the procedure in Fig. 7;
}
```

Fig. 14. Code restructuring algorithm

Table 3. Multiple application execution scenario

Scenario	Running Applications	Number of Arrays	Completion Time (sec)
S-1	swim	14	486.8
S-2	swim + mgrid	18	501.4
S-3	swim + mgrid + applu	20	591.3
S-4	swim + mgrid + applu + apsi	26	670.0

order not to increase the interference among the I/O requests coming from the applications running in parallel, we first assign the disks disjointedly at the application level. After each application is assigned to a subset of disks, we then determine the disk layout of each array at an application level. In determining the most suitable number of disks for each application, we take the same idea of access weight which captures all the number of accesses made to the arrays in the application in question. The second step that determines the disk layout for each array is described in the second phase of Fig. 14.

After the first two phases, we restructure all the application codes using the determined parameters from the above two phases. We present our energy aware prefetching algorithm that considers multiple application scenarios in Fig. 14.

To see the impact of our scheme on the multiple application scenario, we conducted experiments with four different execution scenarios given in Table 3. The second column of this table gives the applications executed simultaneously in each scenario and the third column shows the number of arrays accessed by the applications under consideration. The last column presents the completion time until all the applications in each scenario finish their execution. Since the execution time of the original applications differ from one to another with a large variance, we made them to complete around 500 seconds by changing the dataset size and the corresponding loop bounds of each application. The completion times for the different scenarios shows that, as we execute more applications in parallel, the total execution time also increase proportionally.

Fig. 15 shows the impact of the conventional prefetching scheme (PF) and our energy-aware prefetching scheme (PF+) with several multiple application scenarios on the execution times. In this graph, the bar for a given scenario is normalized with respect to the original execution times (the value given in the last column of Table 3). As we can see, PF increases the maximum execution time when the number of applications running in parallel increases. This is not surprising because, in the PF scheme, each benchmark is modified to insert prefetch instructions without considering the interaction with other applications. Therefore, as we increase the number of benchmarks running in parallel, PF fails to remove I/O stall time successfully. The PF+ scheme, on the other hand, can in general achieve execution time reduction compared to PF because the prefetching for the different applications directed at the separate set of disks and we made modifications to the disk layout accordingly. However, we also observe that the PF+ scheme increases the maximum execution time slightly as we execute more benchmarks in parallel. This is because less number of disks are assigned to each application when more applications are running simultaneously, and as a result of this, it may not be sufficient to meet the I/O requirements of each application.

Fig. 16 gives the normalized energy consumption with four execution scenarios. As we can expect from the increase in execution time, the overall energy consumption also increases as we add the applications executed in parallel for both schemes, PF and PF+. We also see that the energy behavior of PF degrades significantly when we run more applications at the same time. The main reason for this trend is the significant increase in execution time. Since the PF scheme does not consider multi-speed disks, i.e., all disks are running with the highest rotational speed, it consumes a significant energy, whereas PF+ saves energy under the multiple application scenario. These results clearly show that our scheme can be applied to multiple application scenario successfully in terms of execution cycle reduction and and energy savings. This multiple application scheme can be embedded into a runtime system that executes on top of a parallel file system such as PVFS [4].

8   Concluding Remarks and Future Work

The main contribution of this paper is a compiler-directed energy-aware prefetching scheme for disk-intensive scientific applications. The proposed approach determines, in a unified setting, the prefetch distances for disk access (I/O) instructions, the disk speeds for all disks in the storage system, and the data (array) layouts on the disks, given an application program. To test the effectiveness of the proposed strategy, we implemented it within an optimizing compiler and conducted experiments with four applications that manipulate disk-resident data arrays. The results obtained so far from our experiments under both the

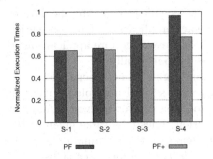

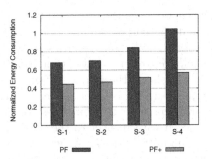

Fig. 15. Normalized execution time for each scenario to complete

Fig. 16. Normalized energy consumption for each scenario to complete

single and multiple application scenarios are very encouraging and show that the energy-aware prefetching brings significant energy benefits over a state-of-the-art (performance oriented) I/O prefetching scheme, without degrading the performance of the latter. Our ongoing work involves integrating this optimization with well-known I/O optimizations such as collective I/O [28] and caching. We also plan to enhance our approach to accommodate disk spin-downs as well, in addition to multi-speed disks.

References

1. Omega library. http://www.cs.umd.edu/projects/omega.
2. A. D. Brown, T. C. Mowry, and O. Krieger. Compiler-Based I/O Prefetching for Out-of-Core Applications. *ACM Transactions on Computer Systems*, 19(2):111–170, May 2001.
3. J. S. Bucy, G. R. Ganger, and Contributors. The DiskSim Simulation Environment Version 3.0 Reference Manual. Technical Report CMU-CS-03-102, CMU, January 2003.
4. P. H. Carns, W. B. L. III, R. B. Boss, and R. Thakur. PVFS: A Parallel File System for Linux Clusters. In *Proceedings of the 4th Annual Linux Showcase and Conference*, pages 317–327, October 2000.
5. E. V. Carrera, E. Pinheiro, and R. Bianchini. Conserving Disk Energy in Network Servers. In *Proceedings of the 17th International Conference on Supercomputing*, pages 86–97. ACM, June 2003.
6. J. Chase, D. Anderson, P. Thackar, A. Vahdat, and R. Boyle. Managing Energy and Server Resources in Hosting Centers. In *Proceedings of the 18th Symposium on Operating Systems Principles*, pages 103–116, October 2001.
7. J. Chase and R. Doyle. Balance of Power: Energy Management for Server Clusters. In *Proceedings of the 8th Workshop on Hot Topics in Operating Systems*, page 165, May 2001.
8. P. M. Chen, E. K. Lee, G. A. Gibson, R. H. Katz, and D. A. Patterson. RAID: high-performance, reliable secondary storage. *ACM Computing Survey*, 26(2):145–185, 1994.
9. D. Colarelli and D. Grunwald. Massive arrays of idle disks for storage archives. In *Proceedings of the 2002 ACM/IEEE conference on Supercomputing*, July 2002.

10. F. Douglis, P. Krishnan, and B. Bershad. Adaptive Disk Spin-down Policies for Mobile Computers. In *Proceedings of the 2nd Symposium on Mobile and Location-Independent Computing*, pages 121–137, 1995.

11. F. Douglis, P. Krishnan, and B. Marsh. Thwarting the Power-Hungry Disk. In *Proceedings of the USENIX Winter Conference*, pages 292–306, 1994.

12. M. Elnozahy, M. Kistler, and R. Rajamony. Energy-efficient Server Clusters. In *Proceedings of the Second Workshop on Power Aware Computing Systems*, February 2002.

13. M. Elnozahy, M. Kistler, and R. Rajamony. Energy Conservation Policies for Web Servers. In *Proceedings of the 4th USENIX Symposium on Internet Technologies and Systems*, March 2003.

14. S. Gurumurthi, A. Sivasubramaniam, M. Kandemir, and H. Franke. DRPM: Dynamic Speed Control for Power Management in Server Class Disks. In *Proceedings of the International Symposium on Computer Architecture*, pages 169–179, June 2003.

15. M. W. Hall, J. M. Anderson, S. P. Amarasinghe, B. R. Murphy, S.-W. Liao, E. Bugnion, and M. S. Lam. Maximizing Multiprocessor Performance with the SUIF Compiler. *Computer Magazine*, 29(12):84–89, December 1996.

16. T. Heath, E. Pinheiro, J. Hom, U. Kremer, and R. Bianchini. Application Transformations for Energy and Performance-Aware Device Management. In *Proceedings of the International Conference on Parallel Architectures and Compilation Techniques*, pages 121–130. IEEE, September 2002.

17. IBM. Ultrastar 36z15 hard disk drive. http://www.hitachigst.com/hdd/ultra/ul36z15.htm 2001.

18. R. K. K. Li, P. Horton, and T. Anderson. A Quantitative Analysis of Disk Drive Power Management in Portable Computers. In *Proceedings of the USENIX Winter Conference*, pages 279–292, 1994.

19. K. Okada, N. Kojima, and K. Yamashita. A novel drive architecture of HDD: multimode hard disc drive. In *Proceedings of the International Conference on Consumer Electronics*, pages 92–93, June 2000.

20. A. E. Papathanasiou and M. L. Scott. Energy Efficient Prefetching and Caching. In *USENIX Annual Technical Conference, General Track*, pages 255–268, 2004.

21. E. Pinheiro and R. Bianchini. Energy Conservation Techniques for Disk Array-Based Servers. In *Proceedings of the 17th International Conference on Supercomputing*, pages 66–78, June 2004.

22. W. Pugh. A Practical Algorithm for Exact Array Dependency Analysis. *Communications of the ACM*, 35(8):102–114, August 1992.

23. R. B. Ross, P. H. Carns, W. B. L. III, and R. Latham. Using the Parallel Virtual File System, July 2002.

24. S. W. Son, G. Chen, M. Kandemir, and A. Choudhary. Exposing Disk Layout to Compiler for Reducing Energy Consumption of Parallel Disk Based Systems. In *Proc. ACM SIGPLAN Symposium on Principles and Practice of Parallel Programming*, pages 174–185, June 2005.

25. S. W. Son, M. Kandemir, and A. Choudhary. Software-Directed Disk Power Management for Scientific Applications. In *Proc. 19th International Parallel and Distributed Processing Symposium*, pages 4b–4b, April 2005.

26. S. W. Son and M. Kandemir. Energy-Aware Data Prefetching for Multi-Speed Disks. In *Proc. of the Conference on Computing Frontiers*, pages 105–114, May 2006.

27. SPEC. Specfp 2000. http://www.specbench.org/cpu2000/CFP2000/, 2000

28. R. Thakur, W. Gropp, and E. Lusk. Data sieving and collective I/O in ROMIO. In *Proceedings of the Seventh Symposium on the Frontiers of Massively Parallel Computation*, pages 182–189. IEEE Computer Society Press, 1999.

29. M. E. Wolf and M. S. Lam. A data locality optimizing algorithm. In *Proceedings of the ACM SIGPLAN conference on Programming language design and implementation*, pages 30–44, New York, NY, USA, 1991. ACM Press.

30. M. Wolfe. *High Performance Compilers for Parallel Computing*. Addison-Wesley Publishing Company, 1996.

31. H. Yada, H. Ishioka, T. Yamakoshi, Y. Onuki, Y. Shimano, M. U. H. Kanno, and N. Hayashi. Head positioning servo and data channel for HDD's with multiple spindle speeds. *IEEE Transactions on Magnetics*, 36(5):2213–2215, September 2000.

32. Q. Zhu, Z. Chen, L. Tan, Y. Zhou, K. Keeton, and J. Wilkes. Hibernator: Helping disk arrays sleep through the winter. In *Proceedings of the 20th ACM Symposium on Operating Systems Principles*, October 2005.

33. Q. Zhu, F. M. David, C. F. Devaraj, Z. Li, Y. Zhou, and P. Cao. Reducing Energy Consumption of Disk Storage Using Power-Aware Cache Management. In *10th International Conference on High-Performance Computer Architecture*, pages 118–129, 2004.

34. Q. Zhu, A. Shankar, and Y. Zhou. PB-LRU: a self-tuning power aware storage cache replacement algorithm for conserving disk energy. In *Proceedings of the 18th Annual International Conference on Supercomputing*, pages 79–88, 2004.

Reconfiguration Strategies for Environmentally Powered Devices: Theoretical Analysis and Experimental Validation*

Alex E. Şuşu[1], Michele Magno[2], Andrea Acquaviva[1,3], David Atienza[1,4], and Giovanni De Micheli[1,3]

[1] LSI/EPFL, Lausanne, Switzerland
{alex.susu,david.atienza,giovanni.demicheli}@epfl.ch
[2] DEIS/University of Bologna, Bologna, Italy
mmagno@deis.unibo.it
[3] STI/University of Urbino, Italy
acquaviva@urbino.it
[4] DACYA/Complutense University, Madrid, Spain
datienza@dacya.ucm.es

Abstract. Environmental energy is becoming a feasible alternative to traditional energy sources for ultra low-power devices such as sensor nodes. These devices can run reactive applications that adapt their control flow depending on the sensed data. In order to reduce the energy consumption of the platform and also to meet the timing constraints imposed by the application, we propose to dynamically reconfigure the system through the use of Field Programmable Gate Array (FPGA) fabric such that it executes more efficiently the tasks of the application.

In this paper we present a new approach that enables the designer to efficiently explore different reconfiguration strategies for environmentally powered systems. For this we define a stochastic model of a harvesting video sensor node that captures the behavior of the node and of its environment. We use this approach to investigate the impact of different reconfiguration strategies for a video surveillance node on metrics of interest, such as the expected lifetime or downtime of the system.

Then, we create a hardware implementation of an energy-aware reconfiguration manager on top of a custom multi-FPGA board.

Our results show that the systems improve their processing capabilities if suitable reconfiguration strategies are defined for their respective configuration environments.

Keywords: Wireless Sensor Nodes, FPGA, energy harvesting, probabilistic model checking, Markov chains.

1 Introduction

The existing and emerging energy harvesting technologies become feasible solutions to power up small electronic devices [21,24]. Using harvested energy has

---

* This article builds upon a paper prepared for the third conference on Computing Frontiers, 2006.

P. Stenström (Ed.): Transactions on HiPEAC I, LNCS 4050, pp. 341–360, 2007.

pluses and minuses: the energy from the environment is infinite, thus providing opportunity to increase the autonomy of the system, yet it is unpredictable. To cope with the unpredictability of the harvested energy we use power adaptation circuitry and energy storage elements such as rechargeable batteries and super-capacitors, which regulate the supplied power level corresponding to the demand. However, this scheme might not constantly offer the required power because it can happen that there is not enough energy coming from the environment and, also, not enough energy in the storage elements.

In order to meet timing constraints and, subsequently, in order to reduce the energy consumption of the platform, we propose to use low power FPGA logic that can execute more rapidly code that can be parallelized. More exactly, we use a sensor node which includes a small on-chip FPGA [1] that can implement signal processing routines together with a low-power microcontroller. Because of the limited capacity of the FPGA we can dynamically reconfigure it in order to load the most energy efficient task sets depending on the sensor context, for example. However, reconfiguration has a cost in terms of energy and time, so that a suitable strategy must be designed to determine if and when it is worth to perform system reconfiguration. Clearly, the reconfiguration process itself has an energy penalty, but our goal is to amortize this cost due to the future savings offered by the reconfiguration.

Power management policies can be considered another form of system reconfiguration w.r.t. the application context. The focus of generic power management policies for environmentally powered systems is different from the one of battery powered devices: while in the latter case we search to maximize the lifetime of the system, in the former case a good design objective is to increase the availability of the device for long periods of time.

Also, situations might arise where the harvester generates more energy than required by the device after the battery is already full. In this case, the additional energy, which we call *energy slack*, is wasted. This situation is of practical relevance with harvesters such as solar cells, where during long periods with intense external light conditions it becomes difficult to store all the available energy.

The work we present brings two contributions. First, we model realistic reconfigurable systems, using PRISM [17], a probabilistic model checking tool. The model is used to formally assess the impact of reconfiguration strategies on metrics of interest such as the lifetime and the availability of the system. We express quantitatively how various proposed policies improve these metrics.

Second, we describe the implementation of a reconfiguration strategy on a prototype board with FPGA, which uses hardware and software versions of the application tasks. The idea behind this policy is to use the otherwise wasted harvested energy (in case the battery is already full) to reconfigure the system, thus improving the energy efficiency in the future. In order to match the relatively high power requirements of the prototype board when compared to the power generated by practical energy harvesters and, in order to perform experiments in a controllable way, we emulate the harvester with a programmable power generator, which generates energy under the form of bursts of constant power and variable length.

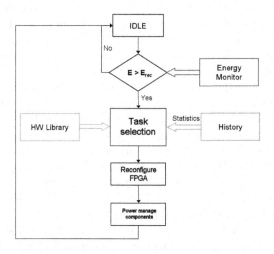

Fig. 1. Generic reconfiguration policy

2   Background Work

Advances in microelectronic technology have been recently exploited to build low-cost and low-power miniaturized sensor nodes that can collaborate together in sensing and relaying the information, building Wireless Sensor Networks (WSN). Such sensor nodes, integrated with harvesting devices, can exploit the environmental energy in order to increase their autonomy [21]. The energy level provided by the harvesting devices is determined by the technology in use. For instance, solar cells provide between $100mW/cm^2$ when directed toward bright sun and $100W/cm^2$ in an illuminated office, while vibrational microgenerators provide $4W/cm^3$ for human motion [21].

A sensor node consists of the following hardware components [12,8,23]: a microprocessor, data storage, sensors, a data transceiver, and an energy source. The processing performance can be increased with a dedicated Digital Signal Processing (DSP) unit, an Application-Specific Integrated Circuit (ASIC) or reconfigurable hardware (e.g., FPGA) that implements computationally demanding or performance constrained tasks.

Currently, most examples of sensor node architectures are microprocessor-based. On the one hand, this provides flexibility for adaptation, since we can implement multi-modal programs on such nodes, or we can even dynamically upload new code on them in order to adapt to a new context.However, a processor executing software is far less efficient in performance, energy consumption and, even in manufacturing cost than an ASIC. On the other hand, ASICs do not have the flexibility for node-level adaptation. Thus, the use of field-programmable hardware, in particular FPGAs, in sensor nodes is a very recent area of research [18,12]. Reconfigurable logic can provide node flexibility with significantly greater energy efficiency than software-only solutions if low-power FPGA platforms are used in combination with suitable reconfiguration strategies. However, because of power and size constraints, suitable FPGAs are limited in the functionality they can implement. This limitation, coupled with the heterogeneous application context makes impractical the trivial solution of mapping simultaneously all the possible tasks on the FPGA. A solution to this problem is to dynamically load in the FPGA the required tasks exactly before being used.

Within the domain of WSN, video sensor nodes hold strong interest for military, security, robotics, and, recently, also, consumer applications [16,19]. However, due to the high computational requirements and energy costs of video coders for processors/microcontrollers, mixed hybrid architectures (i.e., microprocessor with DSP/ASIC/FPGA) with efficient partitioning algorithms have been suggested as a more suitable option to achieve sufficient performance with low energy consumption [22].

A similar hybrid approach is taken in the Low power Energy Aware Project (LEAP) [20]. The LEAP platform is a sensor node that can support intensive processing tasks. The LEAP architecture is composed of two modules: a general purpose computing module used for event-driven computationally intensive processing and a preprocessor module dedicated to low power sensing and energy accounting. The architecture integrates fine-grained energy dissipation monitoring and sophisticated power control scheduling for all subsystems including sensor subsystems. The LEAP architecture enables complex energy-aware algorithm design by providing a simple interface to control numerous platform and sensor power modes and report detailed energy usage information.

Lately, several processing power optimization techniques have been proposed for WSN. In the case of nodes with high duty cycle, one can tune the clock frequency and the supply voltage of the processing units depending on the workload [25]. Also, data aggregation strategies between multiple sensor nodes can reduce the redundant information transmitted and the power used in the network [6]. In addition, power-aware topology control algorithms have been proposed [7]. Another possibility (which is also present in LEAP) is to suspend the microcontroller, the coprocessors or the radio transceiver according to the communication [11] or computation features of the application. The first three methods are complementary to our reconfigurable approach of sensor nodes; thus, they could be used in combination with the reconfiguration strategies we suggest in this paper.

3   Analysis of Environmentally Powered Reconfigurable Systems

In this section we focus on the modeling of nodes, with emphasis on the energy generated by the harvesting device and on the reconfiguration policy. Our goal

Fig. 2. The MicrelEye video surveillance node

is to analyze the model in order to express quantitatively the effectiveness of reconfiguration strategies in the context of environmentally powered devices.

To model the harvested energy, we use traces obtained from a real solar cell [3,9], which consist in the enumeration of the intensity values of the generated current over a period of time. The variation of the energy is periodic w.r.t. the day cycle and is caused by clouds, terrain obstacles from the sun and, in the longer term, by season changes. In Fig. 3 we present an arbitrary trace over 1 day. The voltage of the harvester is almost constant at a value of 5 V.

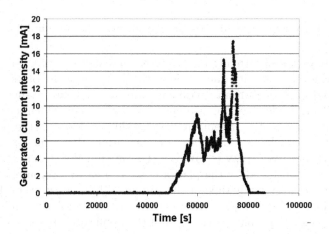

Fig. 3. Trace of the intensity of the generated current by a 5.5x15 cm^2 solar panel, on the roof of one of the buildings at EPFL starting from Nov 14, 2005 18:28, for 24 hours

The unpredictability of the environmental energy source can be modeled stochastically. Using, for example, the solar panel trace presented in Fig. 3, we can build a Discrete Time Markov Chain (DTMC) model for the harvested energy. To each state of the DTMC we associate an interval of energy levels generated in that specific state by the harvester (this is similar to the Power State Machine concept, used in [4] to model power manageable components). To assign

probabilities on the transitions originating in a state of the DTMC, we go over
the solar panel trace and count the occurrences of each transition from that
state (by transition in the trace we understand the jump from one energy level
at a moment, to the level corresponding for the next time instance). Then, we
normalize these frequencies in order to have the sum of probabilities on the
transitions from that state equal to 1.

The choice of the number of states of the DTMC is a compromise between the
accuracy of the DTMC abstraction w.r.t. the real harvester and the tractability
of the analysis of the model, which we introduce in the following paragraphs.
The statistical model can be considered representative for the days of the winter
season in the geographic region of the experiments. Using the same technique,
statistical models for different periods of the year or locations can be generated.
In Fig. 4 we show the DTMC built from the trace in Fig. 3.

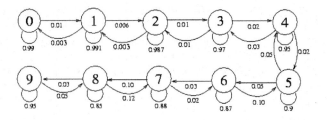

Fig. 4. Discrete Time Markov Chain built from the trace in Figure 3

In order to establish formally various properties like the expected system lifetime, the achievable activity duty cycle or the duration of the blackout periods,
by automated analytical means, without performing expensive simulations, we
use probabilistic model checking. Compared to simulation, which focuses on one
admissible execution of a system, model checking explores all the possible behaviors of the modeled system [14]. One can argue that using a mean value
approximation for the energy received in the time unit by the energy harvester
and the energy consumed by the platform, we can easily compute analytically,
for example, the average lifetime of the system. While this is true, the average
approximation is no longer accurate, and therefore not suitable when we have, for
example, a policy that changes the QoS of the application based on the energy
level coming from the environment or remaining in the battery.

The probabilistic model is defined as the parallel composition of the modules of
the system, such as the harvester, the radio channel and the battery. Each module
has a certain number of states, among which transitions are defined.
The transitions can be either probabilistic, building, for example, DTMCs, or
deterministic.

The tool we use, the probabilistic model checker PRISM [17], is able to infer
properties of the stochastic model through exhaustive exploration, many of them
being non-trivial and amenable only by computer analysis. These properties are
relevant for the hardware and software designers in order to adjust the sizes of

the components, such as the harvester and the battery, as well as designing the software layers. For instance, if we employ backward recovery in order to cope with the blackouts [10] we can tune the checkpointing interval s.t. the average lost computation is minimized by using the average lifetime of the system determined with this method.

In order to instruct PRISM to perform the analysis of a desired property, a query must be built using the Probabilistic Computational Tree Logic (PCTL) temporal logic [5,13]. For example, we can ask the tool to compute the probability that the system runs out of power for a given battery size and initial level of environmental energy. In this case, the tool computes the probability that the battery module reaches the zero energy state. In the following section, we devise a model of a realistic reconfigurable system powered by a solar harvester and a rechargeable battery, the MicrelEye video sensor node used for security applications.

Concerning the reconfiguration policy of the system, we present the flowchart of a generic strategy in Fig. 1. The policy stores runtime statistics regarding the inputs of the application that decide its control flow (e.g., depending if the captured image contains a person or not, the system executes different sets of tasks). Based on these statistics, the policy decides which is the best task candidate for reconfiguration among the available ones and we load it in the FPGA, if it is not already there. The bitstreams of the task candidates are stored in a special module of the reconfiguration manager, namely, the hardware block library, which can be stored in the Flash memory of the available FPGA or in any other storage device directly accessible by the reconfigurable manager. The strategy is also responsible to power manage the components of the system.

The additional energy spent for reconfiguration could prevent the complete execution of a task that would be otherwise finalized if no reconfiguration is performed. But, our assumption is that the reconfiguration cost is amortized in the future by several executions of the more efficient reconfigured task. Moreover, the reconfiguration energy can be provided directly by the harvester at no cost when the battery is full and the power generated is bigger than the consumption.

To validate the proposed reconfiguration policy, we present in Sect. 4.2 a manager that implements such strategy in a proof-of-concept prototype system.

4   Case Studies and Experimental Measurements

In Sect. 4.1 we illustrate the use of PRISM to explore the possible reconfiguration opportunities of the model introduced in Sect. 3 for various hardware-software designs of the MicrelEye video sensor node. Then, in Sect. 4.2, we present the implementation of an energy-aware reconfiguration manager on top of a custom multi-FPGA board and experimental results performed with this platform.

4.1   Evaluation of Reconfiguration Policies Using PRISM

The MicrelEye Node. The MicrelEye (see Fig. 2) is equipped with an Omnivision 7640 video sensor, an ATMEL FPSLIC reconfigurable platform featuring an AVR microcontroller and a 40,000 gates FPGA. FPSLIC is one of the lowest power consuming reconfigurable boards on the market. Its latest version, FP-SLIC II, can put into low-power mode both the microcontroller and the FPGA.

For each captured image, the node performs a set of processing tasks, in order to determine if a human body is present in the viewer of the camera. In the case of a positive outcome, the original image is sent to a basestation for further processing (e.g., face recognition, using a database of features for comparisons). The FPGA is used to perform most of the image processing tasks.

The application running on the platform starts a normal execution cycle by capturing with the camera an image of 320*240 pixels; we call this the Camera Acquisition (CA) task. We apply on the resulting frame a Background Subtraction (BS) function, which removes the background of the image; this is accomplished by using an earlier-captured background frame as a reference. At this moment we can compare the original image (the output of task CA) and the result of the task BS. If the two images are very different, then it means that the original image is mostly background. In this case, we do not perform any more processing of the image, since the image is considered not to be interesting. If the image resulted from the task BS is not discarded, we continue with the Search Algorithm (SA) phase, which returns the position within the 320*240 frame of a 32*16 window that potentially contains a human body, positioned approximately 5 meters away from the camera. On this window of 32*16 pixels we apply the Feature Extraction (FE) function, which performs the average of the pixels for each row and column of the window and stores these values in a vector of size 32+16. This vector is handled by the Support Vector Machine (SVM) task that determines if the input vector corresponds to a human body or not. At the end of the SVM task, we know with a good degree of confidence if the captured image contains a human body.

The CA, BS and SA tasks are very computing intensive. To meet deadlines, since a microcontroller does not provide short execution times for the aforementioned tasks, we have to execute these tasks on the FPGA. Therefore, tasks CA, BS, SA and FE are only executed on the FPGA. We execute the SVM task on the AVR microcontroller, since it can perform fast multiplications, and the SVM task is multiplication intensive.

The characteristics of the tasks of the detection application are given in Table 1. For the energy consumption values, we assume that we suspend the microcontroller or the FPGA whenever they are not used.

We model in PRISM the MicrelEye node as the parallel composition of the following modules: i) the harvesting device (*SolarHarvester*); ii) a rechargeable battery (*Battery*); iii) the consumer part of the video node (*MicrelEyeNode*) that models the energy intake of the camera, microcontroller and FPGA; iv) the "view" of the camera (*CameraView*) that determines if the camera captures a frame only with background information or not. To coordinate the simultaneous execution of the modules we define the *Clock* module. All these modules are synchronized on the *tick* action (the term action comes from the terminology used by PRISM) generated by Clock. The structure of the system can be seen in Fig. 5.

Table 1. Characterization of the Tasks

Task	Execution time [ms]	Energy consumed [mJ]
CA	40	2.64
BS	54.5	12.58
BS2	27.25	6.29
SA	19.2	4.43
FE	0.27	0.0623
SVM	89	33.1881
FPGA Reconfiguration	22	3.63

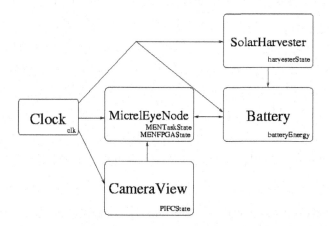

Fig. 5. Block diagram of the system

Battery. The rechargeable battery is modeled as a set of states that represent the battery energy levels with deterministic transitions defined by the energy consumption and generation levels in the current state.

CameraView. We model the view of the camera using two states (the boolean variable PIFCState specifies what is the current state) and probabilistic transitions between them. The transitions represent basically the probability of having a person (or something that is recognized as a person) in the frame captured by the camera.

Clock. The clock module does not correspond to a physical component of the system. The module has two states that generate the actions tick and tock. As previously explained, Clock is used to trigger the activity of the other components through the tick action.

MicrelEyeNode. The node is modeled using the MENFPGAState boolean variable for the two configurations of the FPGA and the MENTaskState variable with 6 states that keeps track which task is the node currently executing. The

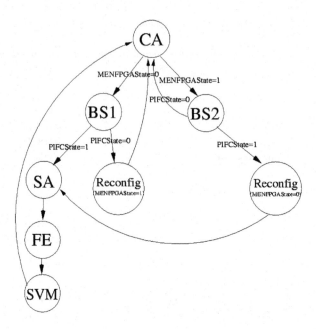

Fig. 6. The task graph of the software application implemented on the MicrelEye node for Policy3

transitions between the states are deterministic and take into account the state of the CameraView and the level of energy in the battery.

The actual specification of the system is done in the Reactive Modules language [2], but we do not present it due to space limitation. We define each module in this language by specifying: i) the variables of the module and their initial values and ii) the behavior of each module by a set of commands, where each describes a guard (a predicate that needs to be true to execute the statement) and one deterministic variable update (transition) or more probabilistic updates with specified probabilities.

The behavior of the model is the following. Initially the battery is full. In every time step we add to the battery energy level (variable *batteryEnergy*) the contribution from the harvester and subtract the energy consumed by the node, which is computed based on the state of the node (MENTaskState and MENF-PGAState). When the battery is full, the system uses directly the energy from the harvester. If this energy is not enough for the given time step, it consumes energy from the battery as well. If the energy from the harvester is bigger than what the platform requires, then the surplus is wasted. If the system runs out of energy (i.e., the system does not have the required energy for executing the current application cycle) it constantly checks the battery level and restarts only when there is enough energy in the battery to be able to execute the initial application cycle.

The Strategies. We consider several operation policies, which we compare quantitatively afterwards. The first two of them disallow runtime reconfiguration, while the following two are variations of dynamic reconfiguration policies.

- *Policy1 (static, FPGA always active)*, which assumes that the system is not able to dynamically reconfigure the FPGA, so it has tasks CA, BS, SA and FE statically mapped on the FPGA. Also, we assume that the FPGA cannot be put into low power mode. On the other hand, the AVR microcontroller is put into sleep mode when it is not used.
- *Policy2 (static, low power FPGA)*: Once again we assume that the configuration of the FPGA is assigned at the beginning and cannot be changed during runtime. We model the use of the FPSLIC II board, and, therefore, the FPGA can be suspended as well, besides the microcontroller.
- *Policy3 (dynamic, low power FPGA)*: This policy takes advantage of the possibility to dynamically reconfigure the FPGA and to suspend the FPGA and the AVR microcontroller, when no longer used. It means that the microcontroller is turned on only during the execution of the SVM task, while the FPGA is suspended only for the tasks CA and SVM.

  The dynamic reconfiguration allows the execution of different versions of a task. For example, since the task BS is the most computing intensive, we can parallelize it by creating two instances of sub-tasks BS that work on half of the image each. Thus, this parallelized version of the task BS (which we call BS2) has almost half the execution time of the original task BS, but this comes at the expense of occupying almost double space on the FPGA. This makes task BS2 to have almost half the energy consumption w.r.t. the original task BS, if we consider that the power of the FPGA is the same for the two different mapping scenarios (tasks CA, BS, SA and FE, versus task BS2). However, the parallelized version of the task BS occupies a big part of the FPGA, and therefore it does not leave space for the SA or the FE tasks.

  Having two different FPGA mapping scenarios, we can make use of one or the other at the right moment by employing dynamic reconfiguration. In the case we detect that the image is not interesting (immediately after running the task BS) we assume that the following images will not be interesting either with a high probability, and, therefore, we execute task BS2 from now on, as long as possible. For doing this, we need to dynamically reconfigure the FPGA with the task BS2, if this task is not already mapped on the FPGA, such that for the future frames we benefit of the lower energy consumption. In case we have mapped task BS2 on the FPGA, which occupies the entire reconfigurable logic estate, and we receive a frame that is declared by BS2 as being valuable, then we are forced to reconfigure the FPGA in order to load the tasks BS, SA and FE on it. This reconfiguration policy is depicted in Fig. 6, where some of the transitions are annotated with predicates which decide if the transition is taken or not.
- *Policy4 (dynamic, low power FPGA, harvester used as sensor)*: This policy enhances Policy3 by sensing the light conditions with the solar panel. If we detect through the solar panel that there is no light in the environment

(i.e., the power from the solar panel is almost zero), then we power down the node. The node restarts when the solar panel captures light and, of course, we have enough energy in the battery to sustain the computations.

We consider Policy2 the baseline non-reconfigurable strategy for our experiments.

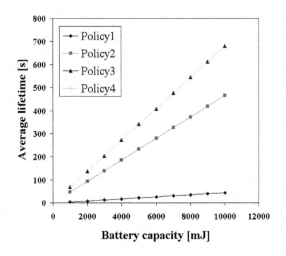

Fig. 7. Variation of the average lifetime for Policy1, Policy2, Policy3 and Policy4 w.r.t. the capacity of the battery. The node is turned on invariably at 11AM.

Exploration Results of the MicrelEye Node. Before presenting the results, we define precisely the terminology we use. By average lifetime we understand the expected period of time from the moment we start the system until the moment it runs out of power (note that the system can sleep during its lifetime). By the downtime of the system over a given period we understand the expected sum of periods of time over the given time frame in which the node cannot run because it does not have enough energy to proceed with the execution. The downtime of the system is the complementary of the uptime for the same period, which can be easily converted in availability. It is important to mention that the average downtime and lifetime are not perfectly complementary: the average downtime is the sum of periods of blackout for the given period of time, while the lifetime is just until the first blackout.

For the experiments we run, we assume a probability of 1% of having a person in front of the camera. In Fig. 7 we present the expected lifetime of the system running each of the defined policies, as a function of the initial (and maximum) capacity of the battery. Clearly, the lifetime depends on the capacity of the battery in a linear way, since we are outside the energy neutral operation mode (i.e., the power consumption, which is dependent on the duty cycle of the application, is higher than the generated power, on average). The initial battery

capacity only affects the initial behavior of the system. We can also see that here
Policy3 and Policy4 are equally efficient. This is so because the node is supposed
to start running at 11AM and, since the power consumption is bigger than the
power generated by the harvester, the system runs out of power in the order of
minutes. Thus, the node is not able to get into a period of darkness and, because
of this, the two policies behave in a similar way.

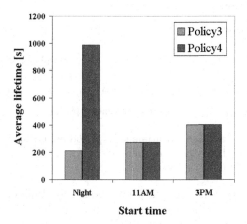

Fig. 8. Variation of the average lifetime for Policy4 w.r.t. the moment of the day when
we turn on the system. The capacity of the battery is 4J.

To test Policy3 and Policy4 in conditions that would differentiate them, we
consider we turn on the node at different hours, in the same day. We show in
Fig. 8 the variation in expected lifetime of the system for the two policies, when
turning on the node at various moments of the day. We can see that only in the
case we turn on the node during the night, the policies are very different: the
lifetime of the node with Policy4 increases 4.7 times when compared to Policy3.
Otherwise, if we turn the node on during the day time, it does not survive until
the night comes, because it runs out of power relatively fast.

In Fig. 9 we present the expected downtime of the system for a period of one
hour, for each of the defined policies. We notice an increase in availability of 37%
for Policy3 w.r.t. Policy2, the baseline non-reconfigurable strategy.

We notice that the dynamic reconfiguration policies reduce the expected
downtime, leading to larger periods of activity of the system with a given environmental energy. This leads to an increased throughput, i.e. number of frames
processed per second.

We also compute the average wasted energy for one hour (we waste energy
when the battery is full and the generated power is bigger than the one consumed) for Policy1: we obtain a value of zero, which is easy to understand since
Policy1 is very power hungry even w.r.t. the maximum power generated by the
harvester.

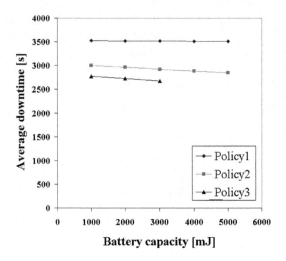

Fig. 9. Variation of the average downtime for a period of one hour for Policy1, Policy2, Policy3, Policy4 w.r.t. the capacity of the battery

We conclude that the reconfiguration strategies, Policy3 and Policy4, can improve the lifetime of the video node at least with 40% when compared to the baseline for non-reconfigurable strategies, Policy2, and the availability up to 37%.

4.2   Proof-of-Concept of the Reconfiguration Manager

For validation purposes we build a hardware implementation of an energy-aware reconfiguration manager on top of a custom multi-FPGA board. The considered platform is equipped with two FGPAs, where one contains a manager that drives the reconfiguration of the other FPGA, which contains the processing logic.

In this set of experiments, we consider a reactive application, which consists of two different tasks. Both tasks implement, either in software or in the FPGA, slightly different versions of a fourth order Finite Impulse Response filter (FIR), and are named accordingly FIR1 and FIR2. The software version is used when a task needs to be executed and its hardware counterpart is not loaded yet in the FPGA, in the idea of completing the task as soon as possible. The choice of the FIR routine is motivated by the following reasons: (i) it is a signal processing algorithm suitable for typical sensor networking application; (ii) it results in a hardware implementation easy to fit in a small-sized FPGA suitable for a low-power device; (iii) it is a workload independent routine, which allows controllable experiments to be performed. In our application, we select for execution one of the tasks FIR1 or FIR2 based on the particular value of a sensor reading.

Clearly, this application is simpler than the one presented in Sect. 4.1. Also, an important difference is the fact that we consider now the environmental energy to come in bursts of different lengths, but of constant power, assumption which holds better for vibrational or indoors photovoltaic harvesters, for example.

In the rest of this section we describe the reconfiguration policy running on the prototype board, then, the implementation of the board, and, in the end, we discuss the results of the measurements that assess the effectiveness of our strategy.

Reconfiguration Policy. The strategy is implemented as code running on the processor of the prototype board. This simple policy, depicted in Fig. 10, allows us to study inherent properties of the reconfiguration strategy in a repeatable and controllable way.

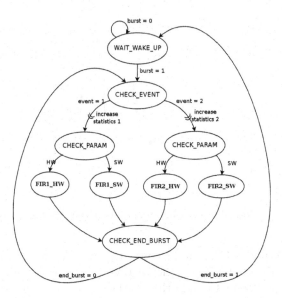

Fig. 10. The event-driven application model

The execution of a task is triggered by the arrival of an energy burst ($burst = 1$). We create fictive sensor readings by using a pseudo-random generator. Depending on the value of the reading, one of two possible events is generated ($event = 1$, or $event = 2$). Each event triggers the execution of one of the two FIR tasks. Along with this, the execution statistics are incremented for the corresponding task. The policy has to select between the hardware and software version of the selected task. This is done by checking a shared memory location ($CHECK\_PARAM$) written by the reconfiguration manager, which stores which routine is actually loaded in the FPGA. The system continues running as long as there is energy available.

For the given implementation, the number of loops executed during an energy burst of constant length becomes a metric for the energy efficiency of the reconfiguration strategy. Obviously, the lower the amount of energy consumed by each loop, the higher the number of loops that get executed within a single energy burst.

Reconfiguration Manager Implementation and Experimental Results.
The custom design board we use to run the reconfiguration policy is equipped
with the URLAP processor [15] (a low power ARM-based processor with 256
KB of internal SRAM), 8MB of external DRAM, 512KB of Flash memory and
two FPGAs. One of the two on-board FPGAs is used for the execution of the
FIR tasks, while the other one is used as a reconfiguration manager. The overall
system architecture is shown in Fig. 11.

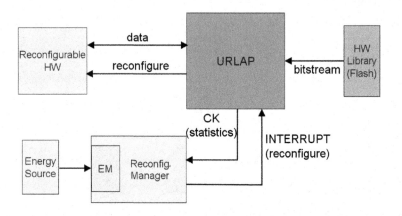

Fig. 11. Reconfigurable system architecture

In this design, the FPGAs can be configured to be either memory-mapped or
to have a coprocessor interface to the URLAP processor. We use the first alternative in our experiments to build the interface to the reconfiguration manager.
The FPGAs and the URLAP communicate through the shared memory view
and interrupt lines. In this case, the reconfiguration of the FPGA can only be
done at run-time by the URLAP, by using two additional CPLDs.

Since the board is not optimized for being powered by a real harvester, we use a
burst emulation system based on the LabVIEW software and a Data AcQuisition
Board (DAQ). A detailed description of the board and the burst emulation
system is beyond the scope of this paper. The hardware reconfiguration manager
is directly connected to the energy source in order to detect the power of the
harvester and the status of the battery, thus being able to detect the energy
slack that might be normally wasted. This component that measures the energy
and power levels is indicated in Fig. 11 as the Energy Monitor (EM).

Since we do not know in advance the size of the energy burst, we start the
reconfiguration process as soon as the power level of the burst is larger than the
reconfiguration power. Moreover, we restrict our analysis to the case where we
always have enough energy to perform the reconfiguration process of the FPGA.

The interface of the reconfiguration manager to the main processor is represented by an interrupt signal (INTERRUPT) and a checkpoint signal (CK).

The first one gives to the reconfiguration manager the capability of issuing a *reconfigure* command to the main processor in the presence of an energy burst. The second one is used in the statistics collection process. We collect statistics by inserting code checkpoints, which write information about the last task execution in a dedicated shared memory location. The reconfiguration manager reads then this information and uses it to update the execution counters of the tasks and other related variables. In order to decide which task to load in the FPGA, we implement a simple moving average filter, which selects the most frequent task from the 15 previous task executions.

We perform now a set of experiments in which we search to obtain efficiency bounds for the proposed reconfiguration policy. In the following paragraphs we use the following terminology: i) the *burst size* indicates the duration of an energy burst; ii) the *event distribution* is the ratio between the number of consecutive events of type 1 and the number of consecutive events of type 2. For instance, an event distribution of 4:6 means that we have four consecutive events of type 1, followed by six consecutive events of type 2.

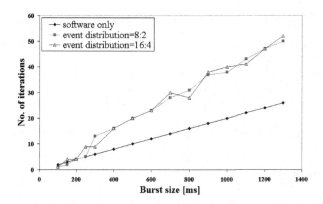

Fig. 12. Number of task executions for various unbalanced event distributions

We evaluate the effectiveness of the dynamic reconfiguration policy for different energy burst sizes. We also measure the energy consumed during the process of reconfiguration process. We find a peak power of 132mW at a frequency of 30 MHz of the reprogrammation of the FPGA, with a reconfiguration time of about 70ms.

In Fig. 12 we report the number of iterations performed per energy burst, for various unbalanced event distributions. The *software only* line represents the number of iterations obtained when we do not employ any reconfiguration policy, for arbitrary event distributions, since both tasks have identical characteristics in software. We can see that the proposed policy is more effective for larger energy bursts, because of the good adaptability of the prediction policy for the actual input event sequence.

In Fig. 13 we present the energy per iteration consumed as a function of the burst size. This energy takes into account the additional energy spent for the reconfiguration process. The plot is performed using a balanced event distribution, for which a history-based prediction algorithm is more effective. In this plot we compare our approach with a *no reconfiguration* case, in which the FPGA is statically programmed with one of the two routines and is never reconfigured.

We conclude that the system using the proposed reconfiguration strategy consumes less energy per iteration than the system using only the software implementation of the tasks, in most of the cases. Since the reconfiguration manager uses a simple prediction policy, with the help of more complex prediction algorithms or of policies that exploit more predictable external events, we should improve the effectiveness of the proposed strategies.

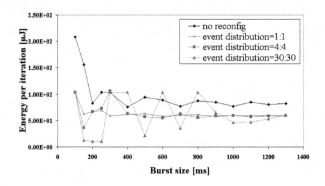

Fig. 13. Energy per iteration with balanced event distribution

5   Conclusions

In this paper we have presented modeling and implementation approaches that use the reconfigurable hardware existing in the latest and forthcoming sensor node architectures. Our goal is to model the energy coming from the environment and the possibilities of reconfiguration that target to maximize the energy efficiency. We have first performed explorations of stochastic models for environmental energy and sensor node architectures and we have shown improvements in the lifetime and the availability of the system of 40% and 37%, respectively, by employing several proposed strategies. Then, we have shown an implementation of the proposed reconfiguration manager architecture using a prototype board with microcontroller and reconfigurable hardware. Our energy efficiency measurements have demonstrated the effectiveness of the employed reconfiguration policies.

As future work we plan to extend our modeling methodology to be able to infer the expected downtime or the energy wasted for more interesting periods of time (e.g., months, years). Also, we plan to analyze additional real-life working environments (e.g., main doors of buildings, bridges, etc.) and types of harvesting devices.

Acknowledgments

We would like to thank Matthias Fruth, Dave Parker, Rajesh Gupta and Andrey Rybalchenko for the insightful discussions regarding the model checking of our prototype system. Also, we would like to thank Henri Dubois-Ferrière and Guillermo Barrenetxea for helping us obtain the traces of the solar panel. This work is partially supported by the Swiss NFS Research Grant 20021-109450/1 and the Spanish Government Research Grant TIN2005-5619.

References

1. FPSLIC (AVR with FPGA) from Atmel, ATMEL Corporation - www.atmel.com/products/FPSLIC/.
2. Rajeev Alur and Thomas A. Henzinger. Reactive modules. *Form. Methods Syst. Des.*, 15(1):7–48, 1999.
3. Guillermo Barrenetxea, Henri Dubois-Ferriere, Roger Meier, and John Selker. A weather station for SensorScope. In *Demo Session, In Information Processing in Sensor Networks (IPSN 2006)*, 2006.
4. Luca Benini, Alessandro Bogliolo, and Giovanni De Micheli. A survey of design techniques for system-level dynamic power management. *IEEE Transactions on Very Large Scale Integration (VLSI) Systems*, 8(3):299–316, June 2000.
5. Andrea Bianco and Luca de Alfaro. Model checking of probabilistic and nondeterministic systems. *FSTTCS: Foundations of Software Technology and Theoretical Computer Science*, 15, 1995.
6. Benjie Chen, Kyle Jamieson, Hari Balakrishnan, and Robert Morris. Span: an energy-efficient coordination algorithm for topology maintenance in ad hoc wireless networks. *Wirel. Netw.*, 8(5):481–494, 2002.
7. Xiuzhen Cheng, Bhagirath Narahari, Rahul Simha, Maggie Xiaoyan Cheng, and Dan Liu. Strong minimum energy topology in wireless sensor networks: Np-completeness and heuristics. *IEEE Transactions on Mobile Computing*, 02(3): 248–256, 2003.
8. David Culler, Deborah Estrin, and Mani Srivastava. Guest editors' introduction: Overview of sensor networks. *Computer*, 37(8):41–49, 2004.
9. Henri Dubois-Ferriere. Sensorscope presentation at NCCR-MICS WG2, 2005.
10. E. N. (Mootaz) Elnozahy, Lorenzo Alvisi, Yi-Min Wang, and David B. Johnson. A survey of rollback-recovery protocols in message-passing systems. *ACM Comput. Surv.*, 34(3):375–408, 2002.
11. Christian C. Enz, Amre El-Hoiydi, Jean-Dominique Decotignie, and Vincent Peiris. Wisenet: An ultralow-power wireless sensor network solution. *Computer*, 37(8): 62–70, 2004.
12. Jessica Feng, Farinaz Koushanfar, and Miodrag Potkonjak. System-architectures for sensor networks issues, alternatives, and directions. *ICCD*, 00:226, 2002.
13. Hans Hansson and Bengt Jonsson. A logic for reasoning about time and probability. *Formal Apsects of Computing*, 6, 1994.
14. Edmund M. Clarke Jr., Orna Grumberg, and Doron A. Peled. *Model checking*. MIT Press, Cambridge, MA, USA, 1999.
15. Ties Kluter. URLAP Processor, EPFL LAP Technical Report, 2004.

16. Greg Kogut, Mike Blackburn, and H.R. Everett. Using video sensor networks to command and control unmanned ground vehicles. In *AUVSI Unmanned Systems in International Security (USIS)*, 2003.

17. Marta Kwiatkowska, Gethin Norman, and David Parker. Prism 2.0: A tool for probabilistic model checking. *QEST*, 00:322–323, 2004.

18. John Lach, David Evans, Jon McCune, and Jason Brandon. Power-efficient adaptable wireless sensor networks. In *International Conference on Military and Aerospace Programmable Logic Devices (MAPLD)*, 2003.

19. Enrico Magli, Massimo Mancin, and Luca Merello. Low-complexity video compression for wireless sensor networks. *Proceedings of the International Conference on Multimedia and Expo, ICME 2003*, 3:585–588, 2003.

20. Dustin McIntire, Kei Ho, Bernie Yip, Amarjeet Singh, Winston Wu, and William J. Kaiser. The low power energy aware processing (leap)embedded networked sensor system. In *IPSN '06: Proceedings of the fifth international conference on Information processing in sensor networks*, pages 449–457, New York, NY, USA, 2006. ACM Press.

21. Joseph A. Paradiso and Thad Starner. Energy scavenging for mobile and wireless electronics. *Pervasive Computing, IEEE*, 4(1):18–27, 2005.

22. Jan M. Rabaey, M. Josie Ammer, Julio L. da Silva, Danny Patel, and Shad Roundy. Picoradio supports ad hoc ultra-low power wireless networking. *Computer*, 33(7):42–48, 2000.

23. Kishore Raja, Ioannis Daskalopoulos, Hamadoun Diall, Stephen Hailes, Tom Torfs, Chris Van Hoof, and George Roussos. Sensor Cubes: A modular, ultra-compact, power-aware platform for sensor networks. In *International Conference on Information Processing in Sensor Networks (IPSN SPOTS)*, April 2006.

24. Shad Roundy, Eli S. Leland, Jessy Baker, Eric Carleton, Elizabeth Reilly, Elaine Lai, Brian Otis, Jan M. Rabaey, Paul K. Wright, and V. Sundararajan. Improving power output for vibration-based energy scavengers. *Pervasive Computing, IEEE*, 4(1):28–36, 2005.

25. Amit Sinha and Anantha Chandrakasan. Dynamic power management in wireless sensor networks. *IEEE Des. Test*, 18(2):62–74, 2001.

Author Index

Lecture Notes in Computer Science

For information about Vols. 1–4327

please contact your bookseller or Springer

Vol. 4374: J.F. Peters, A. Skowron, I. Düntsch, J. Grzymała-Busse, E. Orłowska, L. Polkowski (Eds.), Transactions on Rough Sets VI, Part I. XII, 499 pages. 2007.

Vol. 4373: K. Langendoen, T. Voigt (Eds.), Wireless Sensor Networks. XIII, 358 pages. 2007.

Vol. 4372: M. Kaufmann, D. Wagner (Eds.), Graph Drawing. XIV, 454 pages. 2007.

Vol. 4371: K. Inoue, K. Satoh, F. Toni (Eds.), Computational Logic in Multi-Agent Systems. X, 315 pages. 2007. (Sublibrary LNAI).

Vol. 4370: P.P Lévy, B. Le Grand, F. Poulet, M. Soto, L. Darago, L. Toubiana, J.-F. Vibert (Eds.), Pixelization Paradigm. XV, 279 pages. 2007.

Vol. 4369: M. Umeda, A. Wolf, O. Bartenstein, U. Geske, D. Seipel, O. Takata (Eds.), Declarative Programming for Knowledge Management. X, 229 pages. 2006. (Sublibrary LNAI).

Vol. 4368: T. Erlebach, C. Kaklamanis (Eds.), Approximation and Online Algorithms. X, 345 pages. 2007.

Vol. 4367: K. De Bosschere, D. Kaeli, P. Stenström, D. Whalley, T. Ungerer (Eds.), High Performance Embedded Architectures and Compilers. XI, 307 pages. 2007.

Vol. 4366: K. Tuyls, R. Westra, Y. Saeys, A. Nowé (Eds.), Knowledge Discovery and Emergent Complexity in Bioinformatics. IX, 183 pages. 2007. (Sublibrary LNBI).

Vol. 4364: T. Kühne (Ed.), Models in Software Engineering. XI, 332 pages. 2007.

Vol. 4362: J. van Leeuwen, G.F. Italiano, W. van der Hoek, C. Meinel, H. Sack, F. Plášil (Eds.), SOFSEM 2007: Theory and Practice of Computer Science. XXI, 937 pages. 2007.

Vol. 4361: H.J. Hoogeboom, G. Păun, G. Rozenberg, A. Salomaa (Eds.), Membrane Computing. IX, 555 pages. 2006.

Vol. 4360: W. Dubitzky, A. Schuster, P.M.A. Sloot, M. Schroeder, M. Romberg (Eds.), Distributed, High-Performance and Grid Computing in Computational Biology. X, 192 pages. 2007. (Sublibrary LNBI).

Vol. 4358: R. Vidal, A. Heyden, Y. Ma (Eds.), Dynamical Vision. IX, 329 pages. 2007.

Vol. 4357: L. Buttyán, V. Gligor, D. Westhoff (Eds.), Security and Privacy in Ad-Hoc and Sensor Networks. X, 193 pages. 2006.

Vol. 4355: J. Julliand, O. Kouchnarenko (Eds.), B 2007: Formal Specification and Development in B. XIII, 293 pages. 2006.

Vol. 4354: M. Hanus (Ed.), Practical Aspects of Declarative Languages. X, 335 pages. 2006.

Vol. 4353: T. Schwentick, D. Suciu (Eds.), Database Theory – ICDT 2007. XI, 419 pages. 2006.

Vol. 4352: T.-J. Cham, J. Cai, C. Dorai, D. Rajan, T.-S. Chua, L.-T. Chia (Eds.), Advances in Multimedia Modeling, Part II. XVIII, 743 pages. 2006.

Vol. 4351: T.-J. Cham, J. Cai, C. Dorai, D. Rajan, T.-S. Chua, L.-T. Chia (Eds.), Advances in Multimedia Modeling, Part I. XIX, 797 pages. 2006.

Vol. 4349: B. Cook, A. Podelski (Eds.), Verification, Model Checking, and Abstract Interpretation. XI, 395 pages. 2007.

Vol. 4348: S.T. Taft, R.A. Duff, R.L. Brukardt, E. Ploedereder, P. Leroy (Eds.), Ada 2005 Reference Manual. XXII, 765 pages. 2006.

Vol. 4347: J. Lopez (Ed.), Critical Information Infrastructures Security. X, 286 pages. 2006.

Vol. 4346: L. Brim, B. Haverkort, M. Leucker, J. van de Pol (Eds.), Formal Methods: Applications and Technology. X, 363 pages. 2007.

Vol. 4345: N. Maglaveras, I. Chouvarda, V. Koutkias, R. Brause (Eds.), Biological and Medical Data Analysis. XIII, 496 pages. 2006. (Sublibrary LNBI).

Vol. 4344: V. Gruhn, F. Oquendo (Eds.), Software Architecture. X, 245 pages. 2006.

Vol. 4342: H. de Swart, E. Orłowska, G. Schmidt, M. Roubens (Eds.), Theory and Applications of Relational Structures as Knowledge Instruments II. X, 373 pages. 2006. (Sublibrary LNAI).

Vol. 4341: P.Q. Nguyen (Ed.), Progress in Cryptology - VIETCRYPT 2006. XI, 385 pages. 2006.

Vol. 4340: R. Prodan, T. Fahringer, Grid Computing. XXIII, 317 pages. 2007.

Vol. 4339: E. Ayguadé, G. Baumgartner, J. Ramanujam, P. Sadayappan (Eds.), Languages and Compilers for Parallel Computing. XI, 476 pages. 2006.

Vol. 4338: P. Kalra, S. Peleg (Eds.), Computer Vision, Graphics and Image Processing. XV, 965 pages. 2006.

Vol. 4337: S. Arun-Kumar, N. Garg (Eds.), FSTTCS 2006: Foundations of Software Technology and Theoretical Computer Science. XIII, 430 pages. 2006.

Vol. 4336: V.R. Basili, D. Rombach, K. Schneider, B. Kitchenham, D. Pfahl, R.W. Selby, Empirical Software Engineering Issues. XVII, 193 pages. 2007.

Vol. 4335: S.A. Brueckner, S. Hassas, M. Jelasity, D. Yamins (Eds.), Engineering Self-Organising Systems. XII, 212 pages. 2007. (Sublibrary LNAI).

Vol. 4334: B. Beckert, R. Hähnle, P.H. Schmitt (Eds.), Verification of Object-Oriented Software. XXIX, 658 pages. 2007. (Sublibrary LNAI).

Vol. 4333: U. Reimer, D. Karagiannis (Eds.), Practical Aspects of Knowledge Management. XII, 338 pages. 2006. (Sublibrary LNAI).

Vol. 4332: A. Bagchi, V. Atluri (Eds.), Information Systems Security. XV, 382 pages. 2006.

Vol. 4331: G. Min, B. Di Martino, L.T. Yang, M. Guo, G. Ruenger (Eds.), Frontiers of High Performance Computing and Networking – ISPA 2006 Workshops. XXXVII, 1141 pages. 2006.

Vol. 4330: M. Guo, L.T. Yang, B. Di Martino, H.P. Zima, J. Dongarra, F. Tang (Eds.), Parallel and Distributed Processing and Applications. XVIII, 953 pages. 2006.

Vol. 4329: R. Barua, T. Lange (Eds.), Progress in Cryptology - INDOCRYPT 2006. X, 454 pages. 2006.

Vol. 4328: D. Penkler, M. Reitenspiess, F. Tam (Eds.), Service Availability. X, 289 pages. 2006.